Women's Movements in Asia

This book is a comprehensive study of women's activism across Asia. With chapters written by leading international experts, it provides a full overview of the history of feminism, as well as the current context of the women's movement in twelve countries: the Philippines, China and Hong Kong, Indonesia, Japan, Singapore, Vietnam, Thailand, Cambodia, Korea, India and Pakistan.

Women's movements in Asia were simultaneously transnational in outlook and indigenizing in orientation. This volume provides country-focused case studies that help us understand the contexts within which 'national essence feminism' emerged in Asia. Western feminisms were immediately identified as Other—compelling each Asian country to search for its own unique answers to the 'woman question' by deconstructing how the feminine was constructed not just by culture and religions but also by history and the experiences of colonialism and imperialism. The chapters reveal how Asian activists mobilized transnational forums and protocols to legitimize their specific national campaigns.

Each chapter includes a comprehensive bibliography of key works in the field making it ideal for courses on women and feminism in Asia. It will appeal both to students and specialists in the fields of gender and social and political history.

Louise Edwards is Professor of Modern China Studies at the University of Hong Kong.

Mina Roces is an Associate Professor in the School of History and Philosophy, The University of New South Wales, Sydney, Australia.

Experts in analysing gender issues offer this unique comparative analysis of the evolution of 'national essence feminism' in the context of global feminism. To find out how the women's movement in twelve Asian nations have fought for bodily autonomy, participation in politics and religion, new definitions of womanhood, changed family relations and much more – this book is the best (indeed the only) one to read.

Chilla Bulbeck *Professor emerita and visiting research fellow, The University of Adelaide, Australia*

Women's Movements in Asia

Feminisms and transnational activism

Edited by
Mina Roces and Louise Edwards

Routledge
Taylor & Francis Group

LONDON AND NEW YORK

First published 2010
by Routledge
2 Park Square, Milton Park, Abingdon, Oxon OX14 4RN

Simultaneously published in the USA and Canada
by Routledge
270 Madison Avenue, New York, NY 10016

Routledge is an imprint of the Taylor & Francis Group, an informa business

Typeset in Times New Roman by Glyph International Ltd.
Printed and bound in Great Britain by TJ International Ltd, Padstow,
Cornwall

British Library Cataloguing-in-Publication Data
A catalogue record for this book is available from the British Library

Library of Congress Cataloging-in-Publication Data
Women's movements in Asia: feminisms and transnational activism/
edited by Mina Roces and Louise Edwards.
   p. cm.
Includes bibliographical references and index.
1. Feminism–Asia. 2. Women–Political activity–Asia. 3. Transnationalism.
I. Roces, Mina, 1959– II. Edwards, Louise P.
HQ1726.W695 2010
305.42095–dc22

2009047320

ISBN: 978-0-415-48702-3 (hbk)
ISBN: 978-0-415-48703-0 (pbk)
ISBN: 978-0-203-85123-4 (ebk)

Contents

Acknowledgements

This book is a testament to the value of academic conference networking. It had its origins in a conversation between Routledge Editor, Stephanie Rogers, Mina Roces and Louise Edwards at the International Congress of Asian Scholars in Shanghai in 2005. Once the team of contributors had formed, some authors presented their first drafts at the Asian Studies Association of Australia (ASAA) conference hosted by Monash University in 2008. Yet others presented their work at the ASAA's Women in Asia Conference held at the University of Queensland, also in 2008. At each of these events, colleagues from around the world provided invaluable feedback and interrogation of the concepts and details of the chapters. To those who participated, thank you for your collegiality. You will notice many of your ideas have been incorporated into this final version.

The volume also provides evidence that the transnational nature of feminism is alive and well in the academic community as well as among the activists and organizers discussed in the volume. Contributors to this book are drawn from around the world: Europe, Asia, Australasia and the USA. For some authors, this is their first opportunity to work together on a joint project. For others, it reflects an ongoing commitment to team projects.

All books draw on the time and energies of people beyond the academic authors. The editors would like to thank Samantha Hauw, Claire Moore, Raina Anne Bernardez, Alan Walker, Xi Ping, Steven Xuezhong Su, Darrel Dorrington and Shashim Sharma for their invaluable assistance. Grants from the Australian Research Council supported the project and the Faculty of Arts at the University of New South Wales provided funds for the production of the index. We would also like to acknowledge the enthusiasm and energy provided by Routledge, in particular Stephanie Rogers and her team of Leanne Hinves and Sonja Van Leeuwen.

Finally we would like to thank our partners, Martyn Lyons and Kam Louie for their continued support of our ongoing efforts to promote knowledge of feminism and women's movements in Asia.

Mina Roces, Sydney
Louise Edwards, Hong Kong

Contributors

Susan Blackburn is an Associate Professor in the School of Political and Social Inquiry at Monash University, where she teaches Southeast Asian Politics. In recent years, her research has focused on women in politics and development. She is the author of *Women and the State in Modern Indonesia* (Cambridge University Press 2004).

Alessandra Chiricosta is a Philosopher and Historian of Religions and specializes in Southeast and East Asian Cultures. She focuses on intercultural philosophy, religious and cultural dialogue, Gender Studies and Anthropology and has worked as a consultant for international NGOs and for the Italian Embassy in Vietnam. She has taught at three universities in Italy—La Sapienza, Urbaniana and Roma Tre (where she obtained her European PhD)—as well as the School of Oriental and African Studies and the University of Ha Noi. Her publications include *I sensi del sincretismo* [Meanings of Syncretism], 2004 (with Mazzoleni and Franceschelli) and *Oltre i Confini* [Beyond the Boundaries], 2005, both published by Bulzoni; she also translated and edited Matteo Ricci SJ, *Il vero significato del Signore del Cielo* [The true meaning of the Lord of heaven] (Urbaniana University Press 2006).

Louise Edwards is Professor of Modern China Studies at the University of Hong Kong. Her publications include: *Gender, Politics and Democracy: Women's Suffrage in China* (Stanford University Press 2008); *Men and Women in Qing China* (E.J. Brill 1994, Hawaii University Press 2001); *Censored by Confucius* (M.E. Sharpe 1996, with Kam Louie); and a series of edited volumes with Mina Roces including *The Politics of Dress in Asia and the Americas* (Sussex Academic 2007); *Women's Suffrage in Asia* (RoutledgeCurzon 2004); and *Women in Asia: Tradition, Modernity and Globalization* (Allen & Unwin, Michigan University Press 2000).

Monica Lindberg Falk is a Social Anthropologist and lecturer and researcher at the Centre for East and Southeast Asian Studies, Lund University, Sweden. Her research interests include gender, Buddhism, anthropology of disaster, women's movements, religious movements, development and social change in Southeast Asia. Her scholarship includes extensive fieldwork in Thailand.

She has published a monograph and several articles on themes related to gender and Buddhism. Her current research project is on gender and Buddhism's role in the recovery process after the tsunami catastrophe in Thailand.

Andrea Fleschenberg, PhD, currently works as research associate and lecturer at the Institute of Social Science at the University of Hildesheim, Germany. Previously, she was a research fellow at the Institute of East Asian Studies/ Political Science at the University of Duisburg-Essen and a lecturer at the University of Cologne, Germany. In 2007, she was a visiting professor at the University of the Punjab in Lahore, Pakistan, and in 2006, at the Universitat Jaume I in Castellon, Spain. Her research areas are comparative and third world politics with a particular focus on South and Southeast Asia, democratization and election studies, transitional justice issues, gender and politics, on which she has contributed numerous publications. Recent publications: *Afghanistan's Parliament in the Making. Gendered Understandings and Practices of Politics in a Transitional Country* (Heinrich-Böll-Foundation UNIFEM, Berlin 2009); *The Gender Face of Asian Politics*, co-edited with Aazar Ayaz (Oxford University Press 2009); *Goddesses, Heroes, Sacrifices: Female Political Power in Asia*, co-edited with Dagmar Hellmann-Rajanayagam (LIT Verlag, Zürich/Münster 2008).

Trudy Jacobsen is Assistant Professor of Southeast Asian History at Northern Illinois University. She has published on Buddhism and politics in Cambodia, justice and reconciliation in Southeast Asia, and the history of women and power in Cambodia, most significantly *Lost Goddesses: The Denial of Female Power in Cambodian History* (NIAS Press 2008). Her postdoctoral research project *Intersections of Desire, Duty and Debt: Sexual Contracts in Burma and Cambodia* will be published in 2011.

Kyounghee Kim is an Associate Professor of Sociology and Head of Institute of Sociology at Chung-Ang University, Seoul, Korea. Her major research areas are gender equality policies, care work, and women's movements in Korea from a comparative perspective. Her most recent publications include a comparative analysis of the ERA movement in US and the movement to abolish the family head system in Korea, and the commercialization of care work and motherhood. Her current research is on gender budgets and pay equity in Korea.

Seung-kyung Kim is Associate Professor in the Department of Women's Studies at the University of Maryland, College Park. Her research expertise includes Women and Work, Gender and Labour Politics, Gender and Development, Ethnography, Feminist Theory, and women in East Asia and Asian America. Her publications include: *Class Struggle or Family Struggle?: Lives of Women Factory Workers in South Korea* (Cambridge University Press 1997, 2009); *Feminist Theory Reader: Local and Global Perspective* (Routledge 2003, 2009). She has written articles and book chapters that were published in various journals and anthologies. She is currently working on two book manuscripts: *Women's Movements in Democratic South Korea: The Trajectory* *of Institutionalization and the Loss of Autonomy* which was funded by the Korea Foundation, and *Global Citizens in the Making?: Transnational Migration and Education in Kirogi Families*, which was funded by the Social Science Research Council.

Adelyn Lim is a doctoral candidate from the Department of Anthropology, Research School of Pacific and Asian Studies, the Australian National University. Her doctoral thesis is a comparative analysis of feminist and women's NGOs in Hong Kong and Singapore. Current research interests include feminist and women's movements, marriage and family, and migration in East Asia, Southeast Asia and Australia.

Lenore Lyons is Research Professor in Asian Studies at the University of Western Australia. Recognized as the leading scholar on the feminist movement in Singapore, she was awarded her PhD in Gender Studies from Griffith University. Her book, *A State of Ambivalence: The Feminist Movement in Singapore* (E.J. Brill), was published in 2004. Her work has appeared in a number of edited collections as well as journals including *Women's Studies Quarterly, International Feminist Journal of Politics, Critical Asian Studies, Asian Studies Review, Asia Pacific Viewpoint* and *Citizenship Studies*, among others. She recently completed a major study of citizenship, identity and sovereignty in the Riau Islands of Indonesia (with Michele Ford, University of Sydney) and is currently working on two projects funded by the Australian Research Council—one examines migrant worker activism in support of female domestic workers in Malaysia and Singapore, and the other, skilled migrant women in Australia.

Sumi Madhok is Lecturer in Transnational Gender Studies at the Gender Institute, London School of Economics and Political Science. She is author of *Rethinking Agency: Gender, Developmentalism and Rights* (Routledge 2010).

Barbara Molony, Professor of Japanese History at Santa Clara University (USA), is the President of the American Historical Association Pacific Coast Branch. Her recent work on Japanese women's history includes *Asia's New Mothers* (co-edited with Ochiai Emiko), *Gendering Modern Japanese History* (co-edited with Kathleen Uno), and several articles on Japanese women's suffrage rights, Ichikawa Fusae, gender and the politics of dress, and gender and imperial succession.

Mina Roces is an Associate Professor in the School of History and Philosophy, The University of New South Wales, Sydney, Australia. She is the author of *Women, Power and Kinship Politics: Female Power in Post-War Philippines* (Praeger 1998), and *Kinship Politics in Post-War Philippines, The Lopez Family, 1946–2000* (de la Salle University Press 2001). She has just completed a monograph on women's movements in the Philippines (*Women's Movements and "the Filipino Woman", 1985–2006*) and is Book Series Editor of the Sussex Library of Asian Studies, Sussex Academic Press.

1 Asian feminisms

Women's movements from the Asian perspective

Mina Roces

The international women's movements were pioneers of activism beyond national borders since the fight for suffrage in the late nineteenth century. But it was the second wave of the international women's networks in the 1960s and 1970s and its influence on the United Nations (UN) that fulfilled the potential of cross-border organizing for social change in the increasingly global age (Keck and Sikkink 1998: 167–98). Organizing internationally for women's issues gained momentum during the UN's International Women's Year (1975), its Decade for Women (1975–85) and the three conferences in connection with that special decade (Mexico City 1975, Copenhagen 1980 and Nairobi 1985) were critical in building and consolidating the networks of women's organizations around the world (Keck and Sikkink 1998: 168–69). Although these meetings were platforms for fiery debates that critics often interpreted as a 'split in the sisterhood', the very fact that there was disagreement attested to the fact that women from all over the world were participating in a conversation about women's rights. Women activists from Asia, Africa, Latin America and the Pacific contributed to global women's issues as *international feminists*—using the perspectives from 'home' to participate in fashioning women around the globe.

But is there such a thing as Asian feminisms? For large parts of the twentieth century, Asian women activists disliked the word 'feminism' because it was associated with 'Western feminism' that was caricatured as aggressively individualistic, anti-male, anti-children, and therefore anti-family. 'Western feminism' was immediately branded as alien and thus inapplicable to the 'Asian' context. Opinion leaders and political rulers found it convenient to homogenize a putatively unique 'Asian experience' for nationalist and sometimes anti-colonialist projects that denied Asian women's experience of patriarchy. Western feminists were imagined as 'bra-burning', 'manly and unfeminine women' who could in no way resemble the 'Asian women'. Furthermore, activists that sought to engage with international feminism faced criticisms that they were mimicking Western ideas (Roces 2004; Gangoli 2007), concepts that were not compatible with Asian culture and religion. For example, many Chinese activists 'rejected the label "feminist" since they regarded it as too radical and extreme for their tastes'

(Edwards 2009: 121). In Cambodia, national leaders declared that feminism would destroy Cambodian culture (Jacobsen, Chapter 12); in Singapore ruling elites pronounced that feminism would rupture social morality through the import of decadent 'Western values' (Lyons, Chapter 5); and in Thailand the general consensus was that feminism was 'un-Thai' (Lindberg Falk, Chapter 7).

Asian women activists responded to this fundamental challenge by producing their own brand of 'home-grown' feminism. The development of each Asian country's unique feminist theory was a self-conscious affirmation of their 'difference' from 'the West'. As Maitrayee Chaudhuri explained in her discussion of Indian feminisms, 'the claim for an "indigenous feminism" is the flip side of our persisting legacy of an uneasy relationship with western "feminism"' (Chaudhuri 2004: xxiii). Western feminisms were immediately identified as Other—compelling each Asian country to search for its own unique answers to the 'woman question' by deconstructing how the feminine was constructed not just by culture and religion but also by history and the experiences of colonialism and imperialism.

But, at the same time that Asian activists self-consciously chose to distinguish themselves from Western feminists, these same national movements mobilized transnational forums and protocols to legitimize or to argue for their specific campaigns at home. In particular, this is evident through the invocation of UN conventions such as CEDAW (Convention on the Elimination of Discrimination against Women), DEVAW (Declaration to Eliminate Violence against Women) and the various UN protocols on trafficking, migration and the recent war and gender rights through UN security council resolution 1325 on women, peace and security of 2000 (Blackburn 2008). Transnational networking across national borders gave local movements important and powerful allies. Monica Lindberg Falk (Chapter 7) reveals how, in the face of limited support at home, the Thai movement for women's ordination in the Theravada Buddhist monkhood was compelled to link up with female ordained monks overseas. In the last thirty years, the globalization of the labour force and the feminization of this trend resulted in the exodus (temporary or permanent) of Asian women from their home countries in the search for employment. As the 'Asian woman' moved across national borders, it has become pragmatic, if not essential, for women's organizations to have branches locally and overseas. Women's movements in Asian host countries, such as Singapore, had to confront the 'trans-ethnic' composition of the women in their 'national' population (Lyons, Chapter 5). As feminists all over the world gathered together in special forums to debate the woman question and global patriarchy, the enthusiastic presence of Asian women activists (as government representatives or non-governmental organization (NGO) leaders, for example) meant that they were able to export Asian feminism to the international stage. Some Asian activists enjoyed top international roles. For example, there were four Filipino women who chaired the UN's Commission on the Status of Women and to date three Filipino women have held posts as CEDAW experts (Tripon 2007).

This volume provides country-focused case studies that help us understand the contexts within which 'national essence feminism' emerged in Asia. Women's movements in Asia were also indigenization movements. The title of Chiricosta's chapter on Vietnam (Chapter 8) 'The search for a uniquely Vietnamese women's movement' applies equally to all our Asian case studies. Because each country had a unique grand narrative of the feminine—shaped by religion, culture, history—activists had to interrogate womanhood in each context to come up with Filipino, Chinese, Indian, Indonesian, Pakistani, Thai, Vietnamese, Japanese, Singaporean, Hong Kong, and Korean feminist positions. The diversity of the region meant that there is no such thing as a quintessential 'Asian woman'. Moreover, the variety of political regimes and political contexts experienced in Asia (including democracies, dictatorships, authoritarianism, communism and socialism, as well as the political and social instability produced by war) have set stark limits for activists of any form, feminist or not. While labels familiar to Western or Atlantic feminisms such as liberal, radical feminism, social-democratic, national-democratic, eco-feminist, etc. may have influenced the theoretical developments in the countries discussed in this book, it is also important to underscore the point that in some Asian contexts these labels are not useful, even if activists were pro-active in appropriating certain aspects of the theoretical positions that were compatible with their cultural and religious contexts.

Women's movements in America were classified into three chronological phases: first phase (the suffrage movement), second phase (the deconstruction of patriarchy in the 1960s) and the third phase (the mid-1990s to the present) (Evans 2003). In the Asian context, this periodization of feminist history is problematic. While in a number of Asian countries (i.e. China, Philippines, Indonesia, India, Japan) a suffrage movement comparable with first-wave feminisms in the Atlantic and Australasian worlds did exist in the early twentieth century, the absence of fully enunciated contemporaneous suffrage demands in others did not necessarily mean that they lacked a women's movement. Furthermore, universal suffrage was compromised by the fact that in the second half of the twentieth century many Asian countries experienced dictatorships where human rights violations and the withdrawal of democratic processes meant that both men and women were equally disempowered in formal political practice. The impact of Atlantic second-wave feminisms and the promotion of UN protocols such as CEDAW revitalized many women's movements in Asia. But, in some Asian countries such as China, the first-wave movement was more vibrant and radical than the next phase, while in India a 'third phase' classified as an 'autonomous women's movement' stood out (Edwards 2004, 2008a; Madhok, Chapter 13). Some countries experienced unstable democracies or oscillations between democracy and dictatorships (Philippines, Indonesia, Thailand, for example), and others moved from Third World to First (Singapore, Hong Kong) in the last few decades of the twentieth century. As a result of all of these myriad trends, we are unable to endorse a linear progressive history of women's movements in Asia.

Instead, the struggle for women's equality and empowerment has been a complex and exciting story.

The 'F' word and the 'T' word

On the surface, a non-specialist might be struck by the contradiction between the book's theme on 'Asian feminisms' and Asian activists' aversion for the term 'feminist' because of its Western connotations. Sometimes it was a question of semantics with Malaysia's Sisters in Islam (SIS) for example preferring the word 'womanist' (Stivens 2000: 31), while in Chinese women's studies, the word 'feminology' was used deliberately to distinguish themselves from Western feminist theory (Edwards, Chapter 4). Notable leaders of the Indian women's movement from Sarojini Naidu, who said 'I am not a feminist', to Madhu Kishwar, who explained 'Why I am not a feminist' (quoted in Chaudhuri 2004: xix–xx), demonstrated feminist sociologist Neera Desai's point that 'The term "feminist" was not only not popular, but there was a distinct "allergy" to it and many women, particularly academics, described themselves as WS [Women's Studies] researchers rather than feminist scholars' (quoted in Chaudhuri 2004: xxii). But, just because these activists and researchers were uncomfortable with the term 'feminist' as a self-referent did not mean that they were not in reality, practising feminists, since many of them would agree that they were participants of their particular country's women's movements.

Contributors have grappled with this conceptual dilemma by applying a broad definition of feminisms. Susan Blackburn (Chapter 2) speaks for most contributors when she writes:

> Although few in Indonesia would claim to be feminists, it is legitimate to use the word to apply to much of the women's movement if we understand feminism in a basic sense as 'analysing the problems of women' and 'acting to oppose discrimination against women'.

Lenore Lyons (Chapter 5) writing on Singapore also proposes a similar definition when she describes the organization AWARE as 'an organization that is supportive of women's rights but chooses not to use the term "feminist" to describe its work'. Another broad definition is provided by Mina Roces (Chapter 3) is 'activism centred on altering patriarchal structures of society to remove gender discrimination', while Sumi Madhok's chapter on India (Chapter 13) focuses on the 'rights' discourse and feminism. Cecilia Ng, Maznah Mohamad and Tan Beng Hui, thinking particularly about contemporary Malaysia, point to the evolving meaning of feminism:

> Today, feminism has gone beyond its original meaning of fighting for women's rights and legal reforms in education, property rights and suffrage. Its definition has extended to include an awareness and analysis of women's discrimination and exploitation in the family, at work and in society, as

well as conscious efforts by all—women and men—who wish to end gender inequality.

(Ng, Mohamad and Hui 2006: 3)

These elastic definitions of 'feminisms' have guided our authors in selecting the women's organizations and activists that comprised the women's movements in their respective country studies. For in reality, women activists in Asia (using our broad definitions) have been involved in feminist activism and have been proactive in the project of producing their own brand of feminism appropriate to their local context.

While the body of work that falls under the rubric of 'Women in Asia' is already a distinct research field in its own right (Roces & Edwards 2009: 1–18), the specific topic of Women's Movements in the Asian context is only recently developing a critical mass with the recent publication of book-length country-specific studies on Indonesia (Blackburn 2004; Martyn 2004; Wieringa 2002), Malaysia (Ng, Mohamad and Hui 2006), Singapore (Lyons 2004), Taiwan (Chang 2009), China (Edwards 2008a; Judd 2002; Wesoky 2002; Milwertz 2002), Japan (Mackie 2003; Dales 2009), India (Ray 1999; Chaudhuri 2004; Gangoli 2007), and Korea (Jung 2010). Accompanying this growing list of book-length manuscripts by international academics is a plethora of articles and chapters published by women's organizations in Asia, such as Sisters in Islam and DAWN (Development Alternatives with Women for a New Era). These transnational organizations are now publishing on feminist theorizing from the perspective of the global south (e.g. Othman 2005; Anwar 2009; DAWN 2009). The monographs above have focused on women's movements in action—primarily their engagement with the state in their particular country of study. This current volume adopts broader themes. Contributors have been asked not only to track the history of activist engagement with the state and other institutions (such as religious ones), but also to explore the unique issues, features, activities, and ideologies that characterize the indigenization of the feminist movement in a particular Asian country.

Kumari Jayawardena's book on women's suffrage (Jayawardena 1986) stands as a seminal study of early twentieth-century women's movements in the 'Third World' and remains the only book that has analyzed feminism across Asia. This current anthology is designed as a sequel to Jayawardena's pioneering volume in that it not only analyzes the nature of Asian women's movements across a broad sweep of history (from the first-wave suffragist movement to the first decade of the twenty-first century) but also explores these movements from a transnational perspective. While Jayawardena has eloquently pointed to the characteristic tensions between feminism and nationalism in the Asian, Middle East, Turkey and North African (Egypt) contexts (then still defined in the blanket 1970s framework of the 'Third World'), the view from Asia in 2009 includes a new dimension—the transnational.

The term transnational is understood as the movement of people, ideas, technologies and institutions across national boundaries (Tyrrell 2007: 3). The recently published *Palgrave Dictionary of Trans-national History* declares that its long list of authors are interested in 'links and flows, and want to track people, ideas, products, processes and patterns that operate over, across, through, beyond, above, under, or in-between polities and societies' (Iriye and Saunier 2009: xviii). Ellen Carol DuBois, contributing an entry on women's movements to that idiosyncratic dictionary, points out that 'the intellectual content of women's studies is decidedly transnational' (DuBois 2009: 1120). Indeed, because Asian feminist theories developed partly as a re-thinking of the applicability of Western feminism in local contexts, it might be possible to argue that Asian feminisms were transnationally produced. Ian Tyrrell, for example, has argued that the American nation-state was transnationally produced (Tyrrell 2007). In this volume, we use the term transnational to refer to this movement of ideas about women's status and rights across national borders, as well as the across-the-border organizing between women activists from different countries. Particular advocacies such as trafficking and migration require transnational lobbying and action, as does the 'comfort women' campaign on behalf of victims of enforced military sexual slavery during the Japanese Occupation of large parts of Asia in World War II. However, Molony's chapter in this volume reminds us that even in the early part of the twentieth century, Japanese suffragists were already heavily immersed in transnational activism. In fact, in the peculiar situation of the Japanese empire in the 1930s and 1940s, where involvement with the state meant complicity with the nation's 'bad' actions (Ueno 2004: 60), 'transnationalism in the prewar era gave Japanese and other women a space for influencing state policy in the absence of (national) civil rights' (Molony, Chapter 6). It is this 'space' (a 'mental space') that is the focus of our attention here, as this collection of essays explores the intersection and connections between the local women's movement and the larger international women's movement beyond its borders. Even though the 'transnational politics of location' has been guilty of what Grewal and Kaplan have labelled 'scattered hegemonies' (Grewal and Kaplan 1994: 1–33; Kaplan 1994: 137–51), far from the stereotype of the Asian or Third World country at the receiving end of a 'Western' lecture, we note the proactive, confident, locally informed activist who not only knows Western feminist positions but is also clear about what will or will not work in her country's particular context.

Asian feminists from the early twentieth century until the present were experts at reading the situation 'on the ground' and were not only selective about what aspects of feminist thinking abroad they would adopt but were also passionate about taking their critiques to international platforms. In this volume, we explore how Asian activists engaged with and challenged or modified international feminist theories, and organized across national borders on behalf of 'national women' and women around the world. The process of indigenizing feminisms and modifying international feminisms often occurred in a transnational 'mental space' and organizing and lobbying for legislative change often invoked the help of allies overseas or appeals to international bodies. Although activists in Asia were global actors, and although they were clearly influenced by Western feminisms, the case studies in this volume underscored Amrita Basu's point in her work on India that 'ultimately, the women's movement in India, as in the United States, is more a product of the national than global influences' (Basu 2000). This notion can be extrapolated to the entire Asian region and this volume tells the story of these unique feminist movements.

Women's issues from an Asian perspective

This book explores how women in each individual Asian country developed their own indigenous brands of feminism. After a century of women's activism in Asia it is timely for both scholars and activists to look back and reflect on the history of women's movements in the region. We have defined women's movements as the organized activism by women's groups for the improvement of women's status and asked each contributor to address a number of questions pertinent to their particular national case study. Some of these include: how have women's movements theorized the 'Asian woman'? Who were the leaders and followers of the women's movement? How have specifically local contexts, cultures and religion had an impact on defining the feminine and what challenges have they presented to women activists? How have they tried to disseminate their ideas and how successful have they been in the endeavour to improve women's status in their countries? In what ways have women's movements been transnational movements?

The diversity of the Asian region meant that each chapter would have its own unique answer to the above questions. The plurality of voices within each Asian country also produced additional challenges for authors as they sought to answer the question of who is speaking for which particular 'Asian woman'. The term 'grass-roots women' was prominent in the discourses of Asian women activists who claimed 'up front and centre' that they were interested in the perspective of lower class women. In some cases, this had some basis in reality with activists deploying all sorts of creative strategies in order to build a mass following and to ensure that the voices of the poor were heard. But, as the essays in this volume show, each country's women's movement experienced its own struggles with the issue of class. In some countries such as Pakistan, Singapore and Malaysia, women's organizations failed to increase their membership beyond middle- or elite-class women (Lyons, Chapter 5; Fleschenberg, Chapter 10; Ng, Mohamad and Hui 2006). India was a special case where activists were compelled to tackle caste, a social system unique to that culture (Gangoli 2007: 7). While not all contributors are historians, we asked all of them to adopt a historical perspective to survey, analyze and interpret the women's movement in the twentieth century. The result showed the myriad ways that activists participated in the debates about the 'woman question' and the insights from the local context that have been deployed to modify ideas from abroad.

Not all Asian countries could boast of a clearly organized movement for female enfranchisement. But this did not mean that there were no women's movements there in the 1920s and 1930s. Like their sisters in the Atlantic world, the fight for the vote was also closely tied to the very notion of the 'modern woman' or the 'new woman'. Suffragists in Asia were the elite, educated, intellectual women and it was education that transformed them from 'old' to 'new' (Edwards and Roces 2004: 15). In Korea, for example, the suffrage movement was called the 'new women's movement' (Wells 2004) and there was the New Woman Association formed in Japan (Molony 2004) to further the process of modernizing womanhood. What made Asia different was that the suffrage movement occurred in most cases in a colonial context just at the time when nationalist movements were blossoming. Thus, although the 'modern woman' was a global phenomenon (like ideas about the 'modern girl' around the world, see Weinbaum *et al.* 2008; Edwards 2000), suffragists had to prove that although they were 'modern', they were still 'Asian'. Demanding the female vote in the middle of a nationalist movement inhibited feminists from challenging the grand narrative of woman as bearer and wearer of national tradition (Edwards and Roces 2004; Roces 2004).

Indigenization often involved a rethinking of a Western idea. In India, for example, campaigns on the issue of domestic violence focused on dowry-related murders and the role of mothers-in-law as perpetrators of violence against women (Gangoli 2007: 7). Likewise, Chinese feminists extended the concept of domestic violence from the usually Western concept of 'wife beating' to include child beating, parent beating, husband beating, daughter-in-law abuse and elder abuse (Edwards 2009: 120). Since women held the purse strings in Southeast Asia, the liberal feminist agenda for women's control of the finances had to be readapted to societies where spiritual potency not wealth was the measure of status. In the Philippines, women's health activists asked the question whether women had the capacity to make choices regarding health and reproductive health because they lacked money and access to basic services and feared the judgement of the powerful Catholic Church. In India and China, the two most populous Asian countries that experienced draconian population policies (one-child policy, sterilization programs), activists mobilizing on the issue of contraception had to fight against sex-selective abortion and female infanticide (Basu 2000: 79; Edwards, Chapter 4; Croll 2000; Hudson and den Boer 2004). Sumi Madhok's incisive chapter gave us a unique case study of how rights discourses were adapted in India (Chapter 13).

The great feminist divide over the issue of whether prostitution is 'sex work' or 'violence against women' (VAW) had its Asian variant with activists lined up on both sides of these two camps. But here was another example where the Asian context introduced new perspectives to the debate. Activists argued that poverty, sex tourism, the presence of American military bases and American servicemen on R&R leave as well as the trafficking of Asian women across national borders (all the way to Australia, the USA, Lebanon and Europe) needed to be considered in any discussion about prostitution as a feminist issue (Enloe 1989; Roces 2009; Law 1997; Jeffrey 2002). As cities such as Manila and Bangkok earned reputations as 'sex capitals' of Asia for tourists looking for 'a good time', women's organizations were committed to dismantling the Orientalist narrative that represented Asian women as 'exotic', 'erotic' and submissive women since this powerful myth perpetuated the view that Asian women were 'available' for sex. Activists from

Asia not only had to debunk their local culture's grand narratives of the feminine, they also had to destroy images perpetuated by foreigners (including colonial and imperial powers both Asian and Euro-American) who could not get beyond the sexualized image of the 'Asian woman'. Vera Mackie argued that the transnational feminist networks on the issue of 'comfort women' contributed to the discourses on human rights as militarized sexual violence was openly discussed (Mackie 2004: 250).

Perhaps because they wanted to disassociate themselves from their own stereotyped view that 'feminists' were 'man haters', Asian women activists were careful to send the message that men were potential allies and not enemies of the women's movements. Chinese feminists deliberately acknowledged the importance of the cooperation of men and women in combating social problems (Edwards 2009: 121). This strategy has been fruitful since women were still marginalized in political office and in practical terms activists had to lobby male-dominated legislatures. In the absence of a women's vote and with few women politicians, this has been the best avenue for success (Veneracion-Rallonza 2008). The visible presence of Asian women in the highest offices (as prime minister, president or opposition leader) was not necessarily a barometer for measuring the success of a women's movement since a number of these women acquired these positions through their ties with men (see Roces 1998; Fleschenberg 2008; Iwanaga 2008) and few were imbued with a gender consciousness.

In what seems to be another Asia-wide phenomenon, the issue of sexuality appeared quite late—only from the 1990s onwards. The primary reason for its late arrival in the public discourse was the strong cultural taboos that see sexuality as a very private matter. In Indonesia, the topic of domestic violence was included in the list of 'unmentionables' (Blackburn, Chapter 2). While in America second-wave feminism caused a revolution in American sexual thought when radical feminists publicly discussed orgasm, masturbation and the clitoris (Gerhard 2001), the topic of sex and women's pleasure remained unfathomable in cultures where women were not imagined to be sexual beings capable of experiencing sexual pleasure. In the Philippines where women were not seen to be capable of performing desire (although they were seen as objects of desire), sexuality was raised only in the context of prostitution until the mid-1990s (Roces, Chapter 3), and in Singapore sexuality, including lesbianism, is still considered 'off limits' today (Lyons, Chapter 5). In the last decade, performances of Eve Ensler's play *The Vagina Monologues* (originally performed in New York in 1996 and performed in over eighty countries since) inspired local versions that directly challenge the shame and silence surrounding women's reproductive health, sexual desire and sexuality. Oftentimes these performances were the first times when the word 'vagina' was uttered in a public venue (Edwards 2009; The Libby Manaoag Files 2002). Chinese performances of the play gave birth to an ad hoc group of V-Day activists (from the newly formed Chinese middle classes) 'who link themselves directly to global, high profile and glamorous campaigns on topics of a risqué nature' expressing a feminism that is 'antagonistic, confrontational and demanding of public and peer attention' (Edwards 2008b: 207; Edwards 2009: 114–20).

Despite the region-wide aversion to the imagined stereotype of an aggressive Western 'feminist activist', Asian women activists were not afraid to display a militant face particularly in demonstrations—signature events for most feminists in Asia. From Hong Kong to Indonesia, the Philippines, China, Japan and India—rallies, marches, demonstrations and protests were the visible face of feminism in Asia. From the early twentieth century when women activists in China smashed parliament windows in Nanjing in support of the same act by British suffragists on Bond Street in March 1912 (Edwards and Roces 2004: 1; Edwards 2008a; Edwards, Chapter 4), to the annual International Women's Day Marches held around the world since the first decade of the twentieth century, the spectacle of women protesters called attention to important issues. Women activists have been most creative in organizing colourful events to communicate their agendas. In these cases, they have tapped on theatre, media, the Internet and the semiotics of dress/costume to deliver their demands with a touch of drama. While most events were connected to local issues, some were transnational— when they marched on International Women's Day, they imparted the desire no matter how elusive for a global sisterhood, and when they demonstrated against the war against Iraq, they projected their aim for a world without war. Although some of our contributors have made the observation that Vietnamese (Chiricosta, Chapter 8) and Thai (Lindberg Falk, Chapter 7) feminists were more interested in praxis than theory, the above examples show activists continually testing various theoretical positions, rejecting, modifying or adapting them to specific contexts.

Political contexts

Although the transnational 'mental space' of feminist debate has been important in the development of Asian feminist theories, the political contexts of each country had the power to open or close the doors enabling transnational exchange of ideas or transnational organizing. In China, Louise Edwards (Chapter 4) illustrates how women's movements were greatly affected by the pendulum swings of openness and closure adopted by particular Chinese governments. Although Edwards argues that China presents us with a unique case study of extremes, other countries such as Indonesia, the Philippines, Pakistan, Korea and India (Chapters 2, 3, 10, 11, and 13) who have also lived through the turbulent oscillations between dictatorship and democracy experienced the clear connection between the type of political regime and the tenor of the women's movements there. In this sense, the Asian context differs from Western countries with stable democracies. The case study of China reveals how a xenophobic regime can easily end the transnational contact needed to stimulate and support the local women's movements (Edwards, Chapter 4). Those countries that experienced war (including civil wars and separatist movements) discovered that wartime situations also hampered transnational organizing or connections (see Edwards, Chapter 4; Jacobsen, Chapter 12; Kim and Kim, Chapter 11; and Chiricosta, Chapter 8).

Activists' close connections to 'Nationalist' politics has been both liberating and constraining for them (Blackburn, Chapter 2; Edwards, Chapter 4; Lim, Chapter 9). The women's movements in Asia had the double challenge of opposing colonial and authoritarian regimes as well as the gender discrimination of the nationalist movements they supported. Jayawardena analyzed the tension between feminism and nationalism in the colonial era as activists, already political participants in the independence movements, were pressured into placing the 'national interest' above 'women's issues' in the turbulent fight for liberation from colonial rule (Jayawardena 1986). This tension was once more reproduced in the post-independence dictatorships where the movements for national liberation and the restoration of democratic institutions asked women once again to prioritize national interests over women's issues.

Authoritarian regimes by nature were macho regimes that idealized the masculine and were not particularly sympathetic to women's issues, preferring to redefine the feminine in ways that suited their agendas (Suryakusuma 1996; Fahey 1998; Sunindyo 1998; Heng and Devan 1992; Ungar 2000; Chan 2000; Lyons-Lee 1998; Werner 2004). Communist authoritarian regimes were more conscious about prescribing gender equality but women's issues had to conform to the regime's vision for women, and this prevented them from organizing outside the officially endorsed women's organization. As the authors on China, Vietnam and Korea illustrate, this also stunted the growth of the women's movements there (Edwards, Chapter 4; Chiricosta, Chapter 8; Kim and Kim, Chapter 11). The chapter by Lenore Lyons in this anthology clearly demonstrated the limits of activism in an authoritarian state such as Singapore (Lyons, Chapter 5), while Doris Chang's book on the women's movement in Taiwan argued that during periods of 'soft authoritarianism' autonomous movements emerged but were acting within the political parameters set by the authoritarian regime (much like Singapore), but that in periods of 'hard authoritarianism' women's movements collapsed (Chang 2009: 3). Martial law 'made it virtually impossible for the autonomous women's movement to establish a non-governmental organization' (Chang 2009: 159). On the other hand, in Indonesia, Sukarno's ties with the Indonesian Communist Party (PKI) enabled the women's organization Gerwani to achieve a mass following. But the subsequent military rule of President Suharto (1965–98) destroyed the gains made by the women's movement among the working classes; until this day it has yet to recover its support from this sector of the population (Blackburn, Chapter 2; Weiringa 2002). Hong Kong's handover to PRC-governance has split the women's movement into pro-Democracy and pro-PRC camps, fracturing activists who although they differed in approach were more or less concerned with the same gender issues (Lim, Chapter 9). The negative impact of authoritarian regimes on women's movement in Asia is underscored as women's movements in Indonesia, the Philippines, Pakistan and Korea blossomed when democratic institutions were restored. The global expansion of civil society in the last thirty years epitomized by the proliferation of NGOs, provided another impetus because in many Asian countries women's NGOs were *ipso facto* prime actors in the women's movements.

Transnational secular and religious worlds

The impact of the international feminist movement should not be ignored, as fundamental concepts such as women's suffrage, 'women's rights are human rights'—and shifts in vocabulary from 'reproductive health' to 'reproductive rights' to 'reproductive self-determination' were appropriated by activists all over Asia. Western liberal feminist ideas driving the UN's legislation on women's rights such as CEDAW of 1979, and the DEVAW of 1993 legitimized the agendas of particular activists in the region. In 1946, the Economic and Social Council (ECOSOC) of the UN created a subcommittee under the human rights commission that was renamed the Commission on the Status of Women (CSW) in 1947. Of the forty-five members of this commission, eleven were from Asia (Tripon 2007: 1; see also Commission on the Status of Women 2010) but, if we exclude the Middle East, eight is a more accurate number. In addition, scores of NGOs were allowed to participate in the special NGO sessions of the yearly meetings of the CSW (Tripon 2007: 1). A number of Asian NGOs also acquired consultative status with the UN.

Apart from regular meetings in women's conferences around the world but most especially in New York for the CSW meetings, many NGOs based in Asia received funding from overseas, particularly in the 1990s. While accepting grant money produced its own set of problems including fraught debates among activists about whether or not funding should be taken from particular bodies or Northern countries,[1] the influx of aid required further communications and closer connections with a global community of activists or organizations.

The mere fact that Beijing hosted the Fourth World Conference on Women in 1995 and the related NGO Forum in Huairou identified China, and Asia more broadly, as an important site (not just a venue) for international feminist organizing and discussions. Beijing and Huairou became major turning points in the international feminist movement in terms of the unprecedented numbers of participants (3,340 workshops attended by 30,000 participants (Friedman 1999: 361)) and because it resulted in the proclamation of the Beijing Platform for Action adopted unanimously by 189 countries. That this platform continues to be invoked in international political arenas reiterates the authority of Asia as a benchmark for international goals.

Women activists in Asia also participated in the transnational debates on women and religion as main actors, not just as supporting cast. Religions in Asia have been very influential in defining 'the feminine' and women's movements from the very beginning had to confront religious mores that were prejudicial to women. Where religion was intrinsically linked to notions of national identity such as Thailand (where to be Thai was to be Buddhist), and Malaysia (where to be Malay was to be Muslim), women's movements showed a distinct focus on feminism's connection to religion. The neo-conservative swing, evident from the closing decades of the twentieth century, posed an additional challenge for feminists, particularly those who aspired for women's ordination in Theravada Buddhism and Catholicism, and Muslim women who wanted to work for women's rights within the framework of Islam (Nurmila 2009). This particular stream of women's movements was fundamentally transnational in orientation, structure, advocacy and membership as the religious communities were imagined in global terms.

While nuns and religious women in Western countries were hardly associated with women's studies or feminism, quite the opposite was true in Asia where religious women were among the leading feminist theoreticians. Catholic nuns from religious congregations were automatically connected to their 'mother houses' abroad and, barred from ordination, were free to travel overseas to obtain postgraduate qualifications. Many took advantage of this unique opportunity. They went to the US and Europe to enrol in courses on women and religion, feminist theology, Christology, Philosophy, Missiology and Ecclesiology, for example. The years spent overseas gave them an international perspective while also giving them a chance to establish international perspectives and networks (Roces 2008). When the Ecumenical Association of Third World Theologians (EATWOT) was formed in 1976, Filipino and Korean religious women were participants. In 1981, the women of EATWOT proposed the formation of a Women's Commission 'to promote a theology of liberation from the perspective of women from the Third World, a theology that springs from a critical awareness of women's subjugated position and a commitment to change it' (Fabella 1993: 36). The Women's Commission had an African, Latin American and Asian branch with Asian women theologians Mary John Mananzan (RGS or Religious of the Good Shepherd) and Virginia Fabella (MM or Maryknoll Sisters) from the Philippines, Aruna Granadason from India, Kwok Pui-lan from Hong Kong and Sun Ai Li Park from Korea among the movers and the shakers. When the Women's Commission founded its own journal, *In God's Image*, to focus on doing feminist theology in the Third World, Sun Ai Li Park became editor. It was this unique opportunity to discuss feminist theology in a transnational mental space (the EATWOT conventions, in the journal *In God's Image* and other publications) that enabled nuns and Christian religious women to have a conversation about doing theology as women in Asia, and in doing so had an impact on international feminist theology (a sample of these publications include Kwok 2000, 2002; Fabella, Lee and Suh 1992; Fabella and Park 1989; Fabella 1980; Fabella and Torres 1983; see full list in Roces 2008). In the Philippines, some of these feminist nuns founded important women's organizations and taught women's studies at tertiary institutions (Roces 2008).

The case study of Chatsumarn Kabilsingh, the first Thai woman to receive ordination in the Theravada tradition, demonstrated the tremendous potential of transnational connections. Kabilsingh herself had an international education—her BA in philosophy was from Visva Bharati University in India (1966), her MA in religion from McMaster University in Canada (1971) and her PhD in Buddhist studies at Magadha University in India (1980) (Mananzan 2004: 127). The Thai *sangha* does not recognize women's ordination so she was ordained abroad in Sri Lanka in 2001. Monica Lindberg Falk (Chapter 7) has argued that it was the Sakyaditha transnational network (founded by Kabilsingh now Dhammananda Bhikkhuni and three other *bhikkunis*) that 'has been crucial for the restoration of the *bhikkuni* order'. Despite the disapproval of the Thai *sangha*, Dhammananda Bhikkhuni began the task of establishing a community of female ordained monks in Thailand. Women monks from abroad were important as allies and helpers in the launching of this pivotal and revolutionary project (Lindberg Falk, Chapter 7).

The transnational organization Sisters in Islam (SIS) was founded in Malaysia in 1988 and registered as a NGO in 1993 under the name SIS Forum (Malaysia) Berhad. Its website appealed to the global community of Muslims as well as the national community of Malaysia (Sisters in Islam 2009a). Indeed, the public talks and the plethora of publications including the many edited anthologies produced by SIS explored themes across a wide gamut of countries connecting the Asian region to Egypt, Iran and the Middle East (see, for example, Anwar 2009; Othman 2005) even though there were versions in Bahasa Malaysia language. SIS was founded by Muslim professional women from Kuala Lumpur for the purpose of promoting the rights of Muslim women within the framework of Islam:

> Our mission is to promote an awareness of the true principles of Islam, principles that enshrine the concept of equality between women and men, and to strive towards creating a society that upholds the Islamic principles of equality, justice, freedom and dignity within a democratic state.
>
> (Sisters in Islam 2009b)

It has proposed reforms in the Syariah and campaigned against the implementation of *Hudhud* (Islamic Criminal Laws) (Ng, Mohammad and Hui 2006: 170). It locates itself in the 'precarious middle ground' based on a critical re-examination and reinterpretation of the Islamic texts (the 'true principles of Islam' mentioned in the mission statement) as part of their objectives of eliminating discrimination against women (Ng, Mohammad and Hui 2006: 98–9; Sisters in Islam 2009b). In a 2005 anthology, SIS clearly dissociated itself from what they termed 'religious extremism' or 'Islamic fundamentalism (Othman 2005: 3), referring to themselves as part of Muslim women's movements rather than Malaysian Muslim women's movements (Othman 2005: 8). Identifying themselves as Muslim feminists they described their *raison d'être* as a commitment to changing Islam from within to make it more gentle and friendly towards women (Othman 2005: 8). Indonesian feminists discovered the advantages of tapping into this international network (Blackburn, Chapter 2) for advocacy at home. Andrea Fleschenberg's chapter on Pakistan (Chapter 10) emphasized the importance of religious fundamentalism to the development of the feminist movement where campaigns over *Hudhud* paralleled those led by SIS. As a consequence, the feminist movements in Asia also fundamentally challenged religious movements in those countries.

Track records

After a century of women's activism, how do we evaluate the track record of women's movements in Asia? Each of our authors tries to answer this question for their particular country case study. Clearly, collectively women's activism in

Asia is poly-vocal, vibrant and visible. There are feminist-inspired NGOs all over Asia (literally in the hundreds and thousands) that choose to focus on a myriad number of issues. The strength (in terms of numbers, class representation, ethnic representation, for example) of the women's movements varies from country to country and there is still the question of whether a public presence or numbers translate to actual women's power. The price to pay for having many voices is the propensity for disunity and dissent, another continuing challenge activists must overcome. The advantages of a united front can be seen in the success of the Violence against Women (VAW) campaigns all over Asia.

Activists adopted two specific strategies: lobbying for legislative change and consciousness-raising. The former brought feminist agendas into the public sphere of formal politics (from women's demand for suffrage) and has had a massive impact in countries where pro-women legislation has been passed that fundamentally altered how crimes against women were perceived (such as redefining rape and taking it from a crime against chastity to a crime against person in the Philippines), or laws adapting liberal feminist principles about equality in the workforce and upholding women's reproductive rights (such as maternity leave, menstrual leave and so on). In the last quarter of a century, Asian feminists launched an entire feminist re-education campaign to resocialize their entire countries into rethinking gender. Women's studies courses were being taught in creative ways, all with a national focus. The role of the media (print, television, radio, the internet) was absolutely critical not just in disseminating the new ideologies of feminism in the Asian context but also in removing the cultural taboos about the public discussion of crucial women's issues such as domestic violence, rape, incest, sexuality, contraception, lesbianism and women's desire, sex, abortion, divorce and partner infidelity (to name a few). Mina Roces' chapter discussed how women's movements in the Philippines identified every person as a potential student for their 'women's studies courses', and every venue transformed into a 'classroom' as activists ran workshops in community halls, feminist liturgy practiced in chapels, and theatre as advocacy performed in basketball courts (Chapter 3). Activists were proactive in dismantling cultural constructions of woman in their country.

Were Asian feminists able to build a base of followers? Is it possible to argue that after a century of activism, women's movements in Asia are now mass movements? Each of our contributors attempted to assess this in their country case study. Some countries such as Pakistan (Fleschenberg, Chapter 10) were unable to break the middle-class hold on the women's movement, while a country such as Singapore has not gone beyond a 'one organization' women's movement (Lyons, Chapter 5). A more complex story unfolded in Indonesia where, on the one hand, the big secular mass following built from the 1950s was lost in 1965 but, on the other hand, Islamic women's organizations were able to acquire a huge base, particularly in more recent times (Blackburn, Chapter 2). The issue of ethnicity is another one where more work still needs to be done. Women's movements in Asia still need to pay more attention to the minority and/or indigenous women; a point made by the authors on Indonesia, Singapore and the Philippines.

This book is the first to tackle the task of writing a general history of women's movements in Asia over a century. As such, it is by nature just a starting point for examining Asian feminisms in both the national and the transnational context. In this enterprise, the contributors have documented the ways in which 'feminisms' were indigenized in each Asian country. But since women's movements there were not inward-looking and as activists continue to dialogue in transnational mental spaces and exercise across-the-border organizing, they will continue to have an impact on the international feminist movement. The specific impact of Asian feminists on the international scene is one important area of future research. Leila Rupp's book *Worlds of Women: The Making of an International Women's Movement* (Rupp 1997) pioneered the research in this field for the first half of the twentieth century and the time is ripe for a study on the next period that locates Asian feminists in the wider world of international feminism and acknowledges their contribution. In locating Asian feminisms in transnational spaces, our authors have started the first step towards this important project.

Despite the fact that Asian activists conceived feminisms or feminist theories in binary terms (Asia versus the Western Other), in practice, they were always happy to seek allies abroad (including the 'West') for their advocacies 'at home'. Vera Mackie introduced the concept of 'transnational imaginary' in an essay that focused on the activities of the 'women in black' who protested Japanese atrocities against women in World War II (Mackie 2004: 252). According to Mackie, 'women in black' imagined their transnational links with like-minded activists around the world (ibid.). Asian feminists discovered the power of this 'transnational imaginary', tapping into this 'mental space' in their campaigns to refashion women at home.

Note

1   These same tensions were observed in Venezuela as well; see Friedman (1999).

References

Anwar, Z. (ed.) (2009) *Wanted Equality and Justice in the Muslim Family*, Selangor: Musawah an Initiative of Sisters in Islam.

Basu, A. (2000) 'Globalization of the Local/Localization of the Global Mapping Transnational Women's Movements', *Meridians: Feminism, Race, Transnationalism*, 1, 1: 68–84.

Blackburn, S. (2004) *Women and the State in Modern Indonesia*, Cambridge: Cambridge University Press.

—— (2008) 'The Aftermath for Women Warriors: Cambodia and East Timor', *IIAS Newsletter*, 48 (Summer): 14–15.

Chan, J. (2000) 'The Status of Women in a Patriarchal State: The Case of Singapore', in L. Edwards and M. Roces (eds) *Women in Asia: Tradition, Modernity, Globalisation*, Sydney and Ann Arbor: Allen & Unwin and University of Michigan Press, pp. 38–58.

Chang, D.T. (2009) *Women's Movements in Twentieth-Century Taiwan*, Urbana: University of Illinois Press.

Chaudhuri, M. (ed.) (2004) *Feminism in India*, London: Zed Books.

Commission on the Status of Women (2010) 'Overview: About the Commission'. Online. Available HTTP: <http://www.un.org/womenwatch/daw/csw/> (accessed 24 September 2009).

Croll, E. (2000) *Endangered Daughters Discrimination and Development in Asia*, London: Routledge.

Dales, L. (2009) *Feminist Movements in Contemporary Japan*, London: Routledge.

DAWN website (2009). Online. Available HTTP: <http://www.dawnnet.org/> (accessed 24 September 2009).

DuBois, E.C. (2009) 'Women's Movements', in A. Iriye and P.-Y. Saunier (eds) *The Palgrave Dictionary of Trans-national History From the Mid-19th Century to the Present Day*, New York: Palgrave Macmillan, pp. 1114–20.

Edwards, L. (2000) 'Policing the Modern Woman in Republican China', *Modern China*, 26, 2 (April): 115–47.

—— (2004) 'Chinese Women's Campaigns for Suffrage: Nationalism, Confucianism and Political Agency', in L. Edwards and M. Roces (eds) *Women's Suffrage in Asia: Gender, Nationalism and Democracy*, London: Routledge, pp. 59–78.

—— (2008a) *Gender, Politics and Democracy Women's Suffrage in China*, Stanford: Stanford University Press.

—— (2008b) 'Issue-based Politics Feminism with Chinese Characteristics of the Return of Bourgeois Feminism?', in D.S.G. Goodman (ed.) *The New Rich in China Future Rulers, Present Lives*, London: Routledge, pp. 201–12.

—— (2009) 'Diversity and Evolution in the State-in-Society: International Influences in Combating Violence Against Women', in L.C. Li (ed.) *The Chinese State in Transition:Processes and Contests in Local China*, London: Routledge, pp. 108–26.

Edwards, L. and Roces, M. (eds) (2004) *Women's Suffrage in Asia: Gender, Nationalism and Democracy*, London: Routledge.

Edwards, L. and Roces, M. (2004) 'Introduction Orienting the Global Women's Suffrage Movement', in L. Edwards and M. Roces (eds) *Women's Suffrage in Asia: Gender, Nationalism and Democracy*, London: Routledge, pp. 1–23.

Enloe, C. (1989) *Bananas, Beaches and Bases Making Feminist Sense of International Politics*, London: Pandora.

Evans, S.M. (2003) *Tidal Wave How Women Changed America at Century's End*, New York: Free Press.

Fabella, V. (ed.) (1980) *Asia's Struggle for Full Humanity: Toward a Relevant Theology, Papers from the Asian Theological Conference, January 7–20, 1979, Wennappuwa, Sri Lanka*, Maryknoll, NY: Orbis Books.

Fabella, V.M.M. (1993) *Beyond Bonding a Third World Women's Theological Journey*, Manila: Ecumenical Association of Third World Theologians and Institute of Women's Studies.

Fabella, V. and Park, S.A.L. (eds) (1989) *We Dare to Dream: Doing Theology as Asian Women*, Hong Kong: Asian Women's Resource Center for Culture and Theology and the EATWOT Women's Commission in Asia.

Fabella, V. and Torres, S. (eds) (1983) *Irruption of the Third World Challenge to Theology.* Papers from the Fifth International Conference of the Ecumenical Association of Third World Theologians, 17–29 August 1981. New Delhi, India. Maryknoll, NY: Orbis Books.

Fabella, V., Lee, P.K.H. and Suh, D.K.-S. (eds) (1992) *Asian Christian Spirituality: Reclaiming Traditions*, Maryknoll, NY: Orbis Books.

Fahey, S. (1998) 'Vietnamese Women in the Renovation Era', in K. Sen and M. Stivens (eds) *Gender and Power in Affluent Asia*, London: Routledge, pp. 222–49.

Fleschenberg, A. (2008) 'Asia's Women Politicians at the Top: Roaring Tigresses or Tame Kittens?', in K. Iwanaga (ed.) *Women's Political Participation and Representation in Asia*, Copenhagen: NIAS Press, pp. 23–54.

Friedman, E.J. (1999) 'The Effects of "Transnationalism Reversed" in Venezuela: Assessing the Impact of the UN Global Conferences on the Women's Movement', *International Feminist Journal of Politics*, 1, 3 (Autumn): 357–81.

Gangoli, G. (2007) *Indian Feminisms Law, Patriarchies and Violence in India*, Aldershot: Ashgate.

Gerhard, J. (2001) *Desiring Revolution Second-Wave Feminism and the Rewriting of American Sexual Thought 1920 to 1982*, New York: Columbia University Press.

Grewal, I. and Kaplan, C. (1994) 'Introduction: Transnational Feminist Practices and Questions of Postmodernity', in I. Grewal and C. Kaplan (eds) *Scattered Hegemonies Postmodernity and Transnational Feminist Practices*, Minneapolis: University of Minnesota Press, pp. 1–33.

Heng, G. and Devan, J. (1992) 'State Fatherhood: The Politics of Nationalism, Sexuality and Race in Singapore', in A. Parker, M. Russo, D. Sommer and P. Yaeger (eds) *Nationalisms and Sexualities*, London: Routledge, pp. 343–64.

Hudson, V. and den Boer, A.M. (2004) *Bare Branches Security Implications of Asia's Surplus Male Population*, Cambridge, MA: The MIT Press.

Iriye, A. and Saunier, P.-Y. (2009) 'Introduction The Professor and the Madman', in A. Iriye and P.-Y. Saunier (eds) *The Palgrave Dictionary of Trans-national History From the Mid-19th Century to the Present Day*, New York: Palgrave Macmillan, pp. xvii–xx.

Iwanaga, K. (2008) 'Introduction: Women and Politics in Asia: A Comparative Perspective', in K. Iwanaga (ed.) *Women's Political Participation and Representation in Asia*, Copenhagen: NIAS Press, pp. 1–22.

Jayawardena, K. (1986) *Feminism and Nationalism in the Third World*, London: Zed Books.

Jeffrey, L.A. (2002) *Sex and Borders: Gender, National Identity and Prostitution Policy in Thailand*, Vancouver: University of British Columbia Press.

Judd, E.R. (2002) *The Chinese Women's Movement between State and Market*, Stanford: Stanford University Press.

Jung, K. (2010) *Practising Feminism in South Korea*, London: Routledge.

Kaplan, C. (1994) 'The Politics of Location as Transnational Feminist Cultural Practice', in I. Grewal and C. Kaplan (eds) *Scattered Hegemonies Postmodernity and Transnational Feminist Practices*, Minneapolis: University of Minnesota Press, pp. 117–52.

Keck, M.E. and Sikkink, K. (1998) *Activists Beyond Borders*, Ithaca: Cornell University Press.

Kwok, P.-l. (2000) *Introducing Asian Feminist Theology*, Cleveland: The Pilgrim Press.

—— (2002) 'Feminist Theology as International Discourse', in S.F. Parsons (ed.) *The Cambridge Companion to Feminist Theology*, Cambridge: Cambridge University Press, pp. 23–39.

Law, L. (1997) 'A Matter of "Choice": Discourses on Prostitution in the Philippines', in L. Manderson and M. Jolly (eds) *States of Desire Economies of Pleasure*, Chicago: University of Chicago Press, pp. 233–61.

Lyons, L. (2004) *A State of Ambivalence: The Feminist Movement in Singapore*, Leiden: E.J. Brill.

Lyons-Lee, L. (1998) 'The "Graduate Woman" Phenomenon, Changing Constructions of the Family in Singapore', *Sojourn*, 13, 2 (October): 309–37.

Mackie, V. (2003) *Feminism in Modern Japan Citizenship, Embodiment and Sexuality*, Cambridge: Cambridge University Press.

—— (2004) 'Shifting the Axis Feminism and the National Imaginary', in B.S.A. Yeoh and K. Willis (eds) *State/Nation/Transnation Perspectives on Transnationalism in the Asia-Pacific*, London: Routledge, pp. 238–56.

Mananzan, M.J. (2004) *Woman, Religion & Spirituality in Asia*, Pasig City: Anvil.

Martyn, E. (2004) *The Women's Movement in Postcolonial Indonesia: Gender and Nation in a New Democracy*, London: Routledge.

Milwertz, C. (2002) *Beijing Women Organising for Change: A New Wave of the Chinese Women's Movement*, Copenhagen: NIAS Press.

Molony, B. (2004) 'Citizenship and Suffrage in Interwar Japan', in L. Edwards and M. Roces (eds) *Women's Suffrage in Asia. Gender, Nationalism and Democracy*, London: Routledge, pp. 127–51.

Ng, C., Mohamad, M. and Hui, T.B. (2006) *Feminism and the Women's Movement in Malaysia An Unsung (R)evolution*, London: Routledge.

Nurmila, N. (2009) *Women, Islam and Everyday Life: Negotiating Polygamy in Indonesia*, London: Routledge.

Othman, N. (ed.) (2005) *Muslim Women and the Challenge of Islamic Extremism*, Selangor: Sisters in Islam.

Ray, R. (1999) *Fields of Protest Women's Movements in India*, Minneapolis/London: University of Minnesota Press.

Roces, M. (1998) *Women, Power and Kinship Politics in Post-War Philippines*, Westport, CN: Praeger.

—— (2004) 'Is the Suffragist an American Colonial Construct? Defining "the Filipino Woman" in Colonial Philippines', in L. Edwards and M. Roces (eds) *Women's Suffrage in Asia: Gender, Nationalism and Democracy*, London: Routledge, pp. 24–58.

—— (2008) 'The Filipino Catholic Nun as Transnational Feminist', *Women's History Review*, 17, 1 (February): 57–78.

—— (2009) 'Prostitution, Women's Movements and the Victim Narrative in the Philippines', *Women's Studies International Forum*, 32, 4 (July–August): 270–80.

Roces, M. and Edwards, L. (2009) 'Women in Asia as a Distinct Research Field', in L. Edwards and M. Roces (eds) *Major Works on Women in Asia*, vol. 1, London: Routledge, pp. 1–18.

Rupp, L.J. (1997) *Worlds of Women: The Making of an International Women's Movement*, Princeton, NJ: Princeton University Press.

Sisters in Islam (2009a) 'Sisters in Islam'. Online. Available HTTP: <http://www.sistersinislam.org.my/BM/index.htm/> (accessed 24 September 2009).

—— (2009b) 'Mission'. Online. Available HTTP: <http://www.sistersinislam.org.my/BM/mission.htm> (accessed 24 September 2009).

Stivens, M. (2000) 'Becoming Modern in Malaysia: Women at the End of the Twentieth Century', in L. Edwards and M. Roces (eds) *Women in Asia: Tradition, Modernity and Globalisation*, Sydney and Ann Arbor: Allen & Unwin and University of Michigan Press, pp. 16–38.

Sunindyo, S. (1998) 'When Earth is Female and the Nation is Mother: Gender, the Armed Forces and Nationalism in Indonesia', *Feminist Review*, 58: 1–21.

Suryakusuma, J.I. (1996) 'The State and Sexuality in New Order Indonesia', in L. Sears (ed.) *Fantasizing the Feminine in Indonesia*, Durham and London: Duke University Press, pp. 92–119.

The Libby Manaoag Files (2002) *The Libby Manaoag Files Ang Paghahanap sa Puwertas Princessas, Birthings A Journal of Shared Lives A Nationwide Performance Tour on Women's Health and Reproductive Rights*, Quezon City: PETA.

Tripon, O.H. (2007) *Shaping the Women's Global Agenda Filipino Women in the United Nations Commission on the Status of Women/CEDAW Committee*, Manila: NCRFW.

Tyrrell, I. (2007) *Transnational Nation United States History in Global Perspective since 1789*, New York: Palgrave Macmillan.

Ueno, C. (2004) *Nationalism and Gender*, trans. B. Yamamoto, Melbourne: Trans Pacific Press.

Ungar, E. (2000) 'Re-gendering Vietnam: From Militant to Market Socialism', in L. Edwards and M. Roces (eds) *Women in Asia: Tradition, Modernity and Globalisation*, Sydney and Ann Arbor: Allen & Unwin and University of Michigan Press, pp. 291–317.

Veneracion-Rallonza, L. (2008) 'Women and the Democracy Project: A Feminist Take on Women's Political Participation in the Philippines', in K. Iwanaga (ed.) *Women's Political Participation and Representation in Asia*, Copenhagen: NIAS Press, pp. 210–52.

Weinbaum, A.E., Thomas, L.M., Ramamurthy, P., Poiger, U.G., Yue Dong, M. and Barlow, T.E. (eds) (2008) *The Modern Girl Around the World: Consumption, Modernity, and Globalization*, Durham and London: Duke University Press.

Wieringa, S. (2002) *Sexual Politics in Indonesia*, Basingstoke and New York: Palgrave MacMillan; The Hague: Institute of Social Studies.

Wells, K. (2004) 'Expanding Their Realm: Women and Public Agency in Colonial Korea', in L. Edwards and M. Roces (eds) *Women's Suffrage in Asia: Gender, Nationalism and Democracy*, London: Routledge, pp. 152–69.

Werner, J. (2004) 'State-Subject Making and Womanhood in the Red River Delta of Vietnam', *Asian Studies Review*, 28 (June): 115–31.

Wesoky, S. (2002) *Chinese Feminism Faces Globalisation*, New York and London: Routledge.

Wieringa, S. (2002) *Sexual Politics in Indonesia*, Basingstoke: Palgrave Macmillan.

2 Feminism and the women's movement in the world's largest Islamic nation

Susan Blackburn

Indonesia is a country of some 230 million people of whom almost 90 per cent claim to be Muslim, making it the largest Islamic nation in the world. One would expect that the character of its women's movement would differ from non-Islamic countries and have something in common with other Islamic countries. Unlike some Islamic countries, however, Indonesia is not an Islamic state, meaning that its governments have never, like those in Iran or Pakistan, been committed to the enforcement of Islamic law, with its many negative consequences for women.[1] This chapter will attempt to identify what is special about feminism and the women's movement in Indonesia. Although few in Indonesia would claim to be feminists, it is legitimate to use the word to apply to much of the women's movement if we understand feminism in a basic sense as 'analyzing the problems of women' and 'acting to oppose discrimination against women'. In some important respects, the Indonesian situation resembles that in other Asian countries, and I will discuss these similarities before explaining the combination of circumstances that make Indonesia unique.

What is similar to elsewhere in Asia

Indonesia, known as the Netherlands Indies before the World War II, was colonized by the Dutch, who did not transfer sovereignty to the Indonesian Republic until 1949. The origins of feminist thinking and the women's movement in Indonesia resembled those in most other colonized parts of Asia: they coincided with the rise of nationalism, and the women's movement was closely intertwined with the nationalist struggle for many years. Receiving a Western education stimulated both nationalists and early Indonesian feminists such as Raden Ajeng Kartini (1879–1904) to view their own society in a new light. In Kartini's case, that education led to correspondence with Dutchwomen of a feminist persuasion and caused her to rebel against the restrictive customs imposed on upper-class women among the Javanese, the largest single ethnic group in a multi-ethnic country (Cote 1992).[2] The first women's groups, formed from the 1910s onwards, followed in her footsteps, but as nationalism swept through the ranks of educated Indonesians in the 1920s, the women's organizations joined forces with it. The first congress of women's organizations, held in 1928, was overtly nationalist as well as feminist. It gave rise to a federation of women's organizations that spoke on behalf of Indonesian women.

Although some influential Dutch feminists had close relations with Indonesian women in the early twentieth century, relations declined as nationalism grew and colonial policy hardened against Indonesian political activists. The role of the Women's Suffrage Association is a case in point. In 1908, Dutchwomen created a branch in the Indies of the Women's Suffrage Association, with both Dutch and Indonesian members. Initially part of the struggle for suffrage for women in the Netherlands, after that was gained in 1919 the Indies organization turned its attention to representative assemblies that were being established in the colony, notably the People's Council, formed in 1918, which was partially elected by men of different races. In order to strengthen its case for women's right to vote, the Association sought the support of Indonesian women and gained a few prominent recruits, including one of Kartini's sisters (Roekmini Santoso) and Chailan Sjamsoe Datoe Toemenggoeng, who was active in the women's movement as a leader of an organization for the wives of civil servants. However, few in the Indonesian women's movement took an interest in suffrage until the late 1930s, partly because most women's organizations were more concerned with pressing social issues and partly because the nationalist movement regarded representation in colonial institutions as a waste of time when the authorities were so implacably opposed to negotiating the steps leading to independence. When the radical nationalists were all excluded from political activity by government measures (most of the leaders being held in internal exile), the rump of the more moderate nationalists took a more conciliatory line and began to push for democratic reforms, including universal suffrage. By this stage (late 1930s), the women's movement also endorsed women's suffrage. Just before the Japanese Occupation in 1942, the People's Council won over the government to support the extension of limited voting rights to women, but no elections were held until after the war (Blackburn 2004b; Locher-Scholten 2000; Martyn 2005).

Being so closely associated with nationalism was both liberating and constraining for Indonesian women, as Asian women found elsewhere. It meant that they had to be careful about their relationship to Western feminism, since the nationalist movement was suspicious of foreign influences, particularly as they might affect women who were supposed to be the bearers of all that was good in Indonesian tradition. One could see this caution at work in the first women's congress in 1928. None of the participants called themselves feminist, and some chose to distance themselves from Western women's movements. While they spoke admiringly of the progress achieved by Western women, they felt the methods used by some feminists (particularly the British suffragettes) were 'excessive'. They also warned Indonesian women not to lose respect for their own Eastern culture, even though there were many aspects within it, such as unequal marriage customs, that needed to be changed. Moreover, these Indonesian women had also examined the position of Western women closely and were aware that in some respects Indonesian women's rights were superior; for instance, in relation to property within the family (speeches of Sastrowirjo, Goenawan, Djojoadigoeno and Sastroamidjojo in 1928 Women's Congress cited in Blackburn 2008). Identifying with nationalism also constrained the relations of Indonesian women with groups of women who were deemed to be 'non-Indonesian', including not only the Dutch but also Eurasians and Chinese Indonesians, neither of whom were admitted to women's congresses.[3]

On the other hand, being nationalists was also liberating for women because it legitimized their taking part in public political life, learning to make speeches and participating in organizations alongside men as well as within their own groups. This was all part of modern life, and women (as well as many nationalist men) argued strongly that in order for Indonesia to advance, it would have to modernize in many respects, including in relation to women.[4] In a country where women have not suffered as much discrimination as in many other parts of Asia, it was not so difficult for women to take public roles, but it was a greater struggle for many women in the upper ranks of society (such as Kartini) where the restrictions had been greater than for ordinary women, and it was harder for women in strictly Islamic circles. By the late 1920s, however, women were making speeches in Bahasa Indonesia, based on Malay, one of the many languages of the archipelago, a language which the nationalist movement had chosen as its lingua franca in 1928 and which most Indonesians had to make a special effort to learn. By the 1930s, a number of prominent women leaders had emerged, such as the fiery feminist nationalist Suwarni Pringgodigdo, and the legal reformer Maria Ullfah Santoso (Vreede-de Stuers 1960). Whereas the former took a hard line on many issues, such as opposition to polygamy, the latter was prepared to move towards fundamental change by laying the ground through negotiating legislative reform and counselling women experiencing marital problems.

By the end of the colonial period, the nationalist movement, although dominated by men, had come to accept such feminist notions as female suffrage. After all, most male nationalists, as in other Asian countries, were themselves strong supporters of some women's rights which they held to be essential in shaping a modern nation. The Islamic leader Haji Agus Salim, for instance, opposed the segregation of the sexes at meetings of Islamic organizations (Blackburn 2002: 26) and the moderate secular nationalist Dr Sutomo campaigned against early marriage (Blackburn 2002). This did not prevent nationalist leaders such as Sukarno (later the first president of Indonesia) from warning women that the first priority always was national independence (Brown 1981).

Nationalist ambivalence towards feminism continued even after independence, as it has done elsewhere in Asia. From early days, Indonesian women's organizations have been careful to distinguish valued aspects of what is seen as 'Indonesian culture' that are regarded as incompatible with an often caricatured version of Western feminism. As one well-known Indonesian feminist, Saparinah Sadli, has noted,

> The terms 'feminism', 'feminist' and even 'gender' are still questioned by the majority of Indonesians. They are considered by many to be non-indigenous

concepts that are irrelevant to Indonesian values. Certain assumptions remain common: feminism is a Western or northern concept; it is anti-men; it perceives men to be the source of all gender inequity; it promotes the acceptance of lesbianism and so forth.

(Sadli 2002: 80–1)[5]

Thus there has been reluctance amongst Indonesians to focus on the family as a source of oppression, and a similar reluctance to address issues of sexuality which are deemed to be too private for public discussion. Not until the last decade or so have women's organizations engaged with issues such as rape and domestic violence that were regarded as 'un-Indonesian' in the past. And yet, as Saparinah Sadli says, 'The spirit of feminism has always informed the Indonesian women's movement' (Sadli 2002: 90).

This recent increased willingness to take on controversial issues is a sign of the declining dominance of nationalism in Indonesia and increasing cosmopolitanism. Other Asian countries share this experience as the distance from the gaining of independence grows and communications improve with the rest of the world. The International Decade of Women 1975–85 increased awareness of discrimination against women around the world, and conferences have made it easier for governments and women's organizations to exchange information and learn more about women's issues. Undoubtedly as a response to international pressure, since 1978 Indonesia has had Ministers for Women's Affairs, although their powers are very limited, and Women's Studies centres in universities, focusing mainly on 'women and development' issues. Ever since the New Order regime took power at the end of 1965, Indonesia has also been a major recipient of foreign aid, and donors have imposed their own gender equity policies as conditions of development assistance. A number of foreign organizations such as the Ford Foundation and the Asia Foundation have funded feminist activities such as those related to reproductive health and (since 1998) political education of women.

The final feature of Indonesian feminism and the women's movement, which is similar to elsewhere, is their often-strained relationship with the State. Indonesia has experienced many kinds of states—colonial, democratic and authoritarian— and most of them have held strong views about gender relations that have not always coincided with the aims of the women's movement. Under colonialism, the Dutch were reluctant to intervene in gender relations for fear of alienating Islamic sensitivities, but they did introduce a few changes sought by women's organizations, such as (limited) schooling for girls and (feeble) efforts to combat child marriage.[6] Since independence, some Indonesian regimes have sought to coopt the women's movement for their own purposes, which have offered some opportunities but more restrictions for women's organizations. In the late 1950s and early 1960s, President Sukarno sought to harness women behind his aggressive form of nationalism, and President Suharto wanted them to cooperate in carrying out his development plans from the 1970s to the 1990s. Both Sukarno and Suharto espoused an autocratic and corporatist style of rule in which society was viewed as consisting of 'functional groups' representing different social interests. Women were recognized as one such group and were therefore represented and consulted on issues that the government considered concerned them, but women were regarded as a homogeneous group of mothers whose main duties were to support their families and carry out government policies (Douglas 1980; Suryakusuma 1987).

While Sukarno's state offered little to women, Suharto at least succeeded in providing a better standard of living, access to free contraception under its Family Planning Program, and a uniform marriage law which women's organizations had sought for decades. Up until then, marriage was governed by customary and religious practices, often administered in a haphazard fashion. Arguably, it was possible to get a Marriage Law in 1974 because dissident voices within the women's movement were muted and because the most active women's organizations, which were pushing for a marriage law, took a conservative and pro-government stance. The Law itself satisfied most women's organizations at the time because it regulated marriage in a more predictable and equitable fashion, stated that the marriage norm was monogamy, and made it difficult for men to enter into polygamous marriages. Continuing disadvantages of the Law are that it reinforces stereotypes about husbands as heads of families, and still defines marriage as based on religion, making it legally impossible for people of different religions to marry (Blackburn 2004a).

During its democratic phases, in the 1950s and now since 1998, the Indonesian state has allowed the greatest freedom for women's organizations but has not been very responsive to many of their demands, partly because of the low level of women's representation in Indonesian parliaments, and partly because democratic governments have depended on coalitions which could be fractured by controversial issues such as marriage law reform. These situations can be found elsewhere in the world. After Indonesian nationalist leaders declared independence in 1945, women for the first time were able to form organizations freely and participate in government and elections during the period of liberal parliamentary democracy that lasted until 1958. Although women turned out enthusiastically to vote in the first national elections in 1955, there were relatively few women candidates and even fewer women elected since the main parties (secular nationalist and Islamic) were very male dominated. Governments during the democratic phase contained only a couple of women ministers (Maria Ullfah Santoso and S.K. Trimurti in the late 1940s). After President Sukarno introduced his dictatorship in 1958, there were no more elections until 1971 when the New Order began staging carefully managed 'festivals of democracy' in which its own electoral machine, Golkar, won easily at every five-year election until Suharto finally resigned in 1998 during the Asian Financial Crisis. When free and fair elections resumed in 1999, women found it hard to gain positions as candidates and their representation in parliament actually dropped to nine per cent compared with 11 per cent at the end of the New Order period. As in other parts of the world, women's organizations then began campaigning for the parliament to adopt legislation requiring all parties to have women as 30 per cent of their candidates.

A law in 2003 watered this down to merely recommend that parties adopt this policy, and in the 2004 election slightly more women were elected, bringing their representation in parliament back to 11 per cent.[7]

It was ironic that at a time when women are struggling to gain reasonable representation, Indonesia for the first time gained a woman president in the person of Megawati Sukarnoputri (2001–3), a daughter of former president Sukarno. Although very popular, she showed no interest in women's affairs. The fact that her leadership depended heavily on her relationship to a powerful male figure and her failure, in a male-dominated political arena, to take action on behalf of women, puts Megawati in the category of a number of female Asian heads of government, such as Benazir Bhutto and Sirimavo Bandaranaike.[8]

In many respects, therefore, the women's movement and notions of feminism in Indonesia bear resemblances to elsewhere in Asia, if not in the world. As a foreign idea, feminism has not been well understood or accepted but notions of gender equality and women's rights have gained cautious support. Women's experiences as citizens have varied under different regimes, and with the restoration of democracy they have greater prospects of equality, despite the legacy of male-dominated governments and party systems. Emerging in tandem with nationalism, the women's movement has had periods of autonomy interspersed with co-optation and control by the state.

What is particular about Indonesia?

What is distinctive about Indonesia is the variety of feminisms and women's organizations that have featured in its history over the last century. There have been three main forms of feminism: secular liberal, socialist and Islamic. We can deal most quickly with socialist feminism, since it was prominent in Indonesia only for a couple of decades, from the late 1940s to 1965, during the first period of liberal democracy and under Sukarno's dictatorship. In its heyday it was a strong force, led by Gerwani, the women's organization that became affiliated with the Partai Komunis Indonesia (PKI), the Indonesian Communist Party. With a membership of some 1.5 million women, Gerwani concerned itself with the living and working conditions of the peasant and urban working women who made up the bulk of its members. Two of its best-known leaders were Umi Sarjono (a member of parliament for the PKI) and S.K. Trimurti, who was Minister for Labour in an early Indonesian cabinet. Gerwani, along with the other 'popular front' organizations of the PKI, was wiped out in the extermination of communists that occurred during the wholesale massacres and arrests in 1965–6 (Wieringa 2002). Largely as a result, Indonesia has since lacked any women's organization that has succeeded in recruiting poor women with the aim of improving their livelihoods.

The New Order regime of President Suharto was implacably opposed to the resurgence of any organization that tried to mobilize people 'at the grassroots' of Indonesian society. The only organizations permitted to exist at the village level were those controlled by the regime. Thus the New Order created a nationwide organization for women called the PKK (Pembinaan Kesejahteraan Keluarga or Family Guidance Movement) into which women were drafted to support its development plans, notably its rigorous family planning programme aimed at reducing the birth rate. The PKK could not be called feminist, since it was always subordinated to the male-dominated state, as reflected in its structure: its leaders had to be the wives of government officials.[9] Not until the 1990s were women's organizations again able to win public attention for matters concerning women at work, such as sexual harassment and the mistreatment of migrant women workers. Even then, it was largely a matter of middle-class women speaking on behalf of working-class women: the Indonesian women's movement has not yet recovered the skills exercised by Gerwani in mobilising poor working women.

The women's organizations with the longest continuous history in Indonesia are the Islamic ones and those loosely identifiable with secular liberal feminism. Secular liberal organizations were the first to form, and they soon became intertwined with nationalism, as I have mentioned. Such organizations were prominent in the 1930s, before the Japanese Occupation banned them, and again after 1945 until the New Order regime asserted control over the women's movement. Examples of prominent secular women's organizations, which took independent and outspoken stands on issues such as equality in marriage, were Istri Sedar (Aware Women) in the 1930s, led by Suwarni Pringgodigdo, and Perwari (Indonesian Women's Association), led by Suyatin Kartowiyono in the 1950s. Their leaders and members were largely women who had been privileged to gain a modern education, something quite rare in colonial Indonesia. Secular liberal feminists could also be found outside the ranks of the organizations; for instance, Herawati Diah was for decades a well-known feminist journalist. For some decades their main concerns remained the same: to make education accessible to girls, to combat early marriage, and to fight for more equitable marriage laws.

Although secular women's organizations were restricted under the New Order regime, by the 1990s new overtly feminist NGOs began to form under the leadership of well-educated young women who pursued various aspects of women's rights, some of them new to Indonesia such as opposition to sexual harassment and support for reproductive health. With the freedom that accompanied democratization since 1998, yet more such NGOs have emerged. Most are small and localized, but a number are well-known nationally such as Solidaritas Perempuan (Women's Solidarity) and LBH-APIK (Women's Association for Justice). The concerns of secular organizations tend to reflect those found at the international level of the women's movement, a trend that is strengthened by the importance of foreign funding for a number of Indonesian NGOs. Thus, for instance, issues of sexuality and sexual violence have featured on their agendas since the 1990s for the first time in Indonesian history. An overtly feminist presentation of these ideas can be found in the periodical *Jurnal Perempuan* ('Journal of Women').

Disputes between secular and Islamic women's organizations began in the colonial period and continued after independence. In 1917, the large modernist

Islamic organization Muhammadiyah established a women's wing, Aisyiyah, and the even larger traditionalist Nahlatul Ulama (NU) followed suit in 1946 with Muslimat NU to carry on their religious work among the female population. Being subservient to male-dominated Islamic organizations, the Islamic women's groups felt constrained by the views of the male leadership, which for many decades were very conservative on women's issues. In the women's federation during the 1920s and 1930s, women from Islamic organizations clashed with secular women such as Suwarni Pringgodigdo who spoke out strongly on issues such as polygamy. Although practised by only a tiny minority of Indonesians, polygamy (or, more correctly, polygyny) has long been a flashpoint in relations between secular and Islamic Indonesians. Islamic women's groups felt obliged to defend the honour of Islam as a religion that protects women.[10]

Even during the colonial period, however, one could discern in the ranks of the Islamic women's organizations the beginning of an assertiveness of women's rights against discriminatory practices within Islam. Journals of the major Islamic women's groups were discreetly criticizing unequal marriage practices and supporting women's suffrage.[11] Nor was the Islamic movement as opposed to women's rights as in some other parts of the world. For instance, in the 1950s it accepted the appointment of women judges in religious courts, something that was unique to Indonesia. In this respect, one must remember the wider context: Indonesian governments have always been dominated by secular nationalists and political Islam has been weak, either suppressed by authoritarian governments or failing to unite or gain majority support in elections. Indonesian Islam itself has been characterized by moderation, despite the existence of small radical groups that aim to make the country into an Islamic state.[12]

The rise of Islamic feminism was nevertheless slow, and it did not really blossom until the 1990s. The last two decades have witnessed the emergence of overtly feminist Islamic non-government organizations and increasingly feminist stances within Muhammadiyah and NU. Leading Indonesian Islamic feminists, such as Siti Ruhaini Dzuhayatin from Aisyiyah and Siti Musdah Mulia who heads the gender-mainstreaming unit in the Department of Religion, have drawn on foreign reinterpretations of the Koran, such as those by Fatima Mernissi, to challenge local misogynistic teachings and practices. Thus, in order to strengthen their case, Indonesian Islamic feminists have tapped into international networks of scholars and activists such as Sisters in Islam in Malaysia, and indeed they are now at the forefront of international efforts to reshape Islam in more women-friendly ways. The Islamic feminist movement includes several independent NGOs such as Rifka Annisa, which established Indonesia's first women's crisis centre, and Rahima, both of which emerged from the world of NU, and numerous able spokeswomen and spokesmen. In fact, a remarkable feature of Islamic feminism in Indonesia today is the number of its prominent male champions such as Ulil Abshar Abdallah of the Liberal Muslim network. Under pressure from leading women such as Sinta Nuriya Abdurrahman Wahid of Muslimat NU, practices within the major Islamic organizations and their teaching institutions are being reformed to ensure greater equality between men and women, and issues previously unmentionable in Islamic circles, such as domestic violence, have become matters of public debate (van Doorn-Harder 2006).

In this way, the secular and Islamic branches of Indonesian feminism and women's organizations have drawn closer together in recent years. Both secular and Islamic universities have centres for women's studies where many of the same issues raised in other countries concerning gender inequality are debated.[13] Feminists such as Julia Suryakusuma and Maria Hartiningsih are frequently interviewed on television and write for the press. Some of them, such as the well-known women's rights activist Nursyahbani Katjasungkana, are now members of parliament and were active in getting a law against domestic violence passed in 2004.

Moreover, Islamic and secular liberal feminists often join forces to oppose common enemies, notably conservative Muslims who seek to impose greater restrictions on women's mobility and dress, and who advocate polygamy. Since the 1990s, a number of radical Islamic organizations have been formed in Indonesia and have taken advantage of a weakened central government to assert demands for stricter adherence to their version of *shari'ah* or Islamic law. Decentralization legislation in 2000 devolved more power to lower levels of government, some of which have used it to introduce 'public morality' measures that require women to adopt 'Islamic dress' and limit their mobility. In an effort to win over separatist rebels in the strongly Islamic region of Aceh in north Sumatra, the central government also allowed it to enforce *shari'ah*, something which is impossible elsewhere in Indonesia. This has led to restrictions being placed on women's dress and movements. Not only secular feminists but also moderate Islamic ones have monitored these developments vigilantly and have protested strongly against them, as well as against the revival of public polygamy, where prominent men openly take on more than one wife, often in violation of the Marriage Law.[14] There are, nevertheless, continuing areas of disagreement between secular and religious feminists; some of them are the same divisive ones found in other countries, such as the issue of pornography.[15]

Finally, what is distinctive about Indonesian feminism since the end of the New Order regime is that there is now only one kind of mass-based women's organization, and that is the Islamic one. The women's wings of NU and Muhammadiyah, which together claim more than 15 million followers, spread far and wide to cover the nation (Marcoes 2002). Unlike Gerwani, they survived the New Order years because they were not regarded as a threat by the regime: they kept a low public profile and did not espouse controversial views. But secular women's organizations such as Solidaritas Perempuan lack any such broad base. PKK has lost its state sponsorship and rationale, and secular feminists have not yet managed to establish organizations with a mass membership. Hence they are more open to charges of being unrepresentative and elitist and dependent on foreign aid—all good ammunition for those opposed to feminism in Indonesia.

Indonesia has no umbrella organization for the many women's organizations which could be called feminist according to a capacious conception of that word.

While federations of women's organizations have existed since the late 1920s, they have never encompassed all women's groups and during the New Order the large women's federation, Kowani, lost credibility because it was coopted by the state and dominated by so-called 'wives' organizations', or organizations composed of the wives of civil servants and the military. The latest effort at uniting women's organizations across the spectrum is the Koalisi Perempuan Indonesia (Indonesian Women's Coalition) which exists alongside Kowani, demonstrating the divided nature of the women's movement: neither gives strong leadership. Like most NGOs in Indonesia today, women's groups revel in their new-found autonomy and are reluctant to submit to anything that resembles the straitjackets of the past (Budianta 2002).

Although fragmented, the women's movement in Indonesia's now democratic times derives strength from its freedom, vitality and inclusiveness. It represents better than ever before the wide range of women's interests, although lower-class women tend to be neglected. But groups that were excluded in the past, such as lesbians and Chinese Indonesians, now find a place in the ranks of the women's movement, and the regions are much better represented by their own organizations than previously when the movement was more centralized and dominated by Javanese, the largest single ethnic group. The price paid for freedom is that the movement speaks with many voices which is confusing for those it seeks to influence, and provides them with an excuse to ignore women's demands. To counter this diversity, women's organizations have developed a greater ability to form ad hoc networks on particular issues, which can be quite effective, as in the case of the campaign for domestic violence legislation. Moreover, the women's movement now has a quasi-official voice in the form of the National Committee On Violence Against Women (Komnas Perempuan), which was created by the post-Suharto government in 1998 in response to mass rapes that comprised part of the violence accompanying the demise of the New Order.[16] In general, women have had a much higher public profile since 1998, including a number of prominent women ministers such as Khofifah Indah Parawansa, a former Minister of Women's Empowerment (the name of the portfolio was changed to suit her), Sri Mulyani Indrawati (Minister for National Planning) and Mari Pangestu (Minister for Trade).

Conclusion

A veteran Indonesian feminist, Saparinah Sadli, has concluded modestly that there is not yet 'a distinctively Indonesian feminism' (2002: 80). Yet what has distinguished Indonesian feminism and the Indonesian women's movement is that although their ideas have been derived from foreign liberal, socialist and Islamic feminisms, Indonesians have adapted these ideas to their own circumstances in ways that have allowed their organizations to be quite influential at different times. The fortunes of the different streams of feminism have fluctuated along with changes in Indonesia's regimes and in internationally dominant feminist ideas.

At present, what is remarkable is the efflorescence of Islamic feminism which has taken up the fight for women's equality in a time of Islamic resurgence in Indonesia. Since Islamic women's organizations were already well established throughout the country, Islamic feminism has the opportunity to spread its ideas down to the lowest levels of society.

Notes

1 Indonesia is committed through its state ideology (*Pancasila*) to belief in God, but the nature of God is not specified and the state supports five officially recognized religions, including Islam.
2 Kartini's letters to Dutch friends, published posthumously by Dutch sympathizers in 1911, boosted interest in education of girls in particular, since this was one of Kartini's passions. Her letters have been translated by Joost Cote into English as *Letters from Kartini: An Indonesian Feminist, 1900–1904*, Clayton: Monash Asia Institute, 1992.
3 The groups that were rejected as alien by the nationalist movement were the Europeans and Eurasians, and the Chinese and Arabs, each of whom comprised a small minority in the Indies, the Chinese being the largest group with about 5 per cent of the population.
4 This was a common theme in many of the speeches in the 1928 congress.
5 The author headed the women's studies centre at the University of Indonesia before becoming the chair of Komnas Perempuan, the National Committee on Violence against Women, established in 1998.
6 On colonial gender ideology, see E. Locher-Scholten (2000) and A. Stoler (1995). On the complex issue of child marriage see S. Blackburn and S. Bessell (1997).
7 On women's political representation in Indonesia, see *The Implementation of Quotas: Asian Experiences*, Jakarta, International Institute for Democracy and Electoral Assistance, 2002, plus statistical data and references from the website of the International Parliamentary Union.
8 On the phenomenon of Asian women leaders, see M.R. Thompson (2002). On Megawati's early years, see A. McIntyre (1997). There is as yet no good general coverage of her presidency. For some interesting comments, see Mayling Oey-Gardiner, 'And the winner is … Indonesian women in public life', in Robinson and Bessell (2002) (see also Oey-Gardiner and Bianpoen 2000).
9 For an illuminating comparison of the PKK and Gerwani, see S. Wieringa (1992).
10 The tension between different organizations on matters of polygamy and divorce was patent already in the 1928 women's congress (see Blackburn 2008). For more on the longstanding polygamy debate, see Blackburn (2004a: chapter 5). For excellent coverage of Muslimat NU and Aisyiyah and their innovative young women's affiliates, see P. van Doorn-Harder (2006).
11 On the early period of Indonesian Islamic women's activism, see S. Blackburn (2002).
12 There are many texts on the nature of Indonesian Islam, such as R. Hefner (2000).
13 For an interesting discussion of women's studies in Indonesia, see Saparinah Sadli (2002).
14 On the Islamist threat to women, see Kamala Chandrakirana and Yuniyanti Chuzaifah (2005).
15 In 2006, a draft law against pornography was widely discussed. It aroused strong feelings, particularly since it interpreted pornographic behaviour in such broad terms as to outlaw Balinese dancing. There were huge demonstrations in Jakarta involving supporters and opponents of the bill, which has since been revised in a more liberal fashion.
16 There are a number of sources on the rapes of 1998. They include S. Blackburn (1999).

References

Blackburn, S. (1999) 'Gender Violence and the Indonesian Political Transition', *Asian Studies Review*, 23, 4: 433–48.

—— (2002) 'Indonesian Islamic Women Enter the Political Arena', *Kultur: The Indonesian Journal for Muslim Cultures*, 2, 2: 21–46.

—— (2004a) *Women and the State in Modern Indonesia*, Cambridge: Cambridge University Press.

—— (2004b) 'Women's suffrage and Democracy in Indonesia', in L. Edwards and M. Roces (eds) *Women's Suffrage in Asia: Gender, Nationalism and Democracy*, London: RoutledgeCurzon.

—— (trans. and ed.) (2008) *The First Indonesian Conference of 1928*, Clayton: Monash University Press.

Blackburn, S. and Bessell, S. (1997) 'Marriageable Age: Political Debates on Early Marriage in Twentieth Century Indonesia', *Indonesia*, 63: 107–41.

Brown, C. (1981) 'Sukarno on the Role of Women in the Nationalist Movement', *Review of Indonesian and Malay Affairs*, 15: 68–92.

Budianta, M. (2002) 'Plural Identities: Indonesian Women's Redefinition of Democracy in the Post-Reformasi Era', *Review of Indonesian and Malay Affairs*, 36, 1: 35–50.

Chandrakirana, K. and Chuzaifah, Y. (2005) 'The Battle over a "New" Indonesia: Religious Extremism, Democratization and Women's Agency in a Plural Society' in Norani Othman (ed.) *Muslim Women and the Challenge of Islamic Extremism*, Petaling Jaya: Sisters in Islam.

Cote, J. (1992) *Letters from Kartini: An Indonesian Feminist, 1900–1904*, Clayton: Monash Asia Institute.

Douglas, S. (1980) 'Women in Indonesian Politics: the Myth of Functional Interest' in S. Chipp and J.J. Green (eds) *Asian Women in Transition*, University Park: Pennsylvania State University Press.

Hefner, R. (2000) *Civil Islam: Muslims and Democratization in Indonesia*, Princeton: Princeton University Press.

Locher-Scholten, E. (2000) *Women and the Colonial State: Essays on Gender and Modernity in the Netherlands Indies, 1900–1942*, Amsterdam: Amsterdam University Press.

Marcoes, L. (2002) 'Women's Grassroots Movements in Indonesia: a Case Study of the PKK and Islamic Women's Organisations', in K. Robinson and S. Bessell (eds) *Women in Indonesia: Gender, Equity and Development*, Singapore: Institute of South-East Asian Studies.

Martyn, E. (2005) *The Women's Movement in Postcolonial Indonesia: Gender and Nation in a New Democracy*, London: RoutledgeCurzon.

McIntyre, A. (1997) *In Search of Megawati Sukarnoputri*, Clayton: Monash Asia Institute Centre of Southeast Asian Studies working paper no.103.

Oey-Gardiner, M. and Bianpoen, C. (eds) (2000) *Indonesian Women: The Journey Continues*, Canberra: Australian National University.

Robinson, K. and Bessell, S. (eds) (2002) *Women in Indonesia: Gender, Equity and Development*, Singapore: Institute of South-East Asian Studies.

Sadli, S. (2002) 'Feminism in Indonesia in an International Context', in K. Robinson and S. Bessell (eds) *Women in Indonesia: Gender, Equity and Development*, Singapore, ISEAS.

Stoler, A. (1995) *Race and the Education of Desire*, Durham: Duke University Press.

Suryakusuma, J. (1987) 'The State and Sexuality in New Order Indonesia' in L.J. Sears (ed.) *Fantasizing the Feminine in Indonesia*, Durham: Duke University Press.

—— (2004) *Sex, Power and Nation: An Anthology of Writings, 1979–2003*, Jakarta: Metafor Publishing.

Thompson, M.R. (2002) 'Female Leadership of Democratic Transitions in Asia', *Pacific Affairs*, 75, 4: 535–77.

van Doorn-Harder, P. (2006) *Women Shaping Islam: Reading the Qur'an in Indonesia*, Urbana: University of Illinois Press.

Vreede-de Stuers, C. (1960) *The Indonesian Woman: Struggles and Achievements*, Gravenhage: Mouton.

Wieringa, S. (1992) 'Ibu or the Beast: Gender Interests in Two Indonesian Women's Organizations', *Feminist Review*, 41: 98–114.

—— (2002) *Sexual Politics in Indonesia*, Basingstoke: Palgrave Macmillan.

3   Rethinking 'the Filipino woman'

A century of women's activism in the Philippines, 1905–2006

Mina Roces

The celebration of the feminist centennials in 2005 reminded Filipinos of the long history of women's activism. Looking back over a hundred years, the feminist project could be read as a process of rethinking 'the Filipino woman'. The unique historical context—from the pre-colonial, post-colonial and transnational—has framed the debates about the woman question, with activists particularly self-conscious that their theoretical perspectives be 'home-grown' and distinct from what they perceived to be an alien animal called 'Western Feminisms'. And yet, the international and transnational context of the Filipino women's movements was just as vital as the local/national one. The history of colonialism and the economic position of the Philippines in the global south were critical to the analysis of the 'woman question'. International movements and international organizations such as the United Nations (UN) had an impact on activist agendas, with Filipina activists in turn also contributing to global feminist debates.

Filipino feminist theory is hotly contested, reflecting the heterogeneity, and robust nature of women's activism since the 1980s. While the vibrancy of the women's movements today (2009) is testimony to the sheer magnitude and diversity of women's interests, activists are extremely divided over almost every single issue. These differences may be interpreted in a positive light because they display the many voices of the women's movements or 'served as a catalyst for all to work harder and cover all fronts, so to speak, in the struggle to advance women's rights in the Philippines' (Sobritchea 2004: 104). While disagreement is probably not unusual for activist groups and may in fact enrich the women's projects, its negative consequences—most evident in the failure of women's parties to get politicians elected and in the extremely fraught personal relationships between some women's organizations—need to be noted and pose a formidable challenge to what is otherwise arguably one of the most creative, vigorous women's movements in Asia.

Women's activism could be classified into two major phases: women's demand for suffrage in the 1920s and 1930s, and the post-1980s struggle that continues to the present (2009). The suffragists were women from the upper classes who focused primarily on winning the vote and reform of the Spanish Civil Code. The second phase had a more diverse composition of leaders, including a tiny group of feminist Catholic nuns and highly educated middle-class activists who were formerly political activists against the Marcos regime with links with the left, and their allies from the lower classes. Few elite women were members of the more recent women's movements. Women's organizations, however, had a genuine desire to build a mass following epitomized by the self-conscious use of the vernacular language (colloquial Tagalog), and popular culture (comics, theatre as advocacy, radio talk shows, television and drama) in feminist propaganda. While the suffragists engaged primarily with the state, the second-wave activists have been much more proactive in the cultural and educational side of activism, combining these strategies successfully with the persistent lobbying of government. In this sense, feminist propaganda has been deployed not just to represent women for advocacy but also to fashion women—to construct a 'new Filipina'.

This chapter discusses the history of the women's movements as a process of rethinking 'the Filipino woman' over a century. Discourses about 'the Filipina' – who she was, what she is and what she will become – were central to activist ideologies. Representations of 'the Filipina' were used in strategies that included lobbying for legislative changes and criticizing patriarchy in popular ways using media (radio and television, comics, pocketbooks and newsletters), demonstrations, religious liturgy, dress and rituals. The project of interrogating 'the Filipino woman' was absolutely fundamental to the development of Filipino feminist theory/ies, a highly contested process that is still ongoing today.

My analysis of Filipina feminisms comes from archival research and over sixty-five interviews with activists from a number of women's organizations representing several women's sectors and focusing on a variety of issues. I am a Filipina historian based in Australia and I conducted research for a total of over six months in 2002, 2003, 2005, 2007 and 2008. I have read the newsletters, journals and publications of activists and a number of women's organizations from the suffrage movement in the 1920s until 2008 (including feminist nuns), the Constitutional Convention of 1934 debates on women's suffrage, and listened to forty-five episodes of five radio programmes run by three organizations as well as half a dozen television episodes of *XYZ Young Women's Television* and *Womanwatch*. In addition, I have participated in demonstrations, strikes and workshops run by some organizations.

A brief history of women's movements in the Philippines

The Philippines became an American colony from 1902 to 1946 as a consequence of the Spanish defeat in the Spanish–American War. Although Filipino women were actively involved in the revolution against Spain and later America, once the Philippines officially became an American colony, they began to organize as women to investigate the many ways they could make the American colonial project work for them. The first of these organizations was the Asociación Feminista Filipina founded in 1905. It had the following aims: to oppose early marriage, to work for the regulation of work in factories and shops where women and children were employed, to work for the improvement of conditions of domestic service for women and children and to lobby for the nomination of women in the municipal and provincial boards of education (Calderón 1905; Constitution 1905) (women were allowed into universities in 1908). This organization was interested in political and legislative change, and it displayed a feminist agenda because it also lobbied for women's political appointments in the provincial boards of education. A year later, Pura Villanueva Kalaw founded Asociación Feminista Ilonga. But it was only when the National Federation of Women's Clubs (NFWC) launched the campaign for suffrage in 1921 that women's organizations proactively mobilized nationally (in a genuine women's movement) on behalf of women's political citizenship.

The NFWC, though largely composed of elite women (some of whom were among the first university-educated women since women were allowed into universities in 1908, and some were wives and kin of male politicians), had national links all over the country from Aparri to Jolo. The Constitutional Convention of 1934 voted against women's suffrage and women campaigned in favour of a constitution that disenfranchised them because they prioritized Philippine independence or the national interest above women's rights (Alzona 1937: 79). Besides, the constitution contained a provision promising to extend suffrage to women if 300,000 women voted for it in a specially held plebiscite. Faced with what seemed like insurmountable odds (Senator Rafael Palma who was pro-suffrage pointed out that in the 1918 census only 417,000 women were qualified to vote (Palma 1937: 28)), the NFWC led the campaign for the vote using the media and their networks with women's clubs all over the Philippines. Clubwomen encouraged voter registration and the 'yes' vote. Superbly organized, and determined to address women of all classes, the suffragists embarked on a tireless campaign, which gave them the landslide victory of 447,725 votes (44,307 women voted no) (Kalaw 1952: 44).

Women's organizations from independence (1946) until the mid-1970s were mostly civic organizations run by wives or female kin of male politicians and since they usually functioned as support group for the men, they could hardly be classified as 'feminist' in orientation. By the 1960s, student activism injected new life into the dormant women's movement. In the early 1970s, MAKIBAKA (Malayang Kilusan ng Bagong Kababaihan or Free Movement of New Women) was organized as an offshoot of the Kabataan Makabayan (Nationalist Youth). It was founded initially to mobilize women as part of the student activism of the late 1960s and early 1970s, which protested social injustices, the Vietnam War, the USA's influence on domestic affairs, oil prices, inflation, the Marcos government's fascist tendencies, and the wide disparity between the rich and the poor. Under the leadership of Lorena Barros, MAKIBAKA developed a feminist consciousness. But when martial law was declared in September 1972 and the students were forced underground (and Lorena Barros killed by the military), MAKIBAKA was prevented from mutating into a feminist movement with a nationalist orientation or, alternatively, a nationalist movement with a feminist orientation. With the premature silencing of MAKIBAKA, the development of the women's movement experienced a hiatus.

There were, however, some women in the Communist underground whose common experience of gender discrimination in the Communist Party brought them together. This tiny group who began to question the left's treatment of women cadres bonded together to form KALAYAAN (Katipunan ng Kababaihan Para sa Kalayaan or Organization of Women for Freedom) in 1983 (Maranan 1985: preface). This clearly feminist organization tackled issues of rape, domestic violence, pornography and abortion. In 1981, together with another organization, PILIPINA (also composed of left-leaning activists including a feminist Benedictine nun), these two groups revived feminist activism insisting that women's issues be given equal priority in the struggle against the dictatorship. The cohort of women members of KALAYAAN and PILIPINA became the first group of feminist leaders since the 1980s. They pioneered activism with a feminist perspective tackling issues such as sexism in the media, reproductive rights, prostitution and violence against women (Sobritchea 2004: 103).

But just at the time when activists were developing a feminist consciousness, Marcos's chief political opponent, Benigno Aquino Jr, was assassinated in 1983. This sole political act unleashed a tidal wave of protest that culminated in the People Power 1 revolution that ousted President Ferdinand Marcos. The urgent need to devote their energy on the anti-dictatorship struggle in 1983 meant that once again the women's liberation had to be temporarily shelved in order to focus on the movement to oust the dictator.

In March 1984, a group of women's organizations coalesced to form GABRIELA (General Assembly Binding Women for Reforms, Integrity, Equality, Leadership and Action). At its inception, GABRIELA was interested in harnessing women's power for the anti-Marcos dictatorship movement rather than in advocating specific feminist or women's issues. Since the 1986 ouster of the dictatorship, GABRIELA became increasingly more feminist in orientation, viewing issues from a more gendered perspective. But it was after democratic institutions were restored in 1986 that women's activism gained momentum, resulting by the 1980s in what Carolyn Sobritchea has labelled 'a critical mass of highly motivated feminist advocates' (Sobritchea 2004: 105). There were organizations of women of various sectors (such as peasants, urban poor, Muslim women, Cordillera (indigenous) women, migrant women, women workers, women in media, to name a few) and issue-oriented ones (specializing on women's health, reproductive rights and sexuality, domestic violence (including rape and incest), prostitution, women's legal advocacy and services, and 'comfort women'). Women's Media Circle used the potential of tri-media (radio, television and print media), while women's health advocates and feminist lawyers explored the possibilities of alliance building for advocacy. The spectacular growth (literally in the hundreds and thousands) of non-government organizations (NGOs) could be partially explained by the impacts of the international conferences on women and the UN conferences in particular, as well as the funding made available for NGOs in the developing world (Sobritchea 2004: 107). Although GABRIELA tended to receive the lion's share of media and international attention because of its visible presence at demonstrations and in 2003 the formation of its own women's party (see below), by the 1990s the myriad group of women's organizations, including women NGOs, coalitions and professional groups, underscored the point that one could no longer speak of *a* women's movement (Sobritchea 2004: 107; Aguilar 1998: 70). Women were still marginalized in formal politics, with a general average of a mere 11 per cent (from 1986–2006) elected to local and national office (Veneracion-Rallonza 2008: 223–30). Because of these grim statistics, the most common tactic utilized by activists to ensure that pro-women legislative acts were proposed, discussed and passed in the legislature was to draft legislation and then convince their allies in the legislature to sponsor them. But women activists were also interested in claiming power themselves. The first women's party, Kababaihan Para sa Inang Bayan or Women for the Mother Country (KAIBA) (established in 1987), won only one congressional seat (Dominique Anna 'Nikki' Coseteng) in the 1987 election. This congresswoman eventually joined a traditional party (Quimpo 2005: 11). Angeles explained KAIBA's failure in terms of women's relative isolation from patronage politics (Angeles 1989: 201). Eventually KAIBA became moribund.

But in 1995, the passage of the Party-List System Act that classified women as a sector, enabled women's parties to compete in a more level playing field. This legislation provided that 20 percent (at least fifty) of the House of Representatives (250) be reserved for representatives of labour, peasant, urban poor, indigenous peoples, youth, fisherfolk, elderly, veterans, women and other marginalized sectors elected through a party list system (Quimpo 2005: 14). A new system allowing sectors to compete for 'reserved seats' meant that those parties who were deprived of the traditional patronage networks such as women's groups would have a chance at making it in the lower house. A total of six women's parties offered candidates under the women sector although only one party, Abanse! Pinay (composed of PILIPINA members), was able to get a congresswoman (Patricia Sarenas) elected (Veneracion-Rallonza 2008). In July 2003, GABRIELA launched its own women's party. Liza Maza won a seat in the 2004 elections and became the first GABRIELA women's party member to enter congress. In 2007, Luz Ilagan became the second.

The poignant history of Abanse! Pinay could serve as a case study for the challenges faced by the feminists in formal politics. In a peculiar example of déjà vu, Abanse! Pinay shared the same fate as KAIBA (although PILIPINA is still active). The party failed to get a seat in 2004 and 2007, making it ineligible to run again in the party list unless it registered under a new name. Like KAIBA, Abanse! Pinay had a short life span. A candid interview with Patricia Sarenas provided some insights into the reasons for the party's decline. According to her, PILIPINA was always divided over what strategies to employ to increase the membership of the party (Sarenas 2008). These debates within the party itself were never resolved.[1] If one added to this potent mix the personal disputes between members resulting in some members leaving the organization or abandoning the party, the fragile unity of this organization no doubt contributed to its failure to survive in the long term (Legarda 2005; Sarenas 2008). While such disputes were not unusual in the dynamics of Philippine political parties, there is no denying that the consequences for the women's movements were crippling, preventing them from surviving as viable parties in the long term. While GABRIELA women's party seems to be holding ground (at the present writing 2009), it is still too soon to foretell the future. Sadly, elections were not used as sites for feminist debate (Josefa Francisco pointed out that 'not a ripple of debate was felt') even over priority issues such as reproductive rights, sexual rights and women's poverty (Francisco 1998: 12–13). Maybe election campaigns by their very nature—the need to entice potential voters to one's cause—were far from ideal as a venue for challenging patriarchy. The consequence of the silence was that the women's parties missed the opportunity of using elections as a venue for feminist propaganda.

Theorizing 'the Filipina'

Activists were conscious about not merely grafting Western feminist ideologies onto the Philippine context. Hence, although they were very much influenced by the trends of international feminisms and the protocols emerging from international bodies such as the UN, they were careful to ensure that their deconstruction of Filipino womanhood (*pagkababae*) was grounded in the peculiar local context. Feminists were vulnerable to criticism that Western feminism was 'alien' to Filipino culture. Suffragists were accused of being 'Americanitas', mimicking American women who wanted the right to vote and run for political office (Roces 2004: 24–58), and from the 1960s onwards, activists avoided the word 'feminism' because it conjured up stereotypes of 'bra-burning', man-hating, manly unfeminine women (Cahilog 2003; Miranda 2003; Estavillo 2003; Nemenzo 2004; Illo 2003). The first challenge confronted by feminists was how to define their own brand of feminism. As Anna Leah Sarabia of Women's Media Circle disclosed to me in an interview: 'We have to define it [feminism] for them otherwise people will define it for us' (Sarabia 2008). The hundreds of women's organizations that mushroomed in the last two decades more or less guaranteed that many brands of feminisms were proposed. I have applied a very broad definition of feminism—activism centred on altering patriarchal structures of society to remove gender discrimination—partly because I wanted to include as many perspectives as possible and partly because, when interviewed, many organizations and individuals self-identified as feminists but in reality could only be classified as such if a very broad definition was applied.

While no doubt Filipina activists were influenced by the different colours of feminism classified as socialist-feminists, liberal feminists, Marxist feminists, national-democratic feminists, and radical feminists and eco-feminists these labels do not apply to Filipino women's organizations whose ideologies often straddle between these categories. Interviews with leading feminists in the Philippines confirmed that categorizing women's organizations according to these classifications was not useful (Santos 2006; Estrada-Claudio 2006). Instead, what I will do here is to discuss the fundamental issues raised by activists in their quest to articulate a uniquely Filipino approach to the woman question. The first women's studies syllabus was designed in 1985 in a workshop run by the Institute of Women's Studies (Nursia) and the academics were adamant that the readings should reflect the Philippine experience even if it meant they had to do the research and writing themselves. Specifically, activists sought answers to questions such as: (1) Who is 'the Filipina woman' and what sorts of enduring grand narratives of the feminine have been reproduced over the centuries? (2) Where is this 'Filipina woman' located? (3) How to empower her? and finally, (4) What 'new Filipina' or what alternative narratives of women should we propose and fashion?

Criticizing grand narratives and fashioning new ones

Feminists were not unaware of the political uses of history endorsing a feminist historiography that traced women's oppression to the Spanish colonial period and the introduction of Christianity. The pre-colonial era was idealized as a 'golden age' where women enjoyed high status as religious leaders (as priestesses or *babaylan*), had access to divorce and were able to control their fertility. Women's current low status was blamed on Spanish Iberian cultural values that idealized the woman as 'Angel of the Home' and removed her religious power. Suffragists such as Encarnación Alzona, Paz Policarpio Mendez and Dra. Maria Paz Mendoza-Guazon (Alzona 1934; Mendez 1936; Mendoza-Guazon 1951–64) framed the struggle for suffrage in the 1920s as an attempt to recoup rights lost to colonialism, a claim that fitted into the narrative of Filipino nationalism and the demands for immediate independence from the United States (Roces 2004: 42). In the mid-1980s, Mary John Mananzan's seminal essays on women and history revisited these arguments and embellished them further by exploring 'the religious roots of women's oppression'. According to Mananzan, the introduction of the Virgin Mary as woman's 'impossible ideal' fostered a 'victim consciousness' in women (Mananzan 1998: 59–60 and 117). Mananzan's essays became the foundation cornerstone of subsequent histories reproduced by women's organizations. For example, in GABRIELA's version of history, it was the Spanish friars who defined Filipino womanhood in the period from 1521 to 1896 (Arriola 1989: 16). The American colonial period was not singled out as a major watershed in this periodization of women's history, although it was criticized for encouraging the exploitation of women in factories and for perpetuating the definition of woman as mother and queen of the home (Arriola 1989: 55–6; Women's Media Circle 1986; Taguiwalo 1997–98). Women's Media Circle's two-part documentary 'From Priestess to President' (aired as two episodes of *Womanwatch*) in 1986 reproduced this feminist history in television aimed at popular audiences (in the vernacular language—Tagalog). The suffragists wrote primarily in English and Spanish because they addressed male legislators and other educated women of their class. When in the 1980s this interpretation of history was transmitted in popular forms using television (*Womanwatch, XYZ Young Women's Television*), radio (in the half a dozen or so women's radio talk show series), and comic books, colloquial Tagalog language was the language of choice. Mananzan's seminal essay originally published in English was translated into Tagalog and a comic version followed (Mananzan 2001). Given the deep divisions in the women's movements, the absence of serious controversy in the historiography of 'the Filipino woman' was remarkable. The consensus that the Spanish colonial era destroyed the 'golden age' of women's supposedly egalitarian status with men,[2] and was largely responsible for shaping contemporary womanhood, remained unchallenged as late as 2008. This interpretation of women's history had political uses because it deflected criticisms that activists were embracing a foreign or 'Western' feminist viewpoint that was incompatible with Filipino culture since women were only reclaiming rights once enjoyed but lost to colonialism. In this reading of the past, activists could not be represented as 'radicals' because they were 'merely' asking for 'traditional' rights. These arguments, however, could only be effective if the historiography of a 'lost Eden' of women's rights was endorsed. Hence, there has been little interest in writing a more nuanced feminist history.

The impossible ideal of the 'Virgin Mary' as 'Mater Dolorosa' or the woman as martyr was the most important grand narrative feminists hoped to dismantle. Three characters in Jose Rizal's nineteenth-century novels[3] became iconic examples of this ideal. The character of Maria Clara, the beautiful, virginal, convent-school educated, upper-class heroine, was a shy, obedient daughter whose traits also epitomized the perfect woman described in the various 'rulebooks' books published in the Spanish colonial period regulating female conduct (Wright 2004). Women were expected to behave like saints—devoted to prayer and good charitable works (Maria Clara donates her locket to a leper) (Rizal 1912, 1976). That the character of Maria Clara (whether Rizal intended to or not) acquired iconic status from the nineteenth century until the closing decades of the twentieth century attested to the enduring success of the Spanish colonial construction of woman.

Because society chose to adopt her as the classic Filipino woman, Maria Clara has been the target of feminists from the suffragists of the 1920s until the end of the twentieth century. In the 1920s, the lines between pro- and anti-suffrage (at the male Constitutional Convention) were divided according to whether or not one wanted Maria Clara to be the template for 'the Filipino woman'. Those who were against suffrage framed their discussion in terms of a nostalgic plea for the return of Maria Clara to the pedestal while those for suffrage denounced her as a character of fiction who did not resemble the 'real' Filipino women who fought in the revolution and who wanted to contribute to nation-building (Roces 2004: 24–58). As late as the 1960s, journalist Carmen Guerrero Nakpil wrote that the idealization of Maria Clara was the greatest tragedy experienced by the Filipino woman in the last hundred years (Nakpil 1964: 30).

The character of Sisa, in *Noli Me Tangere* (Rizal 1912, 1976), epitomized the suffering (read ideal) mother. She represented the women of the working classes who sacrificed everything for her two boys. Her husband not only neglected to support his wife but also periodically took her wages to support his vices, which included drinking and gambling. Though he showed no concern for his wife and children and was guilty of domestic violence, Sisa never complained. Sisa's nature, consistently portrayed as quiet, hard working, self-sacrificing and submissive, appeared heroic and admirable even though her son's death at the hands of a Spanish friar drove her to madness. The character of Juli represented the peasant woman who had to go into domestic service in order to clear her father's debts. Her life story epitomized the cultural belief system that peasant women were *pambayad ng utang* (or literally repayment of debt) (Santiago 2002: 29; Maranan 1985: 37; Taguiwalo 1992: 15–21).

Activists since the 1980s aspired to replace Maria Clara, Sisa and Juli as role models. They upheld women revolutionaries against Spain, and political activists who fought against the Marcos regime. The underlying premise that women must accept a life of suffering (*pagtitiis,* or endurance) was critiqued vigorously as new slogans such as '*Hindi Kailangan Magtiis*' (It is not necessary to endure), and 'Know Yourself, Trust Yourself, Respect Yourself' were touted by the Women's Media Circle and feminist songs glorified women revolutionaries and activists as new role models. One feminist song actually identified Maria Clara, Juli and Sisa as stereotypes that needed to be rejected and replaced by women revolutionaries and courageous activists (though ironically the women touted—Lorena Barros, Lisa Balando and Liliosa Hilao were all killed by the military and remembered as martyrs) (*Maria* 2000: 35). Suffragists embraced women revolutionaries against the Spanish regime (i.e. those who rejected the Iberian construction of woman) as ideal women. In the task of expanding this pantheon of role models, activists from the 1990s onwards also redefined the category 'heroine' to include survivors of domestic violence, partner infidelity, trafficking, prostitute and exploitation/abuse.

Unfortunately, this feminist history and definitions of womanhood did not apply to all Filipino women. I am referring in particular to the women of the Cordillera highlands and the Muslim women of southern Philippines. Since the Spanish were unable to colonize the highlands or the south, both categories of women escaped Christianization and Hispanization. Cultural constructions of the feminine therefore differed from that of the Christian lowland majority. For example, Cordillera women were traditionally defined as industrious women tied to their vegetable plots with men (before the 1970s) expected to do the domestic work and child care (Resurreción 1999: 131–69). Although there are a number of Muslim and Cordillera women's organizations, some with links to the national women's movements such as GABRIELA, we still need to have a critique of feminine ideals from those who do not come from the majority ethnic and religious groups.

The Cordillera protest against President Marcos's attempts to build the Chico Dam was mythologized by the women's movements (Cariño and Villanueva 1995) but did not succeed in marking the Cordillera woman (untouched by Spanish colonialism and Christianity) as a 'role model' for 'the Filipina'. Instead, activists looked back to the pre-colonial past for a muse. The *babaylan* or the pre-Hispanic priestess became the mythological ideal with feminists (including those in the diaspora) reinventing themselves as 'modern babaylans' (Shahani 2006: 13).

Claiming that the spirit of the *babaylan* was preserved in their 'dangerous collective memory' (Santiago 2002: 4, 45; Mananzan 1997: preface, 5),[4] feminists constructed a genealogical link with these mysterious women. The feminist fascination for the *babaylan* motivated them to search for 'living *babaylans*' in the foothills of Mount Banahaw where a unique Filipino Christian sect called the Ciudad Mistica de Dios was led by a woman who held the title of *Suprema* Isabel (Ligo 2006: 75–91; Alaras 2000: 181–91; Mananzan 2002: 129–35). One book coined the term 'Babaylan Feminism' or 'babaylanism' to mean an 'enlightened female consciousness' (Shahani 2006: 13; Mangahas and Llaguno 2006: 15–17). From this cryptic definition, it may be gleaned that *babaylan* feminism meant 'Filipino feminisms'—signalling the women's movements self-conscious representation of their theories and perspectives as 'home-grown'. Of all the alternative role models proposed by activists, the *babaylan* remains the most powerful icon. Perhaps because she was a woman with religious power she offered an alternative construction of the feminine distinct from the colonial definition (the beautiful, domestic, long suffering woman), as well as the contemporary activist. The woman as intellectual or scholar has never been part of the grand narrative of 'the Filipino woman'. The *babaylan* mystique, her imaginative power, could be traced to her unique subject position as mature, wise woman with religious power—three characteristics that have yet to be associated with the cultural constructions of the feminine in the Philippines.

Locating women

Filipino activists since the 1980s could not be accused of ignoring 'class' because the question of 'which Filipino woman do we claim to represent?' received 'star billing' up front and centre in the published literature of almost all organizations. Feminist discourses from the 1980s onwards were fond of the phrase 'grass-roots women' and practically every NGO that was woman-centered claimed to speak on behalf of lower-class women classified by women's organizations into 'sectors' such as peasants, prostitutes, urban poor, migrants, entertainers, workers, youth, Muslim women and indigenous women. There were a relatively small number of organizations of middle-class professional women that classified themselves as 'feminist' (in opposition to the civic-oriented foundations and organizations led by wives and kin of male politicians, see Roces 1998). Although the cultural construction of woman as 'wife and mother' was never really attacked, the view from below compelled activists to prioritize the woman as worker because for women of the lower classes the reality was that these wives and mothers were also simultaneously women workers.

Since activists operated from a theoretical framework that perceived 'the Filipina' as deeply connected to the world, the premise was that the Filipina postcolonial condition placed her at the bottom rung of the global racial hierarchy as a 'servant of globalization' (to borrow from Rhacel Parreñas, in Parreñas 2001, 2003) epitomized by the women workers in factories (especially in the electronics industries), peasant women, and by the plight of domestic helpers overseas.

Basic women's orientation seminars run by the Center for Women's Resources (CWR) explained the exploitation suffered by women workers as the result of the feudal nature of Philippine society, and the country's Third World status subject to the neo-imperialism of the rich northern countries and their transnational corporations. Understandably, the Women Worker's Movement (Kilusan ng Manggagawang Kababaihan (KMK)) never put forward a claim for equality of wages for men and instead demanded the payment of a just wage for both men and women. According to the KMK Secretary General Nanette Miranda, it was because the wages for men were so low it would be unthinkable to demand equality on that score (Miranda 2003). But while women workers were represented as 'modern day slaves', they were also imagined to be the mass followers of the women's movements, with the potential of becoming the most militant of activists.

The feminization of the global labour force extended the notion of women's work outside the home to its maximum potential (overseas), with women comprising 49.1 per cent of the 1.75 million workers overseas in 2007 (NCRFW 2009). The plight of these workers who were vulnerable to abuse and exploitation has formed an important part of women's activism whose response was to discourage women from migration seen as 'too risky' an adventure (*TNT, Trends, News and Tidbits* 1991–2005)—a position in direct opposition to the state's targets of deploying one million workers overseas per year (from around 2008) as a short-term solution to the unemployment problems at home.

Other issues given high priority were sexual harassment in the workplace (an Anti-Sexual Harassment Act was passed in 1995), the militarization of the provinces affecting peasant women, the working conditions and safety hazards of women working in factories and export processing zones, and a plea for the extension of maternity leave to sixty-five days. The issue of prostitution (the dominant narrative was that prostitution was violence against women and prostitutes were victims of poverty and male desire), trafficking in women, and women overseas contract workers including entertainers to Japan, were prime topics much debated by feminists of all colours who objected to women's commodification not just as sex objects but as breadwinners for the family.

Practices: fashioning women

Feminist theories were disseminated to audiences in many creative ways. Activists used tri-media—radio, television, print—to deliver what one radio show dubbed 'women's studies on the air' (*Tinig ng Nursia*, or the *Voice of Nursia*, the nickname of the Institute of Women's Studies, St Scholastica's College). Television and radio talk show programmes[5] explained the new feminist vocabularies such as 'prostitution' (defined as violence against women), 'trafficking', 'reproductive self-determination', 'sexuality', 'lesbianism', 'domestic violence', 'sexual harassment', 'rape' and 'incest'. Oral testimonies of survivors received appropriate sound bites while 'hot' topics such as 'what is virginity?' were discussed live and audiences invited to participate by calling in. Every person was identified as a potential convert and every venue transformed into a 'classroom' as activists ran workshops in community halls, feminist liturgy practised in chapels, and theatre as advocacy performed in basketball courts. Most women's organizations sent their members to the CWR's basic women's orientation workshops so there was some uniformity in the feminist curriculum studied by new members. Regular publications such as newsletters, journals and comics documented the many activities and successes of each organization. In an innovative move, women's health organizations commissioned PETA (Philippine Educational Theatre Association) to produce two informances: one on domestic violence and one on women's reproductive rights. The shows (*Tumawag Kay Libby Manaoag,* and *The Libby Manaoag Files*) travelled around the country performing to a combined total of 51,000 people between 1998 and 2001 (Barrameda 2000: 36; no author 2002b: 3).

In addition, activists were proactive in fashioning women by transforming former victims or survivors of trafficking, prostitution, domestic violence, rape and exploitation into advocates. Practices such as the use of oral testimonies (for example, by former trafficked women or 'comfort women'), theatre as advocacy (as former survivors become amateur actors), demonstrations and marches became sites for performing feminism or acting as rites of passage as former 'victims' or 'survivors' acquired new militant personas when they delivered their demands sometimes in front of armed police. Dress and deportment were used to fashion new identities as militant women. For instance, former 'comfort women' in their twilight years protested angrily in front of the Japanese Embassy with clenched fists raised above their heads and attired in national dress. Former victims of rape and sexual harassment who were members of GABRIELA's Circle of Friends attended court trials attired in their 'uniforms'—the T-shirt with the organization's logo—to give the former victim support and maybe to intimidate the defendants/perpetrators.

If the main weakness of the women's movements was their disunity, their main forte was their organizational skills. It was the superb organizational skills of the suffragists that produced the stunning result for women's enfranchisement. The successful staging of important feminist events including demonstrations was due to patience and attention paid to detail. Women's organizations also provided services for victims of domestic violence (the Women's Crisis Centre and KALAKASAN acronym for Kababaihan Laban sa Karahasan or Women Fighting Violence, for example), and health care services (such as the health clinics run by Likhaan or Linangan ng Kababaihan). Alliances were also formed to lobby for particular legislation. SIBOL (Sama-samang Inisyatiba ng Kababaihan sa Pagbabago ng Batas ng Lipunan or United Initiative of Women for Changing the Laws of Society), the alliance of women's health organizations and the women's legal organizations such as Women's Legal Bureau (WLB) and WomenLead were instrumental in the campaign to pass the Anti-Rape Act that redefined rape from 'a crime against chastity' to 'a crime against person'. Both WLB and WomenLead also provided legal services, while organizations for overseas workers such as Kanlungan Migrant Centre assisted women who had court cases against illegal recruiters.

One important strategy deployed from the 1920s onwards was the behind the scenes lobbying with politicians. Filipino feminist theories imagined men as allies and not as enemies because activists were self-conscious about not appearing to conform to the widely held assumption that Western feminists were 'man-haters'. Women's groups approached sympathetic politicians and submitted drafts of various types of legislation for them to consider. The Anti-Trafficking Law of 2003, the Anti-Rape Law (1997) and the Anti-Violence Against Women and Children Law (2004) were examples of this successful collaboration. In addition, women's groups were able to pressure for the establishment of Police Desks for women in some major cities. This strategy is now being used in the current the campaign for a Reproductive Health Bill since 2001.

Looking back, looking forward, looking outwards

How far has the process of rethinking the Filipina come? Activists were proactive in launching a campaign to dismantle gender stereotypes. Although the grand narratives of 'wife and mother', beauty queen (some suffragists were beauty queens, Roces 2004) and moral guardian have yet to be seriously problematized, feminists proposed that the 'future Filipina' be someone able to exercise political and economic power, and reproductive rights. In the pursuit of these goals, activists became entangled in complex (and often contradictory) engagements with the Church and the State—its two most formidable 'enemies' (feminists see them as more powerful obstacles than traditional attitudes). There were traces of 'critical collaboration' (to borrow from Sobritchea 2004) with the State. For example, activists were members of the Executive of the National Commission on the Role of Filipino Women (NCRFW) blurring the lines between activist and government representative. Some women's health organizations worked with the Department of Health on reproductive health issues. On the other hand, organizations that focus on migrant workers or prostitution and trafficking were directly opposed to state policies that encouraged migration and tourism. Similar dilemmas occurred in the relationship with the Catholic Church. While the Church's uncompromising stance on contraception, sexuality (lesbianism), divorce and euthanasia is a huge obstacle for women's rights, feminist nuns are one of the important feminist theoreticians and founders of women's organizations. These nuns actually live with the poor and the indigenous people and are able to immerse themselves in full-time activist work to ensure that the voices of the marginalized are heard.

Looking back at a century of feminist activism, the track record displayed a clear and present commitment to the project of remaking 'the Filipina'—from breaking free of the colonial heritage, to a continuing struggle to exercise the power to choose and to have those choices respected. Although the public campaigns (particularly the use of radio and television) succeeded in lifting the cultural taboos on discussions of domestic violence, rape, partner infidelity, prostitution and sexuality, some issues such as divorce and abortion still remain extremely sensitive. Anyone who dared to talk about abortion in whatever limited context was demonized, preventing a public discussion for abortion as a reproductive right.

The Philippines has not had a consistent policy on contraception (Viado 2005: 9), further ensuring that reproductive rights will continue to be a highly contested issue. Because culturally the construction of sexuality was such that men were perceived to be 'naturally' lustful but women were supposed to be incapable of performing desire, as a consequence, until the mid-1990s sexuality was discussed only in the context of 'prostitution'. Only since 1995 have issues such as lesbianism (since the notion that women could desire yet alone desire another woman was culturally unfathomable), and women's desire, including the right to a happy sex life (*XYZone* 2002), been raised in public. The Coalition against Trafficking in Women, Asia Pacific (CATW-AP) problematized men's desire but the problem of mistresses (the Philippine version of unofficial polygamy) has not yet been seriously addressed. Perhaps feminists need to focus also on remaking masculinity as well as femininity since men are the Other of women. There has been no major educational and advertising campaign to include domestic chores as part of masculinity, for example. In fact, one excellent study on changing masculinities in the Ilocos region concluded that it was women's new roles as 'breadwinners' (as overseas domestic helpers), not feminist activism, that transformed men into househusbands overnight (Pingol 2001).

Philippine women's movements must be located in the international arena and the international networking of feminists everywhere. Filipino organizations argued that activism must be global (no author 2002a: 36). They participated in the international women's movements (through international conferences or in meetings with the UN), and were proactive in hosting international conferences in the Philippines. Two important priority feminist issues—trafficking and migration—required networking or lobbying across national boundaries. Activists lobbied several governments from the USA, to Spain, Italy, Greece, Hong Kong, Singapore and the Middle East to name a few, and international organizations such as the UN. Women's organizations relied on a huge international network in their advocacy work and engaged with the world as transnational subjects. I argue that it was precisely their location in the interstices that makes them effective activists. Straddling national borders allows them to have a continuing dialogue with feminists of all colours, injecting Philippine perspectives into international women's movements, and in so doing, impacting on international feminist debates, and international activism on behalf of all women.

Because of sheer logistics alone, activism on behalf of overseas contract workers or overseas migrant workers needed organizational structures across national borders. GABRIELA has chapters in the USA, Australia and Europe. The Centre for Migrant Advocacy has links all around the world. An organization such as DAWN (Development Action Women's Network), for example, that helps former entertainers to Japan and their children, has a branch in Japan. International activists are invited to Philippine 'spaces' such as the Belgians who joined GABRIELA to support the Shoemart Strike and the Filipino-American interns who spent their summers in the offices of the Third World Movement Against the Exploitation of Women (TW-MAE-W) and Likhaan (Linangan ng Kababaihan, a women's health NGO founded in 1994).

This transnational orientation inspired them to 'think globally'. CATW-AP and TW-MAE-W both aimed for 'a world without prostitution' or 'an end to prostitution and trafficking' (Enriquez 2003; de Dios 2003; Perpiñan 2003), while Lila-Pilipina (the organization of former 'comfort women' or victims of sexual slavery during the Japanese military occupation in World War II) hoped to help bring about 'a world without war' (Extremadura 2003; Cortes 2003; Guillermi 2003). TW-MAE-W staked the entire 'Third World' as their territory, while CATW-AP, claimed the 'Asia-Pacific' as their space, with the former having UN Consultative Status and the latter active in the UN conferences in the area of trafficking in women. GABRIELA conceived of hosting a bi-annual Women's International Solidarity Affair (WISAP) because 'the issues that beset people have a global dimension, and the specific concerns of women are worldwide phenomena. Invariably, women are patriotic and feminists must also be internationalists' (no author 1989: x). When women's organizations marched on International Women's Day, they expressed in symbolic terms their wish (no matter how elusive) for a global sisterhood.

This outlook had practical consequences. Feminist nuns and lay leaders of women's organizations lived a peripatetic lifestyle. Filipino feminist nuns, with postgraduate credentials from overseas institutions, were well networked to the 'mother houses' of their religious congregations and frequently travelled to and from the Philippines. Leaders of women's organizations likewise were great travellers attending international NGO conferences, UN meetings and the academic conference circuit.

The impact of Filipina feminist theory and praxis has gone beyond the geographical borders of the state. Four Filipinas have chaired the Commission on the Status of Women of the UN's CEDAW—one was CEDAW committee vice-chairperson and another two serving as CEDAW experts and rapporteurs (Tripon 2007). Interviews with some of these exceptional women revealed that (Licuanan 2008; de Dios 2008) Filipinas were considered international experts in the field of trafficking and migration. At UN meetings and conferences of international NGOs, Filipinas were often approached and asked to be chairs of panels or rapporteurs because they spoke English, were theoretically informed and extremely organized, and had the patience for NGO work. In this sense, activists have already been exporting 'Filipina feminisms' and had an impact on the development of international feminisms because of NGO work, and their important positions in international bodies. One could argue that these nuns and lay women activists refused to be confined by the geographical borders of the nation-state—as feminist nun Amelia Vasquez RSCJ told me in an interview: 'the world should set our agenda' (Vasquez 2003).

Notes

1 One important issue was whether or not the party should include those who were not formally members of PILIPINA (Sarenas 2008).

2 The topic of women in the pre-colonial era is still under-researched. There is still much that is not known about the status of women in that period although women could inherit property and were religious leaders.
3 Jose Rizal is the Philippine national hero whose novels written in the latter half of the nineteenth century inspired the revolution against Spain. The two famous novels are: *Noli Me Tangere* (The Social Cancer) and *El Filibusterismo* (The Subversive).
4 Both Mangahas and Mananzan used the phrase 'dangerous collective memory' in (Mangahas 2006: 42; Mananzan 1994: viiii).
5 I have listened to forty-five episodes of five radio programmes. The programmes and the years they aired were: *Tinig ng Nursia* (1995–7), *Kape at Chika* (2002–3), *XYZone* (1995–2005), *Okay Ka Mare!* (You are All Right Sister!) (1990–2002), and *Babae Ka, May Say Ka!* (You are a Woman, You Have a Say!) (2003–still ongoing in 2006).

References

Aguilar, D. (1998) *Toward a Nationalist Feminism*, Quezon City: Giraffe Books.
Alaras, C.R. (2000) 'Body Narratives, Metaphors, and Concepts in Philippine Indigenous Religion', in Sylvia Marcos (ed.) *Gender/Bodies/Religions*, Mexico: ALER Publication, pp. 181–91.
Alzona, E. (1934) *The Filipino Woman: Her Social, Economic and Political Status 1563–1937*, Manila: Benipayo Press.
—— (1937) 'A History of Women's Suffrage in the Philippines', *The Woman's Home Journal*, XII, 12 April: 15–16, 18, 20–23, 78–80.
Angeles, L. (1989) 'Feminism and Nationalism: The Discourse on the Woman Question and Politics of the Women's Movement in the Philippines', MA Thesis, University of the Philippines.
Arriola, F.C. (1989) *Si Maria, Nena, Gabriela atbp, Kuwentong Kasaysayan ng Kababaihan*, Manila: GABRIELA.
Barrameda, T.V. with contributions from Lea Espellardo (2000) *Breaking Silence: A Nationwide Informance Tour for the Prevention of Violence Against Women in the Family*, Quezon City: PETA and UNIFEM.
Cahilog, E. (2003) interview with author, Quezon City, 18 August.
Calderón, C.F. De G. (1905) *First Report Philippine Woman's Club* (or Dr Fernando G. Calderon, 'The Causes and Remedies of the Infant Mortality in Manila'), Manila: Asociación Feminista Filipina, in Bureau of Insular Affairs, Record Group 350, Box 777, No. 17087, National Archives Records Administration, College Park, Maryland, Washington DC.
Cariño, J. and Villanueva, R. (1995) *Dumaloy ang Ilog Chico And So the Chico River Flows*, Quezon City: GABRIELA.
Constitution of the *Asociación Feminista Filipina* (n.p.), 1905.
Cortes, L.A. (2003) Lila Pilipina interview with author, Quezon City, 9 August.
de Dios, A. (2003) CATW-AP interview with author, Quezon City, 8 August.
de Dios, A. (2008) CATW-AP interview with author, Quezon City, 26 January.
Enriquez, J. (2003) CATW-AP interview with author, Quezon City, 11 August.
Estavillo, C. (2003) interview with author, Quezon City, 23 August.
Estrada-Claudio, S. (2006) interviews with author, Quezon City, 18 September and 6 October.
Extremadura, R. (2003) Lila Pilipina interviews with author, Quezon City, 26 August.

Francisco, J. (1998) *Women's Participation and Advocacy in the Party List Election*, Quezon City: The Center for Legislative Development.

Guillermi, L.V. (2003) Lila Pilipina interview with author, Quezon City, 9 August.

Illo, J.F. (2003) interview with author, Quezon City, 7 August.

Kalaw, P.V. (1952) *How the Filipina Got the Vote*, Manila: [n.p.].

Legarda, K. (2005) interview with author, Makati City, 21 January.

Licuanan, P. (2008) interview with author, Quezon City, 18 January.

Ligo, A.L. (2006) 'Searching for the Babaylan in Ciudad Mistica de Dios', in F.B. Mangahas and J.R. Llaguno (eds) *Centennial Crossings Readings on Babaylan Feminism in the Philippines*, Quezon City: C & E Publishing, pp. 75–91.

Manzanan, M.J. OSB (1994) 'Welcome Address' National Chairperson GABRIELA in *Gaining Ground, Building Strength: Advancing Grassroots Women's Struggles for Liberation, WISAP '94*, Quezon City: GABRIELA, p. viii.

—— (1997) *The Woman Question in the Philippines*, Manila: Institute of Women's Studies.

—— (1998) *Challenges to the Inner Room: Selected Essays and Speeches on Women by Sr. Mary John Mananzan, OSB*, Manila: The Institute of Women's Studies, St Scholastica's College.

—— (2001) *Ang Pangkababaihang Isyu sa Pilipinas*, Manila: The Institute of Women's Studies, St Scholastica's College.

—— (2002) 'Suprema Isabel Suarez', in D.S. Ahmed, *Gendering the Spirit Women, Religion & the Post-Colonial Response*, London: Zed Books, pp. 129–35.

Mangahas, F.B. (2006) 'The Babaylan Historico-Cultural Context', in F.B. Mangahas and J.R. Llaguno (eds) *Centennial Crossings Readings on Babaylan Feminism in the Philippines*, Quezon City: C & E Publishing.

Mangahas, F.B. and Llaguno, J.R. (eds) (2006) *Centennial Crossings Readings on Babaylan Feminism in the Philippines*, Quezon City: C & E Publishing.

Maranan, A.F. Santos (1985) 'Towards a Theory of Feminism: Preliminary Discussions on the Woman Question in the Philippines', unpublished manuscript, University of the Philippines, CSWCD Library.

Maria (song) (2000) in *Change*, IX, 1: 35.

Mendez, P.P. (1936) 'Our Fight for Suffrage', *Woman's Home Journal*, XII, 6: 8.

Mendoza-Guazon, M.P. (1951) *The Development and Progress of the Filipino Women*, Manila: The Government of the Philippine Islands Department of the Interior Office of the Public Welfare Commissioner Manila, 2nd edn (1st edn printed in 1928).

Miranda, N. (2003) interview with author, Quezon City, 26 August.

Nakpil, C.G. (1964) *Woman Enough and Other Essays*, Manila: Vidal Publishing.

NCRFW or National Commission on the Role of Filipino Women (2009) 'Statistics on Filipino Women Overseas Employment'. Online. Available HTTP: <http://www.ncrfw.gov.ph/index.php/statistics-on-Filipino-women/14-f…filipino-women/71-statistics-fs-filipino-women-overseas-employment> (accessed 31 May 2009).

Nemenzo, A.M. (2006) interview with author, Quezon City, 10 October.

No author (1989) *Women's International Solidarity Affair in the Philippines*, Quezon City: GABRIELA National Women's Coalition.

No author (2002a) *Kontrakwalisasyon sa Paggawa, Marso 8*, Quezon City: Center for Women's Resources.

No author (2002b) *The Libby Manaoag Files Ang Paghahanap sa Puwertas Princessas, Birthings A Journal of Shared lives A Nationwide Informance Tour on Women's Health and Reproductive Rights*, Quezon City: PETA.

Palma, Dr R. (1937) 'The Significance of May 14, 1937', *Women's Home Journal*, XII, 12: 28.

Parreñas, R. (2001, 2003) *Servants of Globalization Women, Migration and Domestic Work*, Stanford and Quezon City: Stanford University Press, and Ateneo de Manila University Press.

Perpiñan, S. (2003), RGS, TW-MAE-W, interview with author, Quezon City, 28 July.

Pingol, A.T. (2001) *Remaking Masculinities Identity, Power, and Gender Dynamics in Families with Migrant Wives and Househusbands*, Quezon City: University Center for Women's Studies, University of the Philippines.

Quimpo, N.G. (2005) 'The Left, Elections, and the Political Party System in the Philippines', *Critical Asian Studies*, 37, 1: 3–28.

Resurrección, B. (1999) *Transforming Nature, Redefining Selves Gender and Ethnic Relations, Resource Use, and Environmental Change in the Philippine Uplands*, Maastricht: Shaker Publishing.

Rizal, J. (1912, 1976) *Noli Me Tangere*, translated from the Spanish by C.E. Derbyshire as *The Social Cancer*, Manila: Philippine Education Company.

Roces, M. (1998) *Women, Power and Kinship Politics in Post-War Philippines*, Westport: Praeger.

—— (2004) 'Is the Suffragist an American Colonial Construct? Defining "the Filipino Woman" in Colonial Philippines', in L. Edwards and M. Roces (eds) *Women's Suffrage in Asia: Gender, Nationalism and Democracy*, London: Routledge, pp. 24–58.

Santiago, Q. (2002) *In the Name of the Mother 100 Years of Philippine Feminist Poetry*, Quezon City: University of the Philippines Press.

Santos, A. (2006) interview with author, Makati City, 11 October.

Sarabia, A.L. (2008) interview with author, Manila, 4 January.

Sarenas, P. (2008) interview with author Makati City, 18 January.

Shahani, L.R. (2006) 'Foreword', in F.B. Mangahas and J.R. Llaguno (eds) *Centennial Crossings Readings on Babaylan Feminism in the Philippines*, Quezon City: C. & E. Publishing, p. 13.

Sobritchea, C. (2004) 'Women's Movement in the Philippines and the Politics of Critical Collaboration with the State', in L.H. Guan (ed.) *Civil Society in Southeast Asia*, Singapore and Copenhagen: ISEAS and NIAS Press, pp. 101–21.

Taguiwalo, J.M. (1992) 'Women as Society's Coping Mechanism', *Laya Feminist Quarterly*, 1, 4: 15–21.

—— (1997–98) 'Ina, Obrera, Unyonista, Ang Pagkakaisa at Tunggalian sa Pananaw sa Kababaihang Manggagawa Sa Panahon ng Kolonyal na Paghahari ng Amerikano sa Pilipinas Isang Panimulang Pag-aaral', unpublished paper.

TNT, Trends, News and Tidbits, newsletter of the Kanlugan Migrant Center, December 1991–December 2005.

Tripon, O.H. (2007) *Shaping the Women's Global Agenda Filipino Women in the United Nations Commission on the Status of Women/CEDAW Committee*, Manila: NCRFW.

Vazquez, A. (2003) RSCJ, interview with author, Quezon City, 19 August.

Veneracion-Rallonza, L. (2008) 'Women and the Democracy Project: A Feminist Take on Women's Political Participation in the Philippines', in K. Iwanaga (ed.) *Women's Political Participation and Representation in Asia: Obstacles and Challenges*, Copehagen: NIAS Press, pp. 223–30.

Viado, L.P. (2005) *Reproductive Health Politics, Health Sector Reforms and Religious Conservatism in the Philippines (1964–2004)*, Nigeria: Development Alternatives with Women for a New Era.

Women's Media Circle (1986) 'From Priestess to President: The Story of Women's Struggle in the Philippines', *Womanwatch*, Women's Media Circle.

Wright, M.T.H. (2004) *Rulebook Women*, Manila: De La Salle University Press.

XYZone (2002) 'Dapat Bang Makialam ang Simbahan sa RH Issue?' Broadcast No. 130, 16 November.

4 Chinese feminism in a transnational frame

Between internationalism and xenophobia

Louise Edwards

In 1900, the small cohort of women and men in China seeking to improve the status of women thought it natural to engage with like-minded people in organizations the world over. Their connections were naturally global, their collaborations inherently international. Half a century later, with the formation of the People's Republic of China, these transnational connections were fragmenting, as women's rights advocates were limited to briefly collaborating with a handful of socialist nations. In the 2000s, Chinese conceptions of 'women's issues' have returned to an internationalist perspective as fresh links are now forged at government-to-government and people-to-people levels around a host of new and old issues. These dramatic shifts in international engagement have influenced the shape and form of the women's movement in China. While the women's movement is inherently transnational and implicitly global in the PRC, there have been decades in which these links were impossible to maintain and nationalism incapacitated the movement.

This chapter traces the key events in women's activism aimed at improving women's status in China in relation to the transnational nature of feminism over the course of the twentieth century and into the first decade of the new millennium.[1] In seeking to place the Chinese women's movement within a transnational frame, it shows that progress on women's status takes different forms when international connections are strong compared to those years when they are weak. China provides us with a unique case study for exploring the impact of periods of extremes of openness and closure—most nations with sustained histories of women's activism have avoided these circumstances through the stability provided by a sustained coherency in political systems. China's modern history is marked by constant change, war and revolutions—the country moved between imperial, democratic and communist governments during the hundred years under consideration. This feature enables us to see the impact of a variety of political systems on women's activism. Just as patriarchy has been nimble in its reassertion of men's rights over women across a host of different political structures, feminism has been agile in presenting countervailing views. Chinese feminists' varying accessibility to international organizations changed the methods of their challenge to patriarchy but not their foundational commitment to improving women's status and life opportunities. However, as this chapter shows, nationalistic-inspired suspicion of feminism's global project remains a key current challenge for China's feminists.

Pendulum swings in international engagement

The political events that caused the dramatic swings in Chinese feminism's engagement with the international scene are well known. In 1900, China was in crisis, the centuries-old Imperial system of dynastic rule was crumbling in the face of incursion from a bevy of European powers, the USA and Japan. Reformers seeking to strengthen China saw engagement with, rather than resistance to, the West as the key. The West's economic, military and political might was manifesting the world over through the myriad colonies in Asia, Africa and the Americas. China had avoided colonization but was facing the humiliation of imperialism as the Chinese Imperial government fell into financial, moral and political bankruptcy. Japan had successfully taken a westernization path to modernization from the 1870s and, in 1895, China was abruptly confronted with the success of this modernization plan in her defeat at the hands of a modern Japanese military in the first Sino-Japanese War. Westernization and a serious engagement with new international norms emerged as the single, clear path to reinvigorate China. Feminism and improving the status of women emerged as part of the broader programme of modernizing the nation. It entered China alongside the other political and social reform agendas swirling around the world in the clippers and steamboats that plied the oceans. These ideas included reform of the political system—specifically the abolition of the Qing monarchy and its replacement with republican democracy. In 1911, the Qing collapsed and Asia's first, albeit fragile, republic emerged.

China's new republican leaders faced apparently insurmountable difficulties in their attempts to embed democratic thinking and democratic processes in the country. Through the 1920s, 1930s and 1940s China faced myriad internal and external attacks—warlord destabilization from within China through the 1920s and direct military invasion from Japan from the late 1930s. At a political level, China's erstwhile leadership was riven with internal spats and petty disagreements that provided fertile ground for military instability. Despite all of these major disruptions, these decades are marked by their intellectual and ideological openness to the world (Dikötter 2008). The literate Chinese citizen, particularly those in urban centres, were treated to a plethora of journals, newspapers and treatise on topics as diverse as free choice in marriage, lesbianism and modern family structures through to the rights of citizens (as opposed to duties of subjects), the prospects for communism and the value of anarchism. Urban educated women mobilized to secure equality with their brothers in key areas: voting rights, inheritance rights, education rights, divorce conditions, employment opportunities and wage rates. In their remarkably successful campaigns, they connected with international feminists mobilizing on the same issues and exchanged energy, ideas and tactics in this transnational movement.

In 1949, the Chinese Communist Party (CCP) came to power, defeating the Nationalists in a bloody civil war. The CCP instituted a radical social and political platform to build a strong and prosperous China, but it abandoned the Nationalist Government's multi-party political system and established a one-party nation where the CCP and its military, the People's Liberation Army (PLA) ruled the country and ruthlessly suppressed dissenting voices. Many of the women activists in the 1930s and 1940s were CCP members and they ensured that sex equality provisions were included in the founding documents and early legislative reforms of the new People's Republic of China (PRC). In April 1949, a special women's bureau designed to 'represent and to protect women's rights and interests, and to promote equality between men and women' was formed. Called the All-China Women's Federation (ACWF), its existence was deemed by the CCP to obviate the need for the myriad other women's societies, clubs and associations that had thrived in the 1940s—these groups withered in the face of the ACWF and its 'state feminist' structure (see Wang 2006). Not only was there a consolidation of the feminist movement under a single organization, but also the new political leadership gradually isolated its population from the capitalist West, and by the 1960s Chinese citizens rarely engaged even with citizens in their fellow socialist nations. The 1950s, 1960s and 1970s were marked by the comparative isolation of China's government and citizens from the global community, including isolation from the ideas and energy building among feminists in the wealthy and developing nations in 'second wave feminism'. Despite the explicit internationalism espoused in the global socialist movement (Kirby 2006), China's population was forced into isolation. People with international connections were politically suspect within this nation that nonetheless declared sexual equality and trumpeted the slogan 'Women hold up half the sky'. China's women activists maintained their feminist ideals but in conformity with the CCP's position did so within an explicit rubric of the primacy of class struggle and the importance of distinguishing themselves from the now-derided 'bourgeois' 'Western' feminism.

In 1978, the CCP embarked upon a period of openness, called 'The Open Door Policy'—a decision that would lift millions of people from poverty but also allow them to renew their international links without fear of accusations of treason, espionage or collaboration with bourgeois capitalists. The CCP government embarked upon a new programme to expand its global links and became active in the United Nations (UN) and its affiliate organizations. Today, transnational collaboration is firmly 'back in vogue' and regarded by both China's one-party leaders and population as a whole as underpinning China's revival and ascendency to the world stage as a global leader. China's feminists were quick to take advantage of this new atmosphere and established early links with the UN's various women's agencies (UNIFEM, Division for the Advancement of Women (DAW), Commission on the Status of Women) and international non-governmental organizations (NGOs) (such as the Ford Foundation, Swedish International Development Cooperation Agency (SIDA)). In this liberalized environment, China's feminists again mobilized outside of the

ACWF—they formed women's groups in universities and schools, theatre troops and art communities. The women's agenda in China again grew closer to that circulating internationally. For example, sexual harassment, domestic violence (DV) and sexual assault, emerged on the public stage as newly identified problems with activists proposing practical solutions that mirrored international knowledge of these phenomena.

As an explicitly political movement, feminism must engage with local, national and international power structures that privilege men. Activists variously collaborate and cooperate with or challenge and undermine the status quo power structures in their bid to promote women's rights and expand women's opportunities. For Chinese women activists, the power structures they sought to influence were changing regularly and dramatically over the course of the last hundred years. Accordingly, the dominant voices within the women's movement changed—as leaders of one group exited the public stage, others entered. Despite the turbulent times, and sometime at extreme personal risk, China's women's rights advocates have an impressive history of sustaining a publicly recognized political platform for women's rights. They variously adjusted their programmes, reframed their propaganda and altered their tactics to accommodate these changing circumstances, as the section below reveals.

Building a feminist movement with global partners prior to 1949

By the end of the nineteenth century, a small group of women, along with their male supporters, resolved that the key to strengthening China was through lifting Chinese women from their abject state of dependency. Elite women were cloistered in their homes, segregated from the outside world and unable to make public contributions to the national rebuilding project despite their wealth and, often, enviable erudition. Ordinary women struggled with poverty and illiteracy and found themselves passed from patriarch to patriarch by marriage in a trade that left them vulnerable and marginalized. To China's reformists, the pitiable state of China's women compared to women elsewhere in the world was a mark of considerable shame. Hu Binxia (circa 1887–1920s), one of China's earliest feminists, encapsulates the thinking of the time with her 1903 comment: 'The current weakened state of China cannot be blamed entirely on the faults of men' (Hu 1903: 156–7). Women's inabilities have prevented them from performing their duties as full citizens and, since they comprised half the population of the nation, this weakness impacted negatively on the strength and prosperity of China as a nation, she surmised. Radical feminist republican Qiu Jin (1875 or 1877–1907) sustained these ideas in her damning indictment of her contemporaries in the urban elite.

> Feet bound so tiny, hair combed so shiny; tied, edged, and decorated with flowers and bouquets; trimmed and coiled in silks and satins; smeared with

white powders and bright rouges. We spend our lives only knowing how to rely on men – for everything we wear and eat we rely on men.

(Qiu Jin 1906 or 1907: 11)

Men were also critical of China's weak womenfolk. In 1903, male feminist and educator Jin Songcen (1874–1947) published a clarion call for radical social and political change in China—*A Tocsin for Women* (*Nü jie zhong*). His programme was designed to overthrow the Qing monarchy and install a democratic republic—both aspects required the full participation of women if they were to succeed (Jin 1903; for discussion of his feminist platform see Edwards 1994). While the reformists agreed that the dismal state of China's womenfolk was evidence of the nation's weakened state, identifying a precise programme for enhancing women's participation in China's rebuilding proved more complicated.

Reformists sought international examples of strong women from strong nations. Close at hand were the Western women living and working in China, in particular the Protestant Christian missionaries included large numbers of women. The many women working as teachers, nurses and preachers on mission work provided models of women's public engagement and independence within a rubric of virtue and service. Historical models of strong Chinese women also achieved greater prominence in popular media as educators sought to encourage elite women to leave their sequestered space and ordinary women to 'get educated'. Mencius' mother (who made repeated sacrifices to ensure her son received a top-quality education) and Hua Mulan (who dressed as a man to replace her father in the military and became a general) were promoted as ideals for women's improved engagement with the rebuilding of China. They featured alongside Joan d'Arc and Sofia Perovskaia as models for women seeking to embark upon the path to modernizing and strengthening China (Judge 2008). As a whole, these actual women (the missionaries) and the model women (both Chinese and foreign) represented vibrant new possibilities for women's engagement with the urgent programme to rebuild China.

Reformers also identified a series of specific problems that would need to be overcome to enable China's women to join Joan, Mulan, Sophia and Mencius' mother. Prime among these was the eradication of foot binding—a physical marker of the crippled state of Chinese women's political consciousness. Angela Zito writes 'For nineteenth century missionaries and Chinese reformers, the woman's bound foot came to stand for the sad plight of Chinese culture itself' (Zito 2007: 3). The campaign to eradicate the centuries-old practice drew on a combination of Chinese and foreign efforts. Prominent foreign anti-foot binding campaigners included Mrs Archibald Little (Alicia Bewicke) and Rev. John Macgowan. Inspired by Macgowan, Little established a national association, the Natural Feet Society, to spearhead the campaign in 1895 (Zito 2007: 5).[2] Little's movement tapped into longstanding Chinese campaigns to eradicate the practice. The Qing monarchy had passed numerous injunctions banning the practice in the early 1600s, prominent literati had written in opposition to the practice from the late 1700s, but it continued largely uninterrupted as families sought to enhance their daughter's marriage prospects with this key marker of beauty. When Little and Macgowan entered the scene at the end of the 1800s, China was in disarray and foot binding, despite its deeply embedded cultural roots, appeared increasingly anachronistic—particularly as Chinese reformers became more aware of the negative international attention foot binding attracted. From the end of the nineteenth century, the pace of change increased and the previously unheeded calls to abolish the practice found more receptive ears in Chinese households.

Leadership and modelling from elite families were crucial to the new programme's success. In the 1890s, a group of prominent literati families formed a pact in which they promised not to bind their daughters' feet and, crucially, not to marry their sons to women with bound feet. In so doing, they sought to break the connection between bound feet and 'good marriage prospects'. Families of prominent reformist intellectuals, Kang Youwei, Liang Qichao and Tan Sitong, led the movement. Their respectability and pre-eminence was crucial to its spread. The men were recognized as outstanding patriots with fresh ideas for rebuilding China's position on the international stage. Through the work of these men, their sisters, wives and daughters, 'natural feet' were linked with the healthy, strong women who would produce healthy and strong sons that would in turn ensure the health and strength of the Chinese nation. Kang wrote: 'the reason why Westerners are upright and self-confident is that their mothers do not have bound feet and thus are stronger' (Kang 1898: 509).[3]

As a result of these local and foreign-led campaigns, operated through pamphleteering, public speaking, displaying posters, the foot-bound Chinese woman came to be associated with backwardness (rather than virtue) and crippling (rather than beauty) – she rapidly became less desirable on the marriage market. Concomitantly, the increasing appeal of girls with 'natural feet' sporting Western-style leather shoes, including the high-heeled variety, sealed the fate of foot binding as a practice (Ko 2005). Mothers, initially in small numbers and then more rapidly, ceased binding their toddler daughter's feet. The rapidity with which this change occurred is evident from a 1929 study of Ding County, a rural area just south of Beijing reported by Sidney Gamble. The survey showed that 99.2 per cent of women aged 40 and above (i.e. those born before 1890) were foot bound. This contrasted with 81.5 per cent of women between 25 and 29 years and 59.7 per cent for those aged between 20 and 25. The decline in acceptability of the practice then becomes dramatic for girls born after 1910 – only 19.5 per cent of 15–19 year olds and 5.6 per cent of 10–14 year old girls suffered foot binding (Gamble 1943: 182). In less than one generation, the practice was effectively eradicated – in urban areas the rate would have been even faster.

The second specific problem women's rights activists identified as hampering women's engagement with China's re-strengthening was the low levels of female literacy. The obvious solution was to expand girls' educational opportunities— initially they campaigned for girls' schools outside of the family space, and later they pushed for girls to have access to all the levels of education currently available to their brothers. Unlike foot binding, which was largely eradicated by 1920, the struggle for women's access to education would remain a key concern for decades (Bailey 2006). The reasons women's literacy and formal education were prioritized included the obvious facts that literacy would enable women to participate more fully in the workforce and gain economic independence from men. But it also was important because of longstanding cultural connections between political power and education. For centuries in China, throughout myriad changing dynasties, political power and moral leadership were equated with education. Key power-holders legitimized their rule on the basis of their superior learning; so the activist women who sought increased access to political power and enhanced rights relative to men regarded education as a prerequisite to achieving these broader goals (Edwards 2004). Indeed, male leaders routinely told those activist women seeking public political power to 'go and get an education'.

International links were crucial in this process from the very start of the twentieth century. In the absence of higher education institutions open to women in China, elite women left for overseas. In the first decade of the century, they primarily went to Japan to be teachers at colleges and women's universities. As demand expanded, they sought education in the USA and Europe. The impact of these international experiences, complete with the global networks the women formed while overseas, cannot be underestimated. China's earliest feminists—Qiu Jin, Hu Binxia, Tang Qunying and He Xiangning—all studied in Japan on scholarships in the first decade of the century. They returned to China to spearhead the movement for women-centred political and social reform. Qiu Jin formed women's schools and women's armies before her execution by the Qing government in 1907. Tang Qunying (1871–1937) headed China's leading suffrage organization in the 1910s. He Xiangning (1879–1972) would become a leading campaigner for women within the CCP from the 1920s onwards. Their experiences in Japan provided them with networks to a wide range of reform-minded men, fellow students, as well as links to active political organizations—such as the anarchists, socialists and republicans.

The radical political agenda of the women who studied in Japan during the final years of the Qing was matched by the professional orientation of the first women to attend colleges in the USA. This second wave of Chinese women to study abroad consisted primarily of medical students. Once trained, these women returned to practise and teach Western medicine throughout the country in hospitals and schools (Ye 1994: 321). Later, women studied a wide variety of subjects including education, law, politics, economics, sociology, the sciences and liberal arts. Missionaries also trained women doctors in China. One of China's prominent early feminists, Zhang Zhujun (1879–n.d.), was a Protestant and trained in the American Presbyterian Mission in Guangzhou with John Glasgow Kerr. In the first decade of the twentieth century, she established several schools for girls as well as some hospitals for the poor (Au 1998: 31–13). In 1905, she formed the Women's Chinese-Western Medical College in Shanghai to provide health care to women from women medical professionals. She remained an advocate of women's rights to education throughout her life and stood as one of the first models of a professional career woman.

Hu Binxia's life provides a useful insight into the impact internationalization through education would have on the women's movement in China (Ye 1994: 315–46). She was one of the first women to go to Japan to study in 1902 (Xie 1996: 66) and in 1907 she won a scholarship to Wellesley College, placing her among the first Chinese women to gain a Western degree. While in the USA, Hu presented a highly favourable vision of traditional Chinese womanly virtues of household management to audiences, including promoting the value of feminine virtues of self-sacrifice. But on her return to China, she published less than flattering appraisals of the Chinese family system. Her personal experience in Japan and the USA no doubt gave her particular authority when she critiqued the Chinese family system as rotten and decaying (Hu in Ye 1994: 332) and her articles comparing the Chinese and American family structures called for radical reform of the former (Hu 1916a, 1916b). Hu also took the then-novel path of combining parenthood with a high-profile career as editor in chief of the major woman's magazine of the times, *The Ladies' Journal* (*Funü zazhi*). Her dual competence in both spheres drew favourable comment from visiting American writer Grace Thompson Seton. Ye Weili writes that 'Hu impressed Seton as "an executive," very much like an "American business woman"' (Ye 1994: 333).

International warfare also played a major role in promoting women's access to colleges in the USA and expanding the numbers of China's women's rights activists. In 1901, with China's humiliating defeat in the Boxer Rebellion, the foreign powers billed China for wartime damages. Because they had been forced to defend their diplomatic quarters and economic interests against the Boxer attacks, these foreign governments demanded reparations within the treaty marking the rebellion's end. The amounts required and rates of interest charged far outweighed the actual cost of the war, so, in 1908, the American government resolved to mark a new relationship with China through renegotiating the Boxer indemnity. Money that would have gone to the USA was instead used to fund Chinese students to American universities, and in the first four years of the programme it was envisaged that over 400 Chinese students would be in America by the fourth year of the scheme (Finch 1924: 545). In 1914, this programme was opened to women and the Women's Boxer Indemnity Scholarship Program stood as recognition of the value of women's higher education from both the American and the Chinese governments. Ye Weili notes, 'Every two years thereafter about ten women were sent to America under the programme. Forty-four women were sponsored by this programme in the next decade' (Ye 1994: 342).

Christian missionaries in China were instrumental in promoting women's education both in China and in facilitating their study abroad (Volz 2007). Prior to their departure for Japan and the USA, many of these soon-to-be internationalized women students had extensive experience in missionary-run schools in China. Hunanese suffrage activist Zhang Hanying (1872–1915 or 1916) went to Japan in 1904 after studying in a local missionary girls' school. Henanese journalist Luo Yanbin (1869–n.d.) graduated from a missionary school before heading to Waseda University in 1905. Likewise, leading educator Zhang Mojun (1883–1965) had received her early education at American missionary schools in Nanjing, Suzhou and Shanghai before going to Columbia University in 1918.

China's foreign-educated women would return to assume leading positions in institutions that created opportunities for their China-based sisters. For example, in 1915 *The Suffragist* reported that Wellesley graduate Miss Fung Hin Liu had returned to China 'to direct the women's division of the Canton Christian College. Nothing could show more clearly than this what the republic of China means to its women. After centuries of seclusion they find themselves allowed a freedom of which they have never dreamed' ('Girl will direct Chinese Women's College' 1915: 2).[4] Overseas education also provided already-radicalized women with opportunities to enhance their careers and commitment to expanding women's rights. For example, prior to her studies in Columbia, Zhang Mojun had established herself as a leading women's suffrage activist and, in 1911, had published a pro-Republic newspaper *Great Han News* (*Da Han bao*) even before the fall of the Qing. After the formation of the Republic in 1912, she maintained her campaigning for women's political rights through her Shenzhou Women's Society and its journal but also directed considerable energies to promoting the importance of women's education—establishing a school called the Shenzhou School for Girls. With this already impressive experience of activism secure, at the age of 36 Zhang attended Columbia University in 1918 on a scholarship and on her return she became the principal of the First Women's Normal College in Jiangsu province. Later Zhang would assume senior positions in the Nationalist Government (Lin 1981).

Zhang's biography provides us with an insight into the third key problem women's rights activists identified in these early years of the women's movement—winning women equal access to the suffrage rights granted to men. Indeed, the issue of women's suffrage provided the core focus of international exchange through the 1910s, 1920s and 1930s. Prominent American suffragist Carrie Chapman Catt toured Nanjing, Shanghai and Beijing through September 1912 promoting the International Women's Suffrage Association and connecting with its Chinese counterpart, the Woman's Suffrage Alliance. Tang Qunying headed the Alliance and, like Hu Binxia, she was Japanese educated. Catt's public appearances drew huge audiences with over 1,000 people gathering to hear her speak at the Nanjing rally alone. She took great glee in reporting back to her colleagues in the USA that she had personally witnessed China's first women legislators—ten women were appointed to the first Guangzhou Provincial Parliament in 1912 (only to be barred later in the same year when national legislation overrode that of the province). Catt celebrated their presence in parliament unaware of their impending exclusion with an article published in *Woman's Journal* sporting the title 'She Sits in the Gallery and Looks Down on China's Ten Women Legislators, Who Had Been Called a Myth' (Catt 1912: 314–15).[5] Chinese women's early success was held up as a mirror of shame to suffragists in Europe and the Americas where equal political rights for women remained elusive.

Equally, Chinese women used women's suffrage success in other countries (for example, New Zealand and Australia) as a tool designed to shame their male political leaders. The modern world, the women argued, was one where women and men shared political power and full rights and duties of citizens. China, they argued, was falling behind the international trends. But, these arguments carried limited weight until the 1920s when the UK, Germany and USA appeared on the charts with sex equality in suffrage rights guaranteed in 1918, 1919 and 1920, respectively. China's male national leaders did not aspire to join the ranks of small nations such as New Zealand or Australia.[6] Nonetheless, China's women's suffrage activists celebrated the successes of their sister suffragists around the world with each new constitutional or electoral victory (Edwards 2008).

Women's suffrage activists had lobbied for equal rights before the formation of the Republic of China in 1912, and they continued their struggle until 1913 when President Yuan Shikai banned women's political activity and forced the movement underground.[7] It resurfaced with renewed vigour in 1919 and continued through the 1920s, winning success in numerous provincial parliaments (e.g. Hunan 1921, Guangdong 1921, Zhejiang 1921, Sichuan 1923) and on until 1936 when women's equal political rights with men were guaranteed in the Double Fifth Constitution at a national level. Their movement was at all times well informed of the international situation and tactics were shared around the globe. In March 1912, Tang Qunying and her supporters smashed windows in the Chinese parliament when sex equality was not included in the new national constitution. They did so in direct imitation of British suffragists' actions—over 200 UK suffragists had simultaneously smashed windows in London's political and commercial centre (Kent 1987) in order to win publicity for their cause.[8]

As Chinese activists looked for inspiration and models abroad to the pressing problems of their times, international feminists also looked to China as a location to spread the word on women's rights. Birth control advocate Margaret Sanger visited China in March 1922 (Paisley 2002: 111) and spoke to enthusiastic, large gatherings. The Chinese leaders of the birth control movement included a leading Protestant feminist, Liu Wang Liming (1897–1970). Liu Wang had excelled in her studies as a young woman in missionary schools and, in 1916, won a scholarship to the USA to study biology at Northwestern University. In keeping with the strong links between Protestantism and women's suffrage, Liu Wang was also active in the Women's Christian Temperance Union (WCTU) serving as its president. She was China's primary link to global Christian women's networks for three decades from the late 1920s. As tensions between China and Japan increased as a result of Japanese military incursions into Manchuria in north-east China in 1931 followed by full-scale invasion in 1937, Liu Wang was instrumental in securing global support for China against Japan through the WCTU networks (Ogawa 2007). Previously close connections between China and Japan WCTU delegates fractured as Japan's military adventures proceeded.

Like Liu Wang, many of China's prominent women's rights activists devoted considerable energies to mobilizing international support for China's defence against Japan through the late 1930s and 1940s. But with Japan's defeat in 1945, China descended into a bitter civil war between the Communists and the Nationalists that served to complicate Chinese feminists' international engagement. The period of military instability within China rendered international connections difficult and with the CCP's eventual victory over the Nationalist Government in 1949, the intense spirit of internationalism among women activists that had typified the previous decades would come to a resounding halt on the mainland of China.

Managing state feminism and isolationist nationalism

The communist movement has long had a problematic relationship with feminism. From its formation in 1921, the CCP, like its European and American counterpart movements, regarded feminism with suspicion—a movement that sought to redress inequalities between men and women was at best regarded as a distraction from class inequalities.[9] Chinese Marxists followed the German socialist Clara Zetkin, who had famously renounced her previous engagement with the women's rights movement in 1889 by declaring that the emancipation of labour from capital was the only solution for the emancipation of women. From this point onwards, the non-Marxist woman's movement was regarded with derision as distracting, disruptive 'bourgeois feminism'. The formation of a communist one-party state ensured that the mistrust of extra-CCP feminism would spread through every aspect of public life stymieing the international links non-CCP women had forged and driving activist women into silence or worse.

Liu Wang Liming's experience typifies this shift. Unlike some 'bourgeois' feminists who left for Taiwan with the Nationalist Party in 1949 (such as Zhang Mojun), Liu Wang remained in China and was a member of the second, third and fourth National People's Political Consultative Conference (NPPCC) and a member of the standing committee for the All-China Women's Federation. She represented China at the International Asian Women's Conference of 1954, held in Beijing, and in 1956 led the Chinese delegation to the World WCTU congress, held in West Germany. To this point, it appeared that China's 'bourgeois' (and even Christian) feminists would be able to continue some form of global activism. But only a year later in 1957, the first of what would prove to be many political attacks on alternative voices occurred—the Anti-Rightists Campaign. Liu Wang was labelled a Rightist, stripped of her official roles and sent for re-education. In 1966 she became a target again, as the Cultural Revolution ramped up its attacks on individuals with foreign connections and dangerous beliefs. Already an elderly woman at this point, she was jailed for 'political crimes' and after three and a half years in prison passed away at the age of 74.

Prior to 1949, the CCP had been more flexible in its approach to women with 'bourgeois feminist' positions. Through the 1920s, 1930s and 1940s the CCP had been keen to integrate its comparatively small membership into the much larger women's associations' memberships. The CCP saw the well-organized women's associations (be they suffragist, philanthropic, educational, patriotic or professional) as a crucial avenue into an important segment of the politically active population. Activist women were all potential CCP members, so the CCP sought to harness their skills and energies rather than dismiss them entirely (Gilmartin 1995). However, after their victory in 1949, the need to maintain such niceties subsided—as Liu Wang Liming discovered.

For feminists within the CCP, the situation was also increasingly difficult. Wang Zheng describes the period immediately after 1949 as a brief 'golden period' (Wang 2006: 913–14) for CCP feminists. The ACWF established its institutional structures throughout the country with official endorsement.

> By 1950, women's federations were set up in 83 cities. By 1953 there were already over 40,000 officials of the ACWF system nationwide working at and above the district level. And by 1954 women in many cities had been organized into women's congresses, the grassroots organization of the ACWF. In a matter of a few years, women communists had successfully developed this gender-based organization into the only mass organization that reached down to the rural villages and urban neighbourhoods.
>
> (Wang 2006: 914)

Through these networks, the women promoted knowledge of sex equality and were able to criticize the current situation in their bid to improve women's opportunities. International Women's Day (8 March) continued to be a focus of women's activism and a celebration of women's contribution to society (as it had since the 1920s among left-wing women activists), but after 1949 the ACWF became the sole organizer and coordinator of the now-nationwide programme. It continues this role in the twenty-first century as part of its engagement with global socialist feminism (see Kaplan 1985).

The CCP made a number of dramatic claims about its progressive position on enhancing women's status in these years. It promulgated a Marriage Law on 1 May 1950 that presented a number of 'firsts' but in fact simply reinstated the gains China's feminists had made in the mid-1930s to ensure equality between husbands and wives in marriage and divorce. For example, the CCP's law reiterated the principle of free choice in partner, monogamy and the equal rights of both husbands and wives within marriage and in the decision to divorce already secured in the Nationalist Family Law.[10] In a legal sense, the CCP was merely confirming previously won rights. However, the key difference between the two governments' laws was that through the extensive ACWF networks established into communities and villages more ordinary people came to be aware of their rights and were able to act upon them. Divorces abounded in the first few years after 1950 as a result of the promotion of the law, and the Marriage Law was nicknamed 'The Divorce Law'. Franz Michael argues that the publicizing of the laws was not particularly driven by the CCP's desire to promote women's rights, but rather by their desire to dismantle clan influence over individuals in order to increase party influence (Michael 1962: 140). Neil Diamant's excellent article on the impact of the Law takes this view further by demonstrating that once young peasant women were armed with 'rights talk', they were active in pursuing their personal interests within the new family–state structures (Diamant 2000).

The ACWF's comparatively happy position within the new Party-State institutional apparatus would not continue for long. Wang Zheng notes that by 1957, the same year that Liu Wang Liming found herself subject to re-education, China's communist feminists 'suddenly made a conservative turn' (Wang 2006: 915). Their campaigns moved from mobilizing women to participate in the paid workforce to one that invoked domestic feminine virtues: 'diligently, thriftily build the country and diligently, thriftily manage the family'. The reason for this sudden shift was a May 1957 document written by Mao Zedong that 'merely talking about problems in socialist China could qualify one as a rightist' (Wang 2006: 919); therefore a central rubric of the ACWF's campaigning—the principle that women still suffered oppression resulting from remnants of old 'feudal' thinking—was likely to draw all of them into political disfavour. Thus, by 1957, not only were women with links to transnational feminist groups suspect, so too were China's own communist feminists. The ACWF's leadership duly modified its programme of activities and policy platforms in order to avoid the consequences of 'being accused of committing bourgeois feminist mistakes' and to ensure that the ACWF was not disbanded by a Party-State in which the only safe view to uphold was that men and women have already achieved equal rights in socialist China (Wang 2006: 924, 932).

A key consequence of the increasing fear of facing political attack was the narrowing of the movement. Individual women could not mobilize on women's issues outside of the structures of the Party's official woman's organ—the ACWF. Neither could the ACWF implement policies or programmes that did not have the imprimatur of the central party leadership. The ossification of the previously dynamic Chinese women's movement in Mainland China occurred in less than ten years. Moreover, in that process 'feminism' was tagged as a 'foreign' concept divorced from a 'Chinese' reality. The extensive history of Chinese women's engagement with the global feminist movement, its theory, practice and institutions was denied, dismissed and then forgotten. The PRC created a new conception of women as political actors—one in which they were passive, victims of feudal oppression before 1949; grateful recipients of the CCP's enlightened social policies after 1949; and uniquely 'Chinese' in their rejection of 'Western' feminism.[11] This CCP narrative presents Chinese women as different from other women around the world—effectively denying the principle of women's common political interests based on sex that the transnational feminist movements of the previous one hundred years had dedicated much energy to constructing. Women in the PRC no longer had the conceptual frame within which to mobilize as 'women of the world'—instead they were 'Chinese' women for whom feminism was inappropriate (because it was foreign) and unnecessary (because they were already equal with men).

The precarious position of China's state feminists and the miserable position of her 'bourgeois' feminists and their continued isolation (both actual and philosophical) from global feminist engagement would continue through the 1960s and 1970s. Along with many other institutions, the ACWF ceased operations during the grim years of the Cultural Revolution—but it had escaped the abolition it was threatened with in 1957. In 1978, after the death of the old rulers Mao Zedong and Zhou Enlai, the CCP embarked on an ambitious programme of economic and political liberalization, and organizations such as the ACWF soon returned to operation. China's post-Mao leaders opened the country to new ideas, allowed increasing personal freedoms and generally liberalized the political and commercial environment. For China's feminist movement, this shift would introduce a new energy and fresh international links.

Engaging with the world but hampered by nationalism, 1979–2009

Understandably, after so many decades of isolation and state terror, when the ACWF recommenced its work, the leadership took some time to find a new path in this liberalized new environment. The country moved quickly to embrace the freedoms presented by the so-called 'Open Door Policy' and the ACWF found itself in the precarious position of being regarded as 'old fashioned' and 'irrelevant'—the mouthpiece for the CCP which people no longer needed to heed. To complicate matters further, 1979 saw the start of a major population control programme and the ACWF workers were charged with administering an unpopular programme. Their challenge was to find a meaningful way of engaging with women on matters of concern to women and staying faithful to their party (see e.g. Hsiung *et al.* 2001).

Their key mechanism for gaining relevancy in these new and rapidly changing years was to target specific issues of concern to women. In particular, they prioritized matters of women's welfare—for example, combating domestic violence, providing legal advice and counselling services; promoting public awareness on the problem of kidnapping and sale of women (as wives or prostitutes); improving childbirth and childcare conditions and running training schemes to enhance women's employment opportunities. The latter was particularly important at the start of the reform period when women were often the first to lose their jobs in a state sector that was rapidly restructuring its hitherto unproductive factories. During these post-Mao years, the ACWF focused on women within their families in keeping with the CCP's renewed interest in 'traditional' values as a stabilizing force after decades of social 'revolution' (for details of their activities, see their website 'All-China Women's Federation' 2009).

At the same time, at the end of the twentieth century the ACWF was among the first social groups to make use of the Party-State's then-new interest in legal models of rights and interests to secure 'The Law on Protecting Women's Rights and Interests' in 1992 (*Funü quanyi baozhang fa*). It addressed all key aspects of equality between men and women (e.g. access to employment and equal remuneration for equal work) and reiterated existing bans on discrimination on the basis of sex (see 'Women's Law' 1992; for discussion, see Keith 1997). The effectiveness of the law was severely hampered by the impoverished state of the

Chinese legal and judicial system and while this continues to be a problem in the twenty-first century, the law's existence signals an ongoing recognition of women's rights from the top levels of the Party-State leadership and the ACWF's effective lobbying within that governance structure.

From their renewed position of confidence and in the absence of constraints from the xenophobia of the Maoist years, the ACWF also re-engaged with the international scene. Ron Keith notes that in 1980 China was one of the first countries to endorse the 1979 UN Convention on the Elimination of Discrimination against Women. In 1985, at the end of the UN's Decade on Women it first discussed creating the law on women's rights that was finalized in 1992. The increasing confidence of the Party-State to participate in international agendas on women was most clearly highlighted in 1990 by China's successful bid to host the UN's Fourth World Women's Conference to be held in 1995 (Keith 1997: 31). This was the first major international event China had hosted and signalled the nation's return to international engagement. Sharon Wesoky explains that the Party-State used this event to 'promote a favourable international image' (Wesoky 2002: 11). The event elevated the ACWF's position within the Chinese government and party structures because they had carriage of a prestigious global event. Since this event, the ACWF has been active in other UN-sponsored activities (such as White Ribbon day) and provides a link from the top levels of the Chinese political system into the international arena.

The ACWF serves a crucial role as the 'supervisory unit' (*guakao danwei*) to a number of NGO-like organizations working on women's issues. Without this sponsorship the organizations would be deemed illegal and would therefore be unable to secure international funding.[12] For example DV-net, an organization that draws together policy-makers, educators, welfare agencies, police and legal experts to combat domestic violence, received funding from the Ford Foundation, Swedish International Development Cooperation Agency, University of Oslo and the Netherlands' branch of Oxfam. ACWF sponsorship is crucial to this international relationship.

The precarious political status of women's organizations in the PRC during the 1980s and 1990s is clear from the case of the Women's Research Institute (WRI). Established in 1988 in Beijing, the WRI was the brainchild of recently retired journalist and editor Wang Xingjuan, and its goal was to conduct research into the current status of women in China to understand the impact of the economic and political reforms on women and, on the basis of that research, provide practical assistance to women. The organization needed a supervisory unit in order to operate and found that under the umbrella of the China Academy of Management Science. After half a decade of successful operation, the WRI fell foul of the Party-State. The UN Conference dramatically increased international interest in the status of women in China and the WRI became a major focus for international visitors of all kinds. Journalists, politicians and activists from around the world sought out WRI staff for interviews and meetings—including the then US First Lady Hillary Clinton. The sheer size of the international attention that the WRI attracted drew them into suspicion with the Party-States's

Public Security Bureau. International links and connections, even though they had not been actively sought by the WRI, were still politically problematic in 1995. The Public Security Bureau's investigation resulted in the Academy withdrawing its sponsorship and the WRI found itself suddenly in an illegal and very precarious position. In order to maintain operations, they had to reregister as a business enterprise under a different name—the Maple Woman's Psychological Counselling Centre (Milwertz 2002: 29–50; Milwertz 2003). The process of reconfiguring their organization for registration detracted from activists' time and energy. The international journalists and politicians had inadvertently damaged the operations of an important woman's organization through their lack of appreciation of the depth of xenophobia circulating among the Party–State leadership at that time.

The 1980s and 1990s also saw the emergence of Women's Studies in the education sector but links between these Chinese programmes and the international ones remained limited until the 2000s.[13] Initially, a nationalistic style of 'women's studies' emerged that clearly differentiated the scholars, teachers and students from 'bourgeois feminism' outside of China. A new narrative of China-centred women's studies was created from this search for a local tradition and style. Initially, researchers excavated the comparatively politically safe topic of women's participation in the building of modern China in a series of province-based women's history projects. Later, women's studies researchers would explore a diverse range of topics in keeping with international trends towards examining sexuality and the body, media and representation. Key foundational institutions include: the Institute for Women's Studies, which was established in 1983 under the auspices of the ACWF in Beijing and provincial and city branches followed later (Li and Zhang 1994: 141); Zhengzhou University opened the first tertiary educational unit in the field in 1985 and established curriculum and teaching materials that were instrumental in promoting the field's growth elsewhere. Over the course of the years since, other universities have followed Zhengzhou in forming centres and departments that focus on women's studies. Today, Peking University has one of the largest Women's Studies centres operating and draws its membership from across multiple disciplines and faculties in the university (Wei Guoying pers. communication 2009). Most major universities in China now have some form of women or gender unit operating.

Crucially, these developments are not *transnational*; rather they are national links into an international space. Within these international links and programmes, the overt discourse is one where 'the *Chinese* woman' stands centre-stage as a special category—the nation cannot be extracted from the conversation. China's current day internationally engaged feminists speak as representatives of their nation, providing *the* Chinese perspective. Antagonistic feminism, within this rubric, can be dismissed as being 'un-Chinese' (which suits a Party-State concerned with maintaining the political *status quo*). But more damaging for the transnational feminist project, such positioning undermines those points of solidarity women share internationally in their experiences of living under patriarchy. PRC women activists spoke to and for *Chinese* women in a context that underplayed their many similar interests with women elsewhere in the world and promoted the defence of the PRC's pride through a trumpeting of its 'unique' circumstances and special cultural characteristics.

A classic example of the reluctance by women scholars working on women's issues to engage fully with 'feminism' as a transnational movement at this time is evident in Li Xiaojiang and Zhang Xiaodan's 1994 comment:

> And yet it is interesting to note that the term *feminist* is seldom used to describe women's activities in China, whether governmental or nongovernmental, academic or general. Few women are willing to call themselves feminist and we have not found such a word anywhere except in translations or articles introducing Western feminism. Instead, in Chinese women studies, the word *feminology* is used, and it rarely implies Western feminist theory. For the Women's Federation, the term *feminism* is obviously seen as part of a bourgeois ideology and thus against the principles of Marxism. For scholars in unofficial women's studies groups, however, avoiding the term *feminism* or not identifying their work as 'feminist' is a deliberate and voluntary choice rather than a political consideration. Such scholars respect Western-based feminist theory, and yet they still believe that Chinese women's studies has its own background and circumstances unique to Chinese history and social reality. Western feminist theory is certainly valuable as a rich source of reference, but a Western feminist tradition can hardly provide standardized answers to all Chinese women's questions. Ultimately, Chinese women's studies scholars believe that through their own ways of seeking truth, they may be able to contribute to the Western tradition of women's studies.
>
> (Li and Zhang 1994: 148)

Through the 1980s and 1990s, despite the extensive links with the outside, China's women scholars, cadres and activists still sought to mark themselves as separate from a homogenized Western feminism through an active campaign of indigenization (*bentuhua*).[14] The dynamic feminisms emerging from South Asia and Japan were ignored as China's self-declared non-feminist women activists sought a uniquely Chinese approach to advancing women's status in China. This Sino-centric approach to women's problems was akin to the CCP's key foreign policy position that upholds China's right to be free from 'international interference in domestic affairs' and revealed the depths of insecurity produced among the intellectual and political classes by decades of isolation from the world and the continuing xenophobic form of nationalism generated by the PRC Party-State. Feng Xu describes the situation as 'the desire to indigenize western theories reflects an understandable anxiety on the part of Chinese women's studies scholars to contribute to theory building, so that China is not merely a "case" against which western-based theories are tested' (Xu 2009: 208). The dominant narrative remains that feminism is a hegemonic 'Western' product that China needs protection from rather than as a dynamic, multi-dimensional movement that has myriad global manifestations. In this regard, nationalism has hampered Chinese women's recognition that feminism as a diverse transnational project rather than one of cultural imperialism.

In the 2000s, this defensive position is beginning to change. Li Xiaojiang embraced a notion that globalization would propel Chinese women into greater chances of becoming individuals outside of family, society and nation (Li Xiaojiang 2001: 1277). But for such globalizing trends to impact public rhetoric on feminism in China they had to be accompanied by the Party-State's willingness to lift restrictions on group political activism. Official tolerance of the activism that has emerged in universities and schools around V-day since the early-to-mid 2000s suggests that transnational activism is possible within certain limited parameters. V-day started in the USA in 1998 as a movement to eradicate Violence against Women (VAW), drawing its energy from Eve Ensler's play *The Vagina Monologues*. Each year during the weeks surrounding 14 February (V-day), women around the world participate in public events, including performing the play, posters, lectures and rallies, to promote awareness of VAW ('V-Day: A Global Movement to End Violence against Women and Girls' 2009).

Chinese women activists based primarily in universities have become active participants in this global movement. The play has been frequently performed in Chinese within universities and schools since 2003 even though it was banned from professional public performance on the basis that its explicitly sexual content offended Chinese moral sensibilities (Edwards 2009). The Party-State's tolerance of grass-roots links to global feminist activism is largely limited to educational institutions or welfare agencies (e.g. DV-Net). These bodies ultimately remain beholden to the Party-State through the CCP's dominance of their formal leadership structures. The regulations surrounding the registration of organizations and associations in the PRC is so prohibitive that citizens seeking to establish a feminist organization would find it nearly impossible without ACWF support. Accordingly, the V-day activists do not have a formal structure or membership; instead, women simply gather together to participate in a commonly agreed set of activities at a certain time of year. To do otherwise would attract criticism from the authorities.

Conclusion

For over a century, Chinese women's activism on women's issues has propelled social and political change in China. Women have continued to struggle for policies and practices that enhance women's status across the decades and within vastly different historical circumstances. Their ideas about the best way to enhance women's status have changed along with these myriad different circumstances. At times their programmes have been unrecognizable to feminists working in Europe, Australasia or America as a result of their isolation from the international scene. As a transnational movement, feminists have routinely looked across the shores and past the border posts, to engage with like-minded women elsewhere in the spirit of solidarity. Only with the emergence of Cold War paranoia and xenophobic nationalism during the second half of the twentieth century did China's leaders isolate its women from participation in this global conversation. In the twenty-first century, we see China's tentative shift back towards a comfortable engagement with transnational social movements, such as feminism. The challenge for the immediate future is to dismantle nationalist thinking that inhibits women activists from responding as women with a feminist agenda rather than as *Chinese women* with a *PRC* agenda.

Notes

1 For a discussion of the various terms that have been used for feminism in Chinese and the implications of their myriad changes, see Ko and Wang (2006).
2 In 1908, Little's association was led entirely by Chinese women (Drucker 1981: 187–9).
3 For a discussion of the considerable contribution of women to the 1898 Reform movement, see Qian Nanxiu (2003).
4 The patronizing tone of the title and article content was typical of the infantilizing Orientalism Chinese women were often subject to by their more 'advanced' Western sisters.
5 I am grateful to Mary Chapman for providing me with this article and excerpts from Catt's diary.
6 For a discussion of the various evolving ways women activists used nationalism in their feminist struggles, see Edwards (2005).
7 For a comprehensive discussion of the suffrage movement, see (Edwards 2008).
8 Chinese women were also in attendance at the Pan Pacific Women's Conferences held in 1928, 1930 and 1934 in Honolulu (Paisley 2002). Taiwan remains a member of this association, but the PRC does not participate ('About PPSEAWA' 2009).
9 For an excellent discussion of the history of the tension between Marxism and feminism, see (Boxer 2007).
10 Franz Michael notes that the key difference between the Nationalist and Communist marriage laws was the requirement in the latter that CCP cadres have final authority to approve (or not) all marriages. This requirement effectively inserted CCP control directly into what had previously been a personal or family choice (1962: 138).
11 A good example of this narrative, complete with its erasure of pre-1949 feminist activism and successes can be found in (Li and Zhang 1994: 138–9). They go so far as to describe Chinese women as being 'passive in the liberation process' since 'the context of Chinese women's liberation initiated by male politicians within a male-run political system' (1994: 146). Sharon Wesoky reports this view in her study and notes that China's contemporary feminists identify themselves as 'the second wave' of feminists following the 'first wave' of the 1920s–1930s. But significantly they also claim to be the first 'wave' to be led by women erroneously claiming that men dominated the 1920s and 1930s 'wave' (Wesoky 2002: 55–6). This common view of history denies their predecessor feminists' leadership and agency of their own movement in a remarkable process of politically inspired erasure.
12 For a discussion of women's activism within the context of an emerging civil society in the PRC, see Howell (2003).
13 For discussion of the development of women's studies in the last years of the twentieth century, see Wang Zheng (1997).
14 Karen Offen had earlier exploded the myth of the unitary 'Western' feminist perspective in her 1988 article on the wide divergence in viewpoints within Europe and between Europe and the USA (Offen 1988).

References

'About PPSEAWA' (2009) Online. Available HTTP: <http://www.ppseawa.org/about-ppseawa> (accessed 20 August 2009).

'All-China Women's Federation' (2009) Online. Available HTTP: <http://www.women.org.cn/english/index.htm> (accessed 20 August 2009).

'Girl will direct Chinese Women's College' (1915) *The Suffragist*, 3, 47 (20 November): 2.

'V-Day: A Global Movement to End Violence against Women and Girls' (2009) Online. Available HTTP: <http://www.vday.org/> (accessed 24 September 2009).

'Women's Law' (1992). Online. Available HTTP: <http://www.women.org.cn/english/english/laws/02.htm> (accessed 24 September 2009).

Au, C.K. (1998) 'Zhang Zhujun', in C.W.-C. Ho (ed.) *Biographical Dictionary of Chinese Women: The Qing Period, 1644–1911*, Armonk, NY: ME Sharpe, pp. 310–13.

Bailey, P. (2006) *Gender and Education in China: Gender Discourses and Women's School in the Early Twentieth Century*, London: Routledge.

Boxer, M.J. (2007) 'Rethinking the Socialist Construction and International Career of the Concept of "Bourgeois feminism"', *American Historical Review*, 112, 1: 131–58.

Catt, C.C. (1912) 'The New China: She Sits in the Gallery and Looks Down on China's Ten Women Legislators, Who Had Been Called a Myth', *Woman's Journal*, 5 October (1912): 314–15.

Diamant, N.J. (2000) 'Re-examining the Impact of the 1950 Marriage Law: State Improvisation, Local Initiative and Rural Family Change', *China Quarterly*, 161: 171–98.

Dikötter, F. (2008) *China in the Age of Openness: China before Mao*, Hong Kong: Hong Kong University Press.

Drucker, A.R. (1981) 'The Influence of Western Women on the Anti-Footbinding Movement, 1840–1911', *Historical Reflections*, 8, 3 (Fall): 179–99.

Edwards, L. (1994) 'Chin Sung-ts'en's *A Tocsin for Women*: The Dexterous Merger of Radicalism and Conservatism in Feminism of the Early Twentieth Century', *Jindai Zhongguo funü shi yanjiu*, 2 (June): 117–40.

—— (2004) 'Chinese Women's Campaigns for Suffrage: Nationalism, Confucianism and Political Agency', in L. Edwards and M. Roces (eds) *Women's Suffrage in Asia: Gender, Nationalism, Democracy*, London: Routledge, pp. 59–78.

—— (2005) 'Moving from the Vote into Citizenship: Crafting Chinese Women's Political Citizenship', *Berliner China-Hefte* (December): 5–17.

—— (2008) *Gender, Politics and Democracy: Women's Suffrage in China*. Stanford: Stanford University Press.

—— (2009) 'Diversity and Evolution in the State-in-Society: International Influences in Combating Violence against Women', in L.C. Li (ed.) *The State in Transition: Processes and Contests in Local China*, London: Routledge, pp. 108–27.

Finch, G.A. (1924) 'Remission of the Chinese Indemnity', *American Journal of International Law*, 18, 3 (June): 544–8.

Gamble, S. (1943) 'The Disappearance of Foot-Binding in Tinghsien', *American Journal of Sociology*, 49, 2 (September): 181–3.

Gilmartin, C.K. (1995) *Engendering the Chinese Revolution: Radical Women, Communist Politics and Mass Movements in the 1920s*, Berkeley: California University Press.

Howell, J. (2003) 'Women's Organizations and Civil Society in China', *International Feminist Journal of Politics*, 5, 2: 191–215.

Hsiung, P., Jaschok, M. et al., (eds) (2001) *Chinese Women Organising: Cadres, Feminists, Muslims, Queers*, Oxford: Berg.

Hu Bin[xia] (1903) 'Lun Zhongguo zhi shuairuo nüzi bu de ci qi zui', *Jiangsu*, 156–7.

—— (1916a) 'Meiguo jiating', *Funü zazhi*, 2, 2 (February): 1–8.

—— (1916b) 'Jichu zhi jichu', *Funü zazhi*, 2, 8 (August): 1–12.

Jin Songcen (1903) *Nü jie zhong*, Shanghai: Datong shuju.

Judge, J. (2008) *The Precious Raft of History: The Past, the West, and the Woman Question in China*, Stanford: Stanford University Press.

Kang Youwei (1898; rpt. 1975) 'Qingjin funü guozu zhe', rpt. in Zhang Yufa, Li Youning (eds) *Jindai Zhongguo nüquan yundong shiliao*, Taibei: Zhuanji wenxue chubanshe, p. 509.

Kaplan, T. (1985) 'On the Socialist Origins of International Women's Day', *Feminist Studies*, 11, 1: 163–71.

Keith, R.C. (1997) 'Legislating Women's and Children's "Rights and Interests" in the PRC', *China Quarterly*, 149 (March): 29–55.

Kent, S.K. (1987) *Sex and Suffrage in Britain, 1860–1914*, Princeton, NJ: Princeton University Press.

Kirby, W.C. (2006) 'China's Internationalization in the Early People's Republic: Dreams of a Socialist World Economy', *China Quarterly*, 188 (December): 870–90.

Ko, D. (2005) *Cinderella's Sisters: A Revisionist History of Footbinding*, Berkeley: University of California Press.

Ko, D. and Wang, Z. (2006) 'Introduction: Translating Feminisms in China', *Gender and History*, 18, 3 (November): 463–71.

Li, X. (2001) 'From "Modernization to "Globalisation": Where are Chinese Women?', *Signs*, 26, 4 (Summer): 1274–78.

Li, X. and Zhang X. (1994) 'Creating a Space for Women: Women's Studies in China in the 1980s', *Signs*, 20, 1: 137–51.

Lin Weihong (1981) 'Tongmenghui shidai nü geming zhishi de huodong', in Li Youning and Zhang Yufa (eds), *Zhongguo funü shilun wenji*, Taipei: Shangwuyin shuguan, pp. 129–78.

Michael, F. (1962) 'The Role of Law in Traditional, Nationalist and Communist China', *China Quarterly*, 9 (January–March): 124–48.

Milwertz, C. (2002) *Beijing Women Organising for Change: A New Wave of the Chinese Women's Movement*, Copenhagen: NIAS Press.

—— (2003) 'Activism against Domestic Violence in the People's Republic of China', *Violence against Women*, 9, 6 (June): 630–54.

Offen, K. (1988) 'Defining Feminism: A Comparative Historical Approach', *Signs*, 14, 1: 119–57.

Ogawa, M. (2007) 'Estranged Sisterhood: The Wartime Trans-Pacific Dialogue of World's Woman's Christian Temperance Union, 1931–45', *The Japanese Journal of American Studies*, 18: 163–85.

Paisley, F. (2002) 'Cultivating Modernity: Culture and Internationalism in Australian Feminism's Pacific Age', *Journal of Women's History*, 14, 3 (Autumn): 105–32.

Qian, N. (2003) 'Revitalizing the *Xianyuan* (Worthy Ladies) Tradition: Women in the 1898 Reforms', *Modern China*, 29, 4 (October): 399–454.

Qiu Jin (1906 or 1907, rpt. 1982) 'Jinggao yimeimen (jiexuan)', in Guo Yanli (ed.) *Qiu Jin shiwen xuan*, Beijing: Renmin wenxue chubanshe, pp. 10–13.

Volz, Y.Z. (2007) 'Going Public Through Writing: Women Journalists and Gendered Journalistic Space in China, 1890–1920s', *Media, Culture and Society*, 29, 3: 469–89.

Wang, Z. (1997) 'Maoism, Feminism and the UN Conference on Women: Women's Studies Research in Contemporary China', *Journal of Women's History*, 8, 4 (Winter): 126–52.

—— (2006) 'Dilemmas of Inside Agitators: Chinese State Feminists in 1957', *China Quarterly*, 188: 913–32.

Wei Guoying (2009) 'Personal Communication', Vice-Director of the Peking University Women's Studies Centre (Beijing daxue Zhong Wai funü wenti yanjiu zhongxin), 12 September.

Wesoky, S. (2002) *Chinese Feminism Faces Globalisation*, New York & London: Routledge.

Xie Zhangfa (1996) 'Qingmo de liu Ri nüxuesheng jiqi huodong yu yingxiang', *Jindai Zhongguo funü shi yanjiu*, 4 (August): 63–86.

Xu, F. (2009) 'Chinese Feminisms Encounter International Feminisms', *International Feminist Journal of Politics*, 11, 2: 196–215.

Ye, W. (1994) '"Nü Liuxuesheng": The Story of American-Educated Chinese Women, 1880s–1920s', *Modern China*, 20, 3 (July): 315–46.

Zito, A. (2007) 'Secularizing the Pain of Footbinding in China: Missionaries and Medical Stagings of the Universal Body', *Journal of the American Academy of Religion*, 75, 1 (Spring): 1–4.

5 Transnational networks and localized campaigns

The women's movement in Singapore

Lenore Lyons

In an article published at the end of the twentieth century, I recounted how, in the course of my research on the Singaporean feminist movement, scholars and activists often responded with incredulity when I discussed the subject of my research—'Is there *really* a women's movement in Singapore?' they would ask (Lyons 2000a). Indeed, there was (and still is!), and it traces its origins in the dense web of transnational networks that link its population to countries in Asia and further abroad. In this chapter, I trace the historical origins of these networks from the mid-1880s during the period of British colonialism through to Independence in 1965, and explore the continued role of transnational networks and connections through the latter half of the twentieth century up to 2008. In describing these links as 'transnational', I distinguish between three different meanings of the term—transnational framing, cross-border organizing, and trans-ethnic solidarity. I use the term 'transnational framing' to refer to the process by which ideas circulate between different scales (the international, national and local) and become translated into concrete practices within specific organizational contexts (Desai 2005). The term 'cross-border organizing' is used to refer to instances of campaigns or activities that transcend the national border (Della Porta and Tarrow 2005). Finally, 'trans-ethnic solidarity' refers to the formation of national-level coalitions and alliances that are made up of individuals and/or organizations representing different ethnic and/or national groups. These groups are 'transnational' in the sense that they transcend nationality as the basis for women's organizing.[1] In using these interconnected concepts to trace the history of the women's movement in Singapore, I do not want to underemphasize the importance of the local. Singapore's rich history of women's activism is an indigenous history based on the concerns and actions of women embedded within the particularities of Singaporean society. Contrary to the claims of the patriarchal state and its supporters, women's activism and feminism are not expressions of 'Western values' but reflect the aspirations of multiple generations of Singaporean women (Lyons 2000a).

Activism in the colonial period

The origins of Singapore's women's movement can be traced back to a tradition of activism and reform by Western missionaries and the wives and daughters of colonial administrators and settlers from the mid-nineteenth century onwards. These women set up schools for girls, and provided medical services for women. Many of the girls who received their education in missionary schools went on to become prominent teachers, doctors, nurses and social workers, and continued the legacy of these strong, socially active women. Formed in 1875, the Young Women's Christian Association (YWCA) (the oldest established women's organization in Singapore) played a key role in educating young girls, particularly Europeans, Eurasians and Chinese. European women lobbied to repeal with Contagious Diseases Ordinance (CDO), which was enacted to counter the spread of sexually transmitted diseases through the creation of regulated brothel zones (Arora 2007: 40–1). Their actions were part of a global alliance of women's groups campaigning against the trafficking of women and the invasive and humiliating laws that regulated prostitution. Their efforts to stop the reintroduction of the CDO into Malaya continued up until World War II (Crinis 2004).

Colonial women were not the only ones engaged in education and charitable activities. Many upper-class Chinese women established charities and made significant donations for the establishment of women's medical wards and maternity hospitals, and girls' schools. The Chinese Ladies' Association, later known as the Chinese Women's Association (CWA), provided both a social network and a channel for philanthropic activity for many of these women (Arora 2007). CWA is the oldest existing women's organization founded by local women and is an example of a strong tradition of ethnically based women's groups which include The Kamala Club (whose membership is primarily women of South Asian background) and the Young Women's Muslim Association.

Middle-class and elite women, however, were not the only ones involved in bringing about changes in women's lives in the early twentieth century. The vegetarian houses or anti-marriage associations set up by Chinese women who travelled from Guangdong Province in southern China to Singapore during the early 1900s to work as domestic workers (or *amahs*) are an important pre-cursor of working-class women's activism. These anti-marriage sisterhoods or 'marriage resisters' were based on similar association formed in southern China in the late 1800s (Raymond 1986; Stockard 1989). There were two types of resisters: those who married but refused to consummate the marriage or cohabit with their husbands, and those who never married ('self-combers') (Raymond 1986: 131). In 1955, there were approximately 250–350 vegetarian halls in Singapore, the majority of which were inhabited by marriage resisters from China (Raymond 1986: 137). Some local-born Chinese women also joined the vegetarian halls. Janice Raymond (1986: 137) notes that although the migrant women did not form a cohesive marriage resistance movement in Singapore, they 'preserved much of the spirit and many of the traditions of sworn sisterhood'. This included running associations or clubs which had a mutual aid or social purpose.

The struggle against polygamy

It was not until after World War II that Singapore's women's movement began to take on a more structured form with the establishment of the Singapore Council of Women (SCW). The SCW was the first women's organization in Singapore to specifically identify 'women's rights' as an issue of social and political concern (Chew 1994). It was strongly aligned with the anti-colonial movement and its leaders saw the struggle for women's rights as part of the wider struggle for democracy and equal rights (Lam 1993: 84). Shirin Fozdar, one of the founders of the SCW, was born in India and participated in the All Asian Women's Conference in Lahore in 1934 and then represented the conference on issues of equality of nationality for women at the League of Nations in Geneva (Arora 2007: 55–6). By the mid-1950s, the SCW had a membership of over 2,000 women from different classes, races and religions. It established crèches, a girls' club and a home for the rehabilitation of women and girls involved in prostitution, and offered marriage counselling (Chew 1994: 119). The council is best remembered, however, for its campaign throughout the 1950s to end polygamy. Members of the SCW lobbied the British colonial government as well as members of local ethnic-based advisory boards for many years, but had its greatest success with local politicians and political parties in the lead up to self-government in 1959. The People's Action Party (PAP) was the only political party to specifically include women's rights in its campaign platform and it pledged to introduce a monogamous marriage law if it was elected to power. It kept this promise and in 1961 the Women's Charter, covering laws dealing with marriage, divorce, custody, maintenance, inheritance, property rights and protection against violence, was passed.[2] By insisting that all marriages had to be legally registered, it fundamentally altered the system of customary marriage rites and gave women greater security within marriage.

With the Women's Charter enacted, the SCW lost momentum and it was not until the International Women's Year of 1975 that the women's movement in Singapore gained renewed vigour with the formation of the National Council of Women (NCW). The NCW was a national advisory committee for women's affairs, with the goal of coordinating the activities of women's groups and eliminating discrimination against women (Lam 1993: 93). The number of women's groups affiliated to the NCW remained small and it consequently failed to receive government recognition as a national body representing women. However, interest in establishing a national women's body remained strong and, in 1980, the government-sanctioned Singapore Council of Women's Organizations (SCWO) was established. The SCWO was more successful than the NCW in attracting affiliate groups and there are presently over forty women's groups affiliated to the council, representing over 150,000 women. The SCWO holds regular forums and workshops aimed at examining and improving the status of women. In addition, it runs training programmes for women, and is involved in the development of government policy through its research and legislative arm. Not long after the formation of the SCWO, renewed interest in women's status was sparked amongst Singaporean women in reaction to the 'Great Marriage Debate' of 1983. Prior to this event, interest in women's issues was characterized by what Nirmala PuruShotam (1998: 141–2) calls a 'modern not feminist' or 'modern/liberated' perspective amongst women. It was a position which asserted that equality based on gender complementarity had already been achieved. The Great Marriage Debate challenged this view.

The Great Marriage Debate

The Great Marriage Debate grew as a public reaction to a series of statements by then prime minister Lee Kuan Yew. In a National Day Rally speech in August 1983, Lee called attention to a trend in which graduate women were delaying or forgoing marriage and children for their careers. Lee feared that in a country whose only resource was its people, a decline in birth-rates amongst the well-educated would result in a 'thinning of the gene pool', and thus national economic disaster:

> We must further amend our policies, and try to reshape our demographic configuration so that our better-educated women will have more children to be adequately represented in the next generation ... Equal employment opportunities, yes, but we shouldn't get our women into jobs where they cannot, at the same time, be mothers. ... You just can't be doing a full-time heavy job like that of a doctor or engineer and run a home and bring up children.
>
> (Lee cited in *The Straits Times* 1983)

An avowed eugenicist, Lee argued that while all women can be mothers, better-educated women should be mothers. Lee cited the 1980 census which showed that while women with limited formal education were producing an average of three children, those with secondary or tertiary education had 1.65 children (Saw 1990: 41). Lee referred to this as a 'lop-sided procreation pattern' and the issue was dubbed the 'Great Marriage Debate' by the local press. In a subsequent discussion of this issue, two changes in demographic behaviour were referred to—the increasing number of unmarried women with tertiary education, and the lower reproduction rate among Chinese (particularly those with higher education).

State promotion of marriage and procreation began as a series of mass educational campaigns conducted in the Singaporean media in the mid-1980s. Run under the auspices of the Family Life Education Programme, campaign slogans have included: 'Are you giving men the wrong idea?', 'Life will be lonely without a family. Don't leave it too late' and 'Why not reality? You could wait a lifetime for a dream'. The government encouraged public and private sector employers to act as matchmakers, and introduced a range of financial and social incentives, including tax relief, to encourage women to marry and have children. These schemes deliberately targeted women with secondary school education and above, based on Lee Kuan Yew's eugenicist belief that well-educated mothers would produce more intelligent children. Lee's call for graduate mothers to produce more children was also intrinsically tied to a policy of cultural/racial maintenance; declining birth rates were most apparent among the upper and middle classes who are predominantly Chinese (Heng and Devan 1995).

Singapore's most prominent feminist organization, the Association of Women for Action and Research (AWARE), was established in 1985 in direct response to the Great Marriage Debate. In November 1984, in reaction to government policies aimed at graduate mothers, the National University of Singapore Society (NUSS) held a forum titled 'Women's Choices, Women's Lives'. The challenge to address the issues raised during the forum was taken up by a group that included both the keynote speakers and the members of the audience. Since then, AWARE has advocated for equal employment opportunities for women, access to equal educational opportunities for girls and changes to laws on domestic violence. In addition to its research work, AWARE runs workshops and seminars and operates a volunteer helpline service. Its membership is open to all Singaporean citizens and permanent residents over the age of eighteen, and men and foreign women may join as associate members. It was founded as a multi-ethnic organization based on a political desire to overcome what its founders saw as the increasing ethnicization of civil society by the PAP (Lyons 2004a).

AWARE has strong links with ASEAN-based women's groups, dealing with issues such as violence against women and reproductive health rights. Representatives from AWARE and SCWO frequently travel to regional conferences, participate in women's networks, and host visitors from women's organizations worldwide. The importance of conference attendance and networking activities should not be underestimated. Conferences are not only crucial in shaping the ways that women's rights issues are understood at the national level, but they are also a way of ensuring that locally specific understandings of conditions on the ground are filtered back up into transnational campaigns. In the case of Singapore's women's organizations, however, these kinds of transnational engagements have not been translated into concrete forms of transnational organising. Their focus remains firmly on the national scale, and while they may see themselves as part of an international movement, they describe their activism as very much based in their local experience.

Over the past two decades, AWARE has been confronted with public and media perceptions of feminists as man-haters, lesbians and radicals and with the political association of feminism with encroaching 'Western values' (Lyons 1999, 2000a). In response, the organization often adopts a shifting and fluid identity that changes to suit public and state constructions of feminism, women's rights, equality and social change. In its first decade, the organization was more reluctant to position itself in relation to feminism, leading to a paradoxical situation in which everyone knew that it was feminist, but few members openly acknowledged their feminist colours (Lyons 2000c). As the organization has matured and the state's interaction with civil society has become less heavy handed, both individual AWARE members and the Executive Committee have been more willing to describe the association as feminist. By this, they mean a political commitment to gender equity for all. Supporting this stance has not always been easy and in the 1990s AWARE's commitment to gender equity for non-citizen women was publicly questioned.

The rights of foreign workers

In 1998, AWARE presented a petition to the Indonesian embassy decrying the treatment of ethnic Chinese women in Indonesia who were raped during a series of racial clashes in Indonesia that year. In receiving the petition, a spokeswoman for the Indonesian embassy pointed out that Indonesian women were frequent victims of violent abuse while working as domestic workers in Singapore, an issue that AWARE had not addressed (Zakaria 1998). AWARE was put in the awkward position of explaining why it had not included the rights of resident foreign women in its campaigns against domestic violence. Following this embarrassing episode, AWARE began to make public statements in support of migrant workers, particularly in relation to the need to punish the perpetrators of violence against foreign domestic workers (FDWs).

The reasons why Singapore's women's rights movement had not taken up the issue of foreign domestic workers are many and complex. In particular, the association of foreign workers with the so-called Marxist Conspiracy has meant that few NGOs were willing to address migrant worker rights. 'Marxist Conspiracy' is a term used to describe the arrest and detention under the Internal Security Act (ISA) of twenty-two people in May 1987 for threatening the state and national interests (Barr 2008). Among those arrested were Catholic social workers and lay workers from the Geylang Catholic Centre for Foreign Workers. Like many topics deemed 'too sensitive' or 'taboo' for activist intervention, the issue has never been publicly identified by the state in its official statements as an area that is 'out of bounds' (OB) but this event had a profound effect on AWARE's decision to avoid issues related to foreign workers (Lyons 2007). AWARE and other civil society organizations (CSOs) work within a framework commonly dubbed the 'OB markers'. Ho (2000: 186) describes these as 'issues that are too sensitive to be discussed in public for fear of destabilising or jeopardising public peace and order'. The ruling PAP elite is responsible for determining the limits of the OB markers, a task that it largely performs retrospectively with the result that what actually constitutes 'unacceptable political engagement' is often unclear. Faced with the prospect of inciting government wrath, most NGOs adopt a cautious approach in their activities (Lyons 2000b).

State control of civil society, however, is not the only explanation for AWARE's long-term silence on female migrant workers. The differences posed by class, ethnicity and nationality have proved significant barriers to understanding the problems faced by migrant women.[3] Thus, although AWARE's twenty-year campaign against the state's pro-natalist policies has addressed the factors that drive demand for FDWs (cf. AWARE 2004), it has not focused on the issues that face domestic workers on arrival in Singapore. From AWARE's perspective, eliminating the foreign domestic worker programme would be an indicator of the success of its campaigns to change traditional gender roles. It believes that employing domestic workers is not the solution to the 'crisis in the home'; instead, the government should encourage employers to introduce family-friendly policies and encourage men to take greater responsibility for housework and childcare. It is also important to note that the majority of AWARE members are middle class and many members are employers of FDWs. For these busy women, hiring a live-in domestic worker is a prerequisite for juggling their careers, family responsibilities, and involvement in community activities, including their work in AWARE. Engaging with the question of migrant labour would require AWARE members to address the fraught topic of class location and demand for cheap domestic labour, issues that cut to the core of their own life experiences. Consequently, until very recently, problems faced by female migrant workers were in themselves not conceived of as a feminist issue by AWARE.

This changed in 2001 when the brutal assault and death of a 19-year-old Indonesian domestic worker by her employer sparked a national outcry in Singapore and prompted the formation of a network of concerned Singaporeans who met to discuss the issue of attitudes towards and treatment of domestic workers in Singapore. The group called themselves The Working Committee Two (TWC2) and their aim was to promote the better treatment of domestic workers through public awareness and legislative change (Lyons 2005; Gee and Ho 2006). AWARE was involved as an affiliate organization, and the TWC2 website and bulletin board were hosted on the AWARE website. As its year-long programme reached its conclusion, a new group consisting of former TWC2 members announced that they would be seeking registration under the Societies Act for an organization called Transient Workers Count Too and that they would retain their original acronym (TWC2). Like AWARE, TWC2 is a trans-ethnic and trans-national organization— its membership is open to Singapore citizens and permanent residents and FDWs of all nationalities. Due to state-imposed restrictions on the registration of NGOs, however, the executive structures of both groups are limited to Singapore citizens and permanent residents. Trans-ethnic solidarity is thus inhibited by state policies regulating the operation of CSOs, and consequently migrant women have a limited voice in shaping the activities of both groups.

TWC2's focus on the feminization of transnational labour migration, and its strong association with AWARE, have meant that it is commonly perceived as a pro-feminist organization. In the Singaporean context, this refers to an organization that is supportive of women's equal rights but chooses not to use the term 'feminist' to describe its work. Several prominent members of AWARE were actively involved in establishing the TWC2, and Braema Mathi was president of both organizations during 2004–5. However, TWC2 remains largely focused on migrant women and AWARE on local women, thus reinforcing an 'us and them' divide in public understandings of migrant worker issues (Lyons 2007). This division is reflected in the absence of strong cross-border links between Singaporean-based women's NGOs and groups elsewhere. The nature of state–civil society interactions is a significant factor moderating the cross-border activities of Singapore's NGOs. Many groups are wary of accepting funds from international bodies lest their actions antagonize the Singapore government (Lyons 2000b). It is important, however, not to overplay the role of the state in determining NGO activities. As I have argued elsewhere, such a view is not only premised on the idea of a unitary Singaporean state (i.e. a state that acts consistently in its dealings with all civil society actors) but also underplays the role of class, ideology and NGO histories in shaping organizational goals and objectives (Lyons 2004b).

Recently, the women's movement has begun to build stronger cross-border links, particularly in the area of migrant worker issues (see Lyons 2009). The formation of UNIFEM Singapore represents one of the first direct links between the Singaporean feminist movement and the international women's movement. As an affiliate member of UNIFEM, it has access to information and other resources not normally available to a nationally based women's organization. UNIFEM has a strong interest in issues facing female migrant workers, and a number of its projects in support of migrant women are based in the Asia-Pacific, including the 'Empowering Migrant Women Workers' campaign and its work to assist victims of trafficking. However, UNIFEM's organizational regulations are very clear about who can participate in these campaigns and in what capacity. Although migrant women from the developing world may live and work in Singapore for many years, their collective needs and concerns are dealt with through a regional network based in Bangkok rather than by UNIFEM's Singapore office. Thus, although it is part of an international non-governmental organization which in turn is part of a transnational feminist network working on issues faced by female migrant workers, UNIFEM Singapore itself occupies a fairly marginal position within this network.

Achievements and setbacks

Since the formation of the Family Planning Association of Singapore in 1949, Singaporean women have been actively involved in campaigns to provide women with access to safe contraception. These issues were not only central to the establishment of the SCW in 1952, but were also at the heart of AWARE's formation, and continue to be a central part of its campaign work. In 1989, in response to growing public concern about the direction of government policy aimed at lifting the birth rate, AWARE wrote its first position paper, titled *Population: An Issue of Current Concern*, in which it argued that a comprehensive solution to declining fertility would need to move beyond financial incentives (favoured by the government), to include improved leave schemes and working conditions, better child-care facilities, changes to the educational system, and attitudinal change amongst employers and colleagues (AWARE 1988). Over the course of the next ten years, AWARE continued to lobby for these changes through meetings with government officials, forums and seminars, and via letters to the forum pages of daily newspapers. In particular, it has been concerned with ensuring adequate recognition of the roles of husbands and fathers (through paternity leave and equal sharing of household responsibilities); ensuring government and employer recognition of gender equity in marriage and parenting; highlighting anomalies in existing legislation that impacts on parenting roles; and supporting the role of single women (including single mothers) (AWARE 2004). Despite the organization's strong and persistent stance on population policy, these campaigns have had limited success in changing the ruling party's pro-natalist views or in introducing family-friendly work environments.

AWARE and the SCWO have had greater success in their efforts to address violence against women and girls. Together they have been active in lobbying the police and the government to change the way victims of family violence and rape are treated. The Rape Study Committee organized by the SCWO (of which AWARE is a member) has played an important role in developing standard police procedures on rape management. Following lengthy dialogue with the police throughout 1993 and 1994, changes were made in the way that police handle rape cases, including a policy of referring victims to social agencies for counselling, and dissemination of relevant telephone numbers of counselling support services or shelters to battered women. More recent efforts to address violence against women include Singapore's first White Ribbon Campaign.[4]

Singapore became a signatory (with reservations) to the UN Convention for the Elimination of All Forms of Discrimination Against Women (CEDAW) in 1995. In order to make the government more accountable to the clauses stipulated in CEDAW, AWARE produces an annual Shadow Report as part of its activities to monitor discrimination against women. After many years of lobbying by AWARE and other groups, significant changes have been achieved in areas of active discrimination against women. These include the lifting of quotas on female medical students, changes to citizenship laws and the removal of discrimination in public service entitlements. From 1979 the intake of female students into the Medical Faculty at the National University of Singapore was restricted to one-third of the total intake of medical students irrespective of the academic grades of these female students. The rationale for this active discrimination against women was the claim that too many women 'waste' their medical education when they marry and have children because they resign from medical practice. The quota was introduced to reduce the cost to the government and the university when women retire. The women's movement lobbied both the government and the NUS to change the policy, arguing that such discrimination amounted to priority entry for male students. The quota was finally lifted in 2003.

Another long-term cause championed by the women's movement is the right of Singaporean women married to foreigners to sponsor their husbands to live in Singapore as permanent residents. In 1999, the immigration rules were changed to allow a Singaporean woman to sponsor her husband for citizenship if he had been a permanent resident for at least two years; or to sponsor her foreign husband for permanent residency so long as the family had the means to support itself. Previously, foreign husbands had to qualify for permanent residency on their own merits. However, these laws continue to discriminate against women because the foreign wives of Singaporean men do not face the same requirements; and because the definition of 'family support' implies that only couples with a certain level of income will be able to sponsor the husband. Until 2004 only male Singaporeans could pass on citizenship by descent to their children born overseas. Those born overseas to female Singaporeans had to apply for citizenship by registration. Starting in 1985, AWARE began to lobby the government to change the citizenship laws on the basis that the law discriminates against Singaporean women who marry foreigners, but who may wish for their children to become Singaporeans. After twenty years of constant campaigning, the law was finally changed.

In the same year, changes were made to the work entitlements of civil servants to eliminate discriminatory practices. Prior to 2004, male civil servants were entitled to a subsidy of 60 per cent for their dependants for outpatient treatment. In contrast, however, a female civil servant was not provided with the same benefits unless she was divorced, widowed, or legally separated and had custody of her children. AWARE consistently argued that such a policy discriminates against women and fails to acknowledge the important and equal roles that both husband and wife play as parents and carers. The government's response to these claims, however, was that male civil servants have a special role as 'heads of households' and that the medical benefits policy supports and endorses this role. A change finally occurred when the government acknowledged that men and women play equal roles as joint 'heads of households'.

However, there are still many areas of legislation where the legal position of women is different to that of men, including tax laws and inheritance laws. While the Women's Charter ensures women's basic rights and the Singapore Constitution guarantees protection against discrimination on the basis of religion, race, and place of birth, there is no specific act that protects against discrimination on the basis of sex. The Singaporean Association of Women Lawyers (SAWL 1986) thus argues that discrimination on the basis of sex is constitutionally legal. Examples of such discrimination include different salary rates for men and women employed in the same positions, job advertisements which specify the sex of staff required, and a lack of public housing support for single mothers (AWARE 2007). Although Singapore is a signatory to CEDAW, the government continues to argue that such instances of gender inequality are internal and/or private matters.

One organization movement?

Speaking in the mid-1990s, Singaporean sociologist Vivienne Wee described the women's movement in Singapore as a 'one organization movement'.[5] She said:

> If you come out and say you are a feminist, of one kind or another, whatever kind, it's like you have to join AWARE. What other organization is there in Singapore to join? There is nothing [else]. ... In a way we dominate the women's movement in Singapore.

At the time Wee's comments were certainly accurate. AWARE was commonly viewed as Singapore's only feminist organization and it quickly became the face of the women's movement. This is not to deny that there were many other women's organizations in Singapore throughout the 1980s and 1990s. None of them, however, adopted an avowedly feminist or activist stance, and few attracted the same degree of public and media scrutiny of their activities. AWARE found itself to be not simply 'a' Singaporean women's organization, but 'the' Singaporean women's movement. Not only did this require the organization to become a place in which all women found their natural feminist home, but it also put pressure on the organization to succeed because to have collapsed would represent more than the failure of a women's organization, it would signal the demise of the entire Singaporean women's movement.[6] In AWARE's first decade, success was not only a matter of hard work and perseverance, but a measure of state benevolence. Many members believed that the possibility of de-registration was always just around the corner.[7]

The mothers of the nation, including the women who campaigned against polygamy in the 1950s, are almost never mentioned in these founding narratives. Consequently, for many Singaporeans, feminism did not exist before AWARE. This view is problematic for several reasons. First, it places pressure on AWARE to be the sole face of feminism in Singapore. In an organization characterized by diversity this pressure inevitably leads to tension, and sometimes conflict, over the meanings associated with 'being feminist'. Second, the history of women's activism outside the formal organizational context of AWARE is largely ignored. For example, questions about what women in the SCWO were doing in the early 1980s are left unasked. Prior to the NUSS meeting in 1983, students and academics at the National University of Singapore were active in forming discussion groups and producing newsletters about topics related to women's status, but their stories are subsumed by AWARE's. Some of these women later became active in the pro-tem committee and joined AWARE. Lee Kuan Yew's National Day Rally speech may have been the focus of much anger and consternation, but it was hardly foundational in terms of women's activism in Singapore. By giving the Great Marriage Debate and Lee's statements about women's roles as mothers such central prominence, these accounts overemphasize the role played by the state and overlook the existence of a nascent women's movement dating back well before Independence.

Although the PAP's role as the women's movement's 'founding father' may be overstated, the political and legislative environment it created has certainly been a significant deterrent to the emergence of a broad-based and diverse feminist movement. Issues of sexuality, including the rights of lesbians, religion and the role of Shariah law, and class-based social divisions are commonly regarded by civil society activists as areas that are off limits and to date there have been few attempts to formalize women's activism on these issues. This does not mean, however, that questions of sexuality, religion or class have been ignored by the women's movement. Religion and class have traditionally been pursued through organizational structures that reflect the backgrounds of their advocates—for example, Muslim women advocating for and on behalf of other Muslim women. Sexuality has been the least publicly debated issue, with GLBT (gay, lesbian, bisexual and transgender) groups maintaining a low profile and networking at the individual level and through the internet.[8] AWARE's prominent role as the face of feminism has slowly begun to change as new organizations emerge and the movement itself becomes more diverse.

In describing the character of the women's movement in Singapore, it is important to keep in mind that Singapore is a small city-state of 4.8 million people, of whom 22 per cent are non-residents. State control of the space of civil society has meant that the diversity and richness of women's organizing that characterizes cities of a similar size elsewhere has not emerged. The requirement for all civil society groups to formally register under the Societies Act means that the women's movement is dominated by NGOs. Informal networks and collectives deliberately maintain a low-key status in order to avoid state scrutiny. The internet has facilitated the emergence of a more diverse women's and less formalized women's movement, but even cyberspace has been the subject of state surveillance (Lee 2003). Singapore's small population has affected the character of the women's movement in other ways. A core group of activists drawn from elite and middle-class circles tends to dominate the sphere of civil society. Prominent members of AWARE, SCWO, SAWL, TWC2 and UNIFEM Singapore sit on the same boards and are members of other NGOs and public sector organizations. While this facilitates information sharing and networking, it can also lead to stagnation and entrenched positions, as well as inevitable rivalries between individuals (and in some cases organizations).

Formal alliances or joint campaigns have not been a strong feature of Singapore's women's movement. This lack of alliance-making reflects a sepa-ration between what are often regarded as separate organizational constituencies, as well as different understandings of 'women's issues'. A case in point is the lack of formal alliances on the issues of women's reproductive health. For example, although AWARE, TWC2 and UNIFEM Singapore agree that Singapore's pro-natalist policies have driven demand for FDWs, none have made a link between the state's interest in controlling the reproductive capacity of Singaporean nationals (i.e. a local women's issue) and its intrusive monitoring of FDW sexuality (i.e. a migrant women's issue). Under current labour laws, any FDW found to be pregnant or to have contracted a sexually transmitted disease is forcibly repatriated. The regulation of domestic worker sexuality is enforced through a programme of compulsory six monthly medical check-ups. This issue, however, has largely been ignored because women's groups recognize that the issue would gain little sympathy from either the government or public, which are supportive of the restrictions placed on Singapore's guest workers.

Conclusion

Throughout the last century and a half, Singapore's citizens and residents have actively lobbied for policy and legislative changes to improve women's status. They have frequently faced staunch resistance from the wider public as well as from a patriarchal, authoritarian state. Despite these setbacks, they have succeeded in bringing about important changes, and have played an important role in challenging public perceptions about 'women's roles'. Their actions have frequently drawn harsh criticism and the claim that feminism and women's rights are foreign ideas that do not reflect 'Asian values'. In response to these criticisms, women's rights activists point to a rich and diverse history that draws on the legacy of strong women who were active in promoting the rights of women and girls during the colonial period, and builds on the efforts of women involved in struggles against polygamy, trafficking and pornography during the 1950s. While these campaigns often drew their inspiration from transnational campaigns and networks, they were firmly based in the cultural and historical specificities of local conditions. Although there has been recent interest in exploring the stories of women involved in these campaigns, a great deal of work remains to be done. Formally recorded histories of women's activism have tended to overlook the actions of working-class women, including domestic workers and labourers, and are dominated instead by the stories of middle-class and elite women. These gaps continue to be replicated in recent accounts of the women's movement which are dominated by studies of middle-class NGOs.[9] Consequently, the dense tapestry of women's organizing that occurs at the level of the everyday in Singapore remains to be revealed.

Notes

1 For further elaboration of these terms and the problems associated with their usage, see Lyons (2009).
2 The Women's Charter is unevenly applied to Muslim women who are also covered by Shariah law.
3 AWARE has also been criticized for its lack of engagement with issues faced by Singaporean working-class women (Lyons 2004b).
4 The White Ribbon Campaign is an international programme organized by men whereby ribbon wearers pledge 'never to commit, never to condone and never to remain silent about violence against women' (White Ribbon Campaign 2003). The White Ribbon Campaign was initially managed by TWC2, but was subsequently taken over by AWARE's male chapter.
5 Personal communication with Vivienne Wee, February 1995.
6 It is also important to note that AWARE was the first politicized NGO to emerge post-Independence. Former AWARE president, Constance Singam points out that the implications of AWARE's survival extended beyond its impact on the women's movement to the sphere of civil society as a whole (Personal Communication, August 2005).
7 Playing up the power of the state to give (i.e. the Women's Charter) and take away (i.e. the Great Marriage Debate), became important PAP's strategy of control and containment through the 1990s (Lyons 2008).
8 To date, no GLBT or gay rights organization has been successful in registering under the Societies Act in Singapore.
9 I include my own work in this critique.

References

Arora, M. (2007) 'Women's Activism and Reform in Colonial Singapore', in M. Arora (ed.) *Small Steps, Giant Leaps: A History of AWARE and the Women's Movement in Singapore*, Singapore: Association of Women for Action and Research, pp. 26–57.

AWARE (1988) *Population: An Issue of Current Concern*. Singapore: Association of Women for Action and Research.

—— (2004) *Beyond Babies: National Duty or Personal Choice?*, July, Singapore: Association of Women for Action and Research.

—— (2007) *CEDAW Shadow Report*, May, Singapore: Association of Women for Action and Research.

Barr, M. (2008) 'Singapore's Catholic Social Activists: Alleged Marxist Conspirators', in M. Barr and C. Trocki (eds) *Paths Not Taken: Political Pluralism in Postwar Singapore*, Singapore: National University of Singapore Press, pp. 228–47.

Chew, P.G.L. (1994) 'The Singapore Council of Women and the Women's Movement', *Journal of Southeast Asian Studies*, 25, 1: 112–40.

Crinis, V.D. (2004) *The Silence and Fantasy of Women and Work*, PhD, School of History and Politics, University of Wollongong.

Della Porta, D. and Tarrow, S. (2005) *Transnational Protest and Global Activism*, Lanham: Rowman & Littlefield.

Desai, M. (2005) 'Transnationalism: the Face of Feminist Politics Post-Beijing', *International Social Science Journal*, 57, 184: 319–30.

Gee, J. and Ho, E. (eds) (2006) *Dignity Overdue*, Singapore: John Gee and Elaine Ho.

Heng, G. and Devan, J. (1995) 'State Fatherhood: The Politics of Nationalism, Sexuality, and Race in Singapore', in A. Ong and M.G. Peletz (eds) *Bewitching Women and Pious Men: Gender and Body Politics in Southeast Asia*, Berkeley: University of California Press, pp. 195–215.

Ho, K.L. (2000) 'Citizen Participation and Policy Making in Singapore', *Asian Survey*, 40, 3: 436–55.

Lam, J.L. (ed.) (1993) *Voices and Choices: The Women's Movement in Singapore*, Singapore: Singapore Council of Women's Organisations.

Lee, T. (2003) 'Internet Use in Singapore: Politics and Policy Implications', *Media International Australia Incorporating Culture and Policy*, 107: 75–88.

Lyons, L. (1999) 'Believing in Equality: The Meanings Attached to "Feminism" in Singapore', *Asian Journal of Women's Studies*, 5, 1: 115–39.

—— (2000a) 'Disrupting the Centre: Interrogating an "Asian Feminist" Identity', *Communal/Plural: Journal of Transnational and Crosscultural Studies*, 8, 1: 65–79.

—— (2000b) 'The Limits of Feminist Political Intervention in Singapore', *Journal of Contemporary Asia*, 30, 1: 67–83.

—— (2000c) 'A State of Ambivalence: Feminism and a Singaporean Women's Organisation', *Asian Studies Review*, 24, 1: 1–24.

—— (2004a) 'Organizing for Domestic Worker Rights in Singapore: The Limits of Transnationalism', in L. Ricciutelli, A. Miles, and M. McFadden (eds) *Feminist Politics, Activism and Vision: Local and Global Challenges*, London and Toronto: Zed Books and Inanna, pp. 149–68.

—— (2004b) *A State of Ambivalence: The Feminist Movement in Singapore*, Leiden: EJ Brill.

—— (2005) 'Transient Workers Count Too? The Intersection of Citizenship and Gender in Singapore's Civil Society', *Sojourn: Journal of Social Issues in Southeast Asia*, 20, 2: 208–48.

—— (2007) 'Dignity Overdue: Women's Rights Activism in Support of Foreign Domestic Workers in Singapore', *Women's Studies Quarterly*, 35, 3/4: 106–22.

—— (2008) 'Internalized Boundaries: AWARE's Place in Singapore's Emerging Civil Society', in M. Barr and C. Trocki (eds) *Paths Not Taken: Political Pluralism in Postwar Singapore*, Singapore: National University of Singapore Press, pp. 248–63.

—— (2009) 'Transcending the Border: Transnational Imperatives in Singapore's Migrant Worker Rights Movement', *Critical Asian Studies*, 41, 1: 89–112.

PuruShotam, N. (1998) 'Between Compliance and Resistance: Women and the Middle-Class Way of Life in Singapore', in K. Sen and M. Stivens (eds) *Gender and Power in Affluent Asia*, London: Routledge, pp. 127–66.

Raymond, J. (1986) *A Passion for Friends: Toward a Philosophy of Female Affection*, London: The Women's Press.

Saw, S.-H. (1990) *Changes in the Fertility Policy of Singapore*, Singapore: The Institute of Policy Studies.

SAWL (1986) *Legal Status of Singapore Women*, Singapore: Asiapac Books.

Stockard, J.E. (1989) *Daughters of the Canton Delta: Marriage Patterns and Economic Strategies in South China, 1860–1930*, Stanford: University of Stanford Press.

The Straits Times (1983) 'PM's National Day Rally Speech', *The Straits Times*, 15 August.

White Ribbon Campaign (2003) *About Us*, Online. Available HTTP: <http://www.whiteribbon.ca/about_us/> (accessed 5 December 2003).

Zakaria, Z. (1998) 'Surprise invite for AWARE as petition delivered', *The Straits Times*, 10 September, p. 30.

6 Crossing boundaries

Transnational feminisms in twentieth-century Japan

Barbara Molony

Feminisms in Japan, as elsewhere, have long been imbricated with transnationalism. In Japan, transnational feminism, following a contested status as 'bourgeois' in the interwar period and ostensibly in opposition to the dominant right-wing ideology during World War II, reemerged after 1945 as one of the principal forms of feminism.

Feminism's transnational connotations (and frequently its reality) have been the articulated reason for opposition to feminism in many countries' post-colonial settings. A large body of scholarship places Western feminism at the heart of imperialist privilege (e.g. Mohanty 1984; Spivak 1988; Grewal and Kaplan 1994; Burton 1994; McClintock 1995; Stoler 2002), and transnational feminism, like most other liberatory movements, does not have clean hands. This has provided contemporary conservative opponents of feminism in post-colonial settings with plenty of ammunition and they have used it effectively to promote their own repressive inclinations (Cassman 2007: 140, n. 141). Many post-colonial feminists also eschew certain types of feminisms as inappropriate to their national cultures, especially women's-rights-based feminisms (Cassman 2007: 140–1). And yet, a new type of feminist transnationalism has caught the attention of feminists in many parts of the world. This is the feminism emanating from human rights initiatives promoted through the United Nations' (UN) global conferences and declarations, especially the Convention to Eliminate All Forms of Discrimination Against Women (CEDAW). As some global 'south' feminists have found, human rights is a 'power tool' to achieve women's rights (Desai 1996).

Japan, of course, was not part of the European cultural sphere (into which historians and others place North America and Australia as well) for which we use the shorthand 'the West'. Like feminists in many non-Western societies, late twentieth-century Japanese feminists found the human rights approach useful to prod the Japanese government to pass domestic equal-rights legislation such as the Equal Employment Opportunity Law in 1985 (Molony 1995: 282) and the Basic Law for a Gender-Equal Society in 1999 (Murase 2006: 81). They also employed it to give a theoretical grounding to the movement to redress the gendered violation of human rights by the Japanese military in World War II (Soh 2008: 31–2). Indeed, the wartime sexual violation of Korean, Chinese, Japanese and other women has opened critical doors to examine the challenge posed by human rights discourse to the history of women's rights in Japan, especially the citizenship rights derived in part from transnational origins (Ueno 2004: 22–9; Mackie 2003: Ch. 5). This challenge has significantly influenced the historiography of women's rights in Japan and should be examined before turning to the issue of transnational feminisms.

The state, transnationalism and feminism in Japanese historiography

During the first half of the twentieth century, human rights discourse was not yet applied to sexual victims of war. In the first decades after the war, feminists and historians continued to view women, who did not have formal rights of citizenship such as suffrage before the war, as responsible neither for wartime atrocities, on the one hand, nor for the shame of defeat, on the other, because they saw women as incapable of influencing policy (Narita 1998: 137–42; Ueno 2004: 22–9; Koikari 2002: 24; Koikari 2008: 36–41). Human-rights concepts such as those embedded in the Universal Declaration of Human Rights of 1948 were consistent with the language of rights developed in the context of the nation-state, in which many Japanese feminists had struggled to be included since the Meiji period (1868–1912). Equal employment laws and equality of rights laws were based on equality of citizenship in the nation-state.

Ex post facto applications of human rights notions have in recent years altered the public's, historians', and even governments' views of what went wrong, in terms of gender, during World War II. It is paradoxical that contemporary transnational human rights thought has both enhanced post-war Japanese women's access to inclusion in the nation-state as well as called into question pre-war feminists' attempts to be included in the state. The difference between these two periods is the existence of the empire before 1945. This tainted all marginalized Japanese people's quests for citizenship rights, including women and minorities, as these quests were based on inclusion in a flawed state (Neary 1989: Ch. 8; Molony 2005c: 85).

The paradigm shift in women's history in the 1980s from 'women-as-victims' to 'women-as-agents' occurred just as the consciousness of the 'comfort women' issue exploded in East Asia. (Comfort women, more accurately described as sex slaves used by the Japanese military, were like the purloined letter, known to many but ignored and rendered invisible in human rights discourse.) The historical contingency of these two events in meta-history—the reading of women's history through the lens of women's agency and the almost simultaneous granting of agency and the right to their own bodily integrity to women formerly viewed as shameful, victimized, and symbolic of their nation's or menfolk's humiliation— could not help but open the floodgates of criticism of the whole (national and transnational) rights-based feminist movement in Japan. If pre-war Japanese women had agency, why did they not fight harder against their country's aggressive war? If rights implied membership in the state, why did feminists accept a (limited) role on committees and in mobilization with such enthusiasm? Was this false consciousness—or worse, a Faustian complicity in the evils of the nation-state for limited gains?

Many of the women associated with transnational rights-based feminism responded positively to the wartime government's invitation to join national organizations that they hoped would give women a role in the state by making best use of their skills and hard work (Garon 1993: 7, 38). Some, though not all, appeared to change their rhetoric to express racist or imperialist opinions (Ogawa 2007a: 173). Earlier historiographical approaches that both excused their comments and actions as necessary in the context of the times and applauded the involvement of feminists in national organizations as the first steps towards equality gave way, in the cold, hard light of the widespread exposure of the 'comfort women' issue, to a major reassessment of pre-war feminists and their quest for inclusion as 'public persons' in the state (Oku Mumeo, cited in Narita 1998: 147; Seraphim 2006: 310–11).

Ueno Chizuko calls this reassessment the 'reflexive school of women's history' in her influential study, *Nationalism and Gender*, originally published in Japanese in 1998 (Ueno 2004: 15). Historians who took the reflexive approach re-examined the writings of feminist leaders. They found new incriminating documents and re-read known documents with different eyes (Suzuki 1986). Further, reflexive historians criticized average women on the home front for their inability to problematize the events of their times and for acting as cheerleaders for an unjust cause (Kanō 1987). Ueno suggests that this was unfair, as the nation-state was all that these women knew (Ueno 2004: 55). At the same time, as Andrea Germer notes in her historiographical study (Germer 2003: 25), some Korean feminist historians are interested in moving beyond questions of guilt and responsibility— guilt and responsibility have been established, they contend, so why waste any more time on them?—to examine the more nuanced history of gender during the period (Germer 2003, paragraph 25, notes 80 and 81; see also Ueno 2004: 184). Ueno contends that to really avoid complicity in the nation's bad actions, feminism must be transnational; that is, it should transcend the nation-state. But as Ueno notes, this was difficult in the pre-war period. Feminists and others who avoided involvement with the state generally did so in the name of a transnational entity, such as communists' identification with Moscow, hardly a paragon of morality under Stalin at that time, or global Christianity, which denied equal rights to women within various churches. Feminists' quest for inclusion—what Ueno calls the 'nationalization' of women—was the trap, and the nation-state, with its monopoly of violence, was to blame (Ueno 2004: 60).

Transnationalism in the pre-war era gave Japanese and other women a space for influencing state policy in the absence of (national) civil rights. But transnational organizations moved, by the 1920s, to the forefront of civil rights activism, and it was at that point where they intersected with empire, racism and nationalism. Before rights talk of one sort (transnational human rights) came to be used to critique rights talk of another sort (political rights feminism at the national level), the dominant divide among Japanese feminists was between 'bourgeois' and socialist approaches. The bourgeois-versus-socialist approach was also the main thrust of both feminist politics and the scholars who narrated the story of feminism in most societies, as Marilyn Boxer so gracefully demonstrates in her article on the transnational concept of 'bourgeois feminism' (Boxer 2007). But the 'power tool' of human rights changed all that for Japanese feminist historiography. There was no denying the gendered nature of Japanese colonial and wartime repression. The goal of women's rights was inclusion in the state, and the price of that inclusion was cooperation. Newly liberated from the bourgeois trap, now ensnared in the human rights trap, could women's rights ever win? Any desire for rights, whether of the individual or communitarian sort, has pitfalls: if individual, one makes one's bed with the state; if communitarian, one can fall into totalizing racial, ethnic, religious or other types of 'we-versus-they' othering. Transnational movements could also be guilty of othering, as we shall see.

Have we moved beyond the paradox encountered by pre-war women's movements? After all, transnationalism and state-based feminism continue to be intertwined. Human rights discourse and activism continue to take the nation as the unit of account, and we have not and may not soon be able to move beyond that. Women and others outside the power and protection of the state will continue to seek to be included in the state. Moreover, the crumbling away of the nation, formed as an imagined community in Benedict Anderson's useful framing (Anderson 1983), can only be replaced by universalism; but which universalism? Again, the issue of hegemony or domination arises. While it is true that international treaty systems, international tribunals and other transnational systems have begun the process of superseding the state, even the UN acknowledges the primacy of the state. That is, states are allowed to opt out of parts of conventions and declarations when those parts seem too 'universal' and not consistent with local practice (most opting out occurs in the areas of gender and family).

To borrow the phrase Joan Scott uses in her analysis of the contradictions of feminisms and the modernizing French state (Scott 1996), we have 'only paradoxes to offer' in interpreting modern Japanese feminisms.

Transnational influences and modernity

Japanese feminist transnationalist links, whether through organizations or through shared ideas, were most common with England and the United States, with additional ties to other European countries, China, and Canada in the first half of the twentieth century. Transnationalism took many forms and embraced feminisms with varying primary interests.

I have argued elsewhere (Molony 2000: 649), and other historians have shown (Mackie 2003: passim), that progressives, often influenced by transnational Christianity as well as by overseas movements and rhetoric, embraced rights for women as part of Japan's modernizing project. By the interwar period, Japanese women in global organizations such as the YWCA and the Woman's Christian

Temperance Union (WCTU; also known in Japan as the Women's Reform Society, an abbreviated version of its Japanese name, *Nihon Kirisutokyō Fujin Kyōfūkai*) played important roles in articulating Japanese feminist theories of citizenship (suffrage and other political rights) and community building (labour/social justice, consumer rights, reproductive rights). Many feminists—for example, Kubushiro Ochimi, Katō Ishimoto Shizue and Ichikawa Fusae (Yasutake 2009: 15; Ishimoto 1935: 97; Ichikawa 1974)—were influenced by missionaries; others, such as Miyamoto Yuriko, a socialist writer, travelled abroad (Tanaka 1987: 43). Non-Japanese feminists such as historian and reformer Mary Beard (Hopper 1996: 28) and birth-control advocate Margaret Sanger (Ishimoto 1935: 220–36) lectured in Japan in the 1920s, and much of what they promoted would fall under the rubric of rights-based feminism.

The earliest discussions of women's rights in Japan blended the popular anti-authoritarianism inherited from the Tokugawa era (1603–1868) with ideas of John Stuart Mill and Jean-Jacques Rousseau (Molony 2005a: 225). No words existed in the Japanese language in the early Meiji years for 'women's rights', so new terms were created. The characters for 'rights', *quanli* in Chinese and *kenri* in Japanese, were first suggested by the American missionary-translator W.A.P. Martin in his Chinese translations of Western legal texts (Liu 1999: 148). Japanese progressives adopted Martin's use of the character '*ken*' (rights) to devise neologisms such as *danjo dōken* (male–female equal rights) and *joken* (women's rights). The Chinese and Korean pronunciations of the characters used for concepts of women's rights coined in Japan were soon adopted in China and Korea as well. Transnationalism had many aspects, not all of them modern and not all of them bridging Japan and the West. Transnationalism included the transfer of ideas through a shared, long-term (at least 1500 years old) East Asian writing system that was originally Chinese but came to be naturalized in Japan.

The state was in the process of formation at the same time that rights were being linguistically introduced to Japanese public discourse. In addition, notions of the public sphere as a locus of civic engagement—what scholars and policy-makers often call civil society—developed as members of the Freedom and People's Rights Movement, who advocated a modern state formed on the basis of a Rousseauian social contract, vied with government officials who planned to form a Bismarckian type of modern state. Both the People's Rights members and government officials cited transnational models, just as bureaucrats in the early modern (Tokugawa) period had adapted Confucian statist ideas for Japanese use. The idea of using models from outside Japan was neither new nor despised, an important idea to keep in mind as we examine the reactions to feminisms with foreign connections. As historians of Japan agree, the German strong-state model won the day, and that system was articulated in the Constitution of 1889 and subsequent legislation. Before laws passed in 1889 and 1890 limited voting rights, succession to the imperial throne, and the right of political assembly and party membership to men alone, women had begun to carve out a space in the emerging civil society in the 1880s. Thereafter, the Law on Political Associations and Assembly, later strengthened as the Public Peace Police Law (1890), made women's political assembly illegal through its infamous Article 5 (Sievers 1983: 99–101; Mackie 2003: 5). Women and their advocates found ways to get around the law, but organizing was severely restricted.

In the late nineteenth century, voting and participation in politics and government, activities intrinsic to full citizenship, were not yet envisioned by many advocates of *joken* (women's rights). But *respect* was. Political theorists discussing the historic struggles in American democracy note that the gaining of the right to vote by successively empowered civic groups was no less important than the respect each group sought through inclusion in the state (Shklar 1995: Ch. 2). The same was true for late nineteenth-century Japanese feminists. Voting was not yet an issue—most men could not vote at that time, either, although their gender was not the barrier it was for women. Advocates for women wanted women to be able to hold their heads high in the family, which was no refuge or private sphere of comfort under Meiji law that gave the family patriarch powers not accorded to other members, notably the wife. Women also sought a respected and socially valued civic role as teachers and moral leaders, a role consistent with the building of the modern state as defined in the nineteenth century (Molony 2005b: 471).

Transnational feminism and Christianity

Many rights advocates had privileged backgrounds that allowed them access to education, often in schools run by Christians. Many were influenced by feminist periodicals such as *Jogaku Zasshi* (Women's education journal), edited by a Christian man, Iwamoto Yoshiharu (Noheji 1984). Although few Japanese were themselves Christians, transnational Christianity played a significant role in turn-of-the-century feminisms. The most important Christian women's organization was the Japan Woman's Christian Temperance Union. The Japan WCTU was established in 1886, after the visit to Japan of Mary Leavitt, the World WCTU's international organizer, little more than a decade after the 1874 founding of the WCTU in the United States. Extensive work in English on the WCTU and transnationalism has been done by a number of scholars, most recently by Rumi Yasutake, Manako Ogawa and Elizabeth Dorn Lublin (Yasutake 2004, 2006, 2009; Ogawa 2004, 2007a, 2007b; Lublin 2006). While anti-alcohol temperance was a theme in the Japanese group, it was of much smaller significance—as its Japanese name, Women's Reform Society, implies—than two other types of reforms the group believed Japanese women were uniquely equipped to handle: sexual morality and patriarchal dominance in the family (Mihalopoulos 2009, passim).

Here we see the first step towards a feminist politics of inclusion in the state, although the members of the Japan WCTU would not have expressed it in that manner until 1920, when they embraced suffragism. By the late nineteenth century, many American WCTU members had explicitly linked women's purity and guardianship of the home with the demand for the vote. The members of the Japan WCTU differed from the US-centred world group in another way that is central to the issue of transnationalism. That is, WCTU president, Frances Willard, called for a global morality campaign, but her universalism had a specific American origin and leadership. 'But for the intrusion of the sea the shores of China and Far East would be part and parcel of our own', she claimed in an 1883 address. 'We must no longer be hedged about by the artificial boundaries of states and nations ... The whole world is my parish and to do good my religion' (Yasutake 2006: 98). Transnationalism and nationalism—and, indeed, imperialism—were clearly linked in Willard's thought.

The Japan WCTU, though inspired by much of the religious rhetoric of the American leadership, balked at being treated as the daughters in a mother–daughter relationship the US WCTU liked to extrapolate from its organizational slogan of 'organized mother's love' (Ogawa 2007b: 29). In the 1920s and 1930s, Japanese delegates attended global WCTU meetings, but were consistently treated as if the goal of their participation was to learn from their more liberated Western counterparts. A 1920 article in the WCTU journal *Union Signal,* announcing financial aid to Japan, China and other countries, was entitled 'To Make the Whole World White' (Ogawa 2007b: 31, note 30), referring to the white ribbon that was the WCTU's symbol but perhaps unintentionally signalling its racialism. At the 1920 meeting in London, the Japanese women, who wore kimono, were seen as 'picturesque' (Ogawa 2007b: 34) and thereby gained attention. (To be sure, Japan WCTU founder Yajima Kajiko's advanced age—she was eighty-eight when she travelled halfway around the world to the conference—also drew attention to the Japanese delegation.) What the Japanese delegates did not recognize at the time, but later came to rue, was that Western women saw them as depoliticized and static when they wore kimono. This should not have been surprising. By the 1920s, Western-style clothing was increasingly viewed as a marker of modernity and public influence for women; Japanese men had deracinated Western clothing, considering it simply modern and powerful, since the late nineteenth century (Molony 2007: 94–7). To be taken seriously in a transnational context, Japanese women abroad were forced to reconsider their attire.

Shortly after the London meeting, Gauntlett (Yamada) Tsune, one of the Japan WCTU delegates, travelled on to Geneva to attend the meeting of the International Woman Suffrage Alliance at the invitation of the IWSA president, Carrie Chapman Catt, who wished to make the organization 'truly international' by having non-Western delegates attend (Yasutake 2009: 15). Gauntlett was initially most interested in women's role in promoting world peace, and Catt persuaded her that the vote was women's tool to advance transnational peace. Catt transformed Gauntlett into an advocate for women's suffrage. When Gauntlett returned to Japan, she found a ready ally in Kubushiro Ochimi, grandniece of Yajima Kajiko and secretary of the WCTU. As early as 1917, Kubushiro had bemoaned women's lack of political clout without the vote when the WCTU was unable to prevent the city of Osaka from approving a new red-light district (Molony 2004: 133). In the next few years, Kubushiro helped the New Woman's Association (*Shin Fujin Kyōkai*), founded in 1919 by secular feminists Hiratsuka Raichō, Ichikawa Fusae and Oku Mumeo, to gather petitions to overturn Article 5. In July 1921, Kubushiro argued for votes for women in an article in the WCTU journal *Fujin Shinpō,* and together with Gauntlett and Ebina Miyako founded the Japan Women's Suffrage Association (*Nihon Fujin Sanseiken Kyōkai*) under the umbrella of the WCTU (Nihon Kirisutokyō Fujin Kyōfūkai 1986: 512–30). Gauntlett's strong commitment to transnationalism led her to apply to the IWSA for affiliation, hoping to beat out other Japanese organizations—most notably the YWCA, whose president, Kawai Michiko, had also attended the Geneva conference, as well as the New Woman's Association—for the honour of being the IWSA affiliate in Japan. Despite the appearance of rivalry among women's rights groups for prominence in Japan, however, many did collaborate effectively (Molony 2004: 138–9; Yasutake 2009: 16).

Another movement that by its very nature was transnational was the peace movement. Christian women, including Mary P.E. Nitobe, a Philadelphia Quaker married to Japanese diplomat Nitobe Inazo, founded the Women's Peace Association (*Fujin Heiwa Kyōkai*) in 1921. Members included both secular women intellectuals as well as women who were also members of the WCTU and/or the YWCA (Yasutake 2009: 15–16). The group became the Japanese affiliate of the transnational Women's International League for Peace and Freedom in 1924, and later presidents included the YWCA's Kawai (in 1930) and the WCTU's Gauntlett (in 1934). The Japan WCTU also participated in peace activism, as when the 89-year-old Yajima hand delivered a petition for peace signed by 10,224 Japanese women to American President Warren G. Harding at the time of the Washington Conference in 1921 (Tyrell 1991: 189; Ogawa 2007b: 35). Although Japanese women did not have civil rights at the national level, this petition represented civic engagement by women acting in the international arena.

But transnationalism had its drawbacks, and the Japan WCTU reacted just as some women in post-colonial settings today react to Western-style feminism. They were offended by Western women's expression of racial superiority and the stereotyping behind Western women's requests that they wear kimono at international meetings. Kubushiro was particularly irked by the Western notion of Japanese women as geisha (Ogawa 2007b: 36). Ironically, the Japan WCTU itself had a patronizing attitude towards geisha and women in the sex trades, viewing them as requiring 'salvation' and dragging down Japan's reputation and national standing (Mihalopoulos 2009: 26–7).

Just as the American WCTU linked transnationalism and the nation, the Japanese group expected to be able to use its transnational ties to serve the Japanese national cause. Not having rights as citizens, these Japanese women carved out a space to act as if they would serve the nation by using transnational links. When the United States outlawed Japanese immigration in 1924, Japan WCTU members contacted their American counterparts, many of them well-connected in US society and politics, as well as Secretary of State Charles Evans Hughes to lobby on behalf of their humiliated nation (Ogawa 2007b: 41–3). Kubushiro, Gauntlett and others believed that Japanese prostitutes and footloose, unmarried men had besmirched Japan's reputation in the United States and could be denied immigration rights. But how could respectable Japanese be included in that group? The Japan WCTU's patronizing attitude towards less fortunate Japanese kept them from understanding that anti-Japanese attitudes had become widespread in the United States. Indeed, race trumped class at that time.

And yet, the Japanese group resembled its US counterpart in developing its own sort of ethnic hierarchy. Despite claims of sisterhood with their Chinese WCTU counterparts, the Japan WCTU president, Kubushiro, viewed the Japanese state's diplomatic relationship with China as one of elder brother to younger brother, implying the necessity of the elder (Japan) guiding the younger (China). Kubushiro replicated this in her notion of the relationships of the two countries' WCTU organizations. Unlike the matriarchal (mother–daughter) hierarchical schema of the American WCTU, Kubushiro employed a patriarchal (elder brother–younger brother) hierarchical trope. The Chinese WCTU also had its own national perspectives and issues. Just as the Japanese organization emphasized prostitution while the US group emphasized alcohol, the Chinese group differed from both by focusing on imperialism. These differences were not yet pronounced in the early 1920s, as the Chinese and Japanese WCTU branches in China had little direct contact with one another and thus initially had little conflict. The Japan WCTU set up branches throughout East Asia—in Korea, Taiwan, Manchuria and cities in China with many Japanese residents. Worried about the export of Japanese prostitution to the territories won by Japan in the Sino- and Russo-Japanese Wars, the Japan WCTU branches followed the flag overseas; the organization protested against Japanese vice, not colonialism. Indeed, Japanese colonial regimes and military presence welcomed the presence of the WCTU (Ogawa 2007b: 38), and the WCTU chose to ignore the imperialist encroachment of the Japanese military in China (Hayakawa 2001: 22–5). In this way, even a transnational organization such as the WCTU was unable to escape the bonds of the nation-state—nor did they really wish to do so.

When Japan's presence in China and Manchuria became militarized in the late 1920s (and especially after the Manchurian Incident in 1931), Japanese Christians were torn between transnationalism and nationalism. The WCTU representatives who travelled to the continent to inspect the results of the Manchurian Incident—which they considered, following Japanese government excuses, a defensive action—were stunned by their Chinese counterparts' anger at Japan's military actions (Ogawa 2007a: 165). When their former allies in the United States, the US branch of the WILPF, lobbied the US government to impose sanctions against Japan after the Manchurian Incident, the WCTU's Kubushiro and the YWCA's Kawai lamented in an English-language book intended for a non-Japanese audience that they were scorned for being Christians by increasingly nationalistic Japanese while their country was criticized by Christians in the West (Kawai and Kubushiro 1934: 168). To keep from being marginalized at home, the Japan WCTU severed its ties to the World WCTU at the outset of the Pacific War and worked to persuade the thought police that their patriotism was real (Ogawa 2007a: 175). Their transnationalism was refocused; rather than aligning their transnational activities with the Anglo-American countries, they adjusted their sights towards Asia, consistent with the government's building of a Greater East Asia Co-Prosperity Sphere. Like Western WCTU organizations, the Japan WCTU saw opportunities for Japanese women to help 'liberate'

Korean women from indigenous oppression (Koikari 2008: 46). In China, Japan WCTU efforts included a medical settlement house, schools and social reform projects. WCTU members naively believed these would improve Japan's image in China. But these projects were launched by Japanese military officers and colonial officials, and only tied the knot of imperialism more tightly (Ogawa 2007a: 172).

Immediately after Pearl Harbor, nationalist rhetoric flourished in statements made by previously transnational feminists. Kubushiro claimed it was time to challenge Anglo-Saxons for their arrogant racial superiority, language she had not used before that time (Ogawa 2007a: 173); Gauntlett Tsune also criticized Japan's adversaries. The American WCTU's comments about Japan were also brutally critical until the end of the war, when the Americans reinitiated contacts with Gauntlett and others, leading to their post-war political rehabilitation. Japan WCTU leaders could be portrayed as friends of the West through their mutual Christianity, and the American occupation encouraged their re-emergence and ultimately permitted them to be described through the new language of universal rights. The occupation forces claimed to be instilling universal values that were 'no longer peculiarly American but now belong to the entire human race', in the words of Douglas MacArthur (Koikari 2002: 23). In the historiography of the post-war decades, the Christians' rehabilitation was used to exempt them from being on the wrong side in the war and therefore to be part of the narrative of the women's movement's progress towards citizenship. Although the American occupation of Japan is viewed by some historians as a form of colonialism (Koshiro 1999: 181), right after the war the American imprimatur was sufficient to rehabilitate the WCTU's standing both nationally and internationally.

The YWCA, another Christian transnational organization, provides an informative parallel with the WCTU. Indeed, many of its members were members of the WCTU and other feminist or Christian groups. Also strongly religious, the YWCA had a political agenda that included women's political rights and a downplaying of nationalism in favour of internationalism. The YWCA was one of the associations actively involved in Japan's multi-organization Women's Suffrage Conferences in the 1930s (Ichikawa 1974: 218–19). These conventions, organized by the secular Women's Suffrage League but attended by transnational Christian feminist groups as well as socialist, Buddhist and teachers' organizations, criticized Japanese militarism in 1931 and 1932, but began to soft-pedal those critiques in 1934, even linking the demand for the vote to women's ability to help the government in this time of 'emergency' (Molony 2004: 143).

As the war intensified, government regulations required religious institutions and groups to take part in the 'national spiritual mobilization' campaign, and while some Christian and Buddhist organizations and churches did enthusiastically support the war effort, others were more passive. The YWCA simultaneously expressed opposition to Japan's war in China, on the one hand, and prepared comfort bags for Japanese soldiers and aided women factory workers, on the other (Garner 2004: 202). These actions were consistent with their Christian service to those they saw as oppressed but at the same time supported the war through the kind of home front activities the reflexive school of historians would later condemn. The Japanese YWCA was strongly criticized by their Chinese counterparts. The Japanese YWCA's general secretary, Katō Taka, wrote to the World YWCA general secretary, Ruth Woodsmall, in 1937 that the Chinese officers told her that the Japanese women were 'dumb or insane' for not protesting the bombing of Chinese cities and challenged Katō 'to die for the principles' (Garner 2004: 204).

The Chinese YWCA's antipathy to Japan, even as the world organization promoted Christian transnationalism after Japan's defeat in 1945, continued after the war. Japanese YWCA members were welcomed back into the global movement by others—indeed, the first Japanese allowed to travel to the US was Japanese YWCA president Uemura Tamaki, in May 1946, who adopted a posture of penitence for the Japanese Christian church's failure to resist the wartime government. Although the United States welcomed a contrite member of a defeated nation, the Chinese YWCA continued to express anger. Japanese delegates were denied visas to the YWCA World Council held in China in 1947 (Garner 2004: 211). This is similar to the nationalist responses of post-colonial countries that rejected feminist universalism because it appeared to be a mask for Western ideological dominance. The YWCA was able to reclaim a moral position within Japan because the American occupation authorities praised its penitent stance as a *Japanese* organization—although, paradoxically, it was criticized for showing too much *womanly* submissiveness (Garner 2004: 215–16). As a result, it escaped, for decades, the charge of wartime complicity, except in the eyes of the Chinese.

Transnationalism and secular feminists' quest for political inclusion

Secular icons of women's rights, such as Yamakawa Kikue, the pre-eminent socialist feminist of the pre-war era and the first female high ranking bureaucrat (as head of the newly created Women's and Minors' Bureau in the Ministry of Labour from 1947 to 1963), and Oku Mumeo, one of the founding mothers of the New Woman's Association and later a consumer rights advocate on behalf of proletarian women and a builder of settlement houses for the poor, represented transnational feminist positions before the war but expressed nation-centred positions during the war. Ichikawa Fusae, Japan's foremost suffragist feminist, whose lifelong work was to gain women's inclusion in the state, was the feminist most often criticized for replacing her opposition to the state with close wartime collaboration. To characterize Oku, Yamakawa and Ichikawa as resisters who opportunistically jumped on the imperialist bandwagon in the 1930s is to miss, however, the nuances in their 1920s feminisms and the paradoxes of these and other women's ideologies even before the rise of militarism. For example, Oku and Ichikawa had worked together in the New Woman's Association, but Oku later publically criticized Ichikawa's single-minded suffragism as 'prostitution' when the latter campaigned for male parliamentary candidates in 1928 who supported women's rights, regardless of party affiliation (Ichikawa 1974: 171). Some Christian women, with their temperance agenda, were offended by the smoking and drinking habits of some of their secular collaborators (Ichikawa 1974: 237). Socialist Yamakawa bitterly criticized the New Woman's Association as 'bourgeois' in the 1920s (Loftus 2004: 55), but collaborated on specific goals with middle-class women. Feminism was one cause that women of diverse national and transnational ideologies could promote together. While some post-war scholars highlighted the gulf between pre-war suffragist ('bourgeois') and socialist feminists, diverse groups actually collaborated frequently across the ideological divide.

Yamakawa had for two decades rejected 'bourgeois' feminism as supportive of a state that should be overcome rather than joined but gave her support to that state during a roundtable discussion of feminist leaders in 1937. Not only did she continue to wish to aid women labourers—who were now involved in war production—Yamakawa also stated that as a result of the 'Incident (Japan's war with China), [women] are acting like mobilized persons for the first time. ... They have been mobilized as members of the state and in the process have been found to have a special function as women' (Ueno 2004: 40). Replacing socialist internationalism with joining the state, Yamakawa nevertheless kept an otherwise fairly apolitical profile during the war, retreating to the countryside and writing a feminist history of the women of her family and similar works to support her husband and herself. Her socialism during the 1920s and 1930s and her avoiding, with just a few exceptions, overt support for the war (Mackie 2003: 106) allowed her to earn hero status—as well as the first directorship of a government bureau held by a woman—in the years after the war.

Oku Mumeo maintained her ties with middle-class suffragists, but focused on women as workers and consumers after 1923. Oku's stance was nuanced and complicated. While joining with suffragists on motherhood issues, she joined with socialists on labour issues. What linked Oku's pre-war activism, which appeared to confront the state, with her 'pride' in the state's allowing women to 'advance and clear their own paths' (Oku 1941, cited in Narita 1998: 147) was her communitarian feminism. That is, she focused in the 1920s on 'women's emancipation as a group' (Narita 1998: 145) rather than on individual civil rights. Her 1920s call for women to be 'subjects of the nation' was easily transformed into wartime construction of women as a group that conformed to the demands of the 'national defense state' (Narita 1998: 147). Oku held a number of government posts during the war and viewed the state as supportive of women. In 1947, she ran for and was elected to the House of Councilors and, in 1948, she founded the Housewives Association (*Shufu Rengōkai*), a massive nationwide organization (Tokuza 1999: 215).

Ichikawa Fusae, unlike Oku, Yamakawa and the Christian feminists, was not immediately re-established after the war. Initially purged by the US occupation— one of only eight women to be purged, she was not de-purged until October 1950— she then catapulted to the pinnacle of popularity for three decades as the 'Susan B. Anthony of Japan' and one of the most highly regarded members of parliament. She did not deny, as did many of her compatriots, that she had supported the war (Ueno 2004: 23). Despite or, perhaps, because of that, she was then recast as the stereotypical feminist nationalist who 'sold out' to gain a political voice during the war. Ichikawa's career and that of her Women's Suffrage League are the exemplars of the shifts in historiography concerning political and transnational feminisms.

Ichikawa began her career as a schoolteacher. Later, as a journalist in Nagoya, she attended lectures on Christianity where she was first exposed to feminist ideas. She moved to Tokyo in 1918, where she met Hiratsuka Raichō, and joined Hiratsuka and Oku in founding the New Woman's Association (Molony 2005c: 61–5). Each of the NWA leaders, in a sense, represented a particular approach to women's rights, and as Ichikawa wrote, hers was of complete equality of men and women as the basis for equal rights (Ichikawa 1930, 1981: 32–3). This was reinforced by her contact with Alice Paul, author of America's Equal Rights Amendment and the standard-bearer for the complete political equality position, as opposed to the protectionism position, in American women's rights history. Criticized by Yamakawa for ignoring social and labour issues and by Hiratsuka for her single-minded focus on women's political rights at the expense of 'motherhood protection' (*bosei hogo*) in the early 1920s, Ichikawa was challenged for her 'bourgeois' emphasis on the vote. The NWA's Oku succeeded, after Hiratsuka took a medical leave and Ichikawa departed for a two-year sojourn in the United States, to persuade the government to expand women's access to civic participation by partial amendment of Article 5.

Ichikawa's trip to the US enriched her transnational ties as well as her deep understanding of the diversity of Western feminisms. She met with Jane Addams, Alice Paul and many other American feminists. She observed and commented on the lives of African Americans she met in Chicago. Rushing home to Japan following the earthquake in September 1923, she got a job with the (transnational) International Labour Organization from 1923 to 1927, where she was responsible for women's labour issues. At the same time, she quickly joined with the WCTU's Kubushiro Ochimi, at that time the president of the WCTU-affiliated Women's Suffrage Association, and countless other feminists from across the political spectrum, to carry out earthquake relief. One year later, their relief work done, Ichikawa and Kubushiro used the spirit of cooperation among women to launch an independent suffrage group in December 1924. This was the League for the Realization of Women's Suffrage; following the passage of universal (read: male) suffrage in February 1925, the group shortened its name to the Women's Suffrage League (*Fusen Kakutoku Dōmei*), to highlight the hypocrisy of 'universal' suffrage (*fusen*) without women's suffrage (also pronounced *fusen*, though written with different characters). WSL members were teachers, journalists, housewives, writers and some workers.

Ichikawa kept up her contacts across the Pacific and played an important role in the first Pan Pacific Women's Conference in August 1928 (Ichikawa 1974: 192–7). At the end of the conference, Ichikawa continued on to the United States, where she observed women exercising their rights of citizenship in the 1928 presidential election and where she met Carrie Chapman Catt and Eleanor Roosevelt (Ichikawa 1974: 198–9).

The Pan Pacific Women's Conference was organized by the Pan Pacific Women's Association, an off-shoot of the Pan Pacific Union. The PPU was founded in 1917 by elite white men in Hawaii. The PPU grew throughout the Pacific Rim in the next decade, and by 1928 it seemed timely to call a meeting to discuss women's issues. Invitations were sent out in 1926 via known transnational conduits, such as the YWCA, WCTU and WILPF-affiliated groups such as Japan's Women's Peace Association. Although the members of the Women's Suffrage League were not primarily upper class, as were many of the members of Christian organizations, Ichikawa, with her excellent command of English, was included in the twenty-five-woman Japanese delegation. Ichikawa reported from the conference that the Japanese delegation was quite contentious, with tensions over status and language ability negatively affecting the transnational efforts of diverse Japanese women's groups (Ichikawa 1974: 194). Despite this rocky start, Japan's transnational feminists continued to work together, creating the Japan Women's Committee for International Relations as an affiliate of the Geneva-based Joint Standing Committee of Women's International Organizations (Ichikawa 1974: 191–2; Yasutake 2009: 17). The YWCA's Tsuji Matsu was president, the WCTU's Gauntlett was vice-president, and Ichikawa was secretary of this international relations committee. The group selected a much smaller delegation—eight women—to attend the 1930 PPWC.

Earlier in 1930, male representatives of Great Britain, the United States, Japan, France and Italy met in London for the follow-up meeting to the Washington Conference of 1921–2 on naval limitations. An unofficial international delegation of women, inspired by Gauntlett, met the official representatives to demand peace and arms reduction. Gauntlett handed the men two baskets of petitions signed by 750,000 Japanese women. But Japanese women's ability to press for peace would soon fade away.

Gauntlett, with her strong connections to global Christian organizations, her membership in Japan's WCTU and YWCA, and her presidency of the Japan's Women's Peace Association, was elected president of the Pan Pacific Women's Association in 1934. She was scheduled to preside over the next meeting in 1937 in Vancouver, but the Chinese delegates initially refused to attend due to Japan's military actions in China. Women's transnationalism was severely challenged by Japan's military aggression. By the middle of the decade of the 1930s, women's suffrage was also severely challenged, as Japan's increasingly militarist government kept suffragists under close surveillance (Molony 2004: 143). Ichikawa's criticism of militarism in an issue of the WSL journal *Fusen* led to that issue being banned. In another issue of *Fusen* in 1933, Ichikawa rued Japan's withdrawal from the League of Nations. In the next few years, the WSL turned to such issues as garbage collection, municipal utilities, clean elections and regulating the Tokyo fish market as ways of involving women in governance with official approval (Tamanoi 2009: 824–30). Transnational—and even national—movements and ideology were supplanted by the extremely local. At the same time, the WSL published an English-language journal, *Japanese Women*, from 1938 to 1940, whose purpose was to call for transnational unity among women. Despite these moves towards the local, on the one hand, and the global, on the other, the WSL, like other organizations, was soon to be part of a deeply nationalist trend. Eight major women's groups formed the Federation of Japanese Women's Organizations in 1937, with Ichikawa as the secretary. The annual National Women's Suffrage Convention was supplanted in 1938 by a Women's National Emergency Congress (Nishikawa 1997: 53). When the wartime government invited Ichikawa and many other feminists to serve on commissions and committees, most jumped in. Ichikawa's only complaint was that the government was doing too little to mobilize women in support of a war that she had bitterly opposed a decade earlier (Ueno 2004: 40–1).

Within ten days of Japan's surrender, Ichikawa had found colleagues alive in war-torn Tokyo and re-established the Women's Suffrage League. Ready to work with the new system, even meeting with Lt. Ethel Weed of the US occupation forces, Ichikawa quickly discovered her type of transnational feminism could not be restarted. The American occupation purged her in 1947, and for reasons still not clear, did not release the purge when tens of thousands of her supporters both in Japan and overseas petitioned to release her. Immediately following the occupation, Ichikawa resumed public life, travelling to the United States and running successfully for public office beginning in 1952. She pushed for Japanese membership in the UN and called for female representation. On trips to Okinawa both before and after its return to Japan as well as to the Philippines to receive the Magsaysay Prize for Community Leadership in 1974, she addressed the issues of forced suicide and institutionalized rape by the Japanese military (Molony 2005c: 84; Kodama 1985: 253–4). In the 1970s, she brought together the large women's groups in the International Women's Year Action Group to confront continuing sexism. Feminism, she contended, was global. Ichikawa was widely popular, and her historical place appeared assured at that time. Her assumption of responsibility for her wartime support for the government because it had begun to acknowledge women, even if only in a minimal way, was initially viewed positively. And yet, the problem of transnational, Western-style rights-based feminism, whose goal was full citizenship, led some historians in the 1980s to identify Ichikawa and other suffragists with the misdeeds of the state.

Postscript

Transnational feminisms have flourished in Japan in the six decades since the end of World War II. They have taken new forms that supplement the Christian, socialist and suffragist transnational organizations that characterized the pre-war era. Each of those older types continues to play an important role in Japanese society, but since the 1970s new directions, primarily focused on Asia and Asian feminist solidarity, have joined these originally more Western orientations.

The first years of the American occupation were by definition transnational. All political, economic and social policies concerning women, as well as forms of discourse in the arts, letters and journalism, were either promoted by foreign occupation officers—particularly those who worked with Ethel Weed, head of

the Women's Affairs Branch of the Civil Information and Education Section—
or approved by the CI&E section. The women's rights clauses of the 1947
Constitution were drafted by a very young member of the occupation, Beate
Sirota. To a large extent, Japanese women involved in pre-war transnational
Christian organizations worked closely with American women officials (Koikari
2008: Ch. 3). As in the pre-war years, the Americans believed they had much
to teach their Japanese counterparts. Many Japanese women felt patronized, but
cooperated out of necessity. This allowed transnational groups such as the Japan
WCTU and the YWCA to flourish. Their members were some of the first Japanese
women allowed to travel abroad after the war.

Other women who had espoused a socialist or pro-labour internationalism
before the war were also encouraged to emerge from hiding immediately after
the war. But as the occupation changed course in 1947 with the rise of the Cold
War, socialists and labour activists who sought their models in the Soviet Union or
China were increasingly restricted and unable to obtain visas to attend international
meetings (Koikari 2008: Ch. 4). At the same time, the leading pre-war Marxist
feminist intellectual, Yamakawa Kikue, was the first woman to earn a top position
in the bureaucracy. Having gained the vote and constitutional equality, suffragist
feminists entered electoral politics, academia and professions such as journalism,
medicine and the law. Some, such as Oku Mumeo, founded the Housewives
Association (*Shufuren*), a consumer rights organization with a national rather than
transnational orientation. Others, such as the octogenarian feminists Hiratsuka
Raichō and Hani Motoko, were drawn to the new Mothers' Convention (Hahaoya
Taikai), which first met in 1955, with links to transnational mothers' peace and
anti-nuclear movements (Uno 1993: 308–9).

The 'second wave' of international feminism washed over Japan beginning
in 1970. As in a number of other countries, women active in Japan's New
Left and anti-Vietnam War movements used the rhetoric of liberation of those
movements to articulate their anger at the continuing sexism in their own
organizations. They linked the oppression of Japanese women with the oppression,
by Japan's cooperation with American imperialism, of women elsewhere in
Asia (Mackie 2003: 148). Other new feminists focused on the body and
sexuality. This was promoted in numerous journals, most notably *Onna: Erosu*
(Woman: Eros), published from 1973 to 1982. Taking a different approach, the
journal *Feminisuto/Feminist*, founded in 1977, included reports about women
in Asian countries and excellent brief historical articles about Japanese women.
With English and Japanese editions, *Feminist* was intended for a transnational
audience.

Groups with names such as *Tatakau Onna* (Fighting Women) and the Shinjuku
Women's Liberation Centre characterized the early 1970s. By 1975, the UN
International Women's Year inspired veteran politicians Ichikawa Fusae and
Tanaka Sumiko to call together dozens of women's groups to discuss plans for the
upcoming multinational UN meeting in Mexico City. The huge Japanese gathering
engendered the Women's Action Group, a coalition of organizations that had
played a role in a variety of political actions concerning workplace equality, child

and elder care, reproductive rights and school curricula in the decades since 1975. It maintained global linkages and ties to the increasingly important UN meetings throughout this period as well.

The transnational focus of Japanese feminism began to shift in the 1970s. The concern of young feminists about Japanese 'sex tours' to Korea and Southeast Asia and the exploitation of women from poorer Asian countries recruited as brides for Japanese men inspired feminist activism. Long-standing transnational organizations such as the WCTU and YWCA both became involved in the movement against the global trafficking of women. The WCTU, for example, runs a programme called HELP (Housing in Emergency of Love and Peace) for women who have been trafficked to Japan for sex. Discovering a domestic need as well, HELP has also opened its doors to homeless and battered Japanese women. In addition, the Asian Women's Association, founded in 1977 by prominent feminist journalist Matsui Yayori, called on Japanese women to consider the ways in which their own economic comfort was linked to the global migration of women, the use of cheap female labour in Asia, sex trafficking and other forms of gendered exploitation. Matsui's reports from East and Southeast Asian countries had an explosive effect on Japanese thought. Her best-selling book, originally published in Japanese in 1987, inspired individuals to consider acting as their 'sisters' keepers' (Matsui 1989). Dozens of transnational non-governmental organizations now address global and especially East Asian women's rights.

The focus on Asia is a significant change in Japan's transnational feminism. Japan's wealth, compared to that of its Asian neighbours, made coalitions with those neighbours difficult in the 1970s and 1980s, but collaboration has been increasingly possible in the past two decades. Gendered violence against Asian women by the wartime Japanese military continues to influence Japan's state-to-state relations in the region. But the end of the formal Japanese empire, the linking of abuses of women in Japan to the global migration of women, and especially the redefining of women's rights as human rights has removed much of the stigma from transnational feminism.

References

Anderson, B. (1983) *Imagined Communities*, London and New York: Verso.

Boxer, M. (2007) 'Rethinking the Socialist Construction and International Career of the Concept "Bourgeois Feminism" ', *American Historical Review*, 112: 131–58.

Burton, A. (1994) *Burdens of History: British Feminists, Indian Women, and Imperial Culture, 1865–1915*, Chapel Hill, NC: University of North Carolina Press.

Cassman, R. (2007) 'Fighting to Make the Cut: Female Genital Cutting Studied within the Context of Cultural Relativism', *Northwestern Journal of International Human Rights*, 6, 1: 128–54.

Desai, M. (1996) 'From Vienna to Beijing: Women's Human Rights Activism and the Human Rights Community', *New Political Science*, 18, 1: 107–19.

Garner, K. (2004) 'Global Feminism and Postwar Reconstruction: The World YWCA Visitation to Occupied JAPAN, 1947', *Journal of World History*, 15, 2: 191–227.

Garon, S. (1993) 'Women's Groups and the Japanese State', *Journal of Japanese Studies*, 19, 1: 5–41.

Germer, A. (2003) 'Feminist History in Japan: National and International Perspectives', in *Intersections: Gender, History and Culture in the Asian Context* 9, Online. Available HTTP: <http://intersections.anu.edu.au/issue9/germer.html>

Grewal, I. and Kaplan, C. (eds) (1994) *Scattered Hegemonies: Postmodernity and Transnational Feminist Practices*, Minneapolis, MN: University of Minnesota Press.

Hayakawa, N. (2001) 'Nationalism, Colonialism and Women: The Case of the World Woman's Christian Temperance Union in Japan', in P. Grimshaw, K. Holmes and M. Lake (eds) *Women's Rights and Human Rights: International Historical Perspectives*, New York: Palgrave Macmillan.

Hopper, H.M. (1996) *A New Woman of Japan: A Political Biography of Katō Shidzue*, Boulder, CO: Westview Press.

Ichikawa, F. (1930) 'Arisu Poru joshi no insho', *Fusen* 4.8, reprinted in F. Ichikawa, *Nonaka no ippon sugi*, Tokyo: Shinjuku Shobō.

—— (1974) *Ichikawa Fusae Jiden: Senzen Hen*, Tokyo: Shinjuku Shobō.

—— (1981) *Nonaka no ippon sugi*, Tokyo: Shinjuku Shobō.

Ishimoto, S. (1935) *Facing Two Ways: The Story of My Life*, New York: Farrar and Rinehart.

Kanō, M. (1987) *Onnatachi no 'jūgo'* (Women and the 'home front'), Tokyo: Chikuma Shobō.

Kawai, M. and Kubushiro, O. (1934) *Japanese Women Speak*, Boston: Central Committee of the United Study of Foreign Missions.

Kodama, K. (1985) *Sengo no Ichikawa Fusae*, Tokyo: Shinjuku Shobō.

Koikari, M. (2002) 'Exporting Democracy? American Women, "Feminist Reforms", and the Politics of Imperialism in the U.S. Occupation of Japan, 1945–52', *Frontiers*, 23, 1: 23–45.

—— (2008) *Pedagogy of Democracy: Feminism and the Cold War in the U.S Occupation of Japan*, Philadelphia, PA: Temple University Press.

Koshiro, Y. (1999) *Trans-Pacific Racisms and the U.S. Occupation of Japan*, New York: Columbia University Press.

Liu, L.H. (1999) 'Legislating the Universal: The Circulation of International Law in the Nineteenth Century', in L. Liu (ed.) *Tokens of Exchange: The Problem of Translation in Global Circulations*, Durham, NC: Duke University Press.

Loftus, R. (2004) *Telling Lives: Women's Self Writing in Modern Japan*, Honolulu: University of Hawai'i Press.

Lublin, E.D. (2006) 'Wearing the White Ribbon of Reform and the Banner of Civic Duty: Yajima Kajiko and the Japan Woman's Christian Temperance Union in the Meiji Period', *U.S. Japan Women's Journal*, 30–1: 60–79.

Mackie, V. (2003) *Feminism in Modern Japan*, Cambridge: Cambridge University Press.

Matsui, Y. (1989) *Women's Asia*, London: Zed Books.

McClintock, A. (1995) *Imperial Leather: Race, Gender, and Sexuality in the Colonial Contest*, London: Routledge.

Mihalopoulos, B. (2009) 'Mediating the Good Life: Prostitution and the Japanese Women's Christian Temperance Union, 1880s–1920s', *Gender and History*, 21, 1: 19–38.

Mohanty, C.T. (1984) 'Under Western Eyes: Feminist Scholarship and Colonial Discourses', *Boundary 2*, 12, 3: 333–58.

Molony, B. (1995) 'Japan's 1996 Equal Employment Opportunity Law and the Changing Discourse on Gender', *Signs: Journal of Women in Culture and Society*, 20, 2: 268–302.

—— (2000) 'Women's Rights, Feminism, and Suffragism in Japan, 1870–1925', *Pacific Historical Review,* 69, 4: 639–61.

—— (2004) 'Citizenship and suffrage in interwar Japan', in L. Edwards and M. Roces, (eds) *Women's Suffrage in Asia: Gender, Nationalism and Democracy*, London and New York: RoutledgeCurzon, pp. 127–51.

—— (2005a) 'Women's Rights and the Japanese State, 1880–1925', in G. Bernstein, A. Gordon and K. Nakai (eds) *Public Spheres, Private Lives in Modern Japan, 1600–1950*, Cambridge, MA: Harvard University Asia Center, pp. 221–58.

—— (2005b) 'The Quest for Women's Rights in Turn-of-the-Century Japan', in B. Molony and K. Uno (eds) *Gendering Modern Japanese History*, Cambridge, MA: Harvard University Asia Center, pp. 463–92.

—— (2005c) 'Ichikawa Fusae and Japan's Pre-war Women's Suffrage Movement', in H. Tomida and G. Daniels (eds) *Japanese Women: Emerging from Subservience, 1868–1945*, Folkestone, Kent: Global Oriental, pp. 57–94.

—— (2007) 'Gender, Citizenship and Dress in Modernizing Japan', in M. Roces and L. Edwards (eds) *The Politics of Dress in Asia and the Americas*, Brighton, UK and Portland, OR: Sussex Academic Press, pp. 81–100.

Murase, M. (2006) *Cooperation over Conflict: The Women's Movement and the State in Postwar Japan*, New York and London: Routledge.

Narita, R. (1998) 'Women in the Motherland: Oku Mumeo Through Wartime and Postwar', in Y. Yamanouchi, J.V. Koschmann and R. Narita, (eds) *Total War and 'Modernization'*, Ithaca, NY: Cornell University Press.

Neary, I. (1989) *Political Protest and Social Control in Pre-war Japan: The Origins of Buraku Liberation*, Atlantic Highlands, NJ: Humanities Press International.

Nihon Kirisutokyō Fujin Kyōfūkai (eds) (1986) *Nihon Kirisutokyō Fujin Kyōfūkai Hyakunenshi*, Tokyo: Domesu.

Nishikawa, Y. (1997) 'Japan's Entry into War and the Support of Women', *U.S.-Japan Women's Journal, English Supplement*, 12: 48–83.

Noheji, K. (1984) *Josei Kaihō Shisō no Genryū: Iwamoto Yoshiharu to 'Jogaku Zasshi'*, Tokyo: Azekura Shobō.

Ogawa, M. (2004) ' "Hull-House" in Downtown Tokyo: The Transplantation of a Settlement House from the United States into Japan and the North American Missionary Women, 1919–45', *Journal of World History*, 15, 3: 359–87.

—— (2007a) 'Estranged Sisterhood: The Wartime Trans-Pacific Dialogue of the World's Woman's Christian Temperance Union, 1931–45', *The Japanese Journal of American Studies*, 18: 163–85.

—— (2007b) 'The "White Ribbon League of Nations Meets Japan": The Trans-Pacific Activism of the Woman's Christian Temperance Union, 1906–30', *Diplomatic History*, 31, 1: 21–50.

Oku, M. (1941) *Hana aru Shokuba E*, Tokyo: Bunmeisha.

Scott, J.W. (1996) *Only Paradoxes to Offer: French Feminists and the Rights of Man*, Cambridge, MA: Harvard University Press.

Seraphim, F. (2006) *War Memory and Social Politics in Japan, 1945–2005*, Cambridge, MA: Harvard University Asia Center.

Shklar, J.N. (1995) *American Citizenship: The Quest for Inclusion*, Cambridge, MA: Harvard University Press.

Sievers, S.L. (1983) *Flowers in Salt: The Beginnings of Feminist Consciousness in Modern Japan*, Stanford, CA: Stanford University Press.

Soh, C.S. (2008) *The Comfort Women: Sexual Violence and Postcolonial Memory in Korea and Japan*, Chicago: University of Chicago Press.

Spivak, G.C. (1988) 'Can the Subaltern Speak?', in C. Nelson and L. Grossberg (eds) *Marxism and the Interpretation of Culture*, Urbana, IL: University of Illinois Press.

Stoler, A.L. (2002) *Carnal Knowledge and Imperial Power: Race and the Intimate in Colonial Rule*, Berkeley, CA: University of California Press.

Suzuki, Y. (1986) *Feminizumu to sensō* (Feminism and war), Tokyo: Marujusha.

Tamanoi, M.A. (2009) 'Suffragist Women, Corrupt Officials, and Waste Control in Prewar Japan: Two Plays by Kaneko Shigepi', *Journal of Asian Studies*, 68, 3: 805–34.

Tanaka, Y. (1987) *To Live and to Write: Selections by Japanese Women Writers, 1913–1938*, Seattle, WA: Seal Press.

Tokuza, A. (1999) *The Rise of the Feminist Movement in Japan*, Tokyo: Keio University Press.

Tyrell, I. (1991) *Women's World, Woman's Empire: The Woman's Christian Temperance Union in International Perspective, 1880–1930*, Chapel Hill, NC: University of North Carolina Press.

Ueno, C. (2004) *Nationalism and Gender,* trans. B. Yamamoto, Melbourne: Trans Pacific Press.

Uno, K. (1993) 'The Death of "Good Wife, Wise Mother"?' in A. Gordon (ed.) *Postwar Japan as History*, Berkeley, CA: University of California Press.

Yasutake, Y. (2004) *Transnational Women's Activism: The United States, Japan, and Japanese Immigrant Communities in California, 1859–1920*, New York and London: New York University Press.

—— (2006) 'Men, Women, and Temperance in Meiji Japan: Engendering WCTU Activism from a Transnational Perspective', *Japanese Journal of American Studies*, 17: 91–111.

—— (2009) 'The First Wave of International Women's Movements from a Japanese Perspective: Western Outreach and Japanese Women Activists during the Interwar Years', *Women's Studies International Forum*, 32: 13–20.

7 Feminism, Buddhism and transnational women's movements in Thailand

Monica Lindberg Falk

This chapter explores the transnational influences on the evolution of the women's movement in Thailand. It focuses on two major women-oriented campaigns: the movement to make Buddhist institutional hierarchies accessible to women and the campaigns designed to enhance the lives and opportunities of women working in the prostitution sector. Buddhism is one of the oldest transnational institutions in Thailand since its influence transcends national boundaries and membership reaches beyond the borders of the nation. Equally, prostitution has flourished in recent decades with the expansion of the tourism sector. Prostitution-linked tourism has contributed to the rapid growth of the Thai economy in recent decades and has inserted Thai women into a globalized economic system. This chapter shows that transnational women's movements have been vital in Thai women activists' formulation of questions of gender inequalities and women's rights. It explores the transnationalization of the key organization working with prostitution—Education Means Protection of Women Engaged in Recreation (EMPOWER) and discusses the importance of the transnational Buddhist women's movement in the Thai campaigns to establish a Buddhist female monks' order—a *bhikkhuni* order.

This chapter begins with a discussion of the overarching framework of gender orders in Thailand and then provides a brief historical overview of women's movements in Thailand. The movement has two main divisions—groups that work on advocacy and others that adopt a welfare-oriented approach (Van Esterik 2000). The chapter is based on research on gender and Buddhism in Thailand that I have carried out for more than ten years. I have followed the development of the female monks' movement—the *bhikkhuni* movement—since 1994 and I have done extensive periods of anthropological fieldwork in Thailand on projects on gender in relation to Buddhism, HIV/AIDS, socially engaged Buddhism and Buddhism's role in the recovery process after the tsunami in 2004.[1]

In general, the term 'feminist' has negative connotations in Thailand. This emerges from the widely held misconception that feminists are only interested in helping women rather than working on behalf of the whole community. Moreover, feminism is sometimes considered un-Thai and rooted in Western social values and therefore unsuitable for Thai society. The arguments raised against feminism in Thailand mirror those noted by Kumari Jayawardena for other non-Western contexts (1986: 2–3). Nonetheless, research on gender in Thailand continues and some adopt feminist perspectives.

Gender scholars in Thailand have adopted two main viewpoints on the status of Thai women. The first describes Thai women as different from, but equal to, men. This description is supported by research conducted mainly on the situation of upper- and middle-class Thai women. It maintains that traditionally Thai women have struggled alongside their husbands and at the same time taken care of their children—the roles of men and women are seen as complementary rather than competitive. An opposing feminist perspective argues that Thai women have experienced long periods of exploitation. On this view, upper-class women are regarded as being forcibly limited to the family sphere, and lower-class women have faced exploitation in their workforce as they worked to support their families (see Wongchaisuwan and Tamronglak 2008: 244–5).

These scholars also show that Thai society promotes an ideal for womanhood that is not always upheld by ordinary people in their life choices. The ideal Thai woman is a dutiful daughter to her parents and upon marriage becomes a caring wife and a self-sacrificing mother. Women who reject this family-oriented, reproductive identity directly violate this idealized vision. The prostitutes and nuns (and the women that advocate on their behalf) discussed in this chapter are prime examples of just such a phenomenon. But, these women, despite their deviation from the idea, still hold a certain status within their families because they are seen as fulfilling their debts of gratitude to their parents—a highly prized quality within Thai society. For example, daughters from poor families who provide for their parents and siblings by working in the sex trade are not condemned. They are regarded as nobly sacrificing themselves for the family (Kabilsingh 1991: 78). As the discussion below demonstrates, Thai gender orders are multi-faceted and complex systems, and these have engaged with global women's movements in equally complex forms.

Thai gender orders

Thai society is generally noted for its relatively egalitarian gender relations compared to neighbouring countries in South and East Asia on the basis that women assume important roles in managing household finances and have high rates of participation in the labour market (see Atkinson and Errington 1990). Patterns of land ownership and kinship structures have also been more equitable in Thailand than they are in Confucian cultures, for example. Yet, Thailand also remains a highly androcentric society in both actual and ideological terms. This paradox is manifest most strikingly in the simultaneous presentation of images of strong and competent women alongside evidence of inequalities and discrimination against women. These conflicting positions operate in concert with each other rather than neutralize each other. Many Thai writers recognize the high status of Thai women as a trope that exists alongside representations of Thai women as victims. The paradox is rationalized in everyday thinking by the idea that Thai culture is relatively 'flexible' and tolerant to individual divergences. An alternative explanation for the contradiction revolves either around modernization rhetoric and perceptions of the transformation of 'traditional' Thai culture. Van Esterik has explained that to some commentators the origins of women's oppression lies in traditional cultural norms that need to be modernized. Yet to others, women's oppression emerged as a result of modernization—that is, in the past Thai women had high status and substantial power, but they lost both during the modernization of the country (Pongsapich 1986; Boonsue 1989; Gardiner and Gardiner 1991; Hanks and Hanks 1963; quoted in Van Esterik 2000: 61).

The evidence for both positions is mixed. The legal codes for Thai family law in the nineteenth and early twentieth centuries clearly considered women to be dependents of their male family members, not free agents (Satha-Anand 2004: 27). A woman's social status was defined through her husband's position in life. Some of these cultural patterns continue today and inequities in the family law that disadvantage women remain. For example, infidelity is a ground for divorce if the wife is unfaithful but not if the husband is having affairs, unless he 'honours another woman as his wife' (ibid.: 28).

In recent decades, the socio-economic situation of most Thai women has improved as the country in general has become wealthier. Thai women constitute nearly half of the economically employed population and comprise the majority of workers in the export and tourism industries. However, women's participation in politics and administration is remarkably low and women have always been denied entry into the formal Buddhist congregation, *sangha*. Non-governmental organizations (NGOs) have made efforts to raise the status of women and encouraged women to be politically engaged (Thomson and Bhongsvej 2003). Nonetheless, politics and religion remain male strongholds in Thai society and the invisibility of women as political and religious leaders is striking compared to other countries in the region. Even though Thai women have had political rights since the change of the absolute monarchy to constitutional monarchy in 1932, Thai women have largely been excluded from political leadership. Over the decades, female participation in politics and administration has usually been under 10 per cent. That is below the Asian average of 14 per cent. In the 2005 general election, the proportion of women in the lower house increased to 10.6 per cent, the highest ever in Thailand. However, women occupy only 10 per cent of the seats in the Senate (Iwanaga 2008: 176).

Similarly, in Thailand, Buddhist monks hold the most culturally celebrated position of authority and value in society. And, when Buddhism is evoked in discussions of gender or women in Thailand, it is often considered to be a patriarchal institution that oppresses women. Buddhism is blamed by some authors for the subordination of Thai women and is considered to provide a moral framework for men's hierarchical precedence over women. The ban on women's ordination is the key marker of this inequality in practice and reinforces those who hold the view that Buddhism is concerned with buttressing male hegemony. Women are deemed to be grounded in the material world, rather than the spiritual world. Khin Thitsa (1980: 7) argues that this 'materialistic' image of women legitimates prostitution as a place from which women can fulfil role expectations attached to worldly matters. Kabilsingh (1991), Keyes (1984) and Satha-Anand (1999) contest this view.

Women's movements

The 1930s was a decade for democratic reforms in Thailand and, in 1932, the country went from being an absolute to a constitutional monarchy and women acquired the rights to vote and to stand for election. Before the end of the absolute monarchy, Thai women carried out voluntary activities to promote national security and welfare under royal sponsorship (Satha-Anand 2004: 16–17). Also, early efforts to form women's groups and raise women's issues (1855–1935) resulted primarily in welfare activities (Pongsapich 1986: 1). It was elite women who were engaged in charity activities. Before 1932, well-educated middle-class women raised their voices and called for equality and educational opportunities for women. They criticized patriarchy and polygamy, and argued their case in a series of women's magazines and newspapers (Van Esterik 2000: 50; Barmé 1995). In 1922, the first in a long series of articles that displayed the inequality of the family law was published in magazines. Women expressed a desire for a monogamy law; the argument was that it would reduce the number of broken homes and child prostitutes that was a result of the widespread practice of men having more than one wife. Such men did not support their families and forced some young girls into prostitution (Pongsapich 1997: 21). The women's movement raised issues such as sexual equality and opportunities for women to work outside the home (Satha-Anand 2004: 16–17). In 1935, the monogamy law was promulgated. The struggle for monogamy was crucial because it was clear to many women that a law which gave the husband the opportunity to remarry without first seeking a divorce from his original wife basically strengthened male dominance.

The first recognized women's organization was established in 1890 and later became the Red Cross. In 1932, the Women's Association of Siam was established and was the first women's organization with formal registration. Some of its key aims were 'forging unity among women, and to operate as a place for higher learning' (Pongsapich 1997: 21–2). In practice, the association provided additional education for women's domestic and child-caring activities (Satha-Anand 2004: 17). The association attempted to tackle class discrimination by providing support for women labourers and including membership for female sex workers (ibid.). These women formed the Thai Women's Association of Thailand. It was the first private voluntary women's organization and it still exists today (Tantiwiramanond and Pandey 1991: 27).

Later, many professional associations for women were established, such as the Women Lawyers' Association. The increase of women's associations reflected that time's more democratic climate. The Women's Status Promotion Group was formed as part of the democratic movement in the mid-1970s. Many women's groups were also created in universities to raise awareness of women's equality as a crucial issue for social justice. During that time women's groups were also created outside the walls of the university. Examples of organizations working on issues of women in the development process are: The Thai Girl Guides Association, The Association for the Promotion for the Status of Women, The Women Lawyers' Association of Thailand, The Gender and Development Research Institute, The Association for Civil Liberty and the Christian Women's Association (Pongsapich 1997: 24).

In the climate of political reform between 1973 and 1976, women's studies and gender issues became more prominent. In 1976, the ultra-right government brutally clamped down on all social justice movements. Many of those who survived either fled to the jungles or found refuge in Western universities. In the 1980s, the government abandoned its anti-communist policy and the students could go back to Thailand. Many started working with NGOs engaged in development or civil rights issues. Some women became activists and were inspired by Western feminist theories (Tantiwiramanond 2007: 201).

In the 1980s and 1990s, Thai society saw an increase of non-governmental organizations, many of which focused on women's concerns. The Friends of Women Group, Women's Information Centre, EMPOWER, Foundation for Women and the already mentioned Gender and Development Research Institute were progressive women's NGOs that were developed in the 1980s (Tantiwiramanond and Pandey 1991: 31). The activities of these organizations include non-formal and vocational training programmes for women, rescue and emergency homes for women and children, shelter for prostitutes escaping from brothels, and legal assistance to factory workers. They also provide legal consultations and encourage women's political participation, while still others work for women sex workers (Pongsapich 1997: 25). Groups such as EMPOWER that form around specific concerns, such as prostitution, tend to keep their mandates narrow and select their venues of confrontation with care. NGOs, including women's groups, are viewed as threatening by the Thai government and must be registered. Van Esterik states that Thai women's groups are considered more Western than other NGOs because of their presumed relation with Western feminism (Van Esterik 2000: 51). Thai leaders of women's groups, particularly elite women's groups, are ideal candidates for participating in international forums. The head of the Asia-Pacific Regional planning committee for the Conference for Women in Beijing and the head of the NGO Forum were both Thai women (ibid.: 52).

Over the years, women's movements have become more visible and groups have been formed at all levels. These groups or organizations can be divided into advocacy groups and welfare-oriented groups. The advocacy category contains organizations that work for creating gender equity and equality. Their stand is to lessen oppression and solve women's problems. They work, for example, with awareness-raising activities and policy campaigns. Groups such as Women and Constitution, Stop Violence against Women, Association for the Promotion of the Status of Women and Women's Movement in Thai Political Reform are examples of groups working with these issues. The welfare-oriented organizations primarily aim at improving the conditions of women and some focus on strengthening the capacity of women in economic, social and political development. Among these are alumni associations, professional groups as well as income-generation groups (Vichitranonda and Bhongsvej 2008: 67–8).

Women's studies emerged out of women's movements and became feminism's academic field. It was young urban university-educated women together with academic activists and senior women bureaucrats who contributed to the development of women's studies in Thailand (Tantiwiramanond 2007: 200). In 2000 and 2001, two universities in Thailand initiated a master's degree in women's studies. It was thanks to the persistent effort of Thai women activists and academics, many with international contacts, that women's studies programs were established (ibid.: 204).

Prostitution and Thai sex workers

Prostitution in Thailand has attracted a great deal of attention over recent decades and there have been numerous studies of commercial sex work in Thailand. The focus here is on organizations working on female prostitution and not on male prostitution, child prostitution, or migrant prostitution that have become large issues over the past decade.

Thai prostitute women are often portrayed as innocent victims of a cultural tradition and a capitalist-driven Thai state, or as victims of an international patriarchy, or as materialistic ego-centred women. Historically, prostitution has been situated within the political economy of colonialism, war and sex tourism. Thai feminists who work with prostitution object to the depiction of Thai women as passive victims without agency. Instead of labelling them 'prostitute', they prefer to use the term 'sex worker', which connotes agency and refers to a person capable of making choices and managing her own life. Nevertheless, there is a need to recognize Thai women in the sex trade as mere victims of larger processes. That perspective argues that understanding prostitution requires understanding the international operation of the capitalist economy and its relationship to prostitution. Sex workers are, as Jeffrey points out, victims of an international patriarchy and the product of a capitalist system that positions them as cheap sexual labour (Jeffrey 2002: xix, xvii). Pasuk Phongpaichit's (1982) work was one of the first in-depth studies of women and girls migrating into the Bangkok prostitution trade from the North and the Northeast parts of Thailand. She situated the trade within the uneven economic relationship between rural and urban Thailand.

In contemporary debate, there is a conflict between those who privilege women's agency and the free will of women to enter prostitution versus those who privilege the more structural deterministic constraints that make prostitution a job opportunity for women. That debate is evident where a forced or voluntary theoretical framework permeates discussions of prostitution. The lack of choice for poor women is the most common explanation of why women enter prostitution for both Western and Asian activists. However, Asian activists who do not acknowledge the complexities of prostitution are suspected of identifying too closely with the Western ideology of sex work (Law 2000: 97–8). In the 1970s and 1980s, sex workers who attempted to organize themselves to get better working conditions were suppressed and discouraged from doing so. The government tried to increase controls over sex workers and lower-class or rural women rather than empowering them. The agency of sex workers is problematic. Seen as an agent, the sex worker is considered as spreading an immoral behaviour, while seen as a victim, she is sympathetic but also powerless. In the early years of women's organizing against prostitution, the focus on rural women's migration into sex work either in urban centres or overseas reinforced the role of elites and government in protecting peasant women by disciplining them into proper cultural behaviour as well as proper sexual behaviour (Jeffrey 2002: 87).

Khin Thitsa (1980) constructs prostitution in Western middle-class moral terms and considers prostitution as being degrading and only for women who are already impoverished and legally, socially and religiously degraded; their inferior status is envisioned as being willing to be sex workers. Many Thai female sex workers' self-interpretations as workers and family wage earners are silenced and their calls for better working conditions are ignored. Nerida Cook (1998) addresses Thai middle-class women's moral panic and active campaigns against prostitution. Instead of listening to the sex workers, the urban middle and upper classes call for protective and rehabilitative activities for the sex workers.

The feminist NGOs that came together in the early 1980s were interested in addressing grass-roots women's needs. However, these organizations also operated from middle-class points of view distancing themselves from grass-roots women. The new women's groups viewed prostitution as the product of the globalization of the economy and the increasing dependence of Thailand on the tourist industry as well as on women's lower status and sexual exploitation within a male-dominated society.

While this concern about the role of rising consumerism in leading women into prostitution was widely shared by the media, government and NGOs, some women's organizations pointed to the economic exploitation of women and the poverty of the rural areas as the underlying causes of prostitution. Over the course of the 1980s, these women's groups had begun to recognize the importance of addressing the working conditions surrounding prostitution rather than seeking to abolish prostitution itself. The punishment of sex workers, they argued, only led to further exploitation and abuse of women who, rather than being 'bad girls', simply represented a form of wage-worker struggling to survive within an impoverished economy (Jeffrey 2002: 118–19). Critical feminists argued that viewing sex workers merely as victims was unproductive and, in fact, harmful. They argued that the sex workers tried to escape from the reform institutions and dared to throw off the moral restraints imposed on 'good' women (ibid.: 120).

In Thailand, the 'good' woman and the 'bad' are defined in terms of their relationship to the institution of the family. To be a 'good' woman means to remain loyal to the family and that means to be a dutiful daughter, a faithful wife and an all-giving mother. In the 1980s, human rights activists such as Sukanya Hantrakul tried to break the good girl/bad girl divide. Hantrakul discussed gender inequalities in Thai society, and when she criticized the government's reform institutions and repression of sex workers, she advocated that sex workers should be protected

(Hantrakul 1988: 129). The activists argued that it is important that sex workers receive the same rights as other Thai citizens. Their strategies were not to question the sex worker's choices; instead, they wanted to give them skills to use in their situation. The sex workers opted for English language training and the activists began to provide English lessons (Tantiwiramanond and Pandey 1991: 128–32). Later it developed into an organization for women sex workers named Education Means Protection of Women Engaged in Recreation—EMPOWER. Jeffrey notes that the activists were particularly concerned with respecting sex workers' agency by, for instance, charging tuition for English lessons rather than offering them as a social welfare service. The arguments were that the majority of activities aimed at sex workers included repression, rehabilitation and registration, and were aimed at disciplining women into good 'sexual behaviour' (Jeffrey 2002: 120).

EMPOWER's approach was very much in opposition to the approach of turning prostitute women back into 'good' women. Some elite women's organizations reacted with hostility to the idea of providing English lessons to prostitute women. They sought to abolish prostitution entirely, and it was felt that the English lessons encouraged rather than discouraged the trade (Jeffrey 2002: 120–1). EMPOWER does not focus on ethics or the reasons for prostitution, and its ability to address the needs of sex workers was proved by the early and effective AIDS education it provided first in Bangkok and later more widely (Cook 1998: 275).

EMPOWER continues to provide language classes, health education and career workshops. It publishes a newspaper and produces dramas with and for women working in the sex trade. EMPOWER has nine centres in four provinces in Thailand. They have different profiles responding to the situation in the specific areas. For example, in the north of Thailand, EMPOWER has a campus of migration and the Chiang Mai Empower Drop-in Centre is a multicultural, multilingual centre with members from more than fifteen different ethnicities. Among many things, EMPOWER runs day-care centres, coffee shops and various types of educational activities. EMPOWER has developed into a transnational organization. In 2005, it received support from the Rockefeller Foundation to establish Empower University Mekong Worknet through which it wants to strengthen their communication with sex workers in China, Burma, Laos, Vietnam and Cambodia. One aim is to improve the health situation and prevent HIV/AIDS. Empower University Mekong Worknet had its first Mekong Regional Sex Workers' Forum in 2006 with fifty participants from Laos, China and Thailand. EMPOWER is a respected organization that shares knowledge and experiences with groups and individuals both nationally and internationally. Cook notes that international support may have helped EMPOWER to remain reasonably independent of the criticism of its lack of involvement in the more mainstream women's movement (Cook 1998: 276).

The transnational *bhikkhuni* movement

Buddhist nuns can be seen as the opposite of sex workers. They live simple, quiet, celibate lives. However, both sex workers and nuns challenge the Thai gender orders. Renouncing the world and becoming a Buddhist nun is not in line with what Thai people in general think is an accepted social role. The ideal Thai woman is expected to fulfil the role of wife and mother, and women are not encouraged to become nuns. Thus, Buddhist nuns are women who, in spite of the social convention, choose to ordain violate cultural norms of gender by abandoning their home lives and renouncing the world.

The nuns' role in Thai society is ambiguous and somewhat vague. Women have never been granted membership in the Buddhist congregation, *sangha*. Women are not given *bhikkhuni* ordination and *bhikkhunis* ordained abroad are not accepted by the *sangha* in Thailand. Most women's movements have not struggled against the Thai Buddhist *sangha's* male stronghold. However, there are Thai academics and activists who argue that Buddhism subordinates women morally and socially (Ekachai 1996; Hantrakul 1988: 115–16; Satha-Anand 1999). Other scholars show that Buddhism can be liberating for women (Gross 1993; Kabilsingh 1991; Sponberg 1992). They argue that it is cultural values and the formalized Buddhist institutions that subordinate and exclude women in ways that are not supported by the Buddhist doctrine.

The *bhikkhuni* order could be seen as a transnational movement that spread from India to Sri Lanka. It became transformed into the Mahayana tradition in China and after that spread to Vietnam, Korea and Japan. The *bhikkhuni sangha* was established by the Buddha five years after the establishment of the male order, the *bhikkhu sangha*. The *bhikkhuni* order disappeared from India sometime after the ninth century CE and it existed in Sri Lanka from the beginning of Buddhism in the country, about 247 BCE, and broke down after about 1,300 years together with the *bhikkhu sangha*. The *bhikkhu sangha* was later restored with assistance from Thai and Burmese monks. The *bhikkhuni* order had not spread to the other Theravada countries and it was therefore considered to have disappeared and be irretrievably lost. Those who argue that the lineage still exists refer to the transnational spreading of the female order. They state that it remains in the Mahayana tradition in East Asian countries, since the female monks' order there actually originated from the *bhikkhuni* order in the Theravada tradition. Recently Mahayana *bhiksunis* have helped in the process of reviving the *bhikkhuni* order. In less than ten years, it is once again possible for women to receive *bhikkhuni* ordination in Sri Lanka (Falk 2008).

Over the years, there have been several efforts to establish the *bhikkhuni* order in Thailand. The attempts have not yet been successful and most Thai people are not interested in addressing the inequity in Thai Buddhism. They adhere to their historical legacy and follow the official standpoint that the *bhikkhuni* lineage has become extinct and it is therefore not possible to revive it. The campaign for the establishment of a *bhikkhuni* order challenges the Thai *sangha*, since the *bhikkhunis* would demand entrance into the Buddhist congregation. The majority of Thai people avoid criticizing the Buddhist monks. Thai Buddhist women who consider ordaining as a Buddhist nun have in general not been interested in becoming *bhikkhunis*. The Thai Buddhist nuns, *mae chiis*, have hitherto not shown interest in receiving *bhikkhuni* ordination (see Falk 2007).

In 2001, a well-known Thai professor from one of the leading universities in Bangkok went to Sri Lanka and received novice *bhikkhuni* ordination. Her name was Chatsumarn Kabilsingh, now Dhammananda Bhikkhuni, and she became the first Thai woman to receive ordination in the Theravada tradition. Before that there were only a few Mahayana *bhiksuni*s in Thailand. They had received ordination from Mahayana monks abroad and none of them were recognized by the Thai *sangha*. Over the centuries, the Thai *sangha* has blocked the entry of females. An important example of this was the two sisters Sara and Chongdee, who received novice ordination in 1928. They were arrested and the incident made the *sangha*'s supreme council pass an order forbidding any monks from giving women novice or full ordination as monks (Kabilsingh 1991: 45–8). The rule was implemented in 1928 by the Supreme Patriarch and is still valid in spite of the fact that it violates the constitution, which espouses gender equality and freedom of faith (Falk 2008: 114–15).

It is through international cooperation that women now have the opportunity to receive *bhikkhuni* ordination. In 1987, Dhammananda Bhikkhuni together with three *bhiksuni*s founded the Sakyadhita International Network of Buddhist Women. The female monks were Karma Lekshe Tsomo, Jampa Tsedroen and Ayya Khema (Tsomo 1988, 2000). The first conference on Buddhist female ascetics was held in Bodh Gaya in India. Although there have been some councils since the death of the Buddha, this was the first recorded conference on Buddhist women (Tsedroen 1988: 44–52). The Sakyaditha transnational network has been crucial for the restoration of the *bhikkhuni* order.

In February 2003, Dhammananda Bhikkhuni completed her two years as a novitiate, and on the twenty-eighth day of the same month, she received full ordination in Sri Lanka. The Thai *sangha* persists in not recognizing her ordination and her status as a Theravada *bhikkhuni*. The number of novices and *bhikkhuni*s in Thailand are growing and the largest group of female monks are in Chiang Mai, in the north of Thailand. The *bhikkhuni* movement in Thailand is composed of *bhikkhuni*s scattered around the country without a formal organization. Most of them are linked to broader networks of Buddhist women nationally, as well as internationally, who work for women's rights and gender equality.

Initially, there were several attempts to silence Dhammananda Bhikkhuni's ordination. Her ordination was publicly criticized in the press and her TV interviews were banned (Janssen 2001). Dhammananda has been accused of 'destroying Buddhism' through her ordination. Her opinion is the opposite. She said that she is 'trying to revive the four pillars of Buddhism—*bhikkhu*s, (male monks) *bhikkhuni*s, (female monks), *upasaka*s (laymen) and *upasika*s (lay women) that will sustain the religion into the future' (Achakulwisut 2001). However, in 2004, the National Buddhist Bureau stated in reply to a Senate proposal that there can never be *bhikkhuni* ordination in Thailand due to the irretrievable loss in the lineage of Theravada *bhikkhuni* order and lack of a *bhikkhuni* preceptor. *Bhikkhuni* ordination is today performed in Thailand with assistance from monastics from abroad who are outside the *sangha*'s control. Dhammananda's ambition is to create a following of *bhikkhuni*s in Thailand.

Without the Thai *sangha*'s approval, she has begun establishing a *bhikkhuni* community at her temple south of Bangkok.

Conclusion

Prostitution is particularly threatening because it signals women's failure to stay within their prescribed gender roles both physically and socially. Prostitution has been analysed as the product of a Buddhist-based culture that demotes women to secondary status. Institutional religion often legitimizes values and rules that disempower women. The well-known importance of Buddhism in many Thai women's lives means that secular feminism is often perceived not only as Western but also as lacking cultural relevance. The Thai *sangha* is a male core stronghold and in general Thai women do not challenge it while very few NGOs have taken an interest in the *bhikkhuni* movement. The Thai *bhikkhuni* movement is part of a transnational movement and it is intriguing why the *bhikkhuni* movement gains so little support from Thai people. Criticizing the *sangha* is a sensitive issue. One explanation could be that receiving *bhikkhuni* ordination and the struggle for membership in the *sangha* is more than just demanding social equality and gender justice. The *sangha* is not only a male powerbase but also a cultural institution closely related to constructing masculine identity in Thailand (see Keyes 1986; Falk 2000, 2007). Moreover, Buddhism is deeply rooted in most Thai's identity and stands for more than an institution that exercises structural inequality. Yet, another explanation is that the *bhikkhuni* issue is regarded as something not belonging to the Thai Buddhist realm and voices are raised that the *sangha* would be degraded if women entered it (Falk 2008: 104).

Women's exclusion from the Thai *sangha* and full ordination has social implications. Academics argue that establishing a *bhikkhuni* ordination in Thailand would be an important step in improving women's social status and opportunities more broadly (Ekachai 2001; Kabilsingh 1991; Satha-Anand 1999). There is a concern that many gender-related issues facing women in Thailand, including domestic violence, sex trafficking and HIV transmission, have a religious and cultural dimension that is frequently overlooked.

A report on why feminism has not 'taken off' in Thailand argues that middle-class urban women prefer to deny that male domination exists and prefer to consider Thai society as male-guided rather than male-dominated (Tantiwiramanond and Pandey 1991: 60). Tantiwiramanond explains that women's movements have been weak in Thailand partly because Thai society is highly vertically constructed while its horizontal structures have remained undeveloped (Tantiwiramanond 2007: 205).

Van Esterik refers to a Thai feminist who argues that a valuable approach for Thai feminism would be to build on the complementarity and flexibility that exist and the overlap in male and female values, and to stress Thai women's sources of power, their potential, and their effective female way of working (Van Esterik 2000: 55). The emphasis on Thai women as victims, instead of focusing on women's agency and resistance, may be because middle-class women lack the confidence to participate in feminist work. Van Esterik hints that middle-class businesswomen who join women's groups only work for causes that benefit themselves directly, with little concern for Thai women generally (ibid.).

In Thailand, religion is intertwined with politics and networking is an important and dynamic force among advocacy groups to raise awareness on gender inequalities. The most activist of the Thai women's groups have chosen to focus attention on groups such as sex workers and advocacy groups that are tackling principles of gender equality and political reforms. Thai women's movements tend to address social problems rather than develop indigenous feminist theory.

Transnational relations have been important both for EMPOWER and for the *bhikkhuni* movement. Cook notes that EMPOWER's decision to assist those sex workers who are involved with foreign tourists has protected it from receiving more hostility from the Thai public than it has. Moreover, international support may have shielded it from criticism (Cook 1998: 275–6). The transnational women's Buddhist movement, Sakyaditha, has been essential for the *bhikkhuni* movement and for the revival of the Bhikkhuni Order.

Dhammananda Bhikkhuni, the first Thai *bhikkhuni,* has been heavily criticized for her ordination and the *bhikkhuni* movement has not attracted as large a Thai following as Dhammananda Bhikkhuni initially had hoped for. She has established a female monks' community in Thailand located at her temple, but it is not recognized by the Thai *sangha.* Thai women are receiving novice and full ordination as *bhikkhuni* with assistance from *bhikkhus and bhikkhunis* abroad. A few new *bhikkhuni* centres have recently been established. Dhammananda Bhikkhuni continues to work transnationally. She travels extensively and gives talks, and leads Buddhist retreats. At her temple she focuses on giving international Buddhist courses.

To conclude, the transnational *bhikkhuni* movement and EMPOWER are influenced by Western feminism. They are challenging Thai gender orders in ways that are not in tune with how the mainstream Thai women's movements' are addressing gender issues. Their transnational networks have been imperative for the continuation of their struggles for gender justice and rights in Thai society.

Note

1 The projects have been financially supported by the Swedish Research Council (VR), the Swedish Council for Planning and Co-ordination of Research (FRN), the Swedish Humanities Research Council (HSFR) and by the Swedish International Development Cooperation Agency (Sida/SAREC).

References

Achakulwisut, A. (2001) 'A path less travelled', *Bangkok Post*, 17 April.
Atkinson, J.M. and Errington, S. (1990) *Power and Difference: Gender in Island Southeast Asia*, Stanford, CA: Stanford University Press.

Barmé, S. (1995) 'Talking Women: Early Twentieth Century Discourses on Women in Siam', paper presented at the conference on Gender and Sexuality in Modern Thailand, Australian National University.

Boonsue, K. (1989) *Buddhism and Gender Bias: An Analysis of a Jataka Tale*, Thai Studies Project, Working Paper Series, No. 3, Toronto: York University.

Cook, N. (1998) ' "Dutiful daughters", Estranged Sisters: Women in Thailand', in K. Sen and M. Stivens (eds) *Gender and Power in Affluent Asia,* London and New York: Routledge, pp. 250–90.

Ekachai, S. (1996) 'Crusading for Nun's Rights', *Bangkok Post*, 4 September.

—— (2001) 'The Rules are There to be Tested', *Bangkok Post*, 3 May.

Falk, M.L. (2000) 'Women In Between: Becoming Religious Persons in Thailand', in E.B. Findly (ed.) *Women's Buddhism Buddhism*'s *Women: Tradition, Revision, Renewal*, Boston: Wisdom Publication, pp. 37–57.

—— (2007) *Making Fields of Merit: Buddhist Female Ascetics and Gendered Orders in Thailand,* Washington: University of Washington Press/Copenhagen: NIAS Press.

—— (2008) 'Gender and Religious Legitimacy in Thailand', in W. Burghoorn, K. Iwanaga, C. Milwertz and Q. Wang (eds) *Gender Politics in Asia: Women Manoeuvring within Dominant Gender Orders*, Copenhagen: NIAS Press, pp. 95–120.

Gardiner, H. and Gardiner, O. (1991) 'Women in Thailand', in L. Alder (ed.) *Women in Cross-Cultural Perspective*, New York: Praeger, pp. 175–88.

Gross, R.M. (1993) *Buddhism after Patriarchy: A Feminist History, Analysis, and Reconstruction of Buddhism*, Albany: State University of New York Press.

Hanks, L. and Hanks, J.R. (1963) 'Thailand: Equality between the Sexes', in Barbara Ward (ed.) *Women in the New Asia.* Paris: UNESCO, pp. 424–51.

Hantrakul, S. (1988) 'Prostitution in Thailand', in G. Chandler, N. Sullivan and J. Branson (eds) *Development and Displacement: Women in Southeast Asia,* Clayton, Australia: Monash Papers on Southeast Asia – No. 18: 115–36.

Iwanaga, K. (2008) 'Women in Thai Politics', in K. Iwanaga (ed.) *Women's Political Participation and Representation in Asia: Obstacles and Challenges,* Copenhagen: NIAS Press, pp. 173–209.

Janssen, P. (2001) 'Thai Novice Attempts to Launch Female Monkhood', *Yasodhara*, 17, 3: 15–16.

Jayawardena, K. (1986) *Feminism and Nationalism in the Third World*, London and New Jersey: Zed Books.

Jeffrey, L.A. (2002) *Sex and Borders: Gender, National Identity, and Prostitution Policy in Thailand*, Chiang Mai: Silkworm Press.

Kabilsingh, C. (1991) *Thai Women in Buddhism,* Berkeley, CA: Parallax Press.

Keyes, C.F. (1984) 'Mother or Mistress but Never a Monk: Buddhist Notions of Female Gender in Rural Thailand', *American Ethnologist*, II, 2: 223–41.

—— (1986) 'Ambiguous Gender: Male Initiation in a Northern Thai Buddhist Society', in C.W. Bynum, S. Harrell and P. Richman (eds), *Gender and Religion: On the Complexity of Symbols*, Boston: Beacon Press, pp. 66–96.

Khin Thitsa (1980) *Providence and Prostitution: Image and Reality for Women in Buddhist Thailand*, London: Change International Reports, Women and Society.

Law, L. (2000) *Sex Work in Southeast Asia: The Place of Desire in a Time of AIDS*, London and New York: Routledge.

Phongpaichit, P. (1982) *From Peasant Girls to Bangkok Masseuses*, Geneva: International Labour Office.

Pongsapich, A. (1986) 'Status of Women's Activities in Thailand', in A. Pongsapich (ed.) *Women's Issues, Book of Readings*, Bangkok: Chulalongkorn University Social Research Institute, pp. 134–54.

—— (1997) 'Feminism Theories and Praxis: Women's Social Movement in Thailand', in V. Somsawasdi and S. Theobald (eds) *Women, Gender Relations and Development in Thai Society*, Chiang Mai: Women's, Gender Relations and Development in Thai society, pp. 3–51.

Satha-Anand, S. (ed.) (1999) 'Truth over Convention: Feminist Interpretations of Buddhism', in C. Howland (ed.) *Religious Fundamentalisms and the Human Rights of Women*, New York: St Martin's Press, pp. 281–92.

—— (ed.) (2004) *Power, Knowledge and Justice*, Seoul: Ewha Womans University Press.

Sponberg, A. (1992) 'Attitudes Towards Women and the Feminine in Early Buddhism', in J.I. Cabezon (ed.) *Buddhism, Sexuality and Gender*, Albany: State University of New York Press, pp. 3–36.

Tantiwirmanond, D. (2007) 'The Growth and Challenges of Women's Studies in Thailand', *Interventions: International Journal of Postcolonial Studies*, 9, 2: 194–208.

Tantiwiramanond, D. and Pandey, S.R. (1991) *By Women, For Women: A Study of Women's Organizations in Thailand*, Singapore: Institute of Southeast Asian Studies.

Thomson, V.S. and Bhongsvej, M. (2003) 'Advocating for Women in Politics by NGOs in Thailand', unpublished paper presented at Gender in Asia Conference, Halmstad, Sweden.

Tiyavanich, K. (1997) *Forest Recollections: Wandering Monks in Twentieth-Century Thailand*, Honolulu: University of Hawaii Press.

Tsedroen, J. (1988) 'The Significance of the Conference', in K.L. Tsomo (ed.) *Sakyadhita: Daughters of the Buddha*, Ithaca, NY: Snow Lion Publication, pp. 31–52.

Tsomo, K.L. (ed.) (1988) *Sakyadhita: Daughters of the Buddha*, Ithaca NY: Snow Lion Publications.

—— (ed.) (2000) *Innovative Buddhist Women,* Richmond, UK: Curzon Press.

Van Esterik, P. (2000) *Materializing Thailand*, Oxford: Berg.

Vichitranonda, S. and Bhongsvej, M. (2008) 'NGO Advocacy for Women in Politics in Thailand', in K. Iwanaga (ed.) *Woman and Politics in Thailand: Continuity and Change*, Copenhagen: NIAS Press, pp. 54–94.

Wongchaisuwan, T. and Tamronglak, A.W. (2008) 'Political Participation of Thai Middle-Class Women', in K. Iwanaga (ed.) *Woman and Politics in Thailand: Continuity and Change,* Copenhagen: NIAS Press, pp. 237–64.

8 Following the trail of the fairy-bird

The search for a uniquely Vietnamese women's movement

Alessandra Chiricosta

Is it possible to speak of a uniquely 'Vietnamese' feminist movement? Vietnamese and non-Vietnamese scholars, writing from both inside and outside the country, frequently ponder this question (Duong 2001; Tran Thi Van Anh and Le Ngog Hung 1997; Turner and Phan 1998). In so doing, they explore the peculiar and sometimes ambiguous paths taken by activists in the women's movement as their nation moved from kingdom to colony and through wars to the current Communist Party-led republic. Their project of excavating the particularities of Vietnamese feminism is complicated by the absence of a single word that directly correlates to the English term 'feminism' in the Vietnamese language.[1] In its place they talk of 'a movement that seeks to improve the status of women' within discussions infused variously with nationalist, modernist, socialist and patriotic sentiments. The persistent public narratives about the improvement of women's status in Vietnam attest to the importance of this aspect of social change to national identity in a rapidly globalizing world. This chapter explores the current dominant perceptions of the evolution of the Vietnamese women's movement from its mythic origins through to the present. In so doing, it emphasizes the movement's ambivalent and sometimes contradictory nature. The chapter argues that the ongoing desire to locate a 'uniquely Vietnamese' movement has often simultaneously promoted and obstructed the development of a self-conscious feminism. The 'myth of uniqueness' has drawn upon deep cultural symbols and ideals of femininity that have circulated for generations, but it also resides in longstanding images of female resistance and active participation in social and political movements by women.

The origin of the myth

The myth of 'uniqueness' originates in the legendary figure of Au Co, Mother of the Vietnamese people and the Vietnamese nation. According to one of Vietnam's most popular folk tales, Au Co was a fairy-bird—the daughter of the King of the North and an Immortal. The legend tells of Au Co's love for the Dragon King's son, Lac Long Quan. Disobeying her father's wishes, she elopes with her beloved and eventually marries him. Au Co then gave birth to 100 eggs, from which spring 100 sons. But, their union was not to last. Lac Long Quan wanted to leave

Au Co and announced: 'I am descended from dragons, you from fairies. We are as incompatible as water is with fire. So we cannot continue in harmony.' Thus resolved, the husband and wife parted ways with Lac Long Quan taking fifty of their sons seaward, and Au Co taking the other fifty into the mountains. Her eldest son became Vietnam's first monarch, Hung Vuong.

This legend has been interpreted in myriad different ways, and one of these has emphasized its significance in shaping Vietnam's women's movement. The story of Au Co, it is said, testifies to the presence of an original 'matriarchy' in North Vietnam and led to the double kinship system, which developed there. Such a system combined matrilineal and patrilineal patterns of family structure and assigned equal importance to both lines. Some Vietnamese scholars, such as Thi Tu and Le Thi Nham Tuyet (1978), use this 'matriarchal' aspect of the myth to differentiate Vietnamese society from the pervasive spread of Chinese Confucian patriarchy. A matriarchal social order, they argue, characterized Vietnamese society and marked it as distinctive from the invading Chinese.[2] Archaeological, textual and ritual materials are regularly invoked to support this core feature of Vietnamese distinctiveness (Ngo Duc Thinh 1999). Thus, the uniquely high status of women in Vietnam has become an emblem of national distinctiveness and is buttressed by the power of the national myth of origin. It is now commonly believed that through its long history, Vietnamese women assumed higher status and greater autonomy than women in other societies in East and South East Asia.

Vietnam's histories of war with its dominant neighbour, China, also provide productive space for the elucidation of a narrative wherein the status of Vietnamese women marks the nation as distinctive. Women feature prominently as warriors and defenders 'in a country one-third of whose history of formation is the wars of national liberation and defence' (La Nham Thin in Le Thi Nham Tuyet 2002: 9). The Trung sisters (14–43 CE) and Lady Trieu (226–48 CE), each of whom were leaders of revolts against Chinese rulers, loom large in the pantheon of militant and brave Vietnamese patriots.[3] Women are key icons of heroism in the fight against Chinese cultural and political domination. And resistance to China's colonization of Vietnam, when framed within the view that Vietnam was originally a matriarchy, produces women's struggles for liberation from (Chinese) patriarchy as a metaphor for the entire nation's struggle for Vietnamese independence.

On the one hand, this discursive role contributed to enhancing the significance attributed to 'femininity' in Vietnam but, on the other, it progressively reduced the attention paid to tangible feminine subjugation—women's experiences were more often considered in symbolic terms rather than in concrete, practical reality. The long-term negative consequences of interweaving the narratives of a valiant struggle against gender discrimination and the noble fight against military occupation become clear after Vietnam gained its political independence from the Chinese empire in 938. Confucian values persisted in Vietnam long after the withdrawal of Chinese forces and legendary figures of fighting heroines have progressively been replaced by more compliant and submissive female images as ideals of Vietnamese femininity. Nonetheless, as the following section on political and legal rights demonstrates, Vietnamese women had access to rights that were unimaginable in many other parts of the world.

The political and legal status of women in dynastic Vietnam

Although patriarchal Confucian structures have shaped the Vietnamese court since the third century CE, they were only officially adopted as state doctrine during the tenth century under the Ly dynasty. But, as Le Thanh Tong's (1422–97) *Hong Duc* Code of the fifteenth century shows, Confucianism was altered to fit its new context—the Code guaranteed women's high status in many important aspects of life (Van Tai Ta 1981). It included many distinctly Vietnamese features, mainly in respect of female dignity. For example, the *Hong Duc* Code prohibited marriage without the woman's consent; even after an official announcement, a woman could break her engagement if her future husband was deemed critically ill, found guilty of a serious crime, or if he squandered his family property. After marriage, a wife could divorce her husband if he abandoned her for more than five months, or, if the couple had children together, after a period of one year. A man could not divorce his wife simply on the grounds of illness, and neither could she be divorced if she was judged guilty of minor crimes. Furthermore, a married woman was guaranteed protection from enslavement, and had the right to inherit property from her family. The *Hong Duc* Code also stipulated an equal division of the family inheritance between daughters and sons. Remarkably, in the absence of sons, the first daughter would be allowed to perform the rituals of ancestor worship. As Darce Frenier and Mancini have suggested (Frenier and Mancini 1996), during the thirteenth century women were also able to participate in the exams for entrance to the Mandarinate and to serve the Imperial Court. However, the degree of the women's influence, the length of their Mandarinate and the nature of its functions remain unclear. In each of these respects, the *Hong Duc* Code differs from the laws of dynastic China.

Nonetheless, alongside this comparatively advanced legal code women were still expected to marry, and once married to take care of children, and to obey their husbands and parents-in-law. Preserving 'family harmony' was considered their first duty, because, in good Confucian style, family happiness was deemed to be the base of community and national stability. This concept of 'family harmony' implicitly included the idea of a wife's self-sacrifice for the sake of male family members.[4]

Paradoxically, as memories of Chinese domination grew more distant, the reality of Confucian-style patriarchy grew stronger. The first Nguyen emperor (1808–19) adopted the *Gia-long* Code, inspired by a Qing Legal Code from China that drastically reduced woman's rights, especially at the elite level. This new legal system undermined the comparatively favourable position for women embedded in the preceding *Hong Duc* Code. For example, it removed the women's right to sit the civil service examinations to enter the Mandarinate. The Nguyen-led dynasty promoted a Confucian-inspired book of 'manners', the *Gia Huan Ca* (Family Training Ode). An exposition of 'proper' female behaviour, the *Gia Huan Ca* outlines the principles designed to shape perfect daughters and wives. Summarized into four sections—*cong* (housework); *dung* (appearance); *ngon* (speech); *hanh* (conduct)—these guidelines indicate that women were generally expected to confine themselves to domestic spaces, and to occupy their time taking care of parents, husband, parents-in-law and sons.[5]

A 'double standard' in gender norms emerged where women from the upper echelons of society were expected to uphold these restrictive codes while women from the lower rungs of society were able to function under more relaxed rules. The normative Vietnamese system showed—and to some extent still shows—a strong discrepancy between the laws issued by the central authority and norms adopted in rural areas among ordinary people. The village is regarded as 'the heart and the roots' of Vietnamese society and its local laws carry sustained weight. The popular proverb 'The king's law yields to village customs' encapsulates this idea and underlines the importance of concepts such as 'customs', 'tradition' and 'unwritten laws' in Vietnamese culture. However, these concepts tend to be extremely vague and loosely defined, and therefore difficult to challenge. For example, from a gender perspective the strength of 'unwritten laws' could lead to a lack of critical reflection on ideas such as female 'traditional role', 'natural duties', or 'proper behaviour'.

Rural women's comparatively high degree of freedom is evident in the traditional folk songs, *Ca Dao* (unaccompanied songs). In contrast to the Chinese-influenced poems that circulated in court and among the elites, the *Ca Dao* tell of the everyday life and the concerns of ordinary Vietnamese. The most common theme is relations between the sexes: lost love, husbands complaining about wives, wives whinging about husbands, conjugal fidelity and infidelity, sexuality, marital bliss, critiques of polygamy and arranged marriages. *Ca Dao* were an important cultural phenomena because they allowed women to voice their sometimes critical and ironical opinions on society, morality and men, whereas men and male perspectives dominated the Chinese-influenced 'high literature' of the elites. The current elevated status of the *Ca Dao* as key relics of a Vietnamese national literary heritage, and the major roles of women in the songs, further buttresses the idea that Vietnamese women's active participation in society is fundamental to Vietnamese-ness. However, the arrival of the French colonial forces in 1846 meant that the status of women would enter a startling new phase—not only one of colonial subjugation but also engagement with grand liberationist philosophy.

The colonial period

French colonization in Vietnam had contradictory effects on woman's emancipa-tion. On the one hand, the 'new ideas' of freedom, equality and brotherhood (or, in this case, sisterhood) pronounced in the French Revolution began to circulate among upper classes, opening new avenues of discussion and potential new frontiers for female empowerment. On the other hand, the position of inferiority as colonized subjects that all Vietnamese found themselves in was particularly harsh for women—they were doubly dominated: by Vietnamese male patriarchy and by the arrogant leadership of a colonial regime. The French replaced the Chinese as the dangerous foreign threat to Vietnamese nation and culture. Women's symbolic roles as markers of 'authentic' Vietnamese-ness and as resistance fighters that defended this 'original' Vietnamese national integrity were reaffirmed in this new phase of Vietnam's history. But, the colonizers also brought a 'modernizing' rhetoric of improvement, advancement and expansion to the nation. Embedded in this rhetoric, the French carried the assumption that Vietnamese women, like all non-Western women, required liberating from backward local cultural practices by superior modern, French civilization. Vietnamese women became the 'objects' of French colonial 'improvement' plans.

The French colonial regime targeted women's education as a key arena for their civilizing mission. And, although the access of women and girls to education appeared to improve during the French occupation, it was almost exclusively reserved for women belonging to urban elite. A far smaller proportion of women than men enrolled in schools and female education did not extend to the higher levels. Moreover, the French educational system in Vietnam was characterized by ethnocentrism, native culture being considered less developed and 'evolved' than European, thus contributing to an enhanced sense of inferiority in the Vietnamese consciousness.

Female labour force participation also grew noticeably during these years, albeit from a high base. The commercial sector had blossomed under the pre-colonial Nguyen leadership and women featured prominently in this expansion because the civil service examination system had excluded them from the Mandarinate. Women's inability to access careers in the bureaucracy combined with the low social esteem of merchants resulted in their increased participation in commerce. Under the new colonial regime, women continued to participate in the public economic sphere, reinforcing their status as members of the powerful national bourgeoisie. But social discrimination and gender disparities inside the family persisted, meaning that paid work outside the domestic arena did not relieve women of their duties as wife, daughter-in-law and mother within the home (Marr 1976).

Women's engagement with the colonial order also drew them into contact with a global, but particularly the French, feminist movement. From the start of the twentieth century, small groups of women, largely from the urban elite, began to reflect critically on women's issues and to publish their ideas in books, novels and newspapers. Progressively, by the 1930s the debate moved from theoretical speculation to more practical activities, and the publications of these nascent feminist-groups metamorphosed into serious social and political critiques (McHale 1995). Male scholars and commentators variously praised and condemned the women's literary and political projects. On the one hand, they valued the growth of women's culture but, on the other, they regarded female literature to be 'weak and emotive' because of women's essential '*am* (*yin*) nature'.[6] In opposition to the conservatives, women writers and activists joined the radical reformers of the Phong Trao Tho Moi (the 'Free verse' movement) that rejected the dominance of 'high literature' influenced by Chinese styles and advocated a free metrical style with greater freedoms in literary content. Similarly they were active in the promotion of the use of a Roman alphabet, called *Quoc Ngu*, rather than Chinese characters for the written version of Vietnamese. The women saw their fight against the Chinese poetic model as a revolt against Confucian hegemony and a challenge to male superiority.

A direct fight against patriarchy took place in specialist magazines as well. For example, in Cochinchina in 1919, the *Nu Gioi Chuong* (Women's Bell) appeared. The *Nu Gioi Chuong* was the first magazine run entirely by women in which female issues were directly addressed and discussed. At this time, Vietnam's feminists found inspiration primarily from French feminism, and the colonial authorities viewed the entire operation of feminist publishing with some suspicion, fearing the spread of ideas originating from the French Revolution. Similarly, some upper-class Vietnamese men, many of whom were trained in French or Western schools, also refuted the feminist ideas expressed in these magazines and books. They considered 'Western feminism' to be unsuitable for Vietnamese women. Instead, Vietnam's women were encouraged to find models and values from within their own tradition. Paradoxically, the men who so vociferously prompted the search for 'Vietnamese values' among their womenfolk had received a Westernized style of education.

Regardless of this opposition, the feminist magazine editors and their readers formed, according to several scholars (Duong 2001; Ngo Vin Long 1974), the first, and to some extent, the only, real feminist movement of twentieth-century Vietnam. The popular reach of this movement should not be underestimated. For instance, *Phu Nu Tan Van* (New Literature on Women), first published on 2 May 1929, reached a circulation of 10,000 copies, making it the most widely sold magazine in Indochina (Ngo Vinh Long 1974). *Phu Nu Tan Van* published research and discussion papers concerning women's issues, particularly focusing on subjects which interested urban, middle-class women. As well as promoting the aforementioned literary and linguistic revolution, the magazine's editors directly addressed moral and social issues, such as polygamy and the core Confucian maxims for women known as 'The Three Obediences' that exhorted women to obey their fathers before marriage, their husbands after marriage and their sons in widowhood. Articles published also decried the limited nature of women's access to education, protested inequality in employment options for women and argued against the disparity between men and women's wage remuneration. Significantly, over the course of its publication history, the magazine increasingly sharpened its critique of Vietnam's male-dominated society to include an exploration of the conditions of lower-class women. In this, *Phu Nu Tan Van*'s authors sought to create a notion of 'sisterhood' that transcended class divides.

Writing and reading eventually led to action. By the end of 1929, Vietnam's feminists established the Nu luu hoc hoi (Women Studies Associations), with the goal of raising funds to enable lower-class girls access to education. In addition, thanks to the Nu luu hoc hoi scholarships—often entirely financed by the *Phu Nu Tan Van* editors—several middle-class schoolgirls were able to study in France.

At this time, the women regarded France as being more likely to offer a superior education and be more sensitive to women's issues and equal rights. The intention of Nu luu hoc hoi was to offer a real opportunity for girls to escape from the constraints of Confucian obligations, thus forming a new generation of women capable of enhancing female status in Vietnam. However, this approach was limited by a naïve idealization of the status of Western women, who were in fact far from achieving genuine equality. This reflects the extent to which the Vietnamese feminists had interiorized a 'sense of inferiority' vis-à-vis 'Western feminism' as a result of years of ethnocentric colonial education.

Paradoxically, as the *Phu Nu Tan Van* editors became increasingly interested in the concerns of lower-class women, they adopted a Marxist suspicion of French feminism, which became associated with 'bourgeois' values. Some articles criticized the 'irresponsible' behaviour of Vietnamese women with French education for their imitation of French colonial ways, their preference for speaking French rather than Vietnamese and their penchant for luxury and expensive styles. Such women were accused of arrogantly ignoring the sufferings of their poorer 'sisters' and betraying the Vietnamese feminist cause. Furthermore, they were held responsible for exacerbating the hardships of Vietnam's lower classes by their support of colonial policies and their exploitation of Vietnamese resources for their 'Western-like' individualistic pleasures. These critical perspectives reflected the growing influence of the newly formed Indochinese Communist Party (est. 1930). Led by Ho Chi Minh, the party promoted left-wing anti-colonial ideas and they quickly circulated among a host of social classes. In their view, even French feminism should be rejected as another manifestation of French colonial power that perpetuated social discrimination and divisions in the Vietnamese nation.

Despite the Communist Party's suspicion of 'bourgeois feminism', Vietnam's feminists found more support among socialists than they did among the French-speaking 'bourgeois male' intellectuals. For the socialists, female subordination was evidence of 'feudal' conceptions of relations between the sexes, and was exacerbated by Western capitalist colonialism. Thus, sex equality became one of the goals of the national struggle for socialism. Inspired by Ho Chi Minh's liberationist narrative, Vietnamese feminists increasingly adopted this interpretation of the role of the women's movement within the broader nationalist struggle.

The effects of the international economic depression of the 1930s confirmed the importance of socialist theories of inequality for *Phu Nu Tan Van*'s editors. The depression aggravated women's working and social conditions and spurred women activists to examine the underlying social and political causes of sex inequality and the roles that colonialism, capitalism and 'traditional' Vietnamese culture played in perpetuating women's oppression. The journal published research about life in rural Vietnam, complete with interviews, and revealed to urban readers a distressing scenario of discrimination, poverty and abuses, for which the Vietnamese bourgeois class was held responsible. The magazine increasingly gave space over to peasant women who fiercely criticized the hypocrisy of urban feminists. Vietnam's feminist was increasingly infused with socialist thinking.

As Ngo Vinh Long pointed out, two articles, published in *Phu Nu Tan Van* on 29 March 1934, reveal the new direction chosen by Vietnam's key feminists:

> The question of women is only an aspect of the entire social question. Therefore, in order to solve the question of women, we must first finish solving the question of the society. We do not agree with the 'bourgeois feminist movement'. This movement has become very heated all over the world and has to a certain extent affected our sisters. For the last few years we have heard much discussion by our sisters from the south to the north. ... But the common women of our country will not benefit in any way when a handful of women on the top of a privileged class have the right to enter educational institutions, to work in offices, to become lawyers, judges, etc. ... The bourgeois feminist movement cannot solve the entire question of women. ... We must change the economic system so that we can create a better society in which women and men will not have to be oppressed by any economic or educational forces.
>
> (*Phu Nu Tan Van*, 29 March 1934)

The second article, based on the first, drew the following conclusions:

> If the present economic system is not changed, then when women come out to take jobs from men, there will be fiercer labour competition. This benefits neither men nor women. This is because the special skills of the individuals will decrease in value with that competition and will only profit a small number of owners who have concentrated the means of production in their hands. If the demand is only for equality with men in the professional field, then this equality will not help to eliminate all other inequality in the society.
>
> (*Phu Nu Tan Van*, 29 March 1934; Chiem 1967)

At the end of 1934, the colonial authorities forced the closure of *Phu Nu Tan Van* on the basis that these articles were politically subversive. But, the marriage of feminism with socialism in Vietnam was already confirmed, forged through the passion of national liberation, as the next section reveals.

Feminism's marriage with socialism

Unlike the earlier 'literary feminism', Vietnamese socialism provided women activists legitimate access to participation in the key political struggles of their time (Taylor 1999; Tetreault 1991). Ho Chi Minh's path to socialism was uniquely entwined with the nationalistic struggle for independence both from the French occupation and from a legacy of Chinese cultural hegemony. Ho's path is composed of a mélange of theories and practices drawn from around the world and adapted to the Vietnamese context by the incorporation of elements from local traditions. The 'myth of uniqueness' of the comparatively higher status of Vietnamese woman regained energy within this context as part of these 'local traditions'. It was a powerful rational for enhancing women's status within the Party.[7] The interweaving of the national liberation and women's liberation causes revitalized the figure of Au Co. In this new environment, she came to symbolize the traditional, national essence of femininity and the new, liberated Vietnamese woman. In this rubric, the latter was a return to an original form of Vietnamese womanhood in which women had always held high status.

In linking their struggle with the national cause, Vietnam's feminists once more decided to follow 'the trail of the fairy-bird', and sought to embody the ideals of an 'original Vietnamese femininity' that placed women in an elevated position relative to women elsewhere in the world. Joining the fight for independence and socialism, women expected to achieve equal rights and status in a better and freer society. In keeping with the international socialist trends, Vietnam's feminists adopted the view that an 'independent' (i.e. non-socialist) feminist movement was futile. They accepted that feminism was a limited theory that had originated in a capitalist context to serve 'bourgeois interests' and would not liberate all the nation's women. But, in addition to this then standard socialist position on the limitation of 'bourgeois feminism', Vietnam's socialism linked this futile 'independent' feminism to 'Western' interests and declared its unfitness for Vietnamese women. The authentic 'Vietnamese feminist' path was one embedded within Ho Chi Minh's fight for the nation's 'freedom, independence and happiness'.

As part of the Ho Chi Minh style of socialist national liberation, women fought alongside men (Turley 1972; Eisen 1984), first in the struggle for independence against French colonization and later against the USA (1954–75). The figure of the 'fighting heroine' stood prominently in communist propaganda and drew on the emblematic ancient female figures, such as Lady Trieu, the Trung Sisters and Princess Tien Hung. These patriotic women warriors were repeatedly invoked in speeches at public rallies and were re-workings of a time-proven model of female devotion and self-sacrifice for new circumstances. Moreover, from the formation of the party in 1930 and in conformity with practices in communist parties the world over, a separate structure specifically designed to address women's concerns was embedded in its structure. Called the Vietnamese Women's Union (VWU), this mass organization was founded in order to promote 'equality' because, as Pettus (2003) notes, 'the Indochinese Communist Party (ICP) recognized women as the most exploited members of an oppressed society, as the "slaves of slaves" and explicitly linked women's emancipation to the Vietnamese people's freedom from feudal and capitalistic rule'.

But women's concerns within the ICP could not stand outside of the broader crisis impacting the party, the nation and, indeed, the region in the mid-twentieth century. French colonial control had collapsed in the face of Japan's military expansion in World War II. With the defeat of Japan in 1945, the French sought to reassert their colonial control but found to their surprise a fierce local and highly organized resistance had formed around the ICP and the charismatic Ho Chi Minh. Ho's forces had famously defeated the French at Diem Bien Phu and in the ensuing peace negotiations agreed to a divided nation on the promise of free elections that would eventually unite the nation. The peace terms of the 1954 Geneva Accord divided the nation at the Seventeenth Parallel giving the South to a coalition of local anti-Communist groups supported by the USA and the French. The promised elections never emerged and the country descended into a second but more protracted war. The North emerged victorious in 1975 and the ideals of Vietnam's socialist womanhood were spread nationally.

Prior to unification of the country, in the North the alliance between the women's movement, the national cause and Marxism resulted in a progressive betterment of female rights and status. For example, women won the right to vote, divorce, abortion, education and wage equality. Polygamy and child marriage were outlawed.[8] During the 1950s and 1960s, the party intensified its efforts in giving shape to the 'new female model' that would demonstrate the success of Marxist–Leninist theories in the Vietnamese context and stand as evidence of enlightened socialist leadership (Novelo Vignal 1982). The party promoted public appreciation of women's presence not only in the battlefield but also in politics, in leading agricultural and industrial cooperatives, and in forging scientific and technical careers.

Historical materialism underpinned these legislative changes and the party saw its work on gender as part of a campaign to eradicate 'feudal' attitudes towards women. The Communist Party and later, the party-led government has taken this classic Marxist periodization into its policies aimed at achieving 'equality of men and woman' (Vietnam Women's Union 1997). The nationalist patriotic 'fairy-bird' narrative, wherein Vietnam's women 'originally' held high status, is melded onto the classic Marxist historical materialist notion of a linear progress of history (wherein human history moves from slave society, through feudalism and capitalism to ultimately arrive at socialism and communism). Vietnamese socialism did not aim to completely eradicate 'traditional culture'—rather it sought to find a connection between the traditional past and the socialist present. In this project, the reinterpretation of ancient myths, and sometimes the creation of 'new' ancient myths, played important roles. The implicit idea was to avoid a complete loss of national identity because this could potentially reinforce the Chinese communist influence in Vietnam.

The mass organization targeting women, the VWU, was charged with the duty of promoting popular appreciation of the uniquely Vietnamese model of womanhood within its broad programme of promoting gender equality. The VWU, originally conceived of as a mass organization broadly representing the rights and interests of women in all strata, was very efficient at the grass-roots level. As Schuler (2006) reminds us, through its health, development, educational and cultural activities, the VWU helps to communicate and implement government policies at the local level. Its programmes include health promotion, cultural and educational activities, and a wide range of interventions to support economic development, issuing directives to strengthen the trend towards women's emancipation in work. To give an example, the 1967 Law stipulated that in situations where women comprised 40 per cent of the labour force of a factory or cooperative, the management committee of that workplace must include a woman. When women comprised 50 per cent of a given labour force, the assistant manager must be a woman. Furthermore 'By providing for their training, the directive also encourages women to advance to more skilled positions and to participate more in the work of state offices and enterprises' (Bergman 1974: 214). As the primary vehicle for policy development and for the implementation of gender equality, the VWU has created a vast network for the implementation of a wide variety of programmes to support women's advancement (Khiet 2000). In 1946, the first year women ever voted in Vietnam, women held only ten out of the 403 seats in the National Assembly. By the Fourth National Assembly, in 1970, there were 125 women among 420 members. Women's membership in the district-level councils rose from 26 per cent to 43 per cent between 1965 and 1969, while at the local village level, women were the chairpersons in 4,300 out of a total of 5,000 People's Councils (Bergman 1974). Membership in the union was open to all women over sixteen years old, to special-interest groups (for instance ethnic minorities) and to women's sections within trade unions.

The VWU represents women to the government and the government depends on the counsel and advice of the VWU to defend women's rights, to design new laws and to implement all laws to protect women. A number of the leaders of the VWU are leaders of the government of the Democratic Republic of Vietnam as well. The VWU works to strengthen various services that meet the needs of women: adult education, child care, canteens, community service teams, and health education and maintenance.

The VWU's publicity organ, the magazine *Phu Nu Viet Nam* (Vietnamese Woman), disseminated details of its work nationally and internationally. *Phu Nu Viet Nam* was a key mechanism by which the idea of a particularly Vietnamese 'socialist womanhood' was popularized. In the 1950s and 1960s, the magazine often adopted a pedagogical approach (i.e. reporting personal emblematic experiences and fictional stories with moral messages) and encouraged Vietnamese women towards making personal transformations in their own lives in order to achieve an 'equal and better society'. However, this approach and the model of female ideals promoted were not without their difficulties. Failure to achieve the ideal on a daily basis resulted in many women feeling inadequate or overwhelmed with the burden of the responsibility they were shouldering in the personal and public realm. The problems inherent in these early VWU programmes are exemplified by the 1961 'Five Goods' campaign (*Phong Trào "5 Tốt"*). Aimed at encouraging women to 'do all things, and do all things well', the campaign mirrored the proscriptive and didactic nature of the Confucian 'Four Virtues'.[9] Women were exhorted to:

1   Fulfil the goals of production and economize well.
2   Follow all state policies and laws.
3   Participate in leadership.
4   Advance in their studies.
5   Raise their families and educate their children well.

Women who failed to achieve these goals were considered responsible for damaging the reputation of their families and also the entire nation. Moreover, the recorded personal testimonies of countless Vietnamese women demonstrate that most Vietnamese families were still imprisoned in 'feudal' dynamics that restricted women's ability to achieve the listed goals. However, by labouring under slogans such as 'Our hearts may stop beating, but our machines will not stop running!' or 'Improve your skills, compete to be good workers', Vietnamese women became 'labour heroines'.

On the one hand, the 'Five Goods' campaign succeeded in increasing the social and economic role of women in the society but, on the other hand, it continued to portray heroic women as 'mothers of the nation': a woman was deemed heroic 'not simply because she attained high production levels during bombings, but because she achieved these results while caring for her children on her own' (Pettus 2003: 44).

In 1974, Vietnamese scholar Nguyen Khac Vien made the astute observation that Vietnamese Marxism (as well as its Chinese counterpart) was deeply rooted in Confucianism and therefore continued to reflect some of the 'backward' aspects of this tradition. Several other scholars followed Nguyen's lead and argued that while the party's model of a new socialist woman enabled her to enter public space as workers and warriors, the more traditional values continued to thrive alongside (Mai Thi Tu and Le Thi Nham Tuyet 1978; Ngo Vinh Long 1974). The traditional model persisted not only inside the family, but also in attitudes towards women's roles in the nation-building project. For example, patriarchal codes, albeit in a milder form than in colonial and dynastic times, still shaped female roles. Endurance, faithfulness, compassion and self-sacrifice were considered women's 'natural' virtues and were deemed invaluable to the national-socialist cause. The highest expression of female moral virtue was seen in the traditional role of devout spouse and mother ready to sacrifice her personal interests for the sake of the nation and the collective.

Significantly, the 'domestic role' of a self-sacrificing and compassionate Vietnamese woman was presented as 'natural' and was not linked to a specific historical context. Pettus (2003: 28) describes women's role in the socialist national political consciousness as follows:

> The Vietnamese woman's dual symbolic role as a marker of revolutionary progress and a vessel of timeless tradition situated her at the core of the party's cultural struggle to forge a uniquely national path to socialist modernity and to project this synthesized ideal to the outside world.

The 'unique' Vietnamese female model was the socialist answer to contrast with a notion of Western feminism that was deemed to be 'individualistic and colonialist' in mentality. The resistance by the French and the USA to Vietnam's ambitions for independence further embittered the VWU about Western feminism and its utility for Vietnamese women. The VWU accused Western feminists of hypocrisy and of holding 'imperialist' mentalities. During the 1960s and 1970s, they deemed Western feminism as having little beneficial theoretical utility to Vietnam's particular circumstances.

From 1965, the exigencies of the war further increased the ICP's interest in women's practical participation in society. That same year the VWU launched the *Ba Dam Dang* (Three Responsibilities) campaign in an effort to confirm women's total commitment to the socialist cause, which asked women:

1   To take charge of agricultural and industrial production, and all other work activities left vacant by men.
2   To manage all family affairs and encourage husbands, sons and brothers to join the army.
3   To support soldiers at the front and to take up arms when necessary.
                                    (Mai Thi Tu and Le Thi Nham Tuyet 1978)

The campaign encouraged women to gain experience in work activities formerly almost exclusively reserved for men, and it expanded their access to knowledge and skills in the scientific and technological fields. However, the party recognized a potential threat to social harmony in this more emancipated female behaviour, especially in the younger generation. In 1975, just before the Northern forces successfully reunified the nation, articles in *Phu Nu Viet Nam* began to critically address the negative consequences of 'individualistic' and 'Western' behaviour growing evident among young urban women. The articles reminded them that their education and work should be exclusively aimed at the collective good.

It was not only in the socialist North that the ideals of Vietnamese women's uniqueness and utility to the national cause was mobilized. The non-socialist South also invoked notions of women's contribution to the nation, albeit in far reduced and less actively theorized forms. Ngo Dinh Nhu, sister-in-law of Southern President Ngo Dinh Diem, founded a women's organization called Phong Trao Phu Nu Lien Doi (Movement for the Solidarity of Women). However, this organization was largely regarded as a vehicle for Ngo's political ambitions rather than a spontaneous, grass-roots women's movement. Ngo became known as the 'Dragon Lady' by her detractors for her pro-Western, her anti-communist position and her support of her brother-in-law. She portrayed herself as the 'charismatic leader of Vietnam's women'. The Phong Trao Phu Nu Lien Doi also sought to invoke the myth of Vietnamese women's uniqueness through a blending of the Vietnamese woman as the original 'Mother of the Nation' with Catholicism. The organization invoked conservative Catholic morality through the promotion of the 1958 Family Law bill, also called the 'Morality Laws', which outlawed abortion, contraceptives, divorce, dance halls, beauty pageants, boxing matches and animal fighting, while closing down brothels and opium dens. It simultaneously invoked the 'traditional fighting spirit' of the Vietnamese woman through its paramilitary wing that sought to engage women in the war against the North. But, in the absence of a VWU-like structure or an explicit theorization of a programme for the enhancement of the status of women, Ngo's organization was more a personal vanity project. To enhance her popular appeal and broad credibility, she likened herself to the elder of the revered Trung sisters and even had a statue of the sisters erected in Saigon with her own facial features as the model for the statues. Thus, governments on both sides of the Seventeenth Parallel found it useful to find new ways of using time-honoured visions of the 'unique Vietnamese woman'.

After the South lost the war in 1975, the VWU extended its operations to the newly reunited country and in so doing faced a new set of challenges. Divided by a civil war, women from the North and South had shared the same burden of sufferings, but sometimes from opposite perspectives. Gaining mutual trust and respect was not an easy task (Goodkind 1995). On the one hand, northern women teamed up with southern women to rebuild farms and houses, give support to women left alone by the war and reunify divided families. On the other hand, prejudice on both sides—northerners saw southerners as 'prostitutes' and southerners viewed northerners as 'cruel'—hindered the creation of a common notion of 'sisterhood'.

During the reconstruction of the war-ravaged areas, the VWU's effective and practical aid to women, sometimes in desperate conditions, went hand in hand with the party's preoccupation with the potentially negative influences of the 'Westernized' South Vietnamese female model. The ICP's overarching view that women's interests should be sacrificed for the sake of family and social harmony was reiterated alongside their claims that the socialist unified nation achieved gender equality, contrary to much objective evidence.

Challenges for the women's movement after Đổi Mới (Renovation)

In 1986, the ICP introduced a radical policy shift that liberalized the economy and moved away from a planned socialist system to one that would more effectively engage with a global multi-sector market economy. The predicted impending collapse of the USSR, the major trading partner for Vietnam, combined with recognition of the positive experience of similar reforms in the Peoples Republic of China encouraged the ICP to make radical shifts in its economic policies. Accordingly, after 1986 they began a process of privatizing state enterprises, promoting foreign investment and trade, legalizing private ownership of land and business and more broadly recognizing the 'household' (rather than the state-organized commune or collective) as the basic economic unit of the country. Vietnam's 'Market Socialism' has produced impressive economic gains, with an average 7.5 per cent GDP growth per annum in 1991–2001.[10] However, there are particular challenges to the status of Vietnamese women as the country moves to a more open-market economy.

The precise impact of *Doi Moi* on women's status is a contentious issue since marketization of the economy and the retreat of the state from direct intervention on social issues, such as women's affairs, has the potential to see a revival of practices that privilege men (Thoa Duong 1992). At stake are some impressive gains that had been made over the preceding decade of peace (1975–86). Vietnam had made striking progress in reducing gender disparities in key areas. The nation has high adult literacy rates for men and women and the highest percentage of women in national parliament in the region (27 per cent since 2002). Vietnam also has one of the highest economic participation rates in the world: 85 per cent of men and 83 per cent of women between the ages of fifteen and sixty participated in the labour force in 2002 (Vietnam Development Report 2004).

Since the early 1990s, academics, government researchers and non-governmental organizations have debated whether the changes brought by the renewal have improved women's social, political and economic status or not. Even though all the population benefits from economic growth, according to Werner and Bélanger (2002: 16)

> the notion of femininity has tended to revert back to pre-socialist norms, particularly among younger urban generations influenced by the lifestyle of Western consumer culture … there is a new balance between the public and private spheres, with the latter seen as reasserting its moral and patriarchal authority.

Neo-Liberal approach exponents might argue that a free-market economy leads to a more effective emancipation through the meritocracy of enterprises. Nonetheless, the Vietnamese case clearly shows that even if women are directly involved in the economic growth process, the female role inside the family, as well as in the work places, is still subordinate to man's (Le Thi Nham Tuyet, Le Van Phung, La Nham Thin 1995).

These changed circumstances present new challenges for the VWU's programme of enhancing the status of women in their nation. As a creature of the ICP, the VWU has been active in participating in spreading the *Doi Moi* policies and this has resulted in a diminution of focus on women's public roles and an increasing focus on their domestic and familial roles. For example, the VWU's activities in urban areas are now focused on family planning, health care, helping women in understanding how to educate children and build up a 'happy family' in a new economic setting. Although female education and participation in economic and social development is highly supported, nevertheless 'unwritten laws' suggest that women should adopt a lower profile in order to preserve family and social harmony. There is a disturbing trend in the VWU towards adopting a non-critical approach to concepts such as 'traditional female role' or 'women's proper duties' and this trend is one of the most insidious obstacles to a real female empowerment in the nation today (Thuan Bich Nguyen and Thomas 2004).

The cultural milieu has altered such that Vietnamese women face pressure not to compete with men in 'their fields' and to fulfil the domestic duties even if they have a job outside (Le Minh 1997; Le Thi Nham Tuyet 1998). Moreover, the relation between mothers-in-law and daughters-in-law continues to be very problematic, mirroring the endurance of Confucian rules inside the family (Barry 1996; Croll 1998). Current government development priorities show a frightening lack of attention to the cultural foundations of gender discrimination. For example,

Lisa Drummond's (2004) analysis of new women's fashion magazines reveals how the image of a successful woman is shifting from a patriotic hard-working heroine to a seductive part-time working housewife responsible for the creation of an 'educated family' rooted in Vietnamese traditions and projected into a new market dimension. An urban, educated ideal has displaced the socialist ideals of the active warrior woman and the noble village woman.

This consolidation of 'traditional roles' is evident in recent studies of girls' vocation selection: Hoang Ba Thinh's research (Le Thi Nham Tuyet 2002: 183) shows that although girl students have the right to register at any university or any courses, the actual tendency is to select subjects 'suitable for women'; that is, teacher training, health, or law. The occupational choice often follows the suggestions given by family members and friends, who advise young girls to choose a career compatible with the 'female nature', namely to be a wife and a mother. The number of girls who attend technical and scientific faculties is decreasing alarmingly, leading to a lack of women, in the near future, who can hold important positions in this key sector.

Due to the evolving historical circumstances outlined above, the VWU can be considered the only 'women's movement' in contemporary Vietnam. Although it is still a very effective organization when promoting gender equality, considering its capacity to collaborate with international non-governmental organizations, the movement's lack of a more independent perspective is still a problematic issue. Nevertheless, in the last two decades it seems that the VWU's philosophy is slightly changing, abandoning, to some extent, the myth of 'uniqueness' and recognizing the necessity of adopting more international perspectives. *Doi Moi* has allowed the VWU to shift its attention from class struggles to issues of 'personal interest and awareness of their rights' (Duong 2001: 278). Therefore, several institutes of research and university curricula on gender issues have been opened: the Centre for the Study of Families and Women (1987); the Centre for Gender, Family and Environment in Development (1992); the Faculty of Women's Studies in Ho Chi Minh City (1992); the Centre for Women's Research and Training (1993); the Centre for the Study of Female Labour. Researchers, professors and writers supported by these organizations have joined the international debate, opening possible new paths for the Vietnamese women's movement.

More recently, local non-governmental organizations and academic institutions have formed a partnership for gender equality known as the Gender and Community Development Network (GENCOMNET). Development agencies and the government also belong to a forum called the Gender Action Partnership (GAP), which, however, has lost momentum since 2004. Within this new scenario, members of the VWU are trying to abandon their 'lonely path' and bridge the gap with international women's movements by participating in the UN conferences on women and promoting the adoption in Vietnam of the 1995 Beijing Declaration and Platform for Action.

Thanks to the effort of the VWU, the new Law on Gender Equality, which follows the guidelines established in the Beijing platform, was signed in 2006 and took effect in 2007 ('National Assembly' 2006). The Law defines key aspects of gender equality in all areas of social and family life, measures to promote gender equality, responsibilities of all public and private agencies, and oversight of violations. It has set out five objectives and twenty quantitative targets to eradicate discrimination and ensure women's equal rights in the fields of labour, employment, education and health care. Moreover, this Law aims to improve the quality of women's participation in economic, political and social fields, and enhance the capacity of national machinery for the advancement of women.

The new 'international' trend of the VWU is also testified by a more critical approach vis-à-vis the party's policies. According to Ha Thi Khiet, head of the National Committee for the Advancement of Women in Vietnam (NCFAW), for instance, even though the new Law on Gender Equality would greatly improve the advancement of women:

> gender inequalities remain in education, while new challenges arising from the nation's moves toward a market economy have exacerbated problems relating to prostitution and the trafficking of women. We, as women, are not yet content with many things which are impeding the advancement of women.
>
> (Hong Thuy 2007)

The VWU now recognizes the limits and risks of its 'unique' path, hoping that international countries would help Vietnam address the problem.

Conclusion

The myth of 'uniqueness' of the Vietnamese way to feminism is a double-edged sword. On the one hand, it creates a strong sense of awareness about women's capability to fulfil diverse duties and achieve success, even in extreme conditions. On the other, by linking the women's cause to a sort of 'national destiny', it reconfirms patriarchal stereotypes by invoking 'traditional' values rather than pro-women values. The 'joyful burden', made of sacrifice and endurance, which the Vietnamese women were asked to bear in order to achieve an 'equal society' has limited their chance of holding an independent perspective on their condition, as well as of creating an independent plan of action aimed to promote their cause. Post-colonial studies have shown us that breaking away from an ethnocentric approach on women's issues is crucial to its success, and the Vietnamese 'fairy-bird' path has shown the dangers of relying on one specific notion of femininity constructed within a single cultural tradition.

Notes

1 Wendy N. Duong (2001) notes, 'The conceptual and linguistic structure of the Vietnamese culture contains no framework for feminism as a doctrine. There is no word for *feminism* or *feminist* in the Vietnamese language (the term *Nu Si* traditionally refers to the female literati, and *Nu Anh Hung* is used for a heroine). Vietnamese researchers of women's studies today define the English word *feminism* in shorthand as a social movement 'aim[ing] to improve the social position of women in concrete ways' (Duong 2001: 194).

2 Benard and Moon point out that the concept of 'matriarchy' (theorized for the first time by Bachofen in 1861) has its origins in an 'intellectual tradition that sees history in terms of an unilinear evolution from matriarchy linked with worship of the Goddess to patriarchy and, eventually, the worship of a single God' (Benard and Moon 2000: 6). Therefore, patriarchy is considered more 'evolved' and 'civilized' than matriarchy. Benard and Moon note that this theory influenced Karl Marx's and Friedrich Engels's views on history as well.

3 The Trung sisters led a revolt against Chinese invasion between 40 and 42 CE. Ba Trieu headed an army against the Chinese riding an elephant in 248 CE. She had a famous mark of distinction: her breasts were so long that she had to throw them over her shoulders while riding into battle. Gloriously defeated at the age of 23, she committed suicide rather than suffer the shame of surrender. She is remembered by her words of defiance: 'I want to rail against the wind and the tide, kill the sharks in the sea, sweep the whole country to save the people from slavery, and I will not give up myself to be their servant-concubine.'

4 Another piece of evidence marshalled to buttress the claim to Vietnamese 'uniqueness' is the word order in a common phrase about family harmony. The famous Vietnamese proverb 'the wife and husband can scoop the east sea dry' places 'wife' before 'husband', leading some scholars to conjecture that women held a dominant position in the family—a view that has been roundly discredited.

5 According to the doctrine of Confucius and Mencius, women had to follow 'The Three Obediences and Four Virtues'. The 'three obediences' are 'obedience to the father and the elder brothers when young, obedience to the husband when married and obedience to the sons when widowed'. The 'four virtues' are: first, 'women's virtue', meaning a woman must know her place under the sun and behave herself and act in every way in compliance with the old ethical code; second, 'women's speech', meaning a woman must not talk too much and take care not to bore people; third, 'women's appearance', meaning a woman must pay attention to adorning herself with a view to pleasing the opposite sex; and fourth, 'women's chore', meaning a woman must willingly do all the household chores.

6 '*Am*' is the Vietnamese word for '*yin*' (feminine principle) and is juxtaposed with '*yang*' (masculine principle) in China's *yin yang* philosophy.

7 Nguyen Thi Binh, for instance, is regarded as a symbol of the women's role in the 'Resistance War'. After the communist victory in April 1975, she was appointed minister of education in united Vietnam. She was elected vice-president of the Socialist Republic of Vietnam in 1992 and then re-elected in 1997 and has served as Vietnamese vice-president again since then.

8 The Marriage and Family Law was passed in 1959 and implemented in 1960. For the first time in Vietnamese history, arranged marriages were abolished and both men and women were granted the freedom to make their own decisions; polygamy was declared illegal and monogamy was adopted as the official form of Vietnamese marriage; equality between men and women was to be practised both in the home and in society in general and the basic rights of women and children, such as freedom from abuse and oppression in the home, were to be protected.

9 See note 1 above.

10 *The Comprehensive Poverty Reduction and Growth Strategy* (2003). The Socialist Republic of Vietnam, Ha Noi, November 2003.

References

'National Assembly of the Socialist Republic of Vietnam: 10th Session of the XI Legislature Law on Gender Equality' (2006). Online. Available HTTP: www.wcwonline.org/pdf/lawcompilation/VIETNAMLawGenderEquality.pdf. (accessed 20 August 2009).

Barry, K. (ed.) (1996) *Vietnam's Women in Transition*, London and New York: Macmillan Press.

Benard, E. and Moon, B. (ed.) (2006) *Goddesses Who Rule*, Oxford and New York: Oxford University Press.

Bergman, A.E. (1974) *Women of Viet Nam*, San Francisco: People Press.

Chiem, T. Keim (1967) *Women in Vietnam: Selected Articles from Vietnamese Periodicals, Saigon, Hanoi, 1957–66*, Honolulu: Institute of Advanced Projects, East-West Center.

Croll, E.J. (1998) *Gender and Transition in China and Vietnam*, Stockholm: Swedish International Development Cooperation Agency.

Drummond, L. (2004) 'The Modern "Vietnamese Woman": Socialization and Women's Magazines', in L. Dummond and H. Rydstrøm (eds) *Gender Practices in Contemporary Vietnam*, Singapore: Singapore University Press.

Duong, N.W. (2001) *Gender Equality and Women's Issues in Vietnam: The Vietnamese Woman—Warrior and Poet*, Washington: Pacific Rim Law & Policy Journal Association.

Eisen, A. (1984) *Women and Revolution in Viet Nam*, London: Zed Books.

Frenier, M.D. and Mancini, K. (1996) 'Vietnamese Women in a Confucian Setting: The Causes of the Initial Decline in the Status of East Asian Women', in K. Barry (ed.) *Vietnamese Woman in Transition*, London and New York: Macmillan, pp. 21–37.

Goodkind, D. (1995) 'Rising Gender Inequality in Vietnam Since Reunification', *Pacific Affairs*, 68, 3: 342–59.

Hong Thuy (2007) 'Women Approve of New Gender Law, but Inequality still Rampant' *Vietnam News*, 29 January 2007. Online. Available HTTP: http://vietnamnews.vnanet. vn/showarticle.php?num=02POP290107 (accessed 20 August 2009).

Khiet Ha Thi (2000) 'Women in 2000: Gender Equality, Development and Peace for the 21st Century'. Speech at the UN General Assembly's 23rd Special Session, New York.

Le Minh (1997) 'Some Problems about the Family and Woman Advancement', *Vietnam Social Sciences*, 57: 71–80.

Le Thi Nham Tuyet (1998) 'National Identity and Gender Characteristics in Vietnam (an approach from socio-anthropological perspectives)', *Vietnam Social Sciences*, 67: 31–9.

—— (ed.) (2002) *Images of the Vietnamese Woman in the New Millennium*, Hanoi: The Gioi Publisher.

Le Thi Nham Tuyet, Le Van Phung and La Nham Thin (1995) *Gioi va phat trien o Viet Nam (Gender and Development in VIETNAM)*, Ha Noi: Khoa Hoc Xa Hoi.

Mai Thi Tu and Le Thi Nham Tuyet (1978) *Women in Vietnam*, Hanoi: Foreign Language Publishing House.

Marr, D. (1976) 'The 1920s Women's Rights Debates in Vietnam', *Journal of Asian Studies*, 35, 3: 371–89.

McHale, S. (1995) 'Printing and Power: Vietnamese Debates over Women's Place in Society, 1918–34', in K.W. Taylor and J.K. Whitmore (eds) *Essays into Vietnamese Pasts*, Ithaca, NY: Southeast Asia Program, Cornell University, pp.173–94.

Ngo Duc Thinh (1999) 'The Pantheon for the Cult of Holy Mothers', *Vietnamese Studies,* 131: 20–35.

Ngo Vinh Long (1974) *Vietnamese Women in Society and Revolution*, Hanoi: Vietnam Resource Centre.

Nguyen Khac Vien (1974) *Tradition and Revolution in Vietnam*, Hanoi: Indochina Resource Centre.

Novelo Vignal, A. (1982) 'La participacion de la mujer Vietnamita en la liberacion nacional y el socialmismo (The Role of Vietnamese Women in National Liberation and Socialism)', *Estudios de Asia y Africa*, 17, 3: 491–515.

Pettus, A. (2003) *Between Sacrifice and Desire. National Identity and the Governing of Femininity in Vietnam*, New York and London: Routledge.

Schuler, S.R. *et al.* (2006) 'Constructions of Gender in Vietnam: In Pursuit of the "Three Criteria"', *Culture, Health & Sexuality*, 8, 5: 383–94.

Taylor, S.C. (1999) *Vietnamese Women at War: Fighting for Ho Chi Minh and the Revolution*, Lawrence: University Press of Kansas.

Tetreault, M.A. (1991) *Women and Revolution in Viet Nam*, East Lansing, MI: Michigan State University.

Thoa Duong (1992) 'On the Present Situation of Vietnamese Women's Living and Working Conditions and Orientations for their Improvement', *Vietnam Social Sciences*, 4: 42–52.

Thuan Bich Nguyen and Thomas, M. (2004) 'Young Women and Emergent Postsocialist Sensibilities in Contemporary Vietnam', *Asian Studies Review*, 28, 2: 133–49.

Tran Thi Van Anh and Le Ngog Hung (1997) *Women and Đổi Mới in Vietnam*, Hanoi: Women's Publishing House.

Turley, W.S. (1972) 'Women in the Communist Revolution in Vietnam', *Asian Survey*, 12, 9: 793–805.

Turner, K.G. and Phan Thanh Hao (1998) *Even the Women Must Fight. Memories of War from North Vietnam*, New York: John Wiley & Sons.

Van Tai Ta (1981) 'Status of Women in Traditional Vietnam: a Comparison of the Code of the Le Dynasty (1428–1788) with the Chinese Codes', *Journal of Asian History*, 15, 2: 97–145.

Vietnam Development Report (2004) *Poverty*. Online. Available HTTP: http://www-wds.worldbank.org/servlet/WDSContentServer/WDSP/IB/2003/11/24/000090341_20031124104423/Rendered/PDF/271300VN.pdf (accessed 23 October 2009).

Vietnam Women's Union (1997) *Rules of the Vietnam Women's Union*, Hanoi: Women's Publishing House.

Werner, J. and Bélanger, D. (2002) *Gender, Household, State: Đổi Mới in Vietnam*, Ithaca, NY: Southeast Asia Program, Cornell University.

Womak, S. (1995) 'The Remakings of a Legend: Women and Patriotism in the Hagiography of the Trung Sisters', *Crossroads*, 9, 2: 31–50.

9 The Hong Kong women's movement

Towards a politics of difference and diversity[1]

Adelyn Lim

Feminism is an expansive, multifaceted discursive field of action that takes different forms at different times, in various economic, political and social contexts, and among women of diverse class and racial groups. There is a multiplicity of places and spaces in which individuals who identify as feminists act, and wherein feminist discourses circulate, from raising consciousness in the community to engaging state apparatus and international aid and development establishments, from producing 'women's culture' (art, literature) for internal consumption to providing services to the community (health, lodging, welfare), from giving priority to research on the self and individual differences to those that emphasize 'sisterhood' (Morgan 1984; Jayawardena 1986; Katzenstein 1987; Mohanty 1991; Margolis 1993; Basu 1995; Melucci 1995; Walker 1995; Heywood and Drake 1997; Alvarez 1999). It is possible to appreciate these different representations of feminisms when we look at women's movements, for they vary in intent and form in complex, multiple ways.

This chapter is an ethnography of the Hong Kong women's movement in the context of burgeoning, globally circulating feminist discourses, as well as Hong Kong's transition from a British colony to governance under the People's Republic of China (PRC) as a Special Administrative Region in 1997.[2] The first section of this chapter is an overview of the Hong Kong women's movement in the twentieth century. Although Jayawardena (1986: 2) argues that 'feminism was not imposed on the third world by the west', colonial ties often determine the links between Western feminists and Third World feminists (Bulbeck 1988; Eisenstein 1997).[3] With its history as a British colony, Western intellectual movements and trends moved freely into Hong Kong and, accordingly, the emergence and development of the Hong Kong women's movement mirrors the major phases of feminism in the West (Tsang 1995). It started with the liberal outlook criticizing gender inequalities in the public and private spheres, moved to the more structural approach to gender subordination and then, in recent years, to the multiple bases of oppression in relation to the constantly shifting axes of identity (Bulbeck 1988; Whelehan 1995; Heywood and Drake 1997).

While these influences from international feminist trends are evident, there are also certain elements within the Hong Kong women's movement that are unique. In contrast to the conventional notion of a women's movement as a visibly recognizable movement with a leadership, a membership, a wide following and a political programme (Molyneux 1998), the emergence and development of the Hong Kong women's movement epitomizes a more decentred and diffused form of collective activism.[4] Local women's organizations with different degrees of identification with feminism address a wide range of issues, including economic issues (employment discrimination, valuation of women's work), family issues (household division of labour, maternity and parental leave, provision of childcare, reproductive rights) and sexual issues (domestic violence, rape, sexual harassment, sex worker rights), as well as adopt various strategies, including lobbying and policy formation, public education, research and publications, and service-provision. While this kind of collective activism has no central coordination, the common goal of improving the position of women in society, the extent of participation, and its overall significance have in cumulative terms come to constitute a women's movement.

In the second section, I utilize academic scholarship on social movements to examine the contemporary Hong Kong women's movement. The transfer of Hong Kong's sovereignty from the British to the PRC has left the Hong Kong women's movement divided on its position towards pro-PRC and pro-democracy political factions in Hong Kong. I illustrate how pro-PRC and pro-democracy women's organizations rely on divergent political opportunities and social networks and use opposing discourses, initiatives and strategies in confronting Violence against Women (VAW). In so doing, I demonstrate how movements that employ different strategies vis-à-vis the state have different political opportunities (Tarrow 1994). I also argue how, in the absence of political opportunities, mobilizing structures and framing processes can facilitate collective action among pro-democracy women's organizations. My inquiry is grounded in and provides empirical support for Goodwin and Jasper's (1999) critique of political opportunities. At the same time, exposure to geographically disparate forms of women's activism in the present era of transnational activism continues to encourage the reflexive scrutiny of localized organizational forms and their representation of women's interests. This diversity within the contemporary Hong Kong women's movement shows how we need to be sensitive to the historically shifting and situationally contingent processes and events that give rise to varying forms of collective action within women's movements.

The Hong Kong women's movement in the colonial period

Britain's rule over Hong Kong commenced formally in 1842 and, as they attempted to establish and maintain control over the Chinese community, the colonial authorities were selective in their intervention within Hong Kong's economy and society. They looked to local business and professional elites to provide community services and conflict mediation in the areas of education, healthcare and housing within the Chinese community, and, in return, local elites enjoyed a certain degree of autonomy from colonial interference. However, the governing strategy of selective intervention constituted legislation and policies with gendered implications. In determining the social issues to be addressed in Hong Kong, local elites failed to create effective institutions to deal with local livelihood issues that predominantly impacted women and children, the elderly, and the working class (Fischler 2003; Lee 2003; Lui *et al.* 2005). Matters pertaining to women did not feature on the colonial authority's agenda and the limited activism by women for political and social reform focused on 'maternalist' initiatives, 'a framework for action whereby educated and usually well-to-do women, drawing equally on their faith in women's superior moral and motherly capacities ... sought to represent and protect less fortunate or vulnerable women and children' (Pedersen 2001: 164, in Fischler 2003: 51), rather than seeking alteration in the colonial administration of Hong Kong.[5]

It was only after World War II that women's activism, designed to effect change in the colony itself, became visible. In 1947, the Hong Kong Council of Women (Heung Gong Fu Loi Sae Wui) was formed by elite expatriate British and local Chinese women, with the general aim of eradicating all forms of discrimination against women in the economic, legal and social arenas. Ellen Li, a local woman from the Chinese elite, founded the council and later became the first woman legislator in Hong Kong in 1966. She was the most prominent and vocal feminist of the post-war period. The council was at the forefront of a coalition of more than 140 organizations in a successful campaign for marriage law reform and the abolition of concubinage in 1970 (Ho 1990; Cheung *et al.* 1994; Tsang 1995; Lee 2000; Fischler 2003). However, as C.K. Lee (2000) points out, public discourses surrounding this issue were grounded in a language of familial or maternal needs and welfare rather than a language of gender equality and women's rights. Although Ellen Li emphasized the legal right of women to a monogamous marriage, the council highlighted the advantages of marriage law reform for the family and dependent children. Following the campaign's specific legislative gains, the council lost its impetus primarily because it lacked a permanent organizational base and had no long-term strategy for social transformation (Ho 1990; Tsang 1995).

The late 1970s marked the beginning of a broader-based women's movement in Hong Kong. The dynamism of second-wave feminism in Britain and the USA invigorated the council and highlighted a host of new gender issues in Hong Kong. Second-wave feminism did not merely concentrate its initiatives on the public sphere, but opened the private sphere as an arena for activism and advocacy. Women began to understand that patriarchy had its origins not only in the realm of public politics, but also in men's control of women's bodies, specifically their reproductive capacities and their sexuality (Mies 1986). This new theoretical and activist perspective on the private sphere resonated with women in Hong Kong. By defining the private sphere of man–woman relationships as a political one, the structural division of society between private and public was challenged. Drawing inspiration from the Western feminist movement, the council launched the 'Against Wife Abuse' and 'War on Rape' campaigns in Hong Kong. With the local context in mind, however, the campaigns adopted a 'community approach' (Cheung *et al.* 1994: 339). The council rejected the strategy of highlighting

Western feminist analysis of violence as male oppression in a male-dominated society. The campaigns also undertook more of a social service rather than a women's rights orientation with an emphasis on public education and service-provision for victims (Cheung *et al.* 1994). Consequently, the council set up Harmony House (Wo Hai Zhi Ga), a shelter for victims of domestic violence, and the Hong Kong Federation of Women's Centres (Heung Gong Fu Loi Zhong Sam Sae Wui), a women's resource centre with counselling services, support groups, as well as educational and retraining programmes (Ho 1990; Cheung *et al.* 1994; Tsang 1995).[6]

In the 1980s, the Hong Kong women's movement diversified further—taking a different course from the council. While the council made attempts to increase its membership base, feminism did not arouse much interest among local Chinese women elites. But other sectors of society were becoming increasingly interested in feminism. In particular, tertiary students and social workers were inspired by Western feminism via feminist literature and/or tertiary education but their interpretation and application of feminist ideology and discourse differed from that of the council. Some of the women in these new groups were involved in student, community, and Christian movements in the 1970s, and they were grounded variously in Marxist social critique and Christian values of equality and justice, and, accordingly, were more inclined to embrace 'protest culture' for effecting social change (Tsang 1995; Choi 2001).

First, these women pointed out that the campaigns concerning abuse and rape ignored the issue of VAW as patriarchal dominance over women, and instead portrayed women as victims and focused on their need for social protection and support. Corresponding to women's movements in the West, they recognized that VAW was not merely an expression of aggression of individual men, but was part and parcel of institutional patriarchy (Walby 1986). Second, while the community approach appealed to the Hong Kong government and society, these women questioned whether this non-confrontational strategy would bring about long-term gains for women. Their experiences of community development programmes taught them that marginal and powerless groups could achieve their goals if they created publicity through popular mobilization and lobbying rather than following bureaucratic procedures of institutional politics. Finally, the knowledge and understanding of Marxist social critique predisposed these women towards a strong identification with the grass-roots. They considered council members, as elite expatriate and local women, ignorant of the cultural and social dynamics of the grass-roots community and unable to speak the language of grass-roots women (Ho 1990; Tsang 1995; Choi 2001).[7]

These women decided to form their own local women's organizations, including the Association for the Advancement of Feminism (AAF: San Fu Loi Sae Zhun Wui) and the Hong Kong Women Christian Council (HKWCC: Heung Gong Fu Loi Gei Dou Tou Sae Wui) (Ho 1990; Cheung *et al.* 1994; Tsang 1995; Choi 2001; Lee 2000; Fischler 2003; Lee 2003). These organizations adopted an expressly 'local orientation'—the designation of 'local' meaning 'an identification with one's own language and culture' and 'an orientation toward the grass-roots' (Choi 2001: 227–8). The AAF and the HKWCC focused their efforts on consciousness-raising. The AAF initially organized exhibitions, street performances and talks in public housing estates. Some of these initiatives were designed to relate women's rights to grass-roots women's daily lives, while others introduced these women to gender-role systems, sexism in the media, and the women's movement in the PRC. The emphasis gradually shifted to policy critique, resource development, and research and publications, reflecting the core members' level of education and professional training. Nevertheless, members continued to liaise with community and social workers, who were in a more visible position to raise awareness of gender issues. The HKWCC promoted the necessity of women's theology within the Church and various Christian organizations, providing the possibility of rethinking the role and situation of women within religious institutions and wider society. Both the AAF and the HKWCC, together with other women's organizations, were also involved in campaigns for women's rights, including abortion, maternity benefits legislation, separate taxation for married women, and land inheritance rights of women in the New Territories.[8] These campaigns were framed as a grand attempt to understand and challenge the structural obstacles to gender equality rather than as one-time material resolutions to specific gender issues (Tsang 1995; Lee 2000).[9]

By the 1990s, the milieu of the Hong Kong women's movement transformed considerably with the formation of women's organizations with different degrees of identification with feminism and specific fields of concerns. This period saw the emergence of women's organizations targeting specific constituencies and mobilizing particular sectors of the grass-roots. For example, the Hong Kong Women Workers Association (HKWWA: Heung Gong Fu Loi Lou Gong Sae Wui), Kwan Fook and Zi Teng focus on consciousness-raising among and mobilization of women cleaners in public housing estates, women survivors of domestic violence, and sex workers respectively. These grass-roots-oriented women's organizations drew attention to the predominantly middle-class and intellectual base of the Hong Kong women's movement during the early 1980s. This is evident from the emphasis on policy critique, research and publications, and the comparatively minimal immediate contact between activists and grassroots women.

Linda To, a tertiary-educated professional working with women workers in the HKWWA, articulated this critique in an AAF conference in 1995. During the conference, 'Strategies of the Hong Kong Women's Movement', she criticized the Hong Kong women's movement for lacking a coherent strategy and consistent commitment in organizing women at the grass-roots level. Grass-roots oriented women's organizations such as the HKWWA, Kwan Fook and Zi Teng, are wary of being involved in policy disputes or political lobbying. They prefer to focus on consciousness-raising among grass-roots women who bear the brunt of structural inequalities in their daily lives, which they believe is the most significant contribution that the women's movement can make to society (Tsang 1995; Choi 2001).

Further tensions in the Hong Kong women's movement became apparent as the date for the transfer of Hong Kong from British colonial control to the PRC drew nearer. Over the course of the 1990s, the PRC government grew increasingly concerned with the formation of oppositional women's organizations (Lui 1997). Fearing that their initiatives would lead to anti-PRC activity, they nurtured the formation of pro-PRC women's organizations. Accordingly, women close to the PRC government and its media organ, the New China News Agency, established the Hong Kong Federation of Women (Heung Gong Gok Gai Fu Loi Lian Hup Sae Zhun Wui) in 1993 to realign pro-PRC forces among Hong Kong women in support of the PRC government (Choi 2001; Lee 2003).[10] The establishment of the federation and the impending hand-over of Hong Kong to the PRC provided the impetus for the whole spectrum of local women's organizations to exploit and build on their differences as a basis for political action. This included effecting desired changes in legislation and policy and securing financial resources for initiatives under PRC-governance, as well as defining a feminist agenda for social change within the wider movement for democracy in Hong Kong. These challenges are illuminated in the next section.

Divisions within the Hong Kong women's movement in the lead-up to 1997

The impending handover of Hong Kong to PRC-governance prompted discernible impacts on the women's movement soon after 1984 when the British and PRC governments signed the Sino-British Joint Declaration. Henceforth, Hong Kong experienced a period of political polarization, as Sino-British conflicts over issues of democratization, human rights and political freedom divided and destabilized the status quo (Lau 2001). The British government was under pressure by the British public and international community to maintain the continuity of Hong Kong's prosperity, sovereignty and stability (Sing 2000). The PRC government, however, envisaged that the continuing success of capitalism in Hong Kong depended on an authoritarian political system combined with a non-interventionist economic doctrine (Lee 2003). Eventually the two countries came to an agreement that Hong Kong would operate under the 'one country, two systems' framework in which Hong Kong enjoys autonomy in governance except in defence and foreign affairs. The 1984 Declaration also stipulates that the territory maintains its capitalist economic system, as well as the rights and freedoms of its people for at least fifty years beyond the transfer of sovereignty. Though freedom of speech and public assembly remains, the resulting electoral system continues to severely limit popular representation in the government. The Hong Kong government is careful in anticipating the interests of the PRC government, and its ruling strategy involves building a support base of conservative upper middle classes and the business community through pro-business economic policies. Consequently, conservative, pro-business and pro-PRC politicians dominate the legislature and maintain an amenable and efficient relationship between the PRC and Hong Kong governments. At the same time, concern with limited popular representation in the Hong Kong government brought about greater involvement of pro-democracy political parties and social movement organizations in oppositional politics, including the participation in elections to various representative assemblies, as well as the organizing of popular mobilization in support of the democratization of the electoral system (Cheng 2005; Pepper 2008).

The political transition has left the Hong Kong women's movement divided on its stance towards pro-PRC and pro-democracy political factions in Hong Kong. The Hong Kong Federation of Women consistently supports the PRC government and opposes the acceleration of democratic reform in Hong Kong. The federation functions as an umbrella women's organization, whose members comprise mainly women's community groups from different geographical regions of Hong Kong. Wealthy married women and community leaders form the majority of its core members. The former are federation council members who understand little about gender issues 'in the grass roots-oriented sense of working with lower-class women' while the latter are involved in grass-roots work but understand little about feminism, the 'theoretical basis' for gender issues (Fischler 2003: 62). The federation focuses primarily on developing 'official' links with individuals and organizations in the PRC, rather than 'informal' networks with transnational feminist groups. Hence federation members are often integrated into the framework of government administration and regulation and are granted privileged access to political decision-making.

In contrast to these pro-PRC women's organizations, there are grass roots-oriented, rights-based women's organizations that believe they have a critical role to play in the democratization of the Hong Kong electoral system. Their perspective of democracy necessitates gender equality as part of the development of the territory. For these groups, women's rights are integral to human rights, and are therefore necessary to any conception of democracy (Ho 1990; Choi 2001). As a form of political opposition, pro-democracy women's organizations are kept distant from the core of the political establishment. Nevertheless, these women's organizations are more active in maintaining a generally liberal civil society, rather than seeking political power. Although they have amicable relations with pro-democracy political parties and social movement organizations and regularly participate in pro-democracy movement initiatives, they are wary of direct alignment with these groups in formal politics. Instead, they assume the role of a pressure group and articulate the interests of marginal communities, including gays and lesbians, middle-aged women workers and sex workers.

The Hong Kong Women's Coalition for Equal Opportunities (Peng Dang Sae Wui Fu Loi Lin Sek) is the most prominent group aligned with the pro-democracy sector. The coalition was established in 1996 to monitor the Equal Opportunities Commission, the Women's Commission and the implementation of the United Nation's (UN) Convention of the Elimination of All Forms of Discrimination against Women in Hong Kong. It is also a platform for member organizations to work together on common gender issues, including VAW, poverty and the political participation of women. Its membership is diverse, including advocacy groups, lesbian groups, religious groups, sex worker rights groups and service-providers. As a loosely organized network of pro-democracy women's organizations, member organizations are obligated to attend meetings, but they can choose whether or not to participate in a specific initiative. For example, representatives from some religious and social-service women's organizations attend coalition meetings to keep themselves current on gender issues, but they do not participate in visible initiatives such as demonstrations and the signing of petitions.

Women's organizations on both sides of the pro-PRC/pro-democracy divide are often concerned with the same gender issues, including education and training, employment, health, political participation, poverty and VAW. However, pro-PRC and pro-democracy women's organizations adopt different approaches to them. For example, they rely on divergent political opportunities and social networks and use opposing discourses, initiatives and strategies in confronting VAW. Since the campaigns concerning abuse and rape initiated by the Hong Kong Council of Women in the 1970s and 1980s, issues relating to VAW have returned to having a low priority on state agenda. This is due in part to traditional Chinese cultural norms, in which VAW is accepted as fate or even condoned as befitting punishment for disobedient wives or delinquent women (Cheung *et al.* 1994). It was only in 2004, when a man stabbed his wife and two daughters to death in Tin Shui Wai, that issues relating to VAW received media and state attention.[11] After repeatedly denying responsibility and claiming that it was merely an unfortunate incident, the police finally admitted that the woman had sought help at a police station just hours before her death. The police officers did not take her fears seriously and told her to return home. Both pro-PRC and pro-democracy women's organizations were alarmed and furious that the police had tried to cover up their involvement in the incident, and demanded an apology be made to the relatives concerned. They also called for an investigation into the police's handling of the case. This dramatic, high-profile incident allowed both pro-PRC and pro-democracy women's organizations to elevate issues relating to VAW to an unprecedented level of public awareness.

In comparing the approaches of pro-PRC and pro-democracy women's organizations to issues relating to VAW, I present an important challenge to the concept of political opportunity offered by academic scholarship on social movements. The selectively inclusive strategy of the Hong Kong government severely restricts opportunities for collective action by pro-democracy women's organizations. In the section below, I argue that collective action by pro-democracy women's organizations emerged not in response to opportunities but to a lack thereof. In fact, the coalition among pro-democracy women's organizations has served as a platform for member organizations to raise consciousness of VAW. Moreover, the assessment of VAW by these women's organizations as one that concerns the individual rights of women facilitated the construction of a frame that equated VAW with patriarchal dominance over women. Hence the empirical discussion below shows how mobilizing structures and framing processes can compel collective action in the absence of political opportunity.

Political opportunities and social networks

Both pro-PRC and pro-democracy women's organizations attempt to bring about changes in legislation and policies concerning women and to secure financial resources for new initiatives. However, they have different political opportunities and use divergent social networks. Pro-PRC women's organizations adopt 'mainstream politics' or effect changes via networking with influential personages, while pro-democracy women's organizations use 'peripheral politics' or the implementation of changes via consciousness-raising, lobbying, mass mobilization, and research and publications (Choi 2001: 229–30).

The role of political opportunity in collective action explains social movement emergence and development in terms of 'consistent—but not necessarily formal or permanent—dimensions of the political environment that provide incentives for people to undertake collective action by affecting their expectations for success or failure' (Tarrow 1994: 85). According to McAdam (1996: 27), these dimensions of the political environment include the relative openness or closure of the institutionalized political system; the stability or instability of that broad set of elite alignments that typically undergird a polity; the presence or absence of elite allies; and the state's capacity and propensity for repression.[12] As mentioned earlier, the Hong Kong Federation of Women did not actually go through the process of first being founded, and then searching for funding for their initiatives. Instead, the federation was founded under the arrangement of the PRC government to propagate patriotic and nationalist passions among local women's organizations. Therefore the presence of elite allies can be said to be present for pro-PRC women's organizations. Although the federation claims to be 'non-political', federation council members have pre-existing and established institutional ties with the PRC and Hong Kong governments.[13] Many of these women are also wives of prominent pro-PRC capitalists, ensuring that the federation is well-financed.

In 2005, ten years after the UN's Fourth World Conference on Women (FWCW) in Beijing, the federation organized a series of activities to commemorate the tenth anniversary of the conference, including a 'Survey on Public Awareness of Women's Issues', a 'Report on the Implementation of the Beijing Platform for Action in Hong Kong', a 'Hong Kong Women in the 21st Century' photo competition and exhibition, and a women's seminar and cocktail reception. The women's seminar and cocktail reception was held at the Ritz Carlton Hotel.[14] It was attended by several prominent Hong Kong women with direct and indirect relations to government administration and regulation, including Salina Tsang, wife of Chief Executive Donald Tsang; Betty Tung, wife of ex-Chief Executive Tung Chee Hwa; Elsie Leung, the Secretary of Justice; Rita Fan, the president of the Legislative Council; and Sophie Leung, the chairperson of the Women's Commission. Peggy Lam, the chairperson of the federation and a pro-PRC legislator, launched the seminar, which included a speech by Gu Xiulian, the president of the Chinese Communist Party's mass organization for women, the All-China Women's Federation (ACWF), and vice-chairperson of the PRC's Standing Committee of the National People's Congress of China. Gu's official presence at this conference marked the PRC government's approval of the event.

However, political opportunities can simultaneously facilitate and constrain collective action, as opportunities may vary for different types of movements (McAdam 1998). For pro-democracy women's organizations, the absence of elite allies has, on occasions, presented obstacles to collective action, whether it is forming alliances to effect change or gaining support for their initiatives. Activists make every effort to lobby the support of pro-democracy politicians and/or political parties who are more concerned with gender issues, creating opportunities for alliance with pro-democracy factions. Kwan Fook has lobbied the support of former legislator and district councillor Cyd Ho, who is also one of the founding members of the pro-democracy political party 'The Frontier' (Qin Xin). In an informal conversation with me, she revealed that she had never 'proactively' taken up gender issues because she had never personally been conscious of unequal treatment—she had been able to receive an education and had been fairly renumerated for her work in the textile industry. Unaware of other people's experiences of gender inequality, she did not incorporate gender issues in her election platform in 1998. But, in her second election in 2000, the Hong Kong Women's Coalition on Equal Opportunities organized an election platform to raise the legislative council election candidates' concern for gender issues, and she realized she had been 'ignorant of women's difficulties'. She was personally approached by Kwan Fook. As members explained their difficulties to her, she came to understand inequality as an institutionalized matter. These women had no opportunity to receive an education and their entire livelihoods were dependent on their husbands. They also had the responsibilities of housework and caring for the family, which the government did not consider as work. They had no income and hence no retirement plan. She decided to include 'women's equality' in her election platform. During her term as a legislator, Kwan Fook continued to provide her with individual case studies to illustrate the problems of various social policies, including health, housing and social welfare, which prevent abused women from leaving their husbands.

However, not all pro-democracy women's organizations have had success in the lobbying of pro-democracy politicians and/or political parties. Zi Teng has had difficulties gaining support from politicians and political parties to curb police harassment and violence against sex workers as they tend to have a different analysis of gender issues from that of pro-democracy women's organizations. According to a Zi Teng staff member, politicians and political parties tend to undertake 'a much more moral position' when it comes to sex workers' rights. In November 2000, legislators and district board councillors from pro-democracy political parties—the Democratic Party (Man Ju Dong) and the Association for Democracy and People's Livelihood (Heung Gong Man Ju Man

Sang Sae Zhun Wui)—mobilized community protest against sex workers in Sham Shui Po.[15] They organized a campaign urging the police to come down hard on sex establishments in the district and promoted a rally of local residents, on the basis that the activities of sex workers have led to harassment of 'good women' living or working in the district (Association for the Advancement of Feminism 2001). Several pro-democracy women's organizations criticized these pro-democracy political parties for their 'hypocrisy'. An AAF member described how these pro-democracy political parties recognized sex workers to be 'disadvantaged' and 'signed a declaration promising to support the rights of these women' before the legislative council elections in September 2000. In mobilizing community protest against sex workers, they had effected a 'u-turn' and were 'using this very vulnerable sector of society to increase their popularity' (Shamdasani and Li 2000). Consequently, some activists prefer to isolate women's organizations from formal politics. Echoing the views of several activists, one HKWWA staff member explained that she is 'more reserved' concerning alliances with politicians and political parties as they are 'focused on their own interests' and 'just want to build up their own image'; they are 'not concerned with grassroots people's rights or women's rights'.

For pro-democracy women's organizations, the Hong Kong Women's Coalition on Equal Opportunities provides a distinct space for women's activism. As McCarthy (1996: 143) observes, mobilizing structures include a wide range of social settings, including a 'wide variety of social sites within people's daily rounds where informal and less formal ties between people can serve as solidarity and communication facilitating structures when and if they choose to go into dissent together.' This role of informal social networks in promoting movement participation is especially significant for pro-democracy women's organizations. There are numerous ties between activists of different pro-democracy women's organizations. Some have had organizing experiences together in the student, community and Christian movements during the 1970s while others have worked in several pro-democracy women's organizations. Subsequently, the formation of the coalition shows that these women's organizations are not responding to political opportunities, but are subjects pursuing their own agendas. Despite individual organizational vision and goals, representatives from member organizations recognize the need to use individual strengths and combine various strategies to achieve the collective goal of 'equal opportunities'. The director of the Hong Kong Women's Federation of Women's Centres explains that member organizations are 'trying to get some support and build up a platform so that some of our agendas can be worked together'. In an interview with me, the director of a group formed to lobby for the rights of sex workers, 'Action for REACH OUT' (Qing Niu), described the relevance of the coalition to member organizations:

> It is important to show solidarity, so what we do every year is to set common themes. Like we're talking about violence, these affect our women [sex workers] as well. Because the law forces them to work alone, it can be very dangerous. The law does not allow them to hire any assistants or bodyguards

or even have two women in the same working place. No matter where they work, it's only on a one-to-one basis. That is why they are more easily exposed to violence by clients or by police. There were times when some women got their throats cut, they got robbed, raped ... So [member] organizations do have their own agendas, but the coalition is able to come up with some common themes that all the organizations are able to work towards, which is the beauty of the coalition.[16]

In the case of pro-democracy women's organizations, therefore, access to political authorities is ambiguous in its effects. Corresponding to Kriesi's (1996) argument on the availability of elite allies, we can observe that support from a powerful ally may provide access to decision-making procedures, important resources and public recognition for pro-PRC women's organizations. On the other hand, a powerful ally may draw resources away from women's organizations, subsume their interests and resources to that of the ally's concern, and alienate important parts of the constituency of women's organizations, as the experiences of pro-democracy women's organizations with pro-democracy political parties and social movement organizations have shown. Moreover, mobilization does not necessarily depend on expanding political opportunities: 'For some challengers, increased political openness enhances the prospects for mobilization, while other movements seem to respond more to threat than opportunity' (Meyer and Staggenborg 1996: 1634). For pro-democracy women's organizations, mobilization is, to use Goodwin and Jasper's (1999: 39) argument, a '*defensive* response to contracting political opportunities'. At the same time, such a focus on political opportunities tends to divert attention away from movements where access to power is not a central objective. Challenging cultural codes is a central goal of certain social movements, even many that are significantly oriented towards the state, as in the case of women's movements (Goodwin and Jasper 1999; Wesoky 2002). As we will see in the next section, pro-PRC and pro-democracy women's organizations draw upon the existing frameworks of their socio-cultural context to articulate their platforms on gender and, in particular, on VAW.

Strategies and symbolic politics

Pro-PRC and pro-democracy women's organizations adopt different strategies and espouse divergent solutions to gender issues in their initiatives. This is due in part to their political opportunities and social networks, or the lack thereof in the case of pro-democracy women's organizations. Through their various initiatives, movements seek to 'frame social problems and injustices in a way that convinces a wide and diverse audience of the necessity for and utility of collective attempts to redress them' (McCarthy, Smith and Zald 1996: 291). This consists of the movement's efforts to influence the state in ways it sees as central to its goals, as well as to spread its viewpoints to the population at large (Snow and Benford 1988). For pro-PRC and pro-democracy women's organizations, different aspects of these arenas are more significant than others.

Pro-PRC women's organizations focus on 'practical work', including service-provision, dialogues with government agencies and participation in international conferences. In view of the challenges faced by women in the area of marriage and family, the Hong Kong Federation of Women provides a women's hotline to offer legal advice in aspects of bankruptcy, inheritance, matrimony, mediation and property. To complement this service, it has also cooperated with the Hong Kong Mediation Centre to launch a Women and Family Disputes Mediation Service in 2006 to provide an alternative for the resolution of family disputes and to reduce cost in litigation procedures. In an interview with me, one federation council member explained how the federation is 'fighting for women's rights in a constructive way, not an aggressive way':

> We don't do things that attract public attention. We don't do exaggerated, superficial things like street drama. Through the federation, the Women's Commission, things can be resolved. We're doing practical work. Like if an abused wife wants a divorce, what are her legal rights? We have a hotline for them. We're doing things in a constructive way to influence the government. Rather than like a pressure group, holding demonstrations, that kind of feminism that happened in the West during the 1960s and 1970s [makes a fist and thrusts her hand in the air]. It is not really the direction of the federation to be a feminist organization. We are more influential, our action-plan is better. What are women's needs, what is the analysis, voice out the needs to the government or present a paper at international conferences. This is the kind of thing we are doing. We do not have a confrontational kind of agenda. We are talking to the central government in China, we are talking to the father. I think it is a more practical, efficient way.

As a service-oriented organization, the federation perceives itself as providing assistance to women in need and, in so doing, participating in activities that are not directly impinging upon state authority. This council member negatively associates feminism with the radical forms of collective action undertaken by feminist activists in Britain and the USA during second-wave feminism. By rejecting this option for the federation, she is perhaps avoiding political suspicion of 'the father'. Instead, she readily accepts the patriarchal social structure and frames the federation as 'cooperative' rather than 'oppositional' in its choice to have dialogues and work in partnership with the state instead of organizing demonstrations and posing an explicit threat to state authority. Since the establishment of the Hong Kong Federation of Women, it has also increasingly aligned itself to and adopted strategies from the ACWF. This council member affirmed, 'We have a very close relationship with the All-China Women's Federation', and even described the organization as 'our partner, our sister'.

As mentioned in the previous section, the Hong Kong Federation of Women organized a series of activities to commemorate the tenth anniversary of the UN's FWCW. With pro-PRC political connections and sufficient financial resources, it coordinated seventy-seven women's organizations, comprising mainly of its member organizations, to form a joint managerial panel to coordinate a series of activities. The 'Report on the Implementation of the Beijing Platform for Action in Hong Kong' summarizes the views and recommendations of representatives from academic institutions, government agencies and women's organizations on ten critical areas of concerns of the Beijing Platform for Action, including VAW.[17] The report outlines the current situation, achievements, gaps and obstacles, and recommendations, and forms a basis for the formulation of legislative and social-service strategies to curb VAW. It reflects a continuing concern with the problems of VAW and, more specifically, acknowledging the need for greater understanding of 'equality, respect, and the handling of emotions' to deal with 'violent behaviours' (Hong Kong Federation of Women 2005).

In keeping with the growing PRC influence over the Hong Kong women's movement, the achievements and recommendations in the Federation Report have similarities to the general approach to VAW taken in the PRC. The core PRC document relating to VAW is the Women's Protection Law of 1992 (All-China Women's Federation 1992), designed to protect women's rights and interests but within the overarching framework of maintaining family and community harmony rather than advocating individual interests.[18] Like the PRC's Women's Protection Law, the achievements and recommendations are centred on the strengthening of the family as a unit of care, rather than the protection of women's interests and rights. The achievements outlined in the federation report described the campaign 'Strengthening Families and Combating Violence' launched by the Social Welfare Department in 2002. This campaign reminded the public of 'the importance of family strengthening' and encouraged 'early help seeking'. The federation report also recommended mandatory treatment and counselling programmes for perpetrators of domestic violence due to the high withdrawal rate and low attendance rate of treatment and counselling programmes (Hong Kong Federation of Women 2005). The primary objective here is not necessarily the protection of women's interests and rights, for treatment and counselling programmes also serve in emphasizing the importance of the reconciliation of the family.

The achievements and recommendations are also focused on mediation through non-governmental organizations (NGOs) concerned with VAW. The achievements outlined in the federation report described the extensive services provided to victims of domestic violence by NGOs, including helplines, women's shelters, self-help groups, treatment and counselling programmes for perpetrators of violence, and outreach programmes to medical professionals and police officers. The federation report also suggested the promotion of universal screening at hospitals carried out by the cooperation between NGOs and medical professionals so as to identify cases of domestic violence successfully. On one hand, domestic violence is no longer perceived to be a private matter that is dealt with from within the family, and public bodies are expected to play a more interventionist role in response to complaints and incidents of domestic violence. On the other hand, the achievements and recommendations illustrate the preference for dealing with problems of domestic violence through mediation between the family and

NGOs rather than through initiatives carried out by the state. This is consistent with general policies in many jurisdictions in the PRC since 1978 (Palmer 2007). Hence political opportunities available to pro-PRC women's organizations suggest a dependence on state forbearance on the range of actions to be taken and the ways in which women's interests are articulated.

Being located on the periphery of the political establishment, 'working loudly' is one of the predominant strategies of pro-democracy women's organizations to gain political influence and raise public awareness. These women's organizations are recognized for their demonstration rallies, protest marches and street performances. Following the Tin Shui Wai tragedy, the Legislative Council steered a motion debate involving the amendment of the Domestic Violence Ordinance, so as to allocate more resources and provide training to improve the ability of front-line personnel to deal with cases of domestic violence. On the day of the debate, the AAF, the Association Concerning Sexual Violence against Women (Guan Ju Fok Loi Seng Bo Lek Sae Wui)[19] and Kwan Fook issued a joint public statement to the media and staged a petition outside the Legislative Council Building to urge government officials and legislators to pass and implement the motion.

In contrast to pro-PRC women's organizations, pro-democracy women's organizations' proposed solutions to VAW are concerned with the individual rights of women. Activists pointed out that current family policies and services were formed on the basis of 'a very conservative definition of the family' and emphasized 'strengthening of families' before 'human rights of the woman'. In strengthening the support for families, 'family unity should not be reinforced at the expense of equality and mutual respect between family members'. They demanded that the government review the direction of current family policies and services and that family policies and services should 'provide women with the conditions to leave an abusive relationship when she chooses to do so'. Despite the lack of political opportunities, the Tin Shui Wai tragedy has provided a way for pro-democracy women's organizations to raise consciousness among individuals beyond their own small circle of leaders and active participants. Through their demonstration rallies, protest marches and street performances, activists can disseminate their ideas and modes for solving problems in relation to VAW to influence the state and the public. Nevertheless, these women's organizations are also constrained to some extent by media and state attention on gender issues in order for them to spread ideas to individuals outside the core of the women's movement. So long as this is the case, a truly open discourse on gender issues will be difficult to achieve.

Pro-democracy women's organizations also emphasize extensive changes in legislation and policies beyond those directly related to VAW. During a workshop on feminism and the Hong Kong women's movement that I participated in, one Kwan Fook founding member shared information about how the self-help group brings together abused women to help one another start a new life.[20] It does not apply 'a top-down management model' and advocates 'self and mutual assistance'. Having 'liberated' herself from her ex-husband's abuse, she described how she takes a long time to listen to abused women, teaches those who are uneducated or do not know their legal rights, helps them in the divorce process and to avoid harassment by ex-husbands, and follows up the situation of those who have come to her or the group. She emphasizes the importance of 'strengthening oneself' and encourages abused women who have overcome their difficult experiences to help the newcomers to the group to 'enhance their self-confidence and self-esteem'. However, she was criticized for 'teaching women to run away from their families' and is perceived as 'a troublemaker for her encouragement of female autonomy and self-protection' by some 'conservative' politicians. She also believes that 'individual power is not enough'. For this reason, Kwan Fook advocates the improvement of various social policies, including health, housing and social welfare, through demonstrations, lobbying of legislators and working with university academics, so as to establish a better environment for abused women and their children.

When movements engage in framing, they are faced with strategic choices as to how they will assume or dispute existing frameworks within their socio-cultural context to their needs (Zald 1996). In this way, movements are both 'consumers of existing cultural meanings as well as producers of new ones' (Tarrow 1994: 123). This is evident when we compare the efforts of pro-PRC and pro-democracy women's organizations to improve the position of women in Hong Kong society. Pro-PRC women's organizations base their solutions to VAW on legislation and policies drawn from the PRC. The PRC government's paternalistic style of governance and the Hong Kong government's acquiesce to the PRC combine to legitimate the pro-PRC women's organization's demands because they incorporate the dominant ideology of both governments. In contrast, pro-democracy women's organizations' proposed solutions to VAW are concerned with the individual rights of women. In so doing, they characterize women's movements which 'pursue women's gender interests … [and] make claims on cultural and political systems on the basis of women's historically ascribed gender roles' (Alvarez 1990: 23). As an oppositional force, these women's organizations perceive the need to demand for privileges, rights, or means to which a group is not entitled to according to dominant state ideology. As Tarrow (1994: 122) argues, 'Out of a cultural toolkit of possible symbols, movement entrepreneurs choose those that they hope will mediate among the cultural underpinnings of the groups they appeal to, the sources of official culture and the militants of their movements—and still reflect their own beliefs and aspirations.'

Conclusion

Any analysis of the women's movement must begin with the recognition that we are discussing 'not one discrete organizational movement but rather a political force that even in a single country has broad ideological variety and a range of organizational expressions' (Katzenstein 1987: 4). This chapter draws attention to the diversity within the contemporary Hong Kong women's movement in relation to political factions and the ways in which women's interests are formulated and articulated.

The comparison between pro-PRC and pro-democracy women's organizations demonstrates how political opportunities vary with regard to a given movement's goals and strategies. Pro-PRC women's organizations, as opposed to pro-democracy women's organizations, are more acceptable to the PRC and Hong Kong governments as they do not pose an explicit threat to state power. More importantly, this comparison illustrates that collective action does not necessarily depend on expanding political opportunities. For pro-democracy women's organizations, collective action emerged in the absence of any favourable opportunities in the political system. It was the lack of opportunity that facilitated the formation of issue-specific coalitions among pro-democracy women's organizations. These coalitions not only provide a platform for these women's organizations to display their unity in a concrete way but also to establish an oppositional frame that represents resistance to the dominant pro-PRC institutions in Hong Kong. At the same time, this comparison also shows the discursive framings of women's interests, reflecting the political positions and priorities of pro-PRC and pro-democracy women's organizations. As Molyneux (1998) argues, the formulation and articulation of women's interests are bound up with the broader political project with which the women's movements are associated.

With emphasis on the diversity within the contemporary Hong Kong women's movement, this chapter shifts the critical perspective from ideological judgements of how women's movements should behave to a systematic observation of the concrete forms and practices of local women's movements and of the challenges that activists experience. It is essential for scholars to explore this complex terrain of historically shifting and situation specific forms of collective action within women's movements so as to understand the redefinitions and renegotiations of the parameters in which these movements operate, and the ways these parameters are changing.

Notes

1   I am grateful to Andrew Kipnis, Louise Edwards, Mina Roces and Tamara Jacka for their constructive criticisms in the development of this chapter, and to Mrs Audrey Lai for the English-to-Cantonese translation of the names of political parties and social movement organizations in this chapter.

2   My understanding of the Hong Kong women's movement is based on participant observation, in-depth interviews and document analysis. During my field research in 2005, I visited women's organizations involved in consciousness-raising and mobilization; expertise-centred research, publications, and policy critique; and/or grass-roots and participatory service-provision. I was involved in various organizational activities and initiatives so I was able to make detailed observations of the ways in which women's organizations work with one another, as well as with other social movement organizations, trade unions, political parties and state apparatus. I also conducted unstructured interviews with thirty-five individuals directly and indirectly involved in various aspects of the women's movement, including organization leaders, members, volunteers, university academics, government officials and politicians. In addition, I drew on documentary research on the women's movement and general issues concerning

women, including pamphlets of women's organizations, the internal newsletters or any other publications of these organizations, government documents, books, newspapers, magazines and scholarly journals.

3 While Hong Kong has been among the world's wealthier nations for several decades, the Hong Kong women's movement does not have the concrete history of feminist ideology and discourse that the Western women's movement has experienced, and activists do not subscribe to any particular feminist ideology.

4 Some important works that focus on more decentred and diffused forms of collective activism include Jayawardena (1986), Moghadam (1994) and Basu (1995).

5 Scholarship on mainland Chinese feminism during the first few decades of the twentieth century also illustrates how Chinese women used 'maternalist' initiatives as a basis for activism, precisely because the Chinese government was vehemently suspicious of collective protest action (Gilmartin 1995).

6 The Hong Kong Council of Women closed down in 1995, and Harmony House and the Hong Kong Federation of Women's Centres have become independent organizations (Choi 2001).

7 The term 'grass-roots' is utilized by both Hong Kong feminist scholars and activists to describe the poorer classes in Hong Kong.

8 In 1898, the rural New Territories became the last and most substantial portion of land acquired by Britain from imperial China. The New Territories Ordinance (NTO) was enacted in 1910 to curb protest by local villagers against the colonial regime's appropriation of land for development purposes. The NTO allowed indigenous residents in the New Territories to preserve their custom of male-only land inheritance, which the British implemented by borrowing from both existing local customs and the Chinese imperial legal system—the Qing code—as it existed at that time (Jones 1995).

9 For an in-depth discussion of the agenda of women's organizations in relation to these issues, see Lee (2000).

10 The Hong Kong Federation of Women has no affiliation with the Hong Kong Federation of Women's Centres established by the Hong Kong Council of Women. The New China News Agency was established in 1931 and operates under the PRC government. Its headquarters are in Beijing and it has offices around the world. Its media releases reflect official policies and promote state programmes.

11 Tin Shui Wai is a residential district in the New Territories.

12 It should be noted that academic scholarship on political opportunities have also employed additional, and often historically and situation specific, political opportunity variables (see Oberschall 1996; Kriesi 1996; Rucht 1996).

13 Among them are members of the high-powered Chinese People's Political Consultative Conference, the National People's Congress, the Chinese government-appointed Hong Kong Affairs Advisors, and the pro-PRC political party Democratic Alliance for the Betterment of Hong Kong (Choi 2001).

14 During the time of my field research, the Ritz Carlton was a five-star hotel located in the Central district in Hong Kong Island, one of the territory's most prestigious business and retail districts. It ceased operations in 2008.

15 Sham Shui Po is a residential district in the Kowloon Peninsula. Street-based sex workers are a common sight in the district at night.

16 Action for REACH OUT is concerned with sex workers' rights. It is involved in advocacy, outreach, public education and research.

17 The UN's Fourth World Conference on Women adopted the 'Beijing Declaration' and the 'Beijing Platform for Action', which specified twelve critical areas of concern instrumental to advancing the goal of equality through removing all obstacles to women's participation in all spheres of private and public life.

18 The Women's Protection Law of the PRC is specified at http://www.women.org.cn/english/english/laws/02.htm.

19 The Association Concerning Sexual Violence against Women is concerned with issues, legislation and policies in relation to rape; sexual abuse of children; sexual harassment and sexual assault; sexual violence in cyberspace, dating, and intimate relationships; and violence against sex workers. It is involved in advocacy, research and publications, and service-provision.

20 This workshop is organized annually by the AAF. Over the course of eight weeks, activists from different aspects of the Hong Kong women's movement are invited to speak about their understandings of feminism and experiences within the Hong Kong women's movement.

References

All-China Women's Federation (1992) *Law of the People's Republic of China on the Protection of Rights and Interests of Women*. Online. Available HTTP: <http://www.women.org.cn/english/english/laws/02.htm> (accessed 30 January 2009).

Alvarez, S.E. (1990) *Engendering Democracy in Brazil: Women's Movements in Transition Politics*, Princeton, NJ: Princeton University Press.

—— (1999) 'Advocating Feminism: the Latin American Feminist NGO Boom', *International Feminist Journal of Politics*, 1, 2: 181–209.

Association for the Advancement of Feminism (2001) *Women's News Digest*, 50/51, (March), Hong Kong: Association for the Advancement of Feminism, p. 5.

Basu, A. (1995) 'Introduction', in A. Basu (ed.) *The Challenge of Local Feminisms: Women's Movements in Global Perspective*, San Francisco and Oxford: Westview Press, pp. 1–21.

Bulbeck, C. (1988) *One World Women's Movement*, London: Pluto Press.

Cheng, J.Y. (2005) 'Introduction: Causes and Implications of the July 1 Protest Rally in Hong Kong', in J.Y. Cheng (ed.) *The July 1 Protest Rally: Interpreting a Historic Event*, Hong Kong: City University of Hong Kong Press, pp. 1–26.

Cheung, F.M., Wan, S.P. and Wan, O.C. (1994) 'The Underdeveloped Political Potential of Women in Hong Kong', in B.J. Nelson and N. Chowdhury (eds) *Women and Politics Worldwide*, New Haven and London: Yale University Press, pp. 327–46.

Choi, P. (2001) 'The Women's Movement and Local Identity in Hong Kong', in P. Lee (ed.) *Hong Kong Reintegrating with China: Political, Cultural and Social Dimensions*, Hong Kong: Hong Kong University Press, pp. 219–38.

Eisenstein, Z. (1997) 'Women's Publics and the Search for New Democracies', *Feminist Review*, 57 (Autumn), pp. 140–67.

Fischler, L. (2003) 'Women's Activism during Hong Kong's Political Transition', in E.W.Y. Lee (ed.) *Gender and Change in Hong Kong: Globalization, Postcolonialism, and Chinese Patriarchy*, Vancouver: UBC Press, pp. 49–77.

Gilmartin, C.K. (1995) *Engendering the Chinese Revolution*, Berkeley, CA: University of California Press.

Goodwin, J. and Jasper, J.M. (1999) 'Caught in a Winding, Snarling Vine: The Structural Bias of Political Process Theory', *Sociological Forum*, 14, 1: 27–54.

Heywood, L. and Drake, J. (eds) (1997) *Third Wave Agenda: Being Feminist, Doing Feminism*, Minneapolis and London: University of Minnesota Press.

Ho, C.A. (1990) 'Opportunities and Challenges: the Role of Feminists for Social Change in Hong Kong', in L. Albrecht and R. Brewer (eds) *Bridges of Power: Women's Multicultural Alliances*, Philadelphia: New Society Publishers, pp. 182–98.

Hong Kong Federation of Women (2005) *Report on the Implementation of the Beijing Platform for Action in Hong Kong*, Hong Kong: Organizing Committee for 'Beijing + 10' Memorial Activities in Hong Kong.

Jayawardena, K. (1986) *Feminism and Nationalism in the Third World*, London: Zed Books.

Jones, C. (1995) 'The New Territories Inheritance Law: Colonization and the Elites', in V. Pearson and B.K.P. Leung (eds) *Women in Hong Kong*, Hong Kong: Oxford University Press, pp. 167–92.

Katzenstein, M.F. (1987) 'Comparing the Feminist Movements of the United States and Western Europe: An Overview', in M.F. Katzenstein and C.M. Mueller (eds) *The Women's Movements of the United States and Western Europe: Consciousness, Political Opportunity, and Public Policy*, Philadelphia: Temple University Press, pp. 3–20.

Kriesi, H. (1996) 'The Organizational Structure of New Social Movements in a Political Context', in D. McAdam, J.D. McCarthy and M.N. Zald (eds) *Comparative Perspectives on Social Movements: Political Opportunities, Mobilizing Structures, and Cultural Framings*, Cambridge: Cambridge University Press, pp. 152–84.

Lau, S. (2001) 'The Hong Kong Special Administrative Region Government in the New Political Environment', in P. Lee (ed.) *Hong Kong Reintegrating with China: Political, Cultural and Social Dimensions*, Hong Kong: Hong Kong University Press, pp. 59–77.

Lee, C.K. (2000) 'Public Discourses and Collective Identities: Emergence of Women as a Collective Actor in the Women's Movement in Hong Kong', in S.K. Wing and T. Lui (eds) *The Dynamics of Social Movement in Hong Kong*, Hong Kong: Hong Kong University Press, pp. 227–57.

Lee, E.W.Y. (2003) 'Introduction: Gender and Change in Hong Kong', in E.W.Y. Lee (ed.) *Gender and Change in Hong Kong: Globalization, Postcolonialism, and Chinese Patriarchy*, Vancouver: UBC Press, pp. 3–22.

Lui, Y. (1997) *The Emergence and Development of the Feminist Movement in Hong Kong from the mid-1980s to the mid-1990s*, MPhil thesis, The Chinese University of Hong Kong.

Lui, T., Kuan, H., Chan, K. and Chan, S. (2005) 'Friends and Critics of the State: the Case of Hong Kong', in R.P. Weller (ed.) *Civil Life, Globalization, and Political Change in Asia: Organizing between Family and State*, London and New York: Routledge, pp. 58–75.

Margolis, D.R. (1993) 'Women's Movements Around the World: Cross-cultural Comparisons', *Gender and Society*, 7, 3: 379–99.

McAdam, D. (1996) 'Conceptual Origins, Current Problems, Future Directions', in D. McAdam, J.D. McCarthy, and M.N. Zald (eds) *Comparative Perspectives on Social Movements: Political Opportunities, Mobilizing Structures, and Cultural Framings*, Cambridge: Cambridge University Press, pp. 23–38.

—— (1998) 'On the International Origins of Domestic Political Opportunities', in A. Constain and A.S. McFarland (eds) *Social Movements and Political Institutions in the United States*, Boulder, CO: Rowman and Littlefield, pp. 251–67.

McCarthy, J.D. (1996) 'Constraints and Opportunities in Adopting, Adapting, and Inventing', in D. McAdam, J.D. McCarthy and M.N. Zald (eds) *Comparative Perspectives on Social Movements: Political Opportunities, Mobilizing Structures, and Cultural Framings*, Cambridge: Cambridge University Press, pp. 142–51.

McCarthy, J.D., Smith, J. and Zald, M. (1996) 'Accessing Public, Media, Electoral, and Governmental Agendas', in D. McAdam, J.D. McCarthy, and M.N. Zald (eds) *Comparative Perspectives on Social Movements: Political Opportunities, Mobilizing*

Structures, and Cultural Framings, Cambridge: Cambridge University Press, pp. 291–311.

Melucci, A. (1995) 'The Process of Collective Identity', in H. Johnston and B. Klandermans (eds) *Social Movements and Culture*, Minneapolis: University of Minnesota Press, pp. 41–63.

Meyer, D.S. and Staggenborg, S. (1996) 'Movements, Countermovements, and the Structure of Political Opportunity', *American Journal of Sociology*, 101, 6: 1628–60.

Mies, M. (1986) *Patriarchy and Accumulation on a World Scale: Women in the International Division of Labour*, London and New Jersey: Zed Books.

Moghadam, V.M. (ed.) (1994) *Identity Politics and Women: Cultural Reassertion and Feminisms in International Perspective*, Boulder, CO: Westview Press.

Mohanty, C.T. (1991) 'Introduction – Cartographies of Struggle: Third World Women and the Politics of Feminism', in C.T. Mohanty, A. Russo, and L. Torres (eds) *Third World Women and the Politics of Feminism*, Bloomington and Indianapolis: Indiana University Press, pp. 1–47.

Molyneux, M. (1998) 'Analysing Women's Movements', *Development and Change*, 29: 219–45.

Morgan, R. (ed.) (1984) *Sisterhood is Global*, Harmondsworth: Penguin.

Oberschall, A. (1996) 'The Great Transition: China, Hungary, and Sociology Exit Socialism into the Market', *American Journal of Sociology*, 101, 4: 1028–41.

Palmer, M. (2007) 'On China's Slow Boat to Women's Rights: Revisions to the Women's Protection Law, 2005', *International Journal of Human Rights*, 11, 1–2: 151–77.

Pepper, S. (2008) *Keeping Democracy at Bay: Hong Kong and the Challenge of Chinese Political Reform*, Lanham, MD: Rowman & Littlefield.

Rucht, D. (1996) 'The Impact of National Contexts on Social Movement Structures: a Cross–movement and Cross–national Comparison', in D. McAdam, J.D. McCarthy and M.N. Zald (eds) *Comparative Perspectives on Social Movements: Political Opportunities, Mobilizing Structures, and Cultural Framings*, Cambridge: Cambridge University Press, pp. 185–214.

Shamdasani, R. and Li, A. (2000) 'Parties Accused of Sex-Trade Hypocrisy', *South China Morning Post*, 4 November.

Sing, M. (2000) 'Mobilization for Political Change—the Pro-democracy Movement in Hong Kong (1980s–1994)', in S.K.C. Wing and T.L. Lui (eds) *The Dynamics of Social Movement in Hong Kong*, Hong Kong: Hong Kong University Press, pp. 21–53.

Snow, D.A. and Benford, R.D. (1988) 'Ideology, Frame Resonance, and Participant Mobilization', in B. Klandermans, H. Kriesi and S. Tarrow (eds) *From Structure to Action: Comparing Social Movement Research across Cultures*, Greenwich, CT: JAI Press, pp. 197–217.

Tarrow, S. (1994) *Power in Movement: Social Movements, Collective Action, and Politics*, Cambridge: Cambridge University Press.

Tsang, G. (1995) 'The Women's Movement at the Crossroads', in V. Pearson and B.K.P. Leung (eds) *Women in Hong Kong*, Oxford and New York: Oxford University Press, pp. 276–91.

Walby, S. (1986) *Patriarchy at Work*, Oxford: Polity Press.

Walker, R. (ed.) (1995) *To Be Real: Telling the Truth and Changing the Face of Feminism*, New York: Anchor Books.

Wesoky, S. (2002) *Chinese Feminism Faces Globalization*, New York and London: Routledge.

Whelehan, I. (1995) *Modern Feminist Thought: From the Second Wave to 'Post-Feminism'*, Edinburgh: Edinburgh University Press.

Zald, M.N. (1996) 'Culture, Ideology, and Strategic Framing', in D. McAdam, J.D. McCarthy and M.N. Zald (eds) *Comparative Perspectives on Social Movements: Political Opportunities, Mobilizing Structures, and Cultural Framings*, Cambridge: Cambridge University Press, pp. 261–74.

10 Military rule, religious fundamentalism, women's empowerment and feminism in Pakistan

Andrea Fleschenberg

> Women's bodies and identities have been, and continue to be, a key site of contestation and definition of self and other in the Pakistani context.
>
> (Rouse 1998: 69)

> Views regarding the women's movement in Pakistan range from outright dismissal of its existence to wholehearted support and admiration for the phenomenon.
>
> (Ali 2000: 55)

Marking the terrain

Gender issues are of a complex and contested nature in Pakistan. There are a variety of national, international and transnational actors that use feminist issues as bargaining chips or vehicles to promote their divergent political–ideological struggles. These include different types of women activists lobbying through national and transnational networks, military rulers, civilian politicians, as well as religious forces. Moreover, feminism in Pakistan has always had to defend itself against charges of Westernization, or of promoting an alien agenda. And it is linked to class interests in a highly stratified society where women activists mainly derive from the (upper) middle class and elite. The class factor is perceived to impact on the agenda, strategies and goals of the women's movement in a multiplicity of ways. Class interests determined the focus and demands of the movement in the early years (Rouse 1998: 55f.). A person's citizenship status is highly contingent on class and rural/urban locality. For instance, in the field of legal rights and access to formal/informal legal institutions, employment options and rights, access to education, impact of law and state–society–citizen relationships, people from different social classes have distinctly different opportunities. For example, middle- and upper-class women reinvigorated the women's movement in the late 1970s and 1980s because they resented the anti-women legislation, Islamization state practices and the religious discourse of the Zia-ul-Haq regime (1977–88) and saw themselves as the main targets of such policies, according to leading women's activist Farida Shaheed (see Shaheed 1998; Rouse 1998). But, given the high stratification and fragmentation of Pakistan's society, with little cross-class interaction, a spill-over of experiences and gains could not take place. Furthermore:

> [c]lass privileges, urban living, and class integration had all cushioned them from other identity-based discriminations, such as ethnicity. By contrast, women who suffer oppression by virtue of class, religion, or ethnic identity, in addition to gender, necessarily have concerns not premised solely on gender.
>
> (Shaheed 1998: 157)

This criticism reflects on the gains achieved by the women's movement regarding delaying or modifying legislative initiatives as well as participating in public and political arenas. For many rural and urban non-elite women, these gains were of little relevance to their own daily realities, and gains in the public domain meant little for predominantly private misogynist practices. Therefore, some critics argue that the patriarchal public–private divide and gender (role) constructions remained uncontested and unchanged by the women's movement—a complicity in 'subservience by privileged women of higher classes' (Jalal 1991: 78; cf. Rouse 1998: 56). Nonetheless, women's activists and feminist scholars such as Khawar Mumtaz and Shaheen Sardar Ali emphasize that the class background of women's activists opened avenues for agency as only elite women had the knowledge of socio-political institutions, access to resources and a cushioned social status to challenge gender norms and misogynist discourses and practices of state and civil society actors (Mumtaz 2005: 67; Ali 2000: 56).

At the same time, the women's rights agenda was always linked to the quest for democratization. National Women's Day on 12 February 1982 dates back to a demonstration of around 300 women in Lahore who protested against the Law of Evidence and faced a brutal police crackdown with baton-charging, teargas and subsequent imprisonments of several women activists such as Hina Jilani and Asma Jahangir. The authority's tough reaction against the women ultimately backfired as it 'generated wide-spread public support for women's cause' (Ali 2000: 50).

In this respect, one needs to consider the set opportunity structures, resources and discourses available for women's activists in a given socio-cultural and political context (Asfar cited in Randall 1998: 192f.). Pakistan's state–civil society institutions and relationships have been placed for the most part of the country's history in a 'hybrid authoritarian context' in which civil society still has 'to emerge as an independent, legally protected public realm of associational and civic activity' (Shah 2004: 357–8). The circumstances of the creation of the Islamic Republic of Pakistan (in partition from British India) as a nation for the Muslims in the South Asian subcontinent led to distinct features, among them the role of religion for state and society in addition to an 'insecurity complex' (Jalal 1991: 86) of the newly born nation vis-à-vis its big neighbour India. In the post-independence nation-building, 'women' took centre stage, because social order, security and societal 'moral underpinnings were symbolized by women'—read: Islamic credentials—and ultimately guaranteed by the state (infusing it with legitimacy) (Jalal 1991: 86). In their engagement with the state, women's groups have to decide between (a) the respect for limits of policy-formulation and co-optation with either modernist or conservative governmental agendas or (b) a confrontational approach by challenging the neo-patriarchal state, which formulates, represents and reproduces gendered, and most often patriarchal, hierarchies, discourses and practices.

> While women leaders in Pakistan during the 1950s and 1960s positioned themselves within the modernist project of the developmental nation-state to demand their rights, the feminist women's movement of the 1980s and early 1990s constructed itself through elite women's disillusionment with the nation-state.
>
> (Jamal 2005b: 59)

In both approaches lies the danger of counter-activism and a 'tendency towards tailism, i.e., allowing the direction of struggle to be determined by the state' (Rouse 1988: 13; cf. Shaheed 1998: 157), which altered to a certain extent from the 1990s onwards.

Civil society itself is a complex and contested playing field for the women's movement—an arena for negotiation, struggle and engagement (Randall 1998: 199). The Soviet occupation of Afghanistan aided the 'proliferation of Islamic charities and seminaries' (Shah 2004: 365), a growing influential movement nowadays with increased participation of women who challenge the progressive, 'liberal' camp of the women's movement in terms of values, agenda-setting, space of agency through adopting similar strategies (e.g. service provisions in education, health, law) and topics (albeit under a divergent ideological framework). In addition, extremist groups 'continue to restrict the socio-political space available to weaker civil organizations. Moreover, they often actively try to replace, and even subvert, opponents in civil society', for instance by anti-NGO campaigns in the North West Frontier Province, which targeted female NGO workers and women's development work (Shah 2004: 373–4).

Women's activists started their struggle in the colonial days for their country's independence from (British) India and, for the last sixty years, undertook efforts to secure an equal citizenship and space for women in Pakistani society with regard to their personal status (such as personal and family law, *Hudood* Ordinances), the assertion and safeguarding of women's human rights (such as violence against women like so-called 'honour killings' and forced marriages) and their political citizenship (right to vote and to stand in elections, and the introduction of reserved seats). The legal and political context, in particular (in)formal state and judicial structures as well as legal pluralism, have been a constant site of struggle and protest for the feminist cause, linking gender, traditions, religion and democracy in an intricate and challenging framing for feminist discourses and practices.

The nexus of religion, culture and tradition has been particularly salient and determined the agenda and agency options as well-presented old and new challenges to Pakistan's women's movement.[1] In fact, 'feminism in Pakistan cannot be understood without considering its antagonistic engagement with Islamization' (Jamal 2005b: 61), in particular from the late 1970s onwards to the present. The glocal effects of 9/11, with a rise in religious fundamentalism at the local and regional level, coincide with developments of international politics and globalization, which undermine the supportive secular and universalist international/transnational sphere and reference system for women activists in countries such as Pakistan (Jamal 2005b: 63). The use of religion as a means of political legitimization by different political regimes resulted in the 'politicization of the "woman's question" and legal constraints on women' and exacerbated issues of identity and strategizing for women's groups (Ali 2000: 41; cf. Rouse 1998: 64). One major question is the use of religion in addressing women's issues, selecting strategies and mobilizing support in a highly religious society, albeit the fact that different opinions on the exercise, public role and status of religion prevail among the populace.

> Feminist movements in Pakistan have drawn on a wide range of strategies in seeking legislative and policy reforms for women. Some have adopted 'insider methodologies', appealing to an egalitarian Islam. Others have adopted secularist strategies refusing to limit their claims to the confines of religious discourse. Opposition to feminist claims has taken many forms. Attempts to reform discriminatory laws have been labelled un-Islamic, unfaithful to and out of touch with Pakistan's inherited traditions. Feminism has been portrayed as a threat to Pakistan's sovereignty, and with it a threat to Pakistan's distinct religious-cultural traditions. ... The 'othering' of feminist discourse has been given an added momentum in recent years with the increasing 'talebanization' of Pakistani society and the rise of religion-based political parties.
>
> (Mullally 2005: 342–3)

Women's groups used religion when pressing for inheritance rights according to the *Shariah* (instead of customary law), conducting Arabic classes to counter charges of Westernization, working on feminist interpretations of Islamic law in response to women-unfriendly Islamist legislation and on Islamic history (e.g. by feminist theologians such as Riffat Hassan). The Pakistan Women Lawyers Association (PAWLA) filed a law suit against a police crackdown on women protestors in Lahore on the grounds that according to Islam the unrelated policemen were not allowed to touch women demonstrators (Ali 2000: 57; cf. Rouse 1998: 54; Haq 1996: 172; Weiss 1985: 876). The Women's Action Forum (Khawateen Mahaz-e-Amal, WAF) declared itself secular in 1991 (Shaheed 1998: 157), but the women's movement remains divided on '[w]hether it should be a secular framework or an Islamic one' (Ali 2000: 57). Secular women's groups challenge the Islamization programme, reject the notion of cultural particularism, stress universal human rights and demand due diligence of the state as neutral arbiter of individual vs. communal interests in the case of violence against women, discriminatory practices as well as protection of victims and endangered activists (Jamal 2005b: 69f., 74). The increased women's activism in Islamist movements— and the combination of a rejection of feminism while demanding more rights and a better status for women along with evoking an Islamic state as the solution— amounts to a 'conceptual crisis for feminism'. Feminist scholars must reconsider 'the assumed dichotomy of secular and religious in women's lives, thereby bringing into question a tradition of women's activism which had upheld secular modernity as the route to women's empowerment' (Jamal 2005a: 53).[2] Are Islamist women and women's groups 'patriarchal women or Islamic feminists' (Moghadam 2003: 168)? Have they decided to join fundamentalist groups and veiling in support of patriarchal fundamentalism or do they work for change within the frame of Islamic culture and religion as feminist reformers, maybe even in possible alliances with secular feminists adhering to universal discourses (Hélie-Lucas cited in Moghadam 2003: 168)?

Inextricably linked to the nexus of religion, state and women's issues are questions of culture and traditions as evident in one of the major rallying points of the women's and human rights movements for numerous years: the so-called 'honour killings' (see Warraich 2007: 78–110). Originally used to sanction and socially control cases of adultery, this practice widened to cover women's expressions of autonomy such as seeking marriage of own choice or divorce, and is furthermore used to settle family feuds or exercise revenge acts, irrespective of the women victims' 'alleged dishonourable behaviour'. Warraich describes it as 'a virtual licence to kill their women on the pretext of "honour"'—irrespective of provisions in the Quran and the Sunnah (2007: 79, 83–4). Women's groups lobbied members of government and parliament in recent years to issue respective protective and penal laws, and even prepared a draft law in cooperation with human rights groups, lawyers and retired judges in 2003 (Warraich 2007: 101, 110). The government did eventually sponsor a bill on 'honour crimes' (effective from January 2005), but women's and human rights groups criticized it for lacking a mandatory minimum sentence irrespective of victim–perpetrator relationship and allowing a reduced sentencing when both parties agree (Warraich 2007: 106).

In the following sections, the women's movement, as it developed in Pakistan, will be analysed according to different phases along the lines of Pakistan's democratic and authoritarian political regimes, outlining pertinent socio-political challenges, corresponding agendas and strategies applied in addition to successes and failures by different groups and key actors within the women's movement.

A movement in the making

The roots of the women's movement originate in the pre-independence period under colonial rule in British India, where women participated in political and social struggles for education opportunities for women, women's political citizenship and rallied on issues such as polygamy, legal rights such as personal status and family laws in accordance with Islamic law rather than customary law, denial of inheritance rights granted by Shariah and gender segregation (*purdah*) (Ali 2000: 42; Jalal 1991: 84). In 1947, Pakistan won independence and, as was the case in many nationalist movements around the world, women's activism decreased and women's issues were sidelined post-independence. Moreover, the post-independence activism was characterized by elitism and 'appendage politics'—most women belonged to families of male politicians. For example, Fatima Jinnah, founder of the All Pakistan Women's Association (APWA), was the younger sister of Pakistan's founder, Muhammad Ali Jinnah, and she herself would run for president in the 1960s (Jalal 1991: 84f.). Nonetheless, despite their elite nature and the fact that women's issues were not prioritized by the new state of Pakistan, Ali notes that women's 'large-scale mobilization in support of this cause may be described as a watershed in the break from traditional housebound roles to which Muslim women had been restricted so far' (Ali 2000: 43).

In the first decades after independence, a number of women's groups were formed which largely focused on welfare and education, motherhood and child rearing, but also served as a lobby-cum-pressure group for women's legal rights. The founding of APWA in 1949 was largely supported by the government and received 'government patronage, in fact, in many cities, wives of the government officials tended to head the local chapters' (Haq 1996: 164; cf. Shaheed and Warraich 1998: 274). Other organizations established in its shadow mainly toed its line: the Federation of University Women, Business and Professional Women's Association, Family Planning Association, the United Front for Women's Rights (Jalal 1991: 90–3)[3] or the Marxist-oriented Democratic Women's Association. After the first military coup under Ayub Khan, who followed a 'modernist' agenda (1958–69), more non-political, urban-based and welfare-oriented women's organizations were established (Shaheed and Warraich 1998: 276).

Major issues for women's lobbying with the state fell into the legal realm: inheritance rights, divorce rights, restriction of polygyny and family law reform. In 1948, hundreds of women, many in *purdah*, protested against the passage of the West Punjab Muslim Shariah Act 1948 on the issue of inheritance rights, invoking Islam in their demand for a change from customary to Islamic law (Jalal 1991: 87f.). Women's groups such as the United Front and APWA successfully pressured the government to set up a Commission on Marriage and Family Laws in 1955, which recommended in its report restrictions of polygyny and more divorce rights for women. Due to the military take-over, the report was not followed up by direct government action—a fate for commissions on women's status to be followed by others to come due to lack of political will or change in political regime. Thus in July 1958, APWA and other groups organized a Women's Demand Day for the implementation of the commission's recommendations and a reform of family law. It took until 1961, with the Family Law Ordinance passed by the regime of Ayub Khan, for the recommendations to be legally implemented. The ordinance guaranteed inheritance rights (also of agricultural property), stipulated the need for first wife's approval for second marriage, made divorce more difficult for men, codified women's right to initiate divorce and implemented a system of marriage registration—a victory for the women's movement. But one which suffered, as many other pro-women laws, the substantive legal penetration and application of the law across the rural–urban and class divide and which encountered substantial counter-pressure from conservative societal and political forces (Jalal 1991: 6; Rouse 1988: 6).

Upon the return to civilian rule under Zulfikar Ali Bhutto (1971–7), a number of women's groups emerged in an overall socio-political context of progressive gender policies. In 1972, administrative reforms paved the way for women to enter all government services and the 1973 Constitution strengthened women's legal status by clauses on equality before the law, non-discrimination for public service and reserved seat provisions for legislative assemblies. A Women's Rights Commission was established in 1976, promulgating legal reforms along with women occupying key positions such as governor of Sindh, university vice-chancellor and deputy speaker of parliament (Ali 2000: 44–6). This decade, infused by the International Women's Year in 1975, saw women joining left groups, a re-emergence of the United Front of Women's Rights lobbying for a constitutional reserved seat provision and the founding of Shirkat Gah ('place of participation'), a major player in the Pakistan women's movement until today, where renowned activists and feminist scholars Farida Shaheed and Khawar Mumtaz have their centre of activist gravitation (Shaheed and Warraich 1998: 276–8).

Shirkat Gah was founded in 1975 with the purpose of women's empowerment through increased access to information, resources, skills and decision-making, following a participatory and rights-based approach, including advocacy and capacity building, research, (trans)national and local networking (especially with community based organizations, CBOs, and as South Asia office of Women Living under Muslim Laws, WLUML) and publications. Its programme areas include women, law and status, women and sustainable development, and reproductive health. Strategies of interaction and lobbying include: regular publications and research in English and Urdu on women's issues (e.g. abortion, women's land rights, poverty, religion and social change); a documentation centre for materials on women in Muslim countries, human rights and globalization; and sessions for CBO members on legal literacy and awareness, reproductive health and rights, gender awareness and analysis, advocacy and research methodologies. It interacts with CBOs and local decision-makers through its offices in Karachi, Lahore and Peshawar as well as with regional and international NGO platforms and the UN system ('Shirkat Gah Women's Resource Centre' 2008).[4]

Activists from Shirkat Gah were also instrumental in establishing the Women's Action Forum (Khawateen Mahaz-e-Amal, WAF) (Shaheed and Warraich 1998: 279), the key platform of the women's movement against '*Nizam-e-Mustafa*—the Islamization of the laws and social fabric in Pakistan' (Rouse 1998: 58) under the rule of military dictator Zia-ul-Haq (1977–88) which ousted Zulfikar Ali Bhutto. This decade of military rule and Islamization policies can be considered as the 'most active and vigorous phase of the women's movement' (Ali 2000: 51). Zia's policies included an Islamic dress code for public employees, the 1984 Law of Evidence (*Qanoon-e-Shahadat*) and the infamous 1979 *Hudood* Ordinances, which provided gender discriminations regarding women's testimony for certain types of punishment (*hadd*), evidence in case of adultery (*zina*) and rape (*zina bil jabr*) and a lower age of criminal responsibility for girls (due to a puberty clause) (Ali 2000: 47). The launch of the women's movement was triggered not immediately by the enactment of the *Hudood* Ordinances, but when subsequent legal practices led to trials against rape victims and couples using their right of free choice of marriage being charged with adultery, a punishable offence by the Ordinances, subject to corporal punishments and/or imprisonment (Ali 2000: 48; Jalal 1991: 103).[5]

> In an atmosphere of general repression expected in a martial law regime, women's protests and meetings, newspaper statements, articles, signature campaigns, etc. became the sole voice of defiance in the Pakistan of the early 1980s.
>
> (Ali 2000: 49; cf. Zia 1998: 378f.)

WAF was formed in 1981 as a platform for women's activists and organizations, endorsed by APWA, 'for advocating human rights of Pakistani women, non-Muslim citizens and other marginalized Pakistanis suffering under unjust systems, discriminatory laws, poverty and patriarchy' (*Daily Times* 2006).[6] According to founding member Lala Rukh Khan, WAF did not define itself openly as feminist in order not to alienate otherwise supportive women (cited in Khan 2006: 87). Using a lobbying-cum-pressure group approach, WAF members also decided on a 'non-structured approach in its organization, membership, and parliamentary procedures within the organization', meaning that women's groups rallying under its banner retained their organizational independence, the same applying to its different chapters established in different cities (such as Karachi, Lahore, Islamabad, Peshawar, Quetta) (Jalal 1991: 104–5; Rouse 1998: 7–8). It was also decided not to accept any financial support from governmental or international sources in order to remain independent and avoid possible cooptation. This limited its options in terms of available resources for office infrastructure, outreach and support base, thus WAF remained a kind of umbrella and did not turn into a mass organization (Khan 2006: 88; Shaheed and Warraich 1998: 305). WAF employed a rather confrontational stance vis-à-vis the Islamization policies of Zia-ul-Haq's regime via demonstrations, gatherings, signature campaigns, petitions, seminars on education, health, law and so on, press conferences or its lobbying with trade unions, professional associations or political parties to include women's issues in their agendas. Nevertheless, WAF cooperated with the newly established governmental Women's Division in a special report for the Planning Commission and its Sixth Five-Year-Plan (Shaheed and Warraich 1998: 29ff.; Jalal 1991: 104–5; Rouse 1998: 7–8). WAF was successful in starting a national debate on women's issues and a women's movement, delaying the implementation or achieving a less gender-incriminatory legislation, successfully protesting against a radio programme in which fundamentalist views of Islamic state and society were propagated in 1981 along with publicly denouncing and subsequently reversing some *zina* sentences (Haq 1996: 171).

But the transversal impact of such actions remained largely minimal for average women in rural and urban areas and their legal, socio-economic and political status. The nascent women's movement, which largely rallied around legal issues and its discriminatory practices, reached out to a limited number of women, largely from middle and upper classes; that is, those closer to state institutions. As a study conducted by Farida Shaheed in the late 1980s/early 1990s in Lahore and Karachi indicates, the segmentation of society in terms of state–society relations and interactions meant that hardly any women 'referred to the political discourse so evident in the mass media and the focus of activist women's groups, much less to laws, directives, and policies' (Shaheed 1998: 154). At the same time, opposing women's groups such as the Majlis-e-Khawatin-i-Pakistan endorsed the Islamization policies of Zia-ul-Haq, rejected these women's activists and their reference system (e.g. CEDAW, Universal Declaration of Human Rights) as Westernized and supported the police crackdown on women protestors (so-called 'traitors') in Lahore in 1983 (Jamal 2005a: 61; Weiss 1985: 873–4).

Apart from the umbrella platform WAF, other important women's organizations were established in the 1980s, which continue to be key players in the women's and human rights movement of Pakistan. One example of nation-wide women's organizations with a community-based network approach is the Aurat Publication and Information Foundation, founded in 1986 for women's empowerment and participation of citizens in the governance process by working with CSOs, networks and other rural and urban groups in 100 out of 110 districts. This district-level network is coordinated by offices in all major provincial capitals (Lahore, Islamabad, Peshawar, Quetta and Karachi). Its main areas are information for women and on women's issues, capacity-building and advocacy. Despite organizational, leadership and funding difficulties in recent years, Aurat Foundation managed to establish, since its formation, information network centres with an outreach of 36,400 women in 2,600 urban and rural communities in 100 districts and 680 supportive local organizations, citizens action committees in 70 districts, legislative watch groups and resource centres in 70 districts for women councillors active at the local government levels. Besides this district-level network approach, Aurat Foundation has been active in monitoring and lobbying against violence against women, promoting women's political participation through publications, posters, capacity-building and campaigns with political parties, women politicians and women voters, denouncing unethical electoral practices along with monitoring elections through its citizen's campaigns for women's participation in local and national elections in 2001, 2002 and 2005 and has been a strong advocate of the repeal of the *Hudood* Ordinances (Aurat Foundation website 2008).

In contrast, AGHS Legal Aid Cell was established in 1980 as a human rights and legal aid organization, which cooperates with the human rights movement (primarily the Human Rights Commission of Pakistan, HRCP) and other women's groups, but operates more localized through its law office based in Lahore.

Its activities include advocacy, legal services to women victims in cases of human rights violations, family law or discriminatory laws such as *Hudood* cases, paralegal trainings, urgent actions, drafting of human rights-related legislation and research with a major focus on rights of women, children and minorities in Pakistan. It also runs the women's shelter DASTAK (since 1990 by an own trust) for victims and endangered women, used by partner organizations such as the WAF offspring War Against Rape (WAR). Two of the co-founders, Hina Jilani and Asma Jahangir, are also internationally renowned human rights activists— Jilani currently serves as Special Representative of the United Nations (UN) Secretary General on Human Rights Defenders and as HRCP member (ABC Radio 2008), while Jahangir is the former UN Special Rapporteur on Extrajudicial Killings and current chairperson of the HRCP. Both women have been under police protection for several years following threats on their lives (AGHS website 2008).

The cases of AGHS, WAF and HRCP also illustrate the various associative links and networks set up between different social movements in Pakistan, ranging from influencing political agenda-setting, interaction in the form of demonstrations, petitions or personal linkages in administrative boards, membership or chair-personship in the case of the women's, human rights and pro-democracy movements (e.g. anti-Musharraf lawyer's movement of 2007/08). Several founding or current council members of WAF and known women's activists repeatedly took over HRCP key positions. These linkages are also of strategic interest for the women's movement, because the human rights movement, in particular the HRCP, disposes of a wider constituency and transnational linkages while sharing similar positions on key issues such as violence against women, repeal of Hudood Ordinances or cases of child custody (Ali 2000: 53–3). But differences crystallize between the two movements on several issues:

> In the opinion of Hina Jilani, a founding member of both WAF and HRCP, these tensions surfaced particularly on issues of cultural rights, rights of religious minorities and the use of indigenous institutions for the promotion of human rights. The women's rights movement had a distinct position on the role of culture, tradition and religion in undermining women's social status and legal rights.
>
> (Ali 2000: 53–4)

The political repression and Islamization programme under Zia-ul-Haq also triggered the formation of professional associations dedicated to the protection of human rights, such as the Pakistan Women Lawyer Association (PAWLA) in 1986. Working for women's emancipation and 'empowerment justice', PAWLA offers legal aid by female lawyers, legal awareness trainings and advocates law reforms. Its jail project provides support for those accused of *zina* charges or arranges bail. Cases were filed for free or with a nominal fee for women-initiated dissolution of marriage by *khula* (separation), dowry, child maintenance and custody, criminal cases, wife maintenance or conjugal rights, thus allowing access to formal judicial institutions for many women (Pakistan Women Lawyer Association 2008). With regional offices in all major cities of the country, it also engages with different segments of society through legal awareness film screenings in schools, clinics, parks and remote areas or through plays aired and discussed on Radio Pakistan (Imran 2005: 94–5).

The transition towards a more democratic civilian rule under Benazir Bhutto in 1988 was not without effect on the movement, leading to a different pace and also new forms of agency in the years to come.

> ... the pace of the women's movement slowed perceptibly. Some women simply no longer felt the urgency of the moment and withdrew to return to pick up their lives. Within the movement, the political differences amongst women activists, hitherto submerged in the face of the common enemy of marital law, started to surface leading to divisions on which positions to take in the changed circumstances. A small number of activists decided to join (or reactivate themselves in) political parties. Those who chose to continue their activism within the framework of the women's movement and the general human rights agenda had to go beyond their experience under martial law to start learning the ropes of non-confrontational advocacy strategies.
>
> (Shaheed and Warraich 1998: 280)

As Ali points out, the women's movement needed to broaden and sustain itself by addressing wider developmental issues—such as health, education, political participation—and establishing (trans)national networks with NGOs and other social movements (Ali 2000: 41). One could even speak of a kind of mainstreaming of the feminist women's movement into society and state alike. The protest against the passage of the Shariah Act 1991 is an example of the women's movement's ability to build alliances with lawyer's associations, professional organizations (Pakistan Medical Association), media and opposition politicians. During the seven-year campaign it coorganized seminars, panel discussions, signature campaigns and disseminated material to legislators and lobbied politicians in parliament, at home or even at the parliamentary cafeteria (Zia 1998: 383f.). 'The passage of the bill could not be prevented. Nevertheless the women's movement generated sufficient pressure and enough support amongst the public, the political parties and the Treasury Benches to drastically alter the character of the bill' (Zia 1998: 384).

In its 1988 Charter of Demands, WAF outlined the following agenda: women's constitutionally guaranteed rights as citizens, a repeal of discriminatory laws, commitment to CEDAW, larger women-related budgetary allocations for women-related needs of health, education, social welfare services, non-discrimination in media and employment, property rights, protection against violence in addition to a commitment to peace and non-proliferation of nuclear weapons (Haq 1996: 168; Jalal 1991: 114).

Keeping up the momentum

The decade of the 1990s saw a return to democracy accompanied by three distinct phenomena with regard to the women's movement development and strategies applied. Women's groups started to:

- influence government, ministerial bureaucracy and political parties through advocacy, engagement and dialogue in advisory committees, working groups and workshops—either as activists or professional consultants;
- build linkages with other social movements (e.g. minority rights, anti-nuclear, peace and environment) and to increase their interaction with other societal forces such as professional organizations, emerging grass-roots organizations and the media;
- expand towards gender-sensitive/-specific developmental NGOs due to increased international funding (Mumtaz 2005: 64; Shaheed and Warraich 1998: 299f.; Zia 1998: 384).

During the decade of civilian rule under twice prime minister Benazir Bhutto (1988–90, 1993–6) and Nawaz Sharif (1990–3, 1997–9), Pakistan's civil society saw a 'proliferation of NGOs' with women's groups establishing gender-specific NGOs to work on issues such as 'legal rights, adult literacy, or income-generation' (Weiss 1998: 136–7). Prime examples are organizations such as Rozan,[7] SACHET or UKS[8] which are either watchdog associations, developmental NGOs with a specific gendered approach on issues such as emotional and psychological health, violence against women and children (Rozan) or welfare and development-oriented (SACHET or Al-Huda).[9]

WAF members also established their own NGOs, such as Simorgh, in the 1990s to advance their agenda and to cooperate on issues related with other (trans)national women's and human rights groups; for example, on women's rights, education or religious fundamentalism (Simorgh 2008). One offspring of WAF in the early 1990s was WAR, established by a group of fifteen journalists, women's and NGO activists with many active male members in response to two high-profile rape cases. It handles around five to six rape cases per month and provides rape victims with legal, medical and survival aid, helps to file first incident reports with police and provides counselling, supported by a pool of doctors, lawyers and psychologists. In its focus on sexual abuse and sex crimes, WAR conducts awareness campaigns and cooperates with other women's or minority community NGOs; for example, DASTAK shelter and AGHS (*Irin News* 2004).

Especially during the second tenure of Benazir Bhutto, women's activists were included for governmental policy planning and policy measures such as the establishment of women's police stations, the twenty-year National Plan of Action for Women or the Beijing Process. The Ministry of Women's Development funded hundreds of NGO projects in the area of 'education, health, skill training, and income generation' (Weiss 1998: 138–9; cf. Shaheed and Warraich 1998: 281).

The creation of these NGOs is seen as a double-edged sword. On the one hand, it supplied women's groups and developmental NGOs with funding for women's programmes and increased outreach to women across classes and localities by NGOs and CBOs. Social services, developmental programmes as well as awareness campaigns could link the women's movement to different sectors of society, mainstream it and broaden its base to the grass-roots level. On the other hand, support and overlap with international NGOs (INGOs) and internationalized women's issues not only present a support and reference system, but can also bring charges of Westernization, problems of priority differences and paternalism from international partners. There is also the danger of cooptation of women's agendas 'through a process that funds "safe" issues such as women's health, education, and micro-enterprise. At the same time, women activists have little energy left to organize against gender-biased practices of the state' (Khan 2006: 102–3; cf. Jamal 2005a: 56; Ali 2000: 54–5). In addition, women's rights groups might encounter hostility or resistance in more conservative and tribal areas of the country, which bars them from effective grass-roots work even on 'non-controversial [issues] like educational or health programmes' (Zia and Bari 1999: 100f.).

To counter charges of Westernization by political leaders and conservative forces, women activists tried to position themselves in a 'nationalist anti-colonial project ... and to delegitimize the monopolistic claims of politico-religious parties on cultural authenticity' (Jamal 2005a: 57). In contrast, women active in Islamist movements, such as members of the Jamaat-e-Islami, 'express widespread suspicion of feminist activities in Pakistan, especially projects funded by international aid-dispensing bodies and UN agencies, as promoting a "Western" agenda to undermine Islamic culture and values'(Jamal 2005a: 71).

One major issue of activism was the political mainstreaming of women by lobbying political parties' members, politicians and government officials at provincial and national level to address women's issues (e.g. in party manifestos), the campaign for a 33 per cent gender quota for legislative assemblies with direct universal suffrage, election monitoring and capacity-building of women voters and candidates. Cooperation with human rights groups, trade unions or media activists, dissemination of information material to political parties, candidates or display in public places in addition to community level meetings or media campaigns were the chosen means of these advocacy efforts (Shaheed and Warraich 1998: 304; Zia 1998: 385). Although public pressure resulted in women's sections being included in all major political party manifestos, few promises were upheld by political parties once in power (Ali 2000: 51). When a consensus was reached in 1997, the 33 per cent campaign was endorsed by representatives of nineteen political parties, ministers, two assembly speakers, 1,500 CSOs and thousands of concerned citizens in addition to two supportive provincial assemblies' resolutions—the 'widest support that any issue relating to women has ever received' (Zia 1998: 393). Other major segments of the women's movement concentrated on the monitoring of violence against women through the use of a more gender-sensitized media to prompt the government to set up women's shelters (Ali 2000: 51). Women's issues gradually penetrated the political and public agenda and discourses. But how sustainable are these activities and what is the quality of their impact (Ali 2000: 51)? Does such lobbying and promotion of women's issues and subsequent government measures actually represent substantial change or are these cosmetic measures to satisfy certain groups at home and abroad, while simultaneously appeasing more patriarchal (or even misogynist) segments through non-implementation?

Under Benazir Bhutto's tenures, women's police stations were set up, women judges appointed, a minimum quota set in government employment, women's studies centres at institutions of tertiary education established and CEDAW ratified in 1996 due to successful lobbying by the women's movement.[10] The country report for Beijing included crucial demands from women's groups such as the repeal of discriminatory laws. The Ministry of Women's Development collaborated actively with women's organizations, which themselves conducted cross-party dialogues and engaged with decision-makers at the provincial and national level. This changed significantly during the second tenure of Nawaz Sharif, whose authoritarian NGO policies decreased interaction. The women's movement then became an effective watchdog of all women-related government actions and could—at least in public discourses and in court—challenge certain policies such as the privatization of the development-oriented First Women's Bank (cf. Ali 2000: 52; Zia and Bari 1999: 86; Zia 1998: 386).

The following Musharraf years (1999–2008) were ambiguous times for the women's movement. Should activists engage with a dictator (albeit an allegedly progressive one with an agenda of 'enlightened moderation') in order to advance gender equality? Such engagement saw gains such as the reserved seat provisions (since 2001/02), legal advances such as the Women Protection Bill (2006) and the establishment of a permanent body of women's affairs—the National Commission on the Status of Women (since 2000). Can such achievements be considered sustainable in a socio-political context of power deals with the religious right and the threat of increased Islamization? Can gender democracy be achieved at all via such state–civil society engagements, negotiations or sometimes even cooptations?

There were political parties like the PPP [Pakistan People's Party of slain two-times prime minister Benazir Bhutto, AF] or many women's, rights and liberal groups that saw in the October 1999 military coup a positive move to block the then prime minister Nawaz Sharif's use of his brute parliamentary strength to introduce his own brand of Islamic Shariah in the country. In the early years of his military rule, Gen Musharraf was praised by the country's liberal political and social circles for reversing the obscurantist policies of General Zia-ul-Haq. There was a time that many women's rights groups thought that he was the best thing that had happened to the country in decades. But the same people turned against him when he struck a deal with the religious right to legitimize his rule after the 2002 elections.

(Abbas 2008)

During the recent events of the state of emergency and widespread protests against the sacking of the chief justice in 2007/08, renowned women's and human rights activists such as Asma Jahangir were placed under house arrest; others were jailed, not for the first time. During its two-day convention in Karachi in January 2008, WAF members condemned the authoritarian policies of Musharraf, responsible for the current socio-economic and political crisis (extremism, price hikes, energy crisis) and called for a neutral government of national consensus for democratization (*The News* 2008). At the same time, several gender-related policy plans and programmes, including gender mainstreaming and budgeting initiatives for executives and ministerial bureaucracies, were officially launched under Musharraf; for example, the National Policy for Development and Empowerment of Women in 2002, National Education Policy 1998–2010, Pakistan's Population Policy of 2002, National Health Policy of 2001, MOWD Family Protection Project, Gender Reform Action Plan or the Women's Political Participation Project under which tens of thousands of local women councillors were trained on gender issues, advocacy and constituency servicing. During the 'Beijing Plus Ten' process, a NGO Organizing Committee—comprised of SACHET, Rozan, APWA, Aurat and others—conducted a visible role in dialogues and national consultations with the government and the MOWD from 2001–5 on diverse women's issues such as CEDAW, education and training, health and population, violence against women, economy, power and decision-making as well as women's human rights and legislation (Shaheed and Zaidi: n.d.). Involved women's activists were critical of the gains achieved under the Beijing Platform of Action.

> Many measures are hampered by inadequate budgets and personnel[,] others suffer from flaws and/or lacuna that greatly undercut their potential to have a positive result. Some are undermined by poor execution[,] others are rendered ineffective or less effective because of contradictions … The net result of these shortcomings suggests an unfortunate continued lack of sufficient political will to bring about basic changes that challenge the status quo.
>
> (Shaheed and Zaidi n.d.: x)

> While these have been developments at the official level, it must be mentioned that a major part of the credit for these developments must go to the women's rights movement in Pakistan, which is a dynamic one and has been actively working on all these issues for several decades, also undertaking untiring advocacy at several levels in pursuance of the goal of gender equality and justice.
>
> (Zia 2005: 14)

Furthermore, gender-related legal initiatives took place such as resolutions against 'honour killings' introduced in National, Sindh and Baluchistan Assemblies, the Citizenship Act 2000, landmark judgements by the superior judiciary on cases of violence against women or the establishment of the National Commission on the Status of Women as a statutory body (but without necessary independence and resources to become effective or a governmental/parliamentary follow-up of its recommendations) (Zia 2005: 9–14). An outstanding example is the Women Protection Bill 2006 (WPB) that received a critical reception by women's groups because it does not repeal the *Hudood* Ordinances, denies women's rights of choice of marriage and—as a compromise with religious forces—introduces 'adultery' as an offence in the penal code. The latter could open a new entry point, states WAF, to victimize persons marrying of their own choice instead of using the previous *zina* clause (ABC Radio 2006; Warraich 2007: 103).

At the same time, Islamist parties were co-opted to Musharraf's power base in a move to counter-balance and offset secular opposition parties, among others. This gave rise to a number of women parliamentarians and women's activists within, for instance, the Jamaat-e-Islami women's wing and its organizational affiliations, which approach issues of 'gender equality' and 'women's emancipation' with distinctly different agenda objectives from secular feminists.[11] These activists might share some issues with progressive feminists such as marriage and divorce rights, economic exploitation of women, and better societal status of women, but identify different causes (e.g. gender segregation in public life) (Jamal 2005a: 61, 69–70). Jamaat's Women's Rights Charter is an excellent example because it raises several similar agenda points in order to achieve a 'reformation of society' and change women's societal status.[12] But cooperation between these different camps of the women's movement remains controversial given the divergence in gendered societal visions and value systems along with the perceived appendage agency of Islamist women activists by secular feminists and charges of socially destructive Westernization by the former.

> The influence of western culture has taken its toll. Government machinery is gradually becoming devoid of people who are God-fearing and true representatives of Islam. This has paved the way for un-Islamic forces to penetrate and achieve their nefarious aims. The main target of this clever and organized plan is the Pakistani woman, the last fortress of Islam.
>
> (Jamaat-e-Islami Women Wing Leaflet)

To 'march towards the Islamic Revolution', a variety of publications, social and educational services are offered: monthly stipends for students, material and monetary provisions for widows as well as 'Kashmiri *mujahideen*', arrangements for health care facilities, conduction of Quran classes and circles for women in different towns and villages, mobile rural medical camps, Islamic teaching seminars for medical professionals, counselling and welfare work for female and juvenile prisoners, arbitration in marital disagreements in addition to the establishment of handicraft and skill development centres and self-financing schemes, seminars for technical and management training of working women or income-generating projects (Jamaat website 2008).

The record of the majority of the women's movement to counter social conservatism and religious fundamentalism has been limited. Although it managed to exercise some checks and balances on discriminatory legal and policy practices, it was unable to prevent certain others, namely the *Hudood* Ordinances, Law of Evidence, or *Shariah* Court purview of family laws. The ideological divide between both strings in the women's movement—secular/universalist vs. religious/social conservatives—was repeatedly used by governments for political purposes (Jalal 1991: 105–6). Two examples illustrate the deliberate neglect of the Musharraf regime due to higher ranking interests of national/provincial power politics.[13] The Mera Ghar women's shelter, run by Aurat for victims of domestic violence or forced marriages, was shut down on charges of 'adultery and obscenity' by the Islamist provincial government in Peshawar. Its closure was accompanied by 'a simultaneous character assassination campaign … against workers of Aurat' (Brohi 2006: 61–2). It could have remained open as a shelter for aged women and women beggars or under the tutelage of Jamaat-e-Islami NGOs (Brohi 2006: 61–2). In 2005, Hina Jilani and Asma Jahangir coorganized a women's marathon demonstration in protest against Musharraf's janus-faced 'enlightened moderation' policies (while engaging with Islamist parties). During the subsequent police crackdown, a policewoman deliberately attacked Asma Jahangir, stripping her of her clothes in public (*ABC Radio* 2008; *BBC News* 2005a; *BBC News* 2005b).

Tomorrow's agenda—achievements, failures and challenges ahead

Given the outstanding commitment and stamina of the women's movement throughout the last three decades, the women's movement managed to (a) place women on the national agenda and public discourse at an unprecedented level, (b) resist or delay discriminatory laws or amend proposed legislation (e.g. Law of Evidence, Law of Qisas and Dyat), open a debate on Islam and Islamic laws previously considered too sacred to tackle, and (c) catalyse new women's advocacy groups and develop linkages with other social movements as important platforms and support structures, becoming a critical watchdog for human rights and minority rights. As a concrete outcome of the women's movement agency and campaigns stand the ratification of CEDAW, reserved seats provisions for local, provincial and national assemblies, a quota for government jobs, greater government allocations for women's programmes, greater visibility in electronic media, a statutory national commission, a National Policy for Women's Development announced in 2002 along with legislation such the WPB (Khan 2006: 90; Basu 2005: 13, 15; Mumtaz 2005: 64–6; Ali 2000: 56–8; Shaheed 1995: 92).

At the same time, several difficulties and challenges remain for the women's movement to address; for instance, the need to develop into a broad-based movement 'across class boundaries and the urban-rural divide' which addresses common women's daily concerns, such as mobility or access to health, education, employment facilities and familial decision-making through effective campaigns and cross-class collective action (Shaheed 1995: 92–4). The current glocal political environment places militarization and subsequent masculinization of public space as a major site of struggle to achieve gender democracy (Rouse 2004: 141–3). Having said that, the women's movement failed to achieve several crucial agenda items given its composition and strategies, but also given the difficult socio-political context in which it operates. To name but a few are the non-repeal of discriminatory laws, a notable reversal of women's socio-economic status or the lack of inclusion of non-elite urban and rural women and women's organizations at the grass-roots level to break with the legacy of Zia-ul-Haq 'to divide and rule along religious, ethnic and sectarian lines' (Ali 2000: 57–61; cf. Khan 2006: 90).

It remains to be seen if president Zardari will follow the footsteps of the Bhutto legacy in terms of women-friendly policy-making and civil society interaction and endorse some of the women's movements prime demands. Minister of information and former journalist Sherry Rehman herself was the private member bill sponsor of the Women Empowerment Act in 2004. But glocal 'hard portfolio issues' such as economic decline or the fight against terrorism and religious extremism appear to overshadow the struggle of the women's movement for women's development and full citizenship status. At the writing of this chapter, police exhumed the bodies of several women in Baluchistan who had wanted to marry men of their own choice against the wishes of tribal elders. Two senators classified these murders as tribal traditions, but met not only the resistance of protesting women's groups but also of the Senate, and the Ministry of Interior ordered an official inquiry (*BBC News* 2008). Shortly after the first public address by President Zardari, one of the biggest bomb blasts ever in the country's history destroyed a hotel in Islamabad. Needless to say that the so-called 'hard portfolio issues' of international politics and economics are inextricably linked to the quest for democracy, human rights, development, empowerment and participation for half of Pakistan's nation—the challenge remains for the women's movement whose different camps might manifest different priorities, strategies and societal visions to follow.

Notes

1 For a detailed analysis of the nexus of Islam and state in Pakistan and the respective different public discourses (orthodox religious vs. developmental/modernist) on 'women' see Rouse (2004).
2 On the discourse and representation of (veiled) women activists in religious right-wing organisations, see Moghadam (2003, 1992: 35–53), Christiansen (2003: 145–65) and Esposito (2003: 69–100).
3 The United Front for Women's Rights was formed with the help of the two first women legislators and lobbied actively for the enactment of West Punjab Muslim Personal Law (*Shariah*) Application Act 1948, in particular for inheritance rights. The Democratic Women's Association was founded in 1948 and engaged in labour issues of working-class women in factories etc. (Shaheed and Warraich 1998: 273f.).
4 In order to expand the feminist movement to the rural areas and to counter charges of urban-based elitism, in 1994 Shirkat Gah started its Women Law and Status Program to enhance legal literacy at the community level, working annually with around forty-five women's groups and CBOs. Shirkat Gah provided capacity-building in legal awareness

(family law, fundamental rights, police procedures, aspects of criminal law, laws relating to sexual violence), advocacy skills, planning and report writing. Core groups of local partners are identified in each province to receive further paralegal and specialized training (e.g. on human rights and the UN, role of women's movement and its fight for women's rights) (Iqbal 2007: 167–70; cf. Iqbal and Naheed 1998: 449–88). This cooperation facilitated the integration and active participation of grass-roots groups into the Beijing process and enlarged the basis of the women's movement away from its largely urban and middle-class centres (Iqbal 2007: 175).

5   For a study on *zina* cases and female prisoners cf. Khan (2006, 2003) and Zia (1998: 379). Feminist documentary filmmaker Sabiha Sumar portrayed the societal effects and impact of Islamization and the role of governments using religion in documentaries such as 'Who will cast the first stone?' (1988), 'Don't ask why' (1999), 'For a Place under the Heavens' and 'Silent Waters' (2003). Unable to officially release her documentaries in Pakistan, she conducted a film screening tour with 'Silent Waters' in forty-one villages and towns across Pakistan (Sabiha Sumar in Booklet of DVD Silent Waters, British Film Institute, BFIVD722; for a detailed analysis of her documentaries see Imran (2008: 117–54)).

6   '1) Women have the right to life, liberty, dignity, freedom of movement and security of person. 2) Women are equal partners in the development of the country and should be recognized as such. 3) Women have the right to determine their lives according to their own aspirations. 4) Women have the right to participate in recreational activities, sports and all aspects of cultural life. 5) WAF does not believe in the principle of enforced segregation' (WAF Charter, chapter one, as quoted in Haq (1996: 168).

7   Rozan is an Islamabad-based NGO with a staff of primarily psychologists, conducting awareness raising activities, trainings and counselling in five programmes: *Arangan* on child sexual abuse, *Zeest* on VAW, *Rabta* on police trainings, Youth Help Line (emotional and reproductive health) and *Pehchaan* (currently inactive gender resource centre) (www.rozan.org).

8   UKS ('reflection') is an advocacy- and rights-based group working for gender equality and women's development while focusing on the relationship of women, women's issues and the media/media personnel since 1997 through media monitoring, trainings and workshops as well as an independent radio production house with all-female staff since 2003. Radio productions cover issues such as poverty, peace and justice, HIV/Aids, earthquake, water and women's issue or women/honour/murder, aired in different FM stations and university campus radios in Karachi, Lahore, Peshawar, Islamabad/Rawalpindi (www.uksresearch.com).

9   SACHET (Society for the Advancement of Community, Health, Education and Training) was established in 1999 and conducts, for example, a silver ribbon campaign on FAD (Fight Against Dowry) since 2004, aims to promote gender awareness and sensitivity as well as reproductive rights and HIV/Aids, to narrow gender gaps in health, education and economic participation as well as to address gender-based and youth violence (http://sachet.org.pk/home). In contrast, Al-Huda has focused explicitly on Islamic education and welfare since 1994. It offers different courses for women and girls, working women, students and 'domesticated women' on Quranic recitation and sciences, *Hadith* sciences, Islamic jurisprudence etc. It also engages in community education programmes and lectures, rural, jail and hospital programmes, daily morning radio programmes in Karachi, Lahore, Islamabad, publications and social welfare services (marriage bureau, teaching of household chores, welfare programmes with monthly stipends for women and orphans, supply of food items and clothes to 'deserving families'), scholarships for students, prisoner help cell (food, clothing, medicine), patients help cell, guidance and counselling or e-learning courses (75US$/three months) in its branches in Islamabad, Lahore and Karachi (www.alhudapk.com). For a critical portrayal of Al-Huda see Afzal-Khan (2007: 22ff.).

10 The ratification of CEDAW 'was a watershed point for the Pakistan women movement' despite reservations regarding issues of coeducation, inheritance and evidence/legal witness (Weiss 2003: 585, 591).

11 ' "Emancipation of women", "gender equality", and "gender discrimination" are some of the slogans to lure and misguide women folk. ... Women wing of Jamaat-e-Islami is struggling for the establishment of the Islamic order' (www.jamaat.org/womenwing/index.html).

12 The charter demands economic, social, political and legal rights; for example, male maintenance of women's economic needs, inheritance rights according to Shariah, women-friendly employment conditions for women who need to work (e.g. job near home, avoidance of mixed atmosphere), women's education (banning of mixed education), institutions for vocational and professional education, well-equipped women health centres in villages and cities, abolishment of exploitive customs such as marriage with Quran, dowry, so-called 'honour killings', active voting rights and improved process of political representation, legal protection against sexual harassment and violence with severe penalties against offenders, rehabilitation centres for female victims, revision of *Hudood* Ordinances and the prohibition of women-exploitative media portrayals (Leaflet of Women Commission Jamaat-e-Islami Pakistan, Women's Rights Charter).

13 For a detailed analysis of Islamist forces during Musharraf's rule, see Rashid (2008: 145–61).

References

Abbas, Z. (2008) 'Musharraf's mixed legacy', *Dawn*, 19 August 2008. Online. Available HTTP: www.dawn.com/2008/08/19/top3.html (accessed 20 August 2008).

ABC Radio (2006) 'The Law Report: Hina Jilani'; *Daily Times*, 'Women's Action Forum thanks anti-Hudood activists', 19 November. Online. Available HTTP: <http://www.dailytimes.com.pk/default.asp?page=2006\11\19\story_19-11-2006_pg7_27> (accessed 1 September 2008).

—— (2008) 'The Law Report: Hina Jilani', 8 August. Online. Available HTTP: <http://www.abc.net.au/rn/lawreport/stories/2008/2209518.htm> (accessed 11 August 2008).

Afzal-Khan, F. (2007) 'Betwixt and Between? Women, the National and Islamization in Pakistan', *Social Identities*, 1: 19–29.

AGHS website (2008) Online. Available HTTP: http://aghsblog.wordpress.com/about-aghs/ (accessed 11 August 2008).

Ali, S.S. (2000) 'Law, Islam and the Women's Movement in Pakistan', in S. Rai (ed.) *International Perspectives on Gender and Democratisation*, Basingstoke and London: Macmillan, pp. 41–70.

Aurat Foundation website (2008) 'Reports'. Online. Available HTTP: www.af.org.pk (accessed 11 August 2008).

Basu, A. (2005) 'Women, Political Parties and Social Movements in South Asia', UNRISD Occasional Paper 5 (July 2005). Online. Available HTTP: www.unrisd.org/publications/opgp5 (accessed 11 August 2008).

BBC News (2005a) 'Head to Head: Pakistan's Mixed-sex Row', 27 May. Online. Available HTTP: <http://news.bbc.co.uk/2/hi/south_asia/4583955.stm> (accessed 5 September 2005).

—— (2005b) 'Pakistan Police Brutality Claim', 15 May. Online. Available HTTP: <http://news.bbc.co.uk/2/hi/south_asia/4548885.stm> (accessed 5 September 2008).

—— (2008) 'Pakistan Women's Bodies Exhumed', 2 September. Online. Available HTTP: <http://news.bbc.co.uk/go/pr/fr/-/2/hi/south_asia/7593522.stm> (accessed 3 September 2008).

Brohi, N. (2006) *The MMA Offensive Three Years in Power 2003–2005*, Islamabad: ActionAid International Pakistan, pp. 61–2.

Christiansen, C.C. (2003) 'Women's Islamic Activism: Between Self-Practices and Social Reform Efforts', in J.L. Esposito and F. Burgat (eds) *Modernizing Islam. Religion in the Public Sphere in Europe and the Middle East*, London: Hurst & Company, pp. 145–65.

Daily Times (2006) 'Women's Action Forum to Fight for Human Rights', 12 February. Online. Available HTTP: <http://www.dailytimes.com.pk/default.asp?page=2006\02\12\story_12-2-2006_pg7_17> (accessed 1 September 2008).

Esposito, J.L. (2003) 'Islam and Civil Society?', in J.L. Esposito and F. Burgat (eds) *Modernizing Islam: Religion in the Public Sphere in Europe and the Middle East*, London: Hurst & Company, pp. 69–100.

Haq, F. (1996) 'Women, Islam and the State in Pakistan', *The Muslim World*, 2: 158–75.

Imran, R. (2005) 'Legal Injustices: The *Zina Hudood Ordinance* of Pakistan and Its Implications for Women', *Journal of International Women's Studies*, 7, 2: 78–100.

—— (2008) 'Deconstructing *Islamization* in Pakistan: Sabihar Sumar Wages Feminist *Cinematic Jihad* through a Documentary Lens', *Journal of International Women's Studies*, 9, 3: 117–54.

Iqbal, S. (2007) 'Widening the Base of the Feminist Movement in Pakistan', in A. Durán *et al.* (eds) *Building Feminist Movements and Organization: Global Perspectives*, London: Zed Books, pp. 167–77.

Iqbal, S. and Naheed, A. (1998) 'Creating Spaces: Shirkat Gah's Outreach Programme' in F. Shaheed *et al.* (eds) *Shaping Women's Lives. Laws, Practices & Strategies in Pakistan*, Lahore: Shirkat Gah, pp. 449–88.

Irin News (2004) 'Pakistan: Anti-rape NGO Struggles to be Heard', 11 February. Online. Available HTTP: www.irinnews.org/Report.aspx?Report/d=22865 (accessed 21 August 2008).

Jalal, A. (1991) 'The Convenience of Subservience: Women and the State of Pakistan', in D. Kandiyoti (ed.) *Women, Islam and the State*, London: Macmillan, pp. 77–114.

Jamal, A. (2005a) 'Feminist "Selves" and Feminism's "Others": Feminist Representations of Jamaat-e-Islami Women in Pakistan', *Feminist Review*, 81: 52–73.

—— (2005b) 'Transnational Feminism as Critical Practice: A Reading of Feminist Discourses in Pakistan', *Meridians*, 2: 57–82.

Jamaat website (2008). Online. Available HTTP: www.jamaat.org/womenwing/index.html (accessed 13 July 2008).

Khan, S. (2003) '*Zina* and the Moral Regulation of Pakistani Women', *Feminist Review*, 75: 75–100.

—— (2006) *Zina, Transnational Feminism and the Moral Regulation of Pakistani Women*, Karachi: Oxford University Press.

Moghadam, V.M. (1992) 'Patriarchy and the Politics of Gender in the Modernising Societies: Iran, Pakistan and Afghanistan', *International Sociology*, 1: 35–53.

—— (2003) *Modernizing Women. Gender and Social Change in the Middle East*, 2nd edn, Boulder, CO: Lynne Rienner Publishers.

Mullally, S. (2005) '"As Nearly as May be": Debating Women's Human Rights in Pakistan', *Social Legal Studies*, 3: 341–58.

Mumtaz, K. (2005) 'Advocacy for an End to Poverty, Inequality, and Insecurity: Feminist Social Movements in Pakistan', *Gender & Development*, 3: 63–9.

'Pakistan Women Lawyers Association' (2008) Online. Available HTTP: http://www.unic. org.pk/index.php?id=pawla (accessed 20 August 2009).

Randall, V. (1998) 'Gender and Power. Women Engage the State', in V. Randall and G. Waylen (eds) *Gender, Politics and the State*, London and New York: Routledge, pp. 185–205.

Rashid, A. (2008) *Descent into Chaos. The United States and the Failure of National Building in Pakistan, Afghanistan and Central Asia*, New York: Viking, pp. 145–61.

Rouse, S. (1988) 'Women's Movement in Pakistan: State, Class, Gender', *Women Living under Muslim Laws*, Dossier 3, June–July. Online. Available HTTP http://www.wluml. org/english/pubsfulltxt.shtml?cmd[87]=i-87-2519 (accessed 1 September 2008).

—— (1998) 'The Outsider(s) Within. Sovereignty and Citizenship in Pakistan', in P. Jeffery and A. Basu (eds) *Appropriating Gender. Women's Activism and Politicized Religion in South Asia*, New York: Routledge, pp. 53–70.

—— (2004) *Shifting Body Politics. Gender, Nation, State in Pakistan*, New Delhi: Women Unlimited.

Shah, A. (2004) 'Pakistan. Civil Society in the Service of an Authoritarian State', in M. Alagappa (ed.) *Civil Society and Political Change in Asia. Expanding and Contracting Democratic Space*, Stanford: Stanford University Press, pp. 357–88.

Shaheed, F. (1995) 'Networking for Change: The Role of Women's Groups in Initiating Dialogue on Women's Issues', in M. Afkhami (ed.) *Faith and Freedom: Women's Human Rights in the Muslim World*, London and New York: I.B. Tauris, pp. 78–103.

—— (1998) 'The Other Side of the Discourse: Women's Experience of Identity, Religion, and Activism in Pakistan', in P. Jeffery and A. Basu (eds) *Appropriating Gender. Women's Activism and Politicized Religion in South Asia*, New York: Routledge, pp. 143–66.

Shaheed, F. and Warraich, S.A. (1998) 'The Context of Women's Activism', in F. Shaheed *et al.* (eds) *Shaping Women's Lives. Laws, Practices & Strategies in Pakistan*, Lahore: Shirkat Gah, pp. 271–318.

Shaheed, F. and Zaidi, Y. (n.d.) *Pakistan Ten Years into the Beijing Platform for Action. A Civil Society Perspective on Some Critical Areas of Concern*, no publications details available.

'Shirkat Gah Women's Resource' (2008) Online. Available HTTP www.shirkatgah.org/ (accessed 20 August 2009).

Simorgh (2008) Online. Available HTTP www.simorghpk.org (accessed 1 July 2009).

The News (2008) 'WAF Moot holds Musharraf solely Responsible for Present Crisis', *The News*, 13 January. Online. Available HTTP: <http://www.thenews.com.pk/daily_ detail.asp?id=90924> (accessed 1 September 2008).

Warraich, S.A. (2007) ' "Honour Killings" and the Law in Pakistan', in L. Welchman and S. Hossain (eds) *'Honour'. Crimes, Paradigms, and Violence Against Women*, Karachi: Oxford University Press, pp. 78–100.

Weiss, A.M. (1985) 'Women's Position in Pakistan. Sociocultural Effects of Islamization', *Asian Survey*, 8: 863–80.

—— (1998) 'The Slow Yet Steady Path to Women's Empowerment in Pakistan', in Y. Yazbeck and J.L. Esposito (eds) *Islam, Gender, and Social Change*, Oxford: Oxford University Press, pp. 124–43.

—— (2003) 'Interpreting Islam and Women's Rights. Implementing CEDAW in Pakistan', *International Sociology*, 3: 581–601.

Zia, S. (1998) 'Some Experiences of the Women's Movement: Strategies for Success' in F. Shaheed *et al.* (eds) *Shaping Women's Lives. Laws, Practices & Strategies in Pakistan*, Lahore: Shirkat Gah, pp. 371–414.

—— (2005) *Future Vision on 'Empowering Women'. Address to First Meeting of the SAARC Autonomous Advocacy Group of Prominent Women Personalities (SAWAG) on 21–22 June 2004, Islamabad, and Some Excerpts From Her Writings*, Islamabad: Aurat Foundation.

Zia, S. and Bari, F. (1999) *Baseline Report on Women's Participation in Political & Public Life in Pakistan*, Islamabad: Aurat Foundation, pp. 100f.

11 Mapping a hundred years of activism

Women's movements in Korea

Seung-kyung Kim and Kyounghee Kim

Women's movements in Korea, like women's movements in other Asian countries, started as a result of interaction with the West, and political organizations concerned with women's issues arose during Korea's first effort to modernize in the late 1800s. Over the past hundred years, women's movements have ebbed and flowed during periods of Japanese colonial rule, civil war, military dictatorship, and democratization, and developed in conjunction with political movements that focused on broader issues affecting the whole society. Women's movements in Korea have been arenas where groups with varied ideological backgrounds have struggled to advance women's interests according to their differing interpretations of those interests. Thus, the history of women's movements has been 'fraught with tension, antagonism, competition, and cooperation' among different groups revolving around the issues of gender, class and nation (Cho 1996: 5; see also Lee 1996; Sim 1985; Yi 1994).

The first women's movement organization, Ch'anyang-hoe ('Praise and Encouragement Association'), was formed in 1898 with a mission to promote girls' education and, in 2008, there were 232 civil organizations dealing with women's issues registered as members of two umbrella groups—Han'guk yŏsŏng tanch'e yŏnhaphoe (Korean Women's Associations United, KWAU) and Han'guk yŏsŏng tanch'e hyŏbuihoe (Korean National Council of Women, KNCW), both with active websites (www.women21.or.kr; www.kncw.or.kr).[1] These two umbrella groups coordinate nearly all non-governmental organizations' activities dealing with women's issues in Korea. The Korean National Council of Women was established in 1959 by middle-class women, including both housewives and professional women. Its founding platform, 'improving women's status and providing service to the society and the country' (*Han'guk yŏsŏng tanche hyŏbuihoe* 1993) called on women to participate in building a strong nation. The KWAU was established in 1987 as an umbrella organization for progressive women's groups, connecting twenty-one previously existing or newly founded member organizations. It developed out of the democracy movement and took a position that women's problems cannot be separated from other social issues (Cho 1996: 8).

This chapter aims to map the turbulent hundred-year history of women's movements while examining significant issues that came into prominence at specific historical junctures. Within women's movements, various currents of feminism, including Christian, liberal, radical and socialist, predominated at different historical moments. At various times, these currents converged because of their common interests in the status of women in Korean society, and each worked to change women's status. They approached this task from different ideological positions, and their agendas sometimes overlapped but, at other times, were in conflict.

Beginnings

In the second half of the nineteenth century, Korean society was forced to adapt as the territorial aggression of its neighbours drove the country into the international political arena where its weakness left its destiny in the hands of outside powers. At the same time as Korea's political fortunes were waning, foreign missionaries were introducing new ideas that clashed violently with the Confucian ideology that had guided the kingdom for the previous 500 years.[2] This period was marked by an intense questioning of the existing social order, an important part of which was a re-examination of the position of women within Korean society.[3] During this time Western missionaries began establishing a modern education system for girls.[4] Korea's first girls' school, Ewha Haktang, was founded in 1886 by Mary Fitch Scranton, an American Methodist missionary, and this was soon followed by a number of other missionary schools for girls.

During this period, progressive male intellectuals[5] supported equality for women along with other reforms of society. Korea's first vernacular newspaper, *Tongnip Sinmun* ('The Independent Newspaper'),[6] published editorials advocating equality between men and women. An 1896 editorial asserted: 'Women are not inferior to men; men are so uncivilized that they mistreat women without any humane considerations or just cause. Isn't it a sign of primitiveness that they oppress women merely by their physical superiority?' (Kim 1976: 214). The paper also urged education for girls:

> If women are educated and develop interests in society, they would realize that their rights as human beings are equal to men's. They would also find a way to stop the brutality of men. We ask, therefore, that women be educated even better than men in order to educate other women and become an example of behaviour to men.

> (ibid.: 215)

In 1898, a group of upper-class women formed a women's organization, Ch'anyang-hoe, in order to establish a secular girls' school. They published their manifesto in *Tongnip Sinmun* on 9 September 1898, a document that is considered 'the first declaration of women's rights' in Korean history (quoted in Kim 1996: 128). The manifesto laid out their goals to use education for Korean women to achieve equal status with men: 'Modelling ourselves after other countries, we have plans for founding a school for girls to educate them in a variety of subjects, rules and personal bearing, making them equal to men in the future' (quoted in ibid.). After first approaching the government for funding and being rebuffed, Ch'anyang-hoe went ahead with funds from its own members and founded Sunsong girls' school in December 1898 (ibid.: 129). Although Ch'anyang-hoe soon became embroiled in political intrigue and disappeared from the scene, its girls' school served as a model for other private girls' schools that 'mushroomed during the next decade' (ibid.: 130).

Graduates of these schools, armed with Western education and Western values, sought to replace the patriarchal value system of Yi dynasty Korea with gender equality and the ideology of democracy. In particular, Christianity's relative gender equality raised Korean women's awareness of their subordinate position within Confucian ideology. Women, educated by Christian schools, became the leaders of Korea's first women's movement and also played key roles in the independence movement during the subsequent colonial period.

Colonial period (1910–45)

The early 1900s were a chaotic period that saw the demise of the nation, and its incorporation into the growing Japanese empire. In 1905, Japan forced Korea to become a Japanese protectorate and, in 1910, it annexed Korea and established a colonial government. The colonial regime was to last for thirty-five years, during which Korea experienced varying degrees of political repression as its weak farming economy was absorbed into Japan's growing capitalist economy. In addition to reorganizing rural production under Japanese auspices, the colonial regime expanded mining and manufacturing in service of the Japanese economy. The regime also oversaw an increasing urban population and the continued expansion of education. The compulsory universal education system implemented by the colonial government increased the number of schools for girls.

The early years of Japanese rule coincided with the introduction of Western liberalism based on a philosophy of individualism which appealed strongly to the first generation of Korean women to receive a Western-style education. These mostly upper-class, educated women sought to replace the Confucian ideal of womanhood with an alternative modern ideal, *sinyŏsŏng* ('new woman').[7] Their progressive essays published in new magazines and newspapers advocated 'women's self-realization' and 'free choice in marriage' (Cho 1988: 96). Some of these early *sinyŏsŏng* regarded it as their pioneering duty to oppose the traditional family system and tried to live according to their beliefs. These modern women felt they should be free to form relationships based on love, rather than being legally bound into an arranged marriage. The new ideology of *sinyŏsŏng* was expressed in 1922 in a characteristic editorial in the magazine *Puin* ('Woman'). The editorial urges its readers to transform themselves completely, not just superficially:

> Should we only use the word civilization and not adopt its content; … should
> we only be intoxicated by the beautiful words of male and female equality

and not cultivate our capacity for equality ... should we only adopt Western hair styles ... and dress and not create the situation that requires it ... should we only be proud that we do not do sewing and not learn more important skills; and should we only be proud of escaping from ordinary kitchen work and not learn more important work?

(*Puin* ('Woman') 1922 (Park 1977: 109–10))

Three of the most well-known *sinyŏsŏng* of the 1920s—Kim Wŏn-ju, Kim Myŏng-sun and Na Hye-sŏk—were all beneficiaries of the modern education offered by missionaries. Kim Wŏn-ju (1896–1971) attended Ewha Haktang and studied in Japan before returning to Korea. A well-known poet and writer, Kim advocated the new sexual morality of the *sinyŏsŏng* in her article, 'Our Ideal': 'We need to protest against the old sexual morality that disregards our individuality and character. ... We need to get rid of the old idea that if a woman lost her virginity, her love is no longer pure' (quoted in Cho 1988: 97). Kim married twice and divorced twice and was most notorious for her love affair with Yi Kwang-su, a famous writer who was married to another woman. In later years, she retreated from her avant-garde stance and ended her life as a Buddhist nun. Kim Myŏng-sun (1896–1951) also studied at Ewha Haktang before going to Japan to attend Tokyo Women's College. She became a novelist, and her first novel was published in a famous literary magazine, *Ch'ŏngch'un* ('The Heyday of Youth'), in 1917. Her reputation as a writer was overshadowed by her lifestyle of 'free love', and she became a target of society's criticism against *sinyŏsŏng*. Na Hye-sŏk (1896–1948), the first Korean woman professional painter and a reform-minded writer and critic, was another well-known *sinyŏsŏng* during the same period: 'A beneficiary of progressive education in Korea, Japan, and Europe, rarely available to average Koreans of her time, Na enjoyed high social visibility and reputation' (Kim 2002: 1). She attended Jinmyŏng Women's School before leaving for Japan to study painting at the Tokyo Women's Art College. She returned to Korea in 1913, worked as a junior high school teacher, became involved in nationalist politics and married a progressive intellectual. In 1927, she embarked on a tour of Europe and America with her husband, and chose to remain behind in Paris. Na's love affair with Ch'oe Lin in Paris was widely publicized and condemned by society because she was a married woman and a mother of four children (Kwon 1998: 387). As a proponent of 'free love', Na pursued her love affairs despite becoming a target of severe social criticism.[8] Nevertheless, her life was far from a happy one; her husband eventually divorced her, and she died a pauper.

The term *sinyŏsŏng* was first used by women who had received modern education to refer to themselves, but by the end of the 1920s, it came to designate women with loose sexual morality and, in the extreme, implied a high-class call girl. Thus educated women began calling themselves 'inteli' women to distinguish themselves from the others. These first generation women's liberationists faded out at the end of the 1920s without having made noticeable gains for women in society and attacked by both conservatives and progressives (Cho 1988: 97–8).

In addition to women who sought women's liberation through greater personal freedom, many women were active participants in political movements during the colonial period. Women students who were educated at the Ewha Haktang played an especially important role in the anti-colonial movement, 'forming an underground society called the Patriotic Women's League' (Jayawardena 1986: 222). Ewha students were prominent in the March First Movement in 1919 against Japanese occupation. During the March First Movement, many demonstrations were led by women from Ewha. The young woman who became emblematic of the independence struggle was an Ewha student, Yu Kwan-sun, who led the demonstration at her hometown in Ch'ungch'ŏng province. She was arrested and tortured to death by the Japanese at age sixteen. Christian women, who participated in the March First Movement, became more aware of nationalist ideology, but the colonial government's suppression prevented the churches from developing into an overt political movement. Faced with the Japanese repression, Christian women backed away from direct confrontation with the Japanese, but continued nationalist work underground through proselytizing and organizing night classes (Lee 1996: 159).

Women were also important in organizations based on socialist ideas, first introduced to Korea by students educated in Japan (Yi 1989: 264–5). The Korean Communist Party was founded in 1925, and its early leadership included one notable woman, Chŏng Chŏng-Myŏng. Women in this and other socialist organizations set as their main goal, national liberation, and, since they directly challenged Japanese rule, they were suppressed nearly as quickly as they formed (Cho 1988: 98–9).

In 1927, a coalition of missionary and socialist women formed Kŭn'u-hoe, an important new women's organization. Kŭn'u-hoe advocated progressive positions on a variety of social issues and declared in its mission statement that 'the oppression of Korean women is caused by both Confucian patriarchy and the contradictions of modern capitalism' (Yi 1989: 268). Kŭn'u-hoe advocated rights for women, worked at exposing the terrible working conditions endured by Korean women workers, and advocated national independence from Japan. For four years, Kŭn'u-hoe struggled with both internal division and external oppression before breaking up in 1931 (Yi 1989: 269–71; Yi 1994: 235–6). Kŭn'u-hoe is important because it was the first women's organization that claimed to represent all '10 million Korean women' and was the first alliance of progressive missionary-educated women and progressive socialist women.

The Japanese colonial regime also made use of women's organizations to rally support for itself. As Japan mobilized the resources of Korea for its war effort, it established several pro-colonial government women's groups, such as 'Puin kyemong toknyŏban' (1938) and 'Chosŏn imjonbokukdan puinhoe' (1942) to recruit women to support the war. Young women recruited by these groups were among those who ended up as 'comfort women', military prostitutes serving the Japanese Imperial Army (Son 1993: 376).

Throughout the colonial period, women's direct participation in labour increased. As colonial Korea was drawn into Japan's war efforts, men were drafted into the military and to provide labour for factories and mines. Rural women were forced to take over a greater share of farm labour, while urban women took on new roles as wage labourers in factories. The textile industry was the employer of more than 50 per cent of these women industrial workers.[9]

Liberation to the fall of Syngman Rhee

During the last years of Japanese colonial government, national liberation movements were forced underground and the Korean women's movement effectively disappeared. After liberation, however, women's organizations were among the many social and political movements that sprung up in the contest to define Korea's future (see Cumings 1997: 185ff). On 17 August 1945, the first post-liberation women's organization, Kŏnkuk Punyŏ Tongmaeng, was established by women activists representing a broad range of ideologies.

Kŏnkuk Punyŏ Tongmaeng moved steadily to the left, and its more conservative members departed the organization. In December, it renamed itself Chosŏn Punyŏ Ch'ongdongmaeng, affiliated with the Communist Party and began mass orga-nizing. It renamed itself again in 1947, NamChosŏn Minju yŏsŏng Tongmaeng, recasting itself as a parallel organization to the North Korean PukChosŏn Minju yŏsŏng Tongmaeng. Each of these organizations was opposed by the American military government in South Korea, which sought to suppress left-wing organizations (Cumings 1997: 244–5). When the South Korean government was established in 1948, NamChosŏn Minju yŏsŏng Tongmaeng's activities were outlawed. It supported the North during the war and merged with its northern counterpart into Chosŏn Minju yŏsŏng Tongmaeng (ibid.: 245–6).

More conservative women also founded several organizations during the period of American military government. One of the most important of these was Tongnip ch'oksŏng aeguk puindan, which was organized in opposition to Kŏnkuk Punyŏ Tongmaeng in 1946 (Ch'oe 1979: 255). The organization's first president was Pak Sun-ch'ŏn, a participant in the March First Movement who later cooperated with Japanese colonial authorities. These right-wing women's organizations sought to establish a unified, sovereign and anti-communist Korea, but did not receive much mass support because of some of their leaders' pro-Japanese history (Yi 1994: 240–3). Women also formed professional organizations[10] that put forth platforms that advocated 'better status for women', 'gender equality rights' and 'expanding women's rights in order to achieve gender equality' (ibid.: 247). Both left- and right-wing women's organizations thus supported gender equality, but whereas the right wing advocated a narrow agenda of gradual reform and nurturing professional women, the left wing sought a much more sweeping 'complete liberation in political, economic, and social arenas' (ibid.).

When the Republic of Korea was established in 1948, the Constitution guaranteed women equal rights with men, including the right to vote and stand for election. Nevertheless, women were almost completely excluded from political life: 'The membership of the first National Assembly (1948–50) consisted of 199 men and one woman' (Soh 1993: 2). The three other prominent women politicians during this time were Pak Hyŏn-suk who became a minister without portfolio in 1952; Pak Sun-ch'ŏn who was elected to the Assembly in 1950, went on to serve five terms, and became the leader of the opposition party in 1960s; and Kim Whal-ran, who served as a minister in Syngman Rhee's administration in 1950. These pioneering women politicians came 'from the ranks of Christian women who were educated during the Japanese colonization of Korea' (ibid.: 59). Soh traces the political activism of these 'pioneer women' to 'the larger process of the resistance against Japanese rule, especially the March First Movement of 1919, which proved to be the turning point in the lives of the women legislators of the pioneer generation' (ibid.). The achievements of these women, however, remained isolated examples and did not lead to the involvement of large numbers of women in politics (Park 1999: 433).

The Korean War (1950–3) left the peninsula 'a smouldering ruin' (Cumings 1981: xix). The three years of civil war ruined both the southern and northern parts of the country.

> The toll in human lives was staggering. In the South alone, the combined total of military and civilian casualties—Koreans who had been killed, executed, wounded, kidnapped, or gone missing—was about 1.3 million people. Nearly half of the industrial capacity and a third of the housing in the south were destroyed along with much of the public infrastructure.
>
> (Eckert *et al.* 1990: 345)

The lingering effects of the devastating war lasted at least a decade, leaving people in extreme poverty; 'it also left its scars on an entire generation of survivors, a legacy of fear and insecurity that continues even now to affect the two Koreas both in their internal development and in their relations with each other' (ibid.: 346).

Towards the end of the war, several prominent women leaders, including Pak Sun-ch'ŏn, Hwang Sin-dŏk, Yi T'ae-yŏng and Yi Hui-ho, established yŏsŏng munje yŏn'guwŏn (Institute for Women's Issues) in 1952 (Ch'oe 1979: 255). They formed an alliance with other influential women's organizations, such as Taehan Puin-hoe (Korean Women's Organization), YWCA and Taehan Kanhohyŏphoe (Korean Nurses Association), and worked to influence public opinion about improving women's legal status. In the second half of the 1950s, various professional women's organizations were formed and, in 1959, were coordinated under yŏsŏng tanch'e hyob'uihoe (Korean National Council of Women), an umbrella organization with Kim Whal-ran as the president.

Rhee's regime became increasingly dictatorial as he clung to power by rigging elections and amending the constitution in order to hold on to the presidency. Student demonstrations against rigged elections led to Rhee's forced resignation and the founding of the short-lived Second Republic. The student revolution of 19 April 1960 established the student movement as a significant political force in South Korean politics, and students have remained prominent in the pro-democracy movement since then.

Women's movements under military dictatorship (1961–86)

The coup d'état of May 1961, led by Park Chung Hee, established a military dictatorship with policies which led to rapid industrialization and urbanization. Park's regime continued Rhee's anti-communism, but it was even more openly anti-democratic. When he came to power, Park disbanded all political and social organizations, including women's organizations. Later, the Park regime allowed a small number of pro-government, conservative women's groups to organize (Lee 1996: 245). Under the regime's tight political control, these organizations were restricted to improving women's welfare and providing anti-communist education, and they avoided any form of social activism (ibid.: 245–7). Women also formed non-government-sponsored organizations with various agendas during this period in response to these rapid changes in Korean society and the repressive government. Three organizations that were active during this period were Han'guk yŏsŏng tanch'e hyŏbuihoe (Korean National Council of Women), the Christian Academy and Han'guk kyohoe yŏsŏng yŏnhaphoe (Korea Church Women United). Even though Park suppressed workers' rights, this period also saw the rise of women workers' unions.

The KNCW continued to function under Park because its platform of 'improving women's status, and service to the society and the country' did not directly challenge the regime's priorities. With government support, KNCW and its affiliated organizations attracted a large following during the 1960s and 1970s. In preparation for the United Nations' 'International Women's Year' (1975), KNCW chose 'The International Women's Year and Korean Women's Reality' as the theme for its 1974 annual meeting (Lee 1996: 249). Their coalition of women's groups succeeded in obtaining a revision of Family Law in 1977. Organizations such as KNCW that remained narrowly focused on women's issues were later criticized by other social movements as being conservative and even reactionary. Groups with more progressive agendas have argued that the impact of liberal women's organizations was trivial and compromised by their cooperation with the government (Chŏng 1993: 164).

During the Yusin period (1972–9), the Park Chung Hee regime took the initiative in establishing mass organizations to support its agenda. The most important of these was Saemaŭl Punyŏhoe, founded as part of the Saemaŭl movement for rural development. By 1979, Saemaŭl Punyŏhoe had over three million members and nearly 100,000 branch offices (Yi 1994: 307). The government used this and other organizations to promote its policies on education, family planning, consumerism and dietary improvement (Moon 2000).

Despite Park's conservative attitude towards women's organizations and the government's harsh repression of political opposition, the national pro-democracy movement grew in strength during the 1970s. College students and others formed groups to oppose dictatorship and support democracy. The Christian Academy was an important organization that trained a generation of women leaders. It sought to reform the women's movement by unifying young women across class divisions and taught young women from diverse backgrounds. Their position was that the women's movement is a movement for all humanity (Yi 1994: 337–8). Many women who are currently leaders of the women's movement in Korea were members of the Christian Academy in the 1970s (Lee 1996: 250).[11]

Organizations of Christian women were also active during this time. Han'guk kyohoe yŏsŏng yŏnhaphoe (Korea Church Women United) took a leading role in condemning sex-tourism, and exposed the government's complicity in this issue (ibid.: 251). They also provided support to the women workers' labour movement and the pro-democracy movement by holding prayer meetings and supporting families of political prisoners (ibid.: 251–2).

Women also led organizations that were important in promoting the rights of workers during the 1970s. As Park Chung Hee's policy of export-led industrialization took hold, hundreds of thousands of young women joined the industrial workforce with extremely low wages and exploitative working conditions. Concern about the extreme exploitation of these women workers became a focus for political opposition. Women workers reacting to specific abuses in their factories spontaneously organized to resist management and form unions, but, because the industries where they worked were so fragmented, it was only when their actions were publicized and supported by groups such as Han'guk kyohoe yŏsŏng yŏnhaphoe (Korea Church Women United) that their collective actions took on national significance. Other, specifically religious, groups such as the Urban Industrial Mission also gave their support to spontaneously organized women's unions.

The two most important labour conflicts of the 1970s were those at Tong'il Textile Company and the YH Company, both of which had predominantly female labour forces. The militancy of the women's labour movement of the 1970s is especially noteworthy because other forms of political opposition to the Yusin system were so effectively suppressed that women's unions were among the very few social forces able to stand up to the regime (Choi 1993: 37; Kim 1997; Koo 1993: 140, 156; Lee 1989: 264–71; Pak 1983; Sin 1985: 49–60). Ironically, brutal treatment applied to women workers enhanced their political importance. The 1970s produced female martyrs for the labour cause and a thread of continuity throughout a period of severe repression, but workers did not gain any lasting victories at this time. At the end of the Yusin regime, working conditions in South Korea's factories remained poor, workers were still poorly paid, and labour organizing was still difficult and dangerous.

After a brief interlude following Park's assassination, another military dicta-torship was set up by Chun Doo Hwan who continued most of Park's policies. Despite his efforts to repress political opposition, pro-democracy activists grew in numbers and importance and, eventually, forced him to begin a transition to democracy in 1987. The women's movements during this period were distinctly different from their predecessors in that they were clearly social change movements. These social movements played a crucial role in moving Korean society towards democratization. Women workers, professors, college students and college graduates formed many organizations with progressive agendas: yŏsŏng p'yŏng'uhoe (The Association for Women's Equality and Friendship)[12] in 1983, Tto hanaŭi munhwa (Alternative Culture) in 1984, yŏsŏng'ui chŏnhwa (Women's Hotline) in 1983, Han'guk yŏsŏng yŏnhaphoe (Korean Women's Associations United) in 1987, and Han'guk yŏsŏng nodongjahoe (Korean Women Workers Association) in 1987.

The Association for Women's Equality and Friendship described itself as the first organization with a clear programme for women's liberation since the division of Korea, and opened up a new agenda for women's movements in the 1980s (Yi 1994: 341). Its mission statement declares that 'the women's movement should not stop at solving the problems of gender inequality, but work toward social change and national reunification' (ibid.: 342). They maintained that women's liberation was only possible with total social restructuring, but they disagreed among themselves about how to achieve this change. Although members of this group were mostly intellectual women, they were constrained by their position that the main players of the women's movement should be disenfranchised women. Thus, they tried to transform from a middle-class, intellectual women's organization to one based on women workers, poor women and women farmers (Cho 1996: 9). The group fell apart in 1986 because of disputes around these issues. Those who were most concerned with women's issues became the founding members of the Korean Women's Associations United in 1987, and others joined more radical *minjung* groups.

Unlike the Association for Women's Equality and Friendship which emphasized class issues, Tto hanaui munhwa (Alternative Culture) was founded as a feminist organization for consciousness-raising. The founders were academics who had recently returned to Korea after earning PhDs in leading American and European universities.[13] Rather than engaging in politics, the members of Tto hanaui munhwa sought to change the lives of women through writing and publishing (Cho 1996: 7). During the 1980s, they published three anthologies that focused on overcoming Korean society's 'patriarchal hierarchy and gender inequality.' They also considered children's education an important mission of the women's movement, and published two anthologies on this topic (ibid.: 13–14).

Gradual transition to democracy and the role of women's movements (1987–97)

In 1987, following the nationwide uprising for democracy and workers' rights in June, many women's organizations were formed throughout the country. Yŏsŏng tanch'e yŏnhaphoe (Korean Women's Associations United) was established as an umbrella organization for progressive women's groups, connecting twenty-one member organizations. KWAU supported the democracy movement and declared that women's problems could not be separated from the democracy movement (ibid.: 8). The organization also endorsed Kim Dae Jung in the 1987 presidential election. KWAU's platform advocated 'achieving women's liberation, democratization, and autonomy of Korean society' (Yi 1994: 313).

Also in 1987, the Korean Women Workers' Association was established in order to advocate women workers' rights. The founding members of the organization were women workers who were active in the democratic labour union movement from the 1970s and activists from the Association for Women's Equality and Friendship. It became a member organization of the KWAU. The Korean Women Workers' Association was the first national women's organization based on women workers. It promoted the rights of women workers, and took the lead in advocating the Equal Employment Law, which was passed in 1988. Under this law, it became illegal to discriminate against women workers in recruitment or employment.

After the election of the first civilian president in 1992, the broad coalition of social movements advocating the rights of the disenfranchised (women, workers, farmers and the urban poor) was replaced by a less militant and more fragmented set of civil organizations (Abelmann 1996: 227). The unifying themes of 1980s progressiveness in the women's movement—anti-government, pro-labour and pro-democracy—have gradually faded and, in the 1990s, issues regarding *sŏng p'oknyŏk* (sexual violence against women) and *sŏng munhwa* (sex culture) became the central focus of women's activism. A broad spectrum of various women's groups coalesced around these 'women's issues', and sought to create a 'woman's identity' that transcended class. Women's groups with various political agendas formed a coalition and were able to have a Special Law on Sexual Violence against Women enacted in 1992.[14] The movement that lobbied for the Special Law on Sexual Violence against Women was supported by a broad spectrum of civil organizations.

An issue that came into prominence in the 1990s involved forcing the Japanese government to acknowledge its responsibility for recruiting comfort women during World War II. Yoon Chŏng-ok, a professor at Ewha Womans University and a member of the Korea Church Women United, started to research comfort women during the 1980s. In 1990, Han'guk Chŏngsindae munje taech'aek hyŏbuihoe (the Korean Council for the Women Drafted for Military Sexual Slavery by Japan) was organized by a coalition of 37 women's groups (www.womenandwar.net). Relying on survivors' testimonies, they built up a case against the Japanese government and presented it to international human rights NGOs and to the UN Human Rights Committee. As a result, a transnational alliance on comfort women issues was formed in 1992. The group has been staging weekly demonstrations at the Japanese Embassy in Seoul since 1992 in an effort to have the Japanese government accept full responsibility for its actions during the war and to compensate survivors.

Another issue that was important to women's organizations in the 1990s was increasing the representation of women in government. In anticipation of the 1995 local election, KWAU and KNCW led a coalition group, Yŏsŏng Yŏndae, and worked to have women elected to public office. Their efforts did lead to an increase in the number of women in the public office although they fell far short of their goal of filling 20 per cent of the seats.

At the end of the 1990s, the distinction between progressive and conservative women's organizations became ambiguous, especially after 'the KWAU registered with the state as an incorporated body in 1995' (Moon 2002: 490). In 1998, a staff member at the KNCW told us that she no longer saw much difference between the two organizations' agendas. With the establishment of a democratic government, the old political cleavages within society are becoming obsolete.

Women-friendly governments and the institutionalization of women's movements (1998–2007)

The historic peaceful change of government in 1998 established the women-friendly presidency of Kim Dae Jung. During his presidency, he established the President's Special Committee on Women's Affairs, and a position in charge of gender policy was added to each of six ministries (Labour, Education, Law, Health and Welfare, Agriculture and Forestry, and Administration and Local-Government).[15] These newly established positions needed gender specialists, and were filled by women with degrees in women's studies or by women's movement activists. The Special Committee took up gender mainstreaming, and broke away from previous policies on grounds that they were divisive and objectified women as victims (Special Committee 1998). In 2001, the President's Special Committee on Women's Affairs was reorganized and elevated to the cabinet level as the Ministry of Gender Equality,[16] and Han Myeong-sook was appointed as minister.[17] The Ministry of Gender Equality continued to stress gender mainstreaming as its primary strategy. It listed its objectives as: first, to bring about a society with gender equality; second, to increase women's participation in society; and third, to improve women's welfare.

Working closely with the government, KWAU began an aggressive campaign—politics of engagement (*ch'amga ŭi Chŏngch'i*)—for gender mainstreaming in politics, economy and society, designating these areas as priorities in the three-year plan for 1998–2000. KWAU wielded considerable influence over policy-making and decision-making during the Kim Dae Jung administration, and they incorporated feminist ideas into the government's policies. For political mainstreaming, KWAU began a campaign for a quota system for the selection of candidates for the National Assembly under the system of proportional representation,[18] and a quota system for the hiring of civil servants. For economic mainstreaming, they began a campaign to ensure that women workers had standard rights and protections, preventing job irregularization. For social welfare mainstreaming, they sought to eliminate the discriminatory clause in the national pension system, and to provide pre- and post-natal care as part of social welfare.

The effects of KWAU's politics of engagement were most evident in political mainstreaming, and showed up in the increase of the number of women in the government and the National Assembly.[19] Affirmative action was also successful in increasing the number of women civil servants, including professors in public universities.[20] The Gender Equality Employment Act[21] and the Gender Discrimination Prevention and Relief Act[22] provided the most important legal basis for implementing affirmative action. Furthermore, when the Framework Act on Women's Development was revised in 2002, it substituted the term 'affirmative action' for the earlier phrase, 'temporary measure of preferential treatment'. Affirmative action boosted the number of women hired in the Foreign Service from 16.7 per cent in 1998 to 45.7 per cent in 2002; it also increased the percentage of women hired in the Administrative Civil Service from 23.1 per cent in 1998 to 28.4 per cent in 2002. Affirmative action was the most visible achievement of the gender policy during this period, and it exposed and corrected the systematic gender discrimination at every level of society.

The Roh Moo Hyun administration came into power supported by various groups who were active in the pro-democracy movement during the 1980s, thus, many who were involved in these movements came to occupy important government positions. The new administration advocated the 'realization of a society with gender equality' and 'the abolition of the family-head system' as two of the new government's 'national tasks'. In addition, the administration included gender discrimination as one of the six things that need to be eliminated because it contributed to social inequality. Calling itself 'the participatory government' (*ch'amyŏ Chŏngbu*), the Roh Moo Hyun administration emphasized active participation of civil society, and recruited many democratization activists into high government positions. Many women's movements activists were also recruited into government positions: Chi Eun-hee, the president of KWAU resigned her position in order to become the minister of gender equality; Han Myeong-sook, a past president of KWAU and the first minister of gender equality was appointed as the minister of environment; and others were also recruited into high positions in the 'National Human Rights Commission', 'Government Youth Commission', and the Ministry of Environment. KWAU also increased its power in the Women's Policy Advisory Committee, the most important committee within the Ministry of Gender Equality. Nevertheless, the ministry remained the smallest government ministry until 2006 when it was expanded and put in charge of childcare, and its name was changed to the Ministry of Gender Equality and Family.

As minister of gender equality, Chi Eun Hee maintained a close alliance with KWAU. She utilized her network with KWAU and other women's organizations in order to carry out the feminist agenda; KWAU's agenda provided underpinnings for the ministry's gender policy. During the Roh Moo Hyun administration, state feminism strengthened while women's organizations were able to solve important women's issues through policy-making by lobbying and challenging existing laws.

The two most important legal achievements produced by the women's movements' alliance with the government were the Act to Prevent Prostitution in 2004 and the abolition of the Family-Head System in 2005. These two legal changes abolished two systems that were supporting unequal gender relationships and show that the government was taking charge of fundamental social change, and had embraced progressive feminist ideology in its policy. Both abolishing the Family-Head System and preventing prostitution had been on the women's movements' agendas for several decades, but it was not until Roh Moo Hyun's presidency that these legal changes were accomplished. These two changes represent the high point in the power of state feminism and the alliance between KWAU and the Roh Moo Hyun administration.

Neo-Conservative retreat

When the neo-conservative administration of Lee Myung-bak took office in 2008, the Ministry of Gender Equality and Family was stripped of its newly acquired childcare duty, and reverted to its original size as the Ministry of Gender Equality. In order to staff the ministry, Lee's administration appointed career bureaucrats rather than feminist activists. The new minister of gender equality had worked for Lee's administration when he was mayor of Seoul City. The business of family and childcare was transferred back to the Ministry of Health and Welfare, and the promotion of gender equality no longer was at the top of the administration's agenda. The progressive women's policy organization created in 1998 in order to stop discrimination and achieve gender equality is now, in effect, a name only ministry without administrative power to deal effectively with the issues of gender discrimination.

Conclusion

Over the past century, women's movements have achieved remarkable progress in advancing women's rights and status within Korean society. The age-old family-head system, which was a key tenet of Confucian gender ideology,[23] was finally abolished in 2005, the latest step in a process of reform, driven by women's movements and put in place by reform-driven governments. A plethora of new and revised laws regarding women's issues, including affirmative action, equal employment, sexual violence, and prostitution, have also been enacted. These important changes in the legal arena have come about with the rapid transformation of Korea from a rural, agrarian society to an urban, industrialized one.

In Korea, as in many Third World countries, women's movements have been intricately connected with nationalist movements (Croll 1978; Jayawardena 1986; Lazreg 1988; Louie 2000; Moon 2000; Smith 2000; Wang 1999). Korean feminists have, from their beginnings in the 1890s until the democratic government was established in the 1990s, participated in struggles to redefine Korea's national identity within changing geo-political circumstances. Korea's earliest modernizers promoted the idea of gender equality and women's education in a drive to move away from stagnant Confucian traditions. During the early period of Japanese colonial rule, both Christian and secular women were involved in a nationalist movement that culminated in the March First Movement in 1919. The 1920s were marked by continued interest in individual freedom while the effectiveness of the nationalist movement diminished. The rise of *sinyŏsŏng* was the most important characteristic of feminism during this period. Japanese rule became increasingly harsh during its final decade, and liberation saw a sudden explosion of social and political activism. Women's movements during this chaotic period played an auxiliary role to various political factions that were vying for control over the country. During the three decades of military dictatorship, there were two important strands of feminism: liberal feminists who sought to reform society to improve women's status without opposing the government; and socialist feminists who saw establishing a democratic government as the crucial first step, and worked closely with other groups in the pro-democracy movement. When the democratic government was established and there was no longer a single enemy to fight against, the pro-democracy movement splintered into a multitude of single-issue organizations. Following the election of the former political opposition, the women's movement became influential during the women-friendly governments (1998–2007); however, when a neo-conservative government took over in 2008, the momentum for change had shifted.

At the current point in time Korean women's movements are once again in a period of transition. Many of the items that have been on the feminist agenda for decades have been introduced into law, and there is still a government ministry dedicated to gender equality. However, the women who were responsible for these achievements are not part of the current administration and cannot participate in formulating its policies. Furthermore, having achieved so much, the next goals are less obvious. The new generation of young feminists needs to decide for itself what issues and directions are important to them and what organizations and methods are most useful in pursuing them.

Notes

1 The progressive, feminist organization Korean Women's Associations United has 187 member organizations and the more conservative organization Korean National Council of Women has forty-five members. There are other women's organizations that do not belong to either KWAU or KNCW: some want to keep a distance from these two established organizations in order to maintain their organizational freedom; others wanted to become members but were not admitted because of political identity.
2 See Seth (2006: 220–1) for a summary of the introduction of Catholicism to Korea.
3 One of the early efforts to come to terms with the growing influence of the Western powers was the *Tonghak* movement. They advocated gender equality among the reforms that they promoted. See Eckert *et al.* (1990: 214–30) and Cummings (1997: 115–20) for a discussion of *Tonghak*.
4 For an extended discussion of women's literacy and the role of missionaries, see Choi (2000). She argues that 'the primary goal of the missionaries was to convert Koreans to Christianity and the dissemination of literacy was an expedient means for accomplishing this objective' (2000: 99).
5 These Enlightenment-oriented intellectuals include Yu Kil-chun, Yun Ch'i-ho, Pak Yŏng-hyo, and Sŏ Chae-pil.
6 Sŏ Chae-pil (1866–1951) founded this newspaper on 7 April 1896 'for easy accessibility by the masses, particularly women' (Kim 1996: 125).
7 The term *sinyŏsŏng* began to be circulated around the March First Movement when magazine publication was on the rise (Kim 2006: 264).
8 Similar to Kim Wŏn-ju's argument on 'virginity', Na declared that 'virginity is a hobby, and it has nothing to do with morality or law' (Kim 2000: 48).
9 For a detailed discussion of women factory workers during the Japanese colonial period, see Kang (1993).

10 The professional organizations include Chosŏn Women Scientists Association (1946),
    Korean Home Economics Association (1947) and Korean Midwives Association
    (1946).
11 Women who were alumni of the Christian Academy became leaders in politics,
    administration and the academy. They include Han Myeong-sook who became the
    first female prime minister, Yi Mi-kyung who is a leading member of the National
    Assembly, and Chang Pil-wha who headed the Department of Women's Studies at
    Ewha Womans University.
12 The founding members included Lee Hyo-chae and Cho Hyoung who were professors
    at Ewha Womans University, and were also founding members of Ewha's Department
    of Women's Studies.
13 The founding members, Cho Haejoang, Cho Oak-la, Cho Uhn, Cho Hyoung and Chang
    Pil-wha, are currently professors of leading universities and leading feminist scholars.
14 In 1995, college students and women's groups formed a coalition to support a sexual
    harassment case brought to court by a woman teaching assistant at Seoul National
    University.
15 Gender policy was first given a formal cabinet-level position in 1988 when President
    Roh Tae Woo established the Second Ministry of Political Affairs to focus on women's
    issues. The Second Ministry of Political Affairs continued to be in charge of gender
    policy until 1998 when President Kim Dae Jung downgraded the ministry, and replaced
    it with the President's Special Committee on Women's Affairs.
16 The President's Special Committee fell short of its goals for a variety of reasons.
    One was due to its low status—not being a ministry—which placed constraints
    and contradictions on its function, such as a shortage of budget and personnel, and
    contributed to problems with the mainstreaming of gender policy. See Kim (2002) for
    a detailed discussion of the Kim Dae Jung government's gender policy.
17 Han's appointment was widely praised by women's organizations, academics and
    activists. Han had been a long-time activist, starting as a member of the Christian
    Academy in the 1970s, and she also served as the president of KWAU (1993–5). Her
    record of working for Korean women's issues was indisputable.
18 Each party was required to put up a slate of candidates that was 50 per cent male and
    50 per cent female.
19 The number of women in the 299-member National Assembly increased from three in
    1992 to thirty-nine in 2004.
20 The Framework Act on Women's Development established in 1995 provided the legal
    basis for the affirmative action.
21 The Gender Equality Employment Act was first enacted in 1987.
22 The Gender Discrimination Prevention and Relief Act was first enacted in 1999.
23 Important studies of changing gender ideology in Korea include Abelmann (2003),
    Cho (1988), Deuchler (1992), Kendall (1996, 2002), Kim (1997), Lett (1998) and
    Nelson (2000).

References

Abelmann, N. (1996) *Echoes of the Past, Epics of Dissent: A South Korean Social
    Movement*, Berkeley, CA: University of California Press.
——(2003) *The Melodrama of Mobility: Women, Class, and Talk in Contemporary
    South Korea*, Honolulu, HI: University of Hawaii Press.
Cho, H. (1988) *Han'guŭi yŏsŏnggwa namsong* [Korean women and men], Seoul:
    Munhaggwa chisongsa.
Cho, J. (1996) 'Yŏsŏng Chŏngch'esŏng'ŭi Chŏngch'ihak: 80–90nyŏndae han'gug'ŭi
    yŏsŏng undong'ŭl chungsim'ŭro' [Gender Identity Politics: the Case of Women's

Liberation Movement in Korea in 80s and 90s], *Han'gŭk yŏsŏnghak* [Journal of Korean Women's Studies], 12: 138–79.

Ch'oe, M. (1979) 'Han'guk yŏsŏng undong sosa' [History of Korean Women's Movement], in Hyo-chae Lee (ed.) *Yŏsŏng haebang'ui iron'gwa hyŏnsil* [Theory and Reality of Women's Liberation], Seoul: Ch'angjakgwa Pip'yŏngsa.

Choi, H. (2000) 'Women's Literacy and New Womanhood in Late Chosŏn Korea', *Asian Journal of Women's Studies*, 6, 1: 88–105.

Choi, J. (1993) 'Political Cleavages in South Korea', in H. Koo (ed.) *State and Society in Contemporary Korea*, Ithaca: Cornell University Press.

Chŏng H. (1993) 'Pyŏnhwahanŭn segyewa yŏsŏng haebang undong'ŭi mosaek' [Changing World and the Search for the Theory of Women's Liberation Movement], *Yŏsŏng'gwa sahoe* [Women and Society], 4: 138–65.

Croll, E. (1978) *Feminism and Socialism in China,* London: Routledge and Kegan Paul.

Cumings, B. (1981) *The Origins of the Korean War: Liberation and the Emergence of Separate Regimes*, Princeton, NJ: Princeton University Press.

——(1997) *Korea's Place in the Sun: A Modern History*, New York: W.W. Norton & Company.

Deuchler, M. (1992) *The Confucian Transformation of Korea: A Study of Society and Ideology*, Cambridge, MA: Council on East Asian Studies, Harvard University.

Eckert, C. *et al.* (1990) *Korea Old and New: A History*, Cambridge, MA: Korea Institute, Harvard University.

Jayawardena, K. (1986) *Feminism and Nationalism in The Third World*, London: Zed Books.

Kang, I. (1993) '1920–60nyŏn han'guk yŏsŏngnodongsijang kujoui sajŏk pyŏnhwa'[A Historical Overview of the Korean Women's Labor Market Structure, 1920s–1960s], *Yŏsŏnggwa sahoe* [Women and Society], 4: 166–209.

Kendall, L. (1996) *Getting Married in Korea: Of Gender, Morality, and Modernity*, Berkeley, CA: University of California Press.

——(ed.) (2002) *Under Construction: The Gendering of Modernity, Class and Consumption in the Republic of Korea*, Honolulu, HI: University of Hawaii Press.

Kim K. (2000) 'Iljehaui sinyŏsŏng yŏn'gu: sŏng'gwa sarang'ŭi munjerŭl chungsim'ŭro' [Study of New Women during the Japanese Colonial Period: Issues Related to Sex and Love], *Sahoewa yŏksa* [Society and History], 57: 45–78.

Kim, S.J. (2006) 'Sinyŏsŏngdamnon saengsan'ŭi sikminjijok kujowa sinyŏsŏng' [The Day of the New Woman: Women's Magazines in Colonial Communication Field of Korea], *Kyŏngjewa sahoe* [Economy and Society], 69: 255–84.

Kim, S.K. (1997) *Class Struggle or Family Struggle?: Lives of Women Factory Workers in South Korea*, New York: Cambridge University Press.

——(2002) 'Gender Policy and the New Status of Women in Korea', in C. Moon and D. (eds), *Korea In Transition: Three Years Under the Kim Dae Jung Government*, Seoul: Yonsei University Press.

Kim, Y.C. (1976) *Women of Korea: A History from Ancient Times to 1945*, Seoul: Ewha Womans University Press.

Kim, Y.H. (1996) 'Under the Mandate of Nationalism: Development of Feminist Enterprises in Modern Korea, 1860–1910', *Journal of Women's History*, 7, 4: 120–36.

——(2002) 'Creating New Paradigms of Womanhood in Modern Korean Literature: Na Hye-sŏk's Kyŏnghŭi', *Korean Studies*, 26, 1: 1–60.

Koo, H. (ed.) (1993) *State and Society in Contemporary Korea*, Ithaca: Cornell University Press.

——(2001) *Korean Workers: The Culture and Politics of Class Formation*, Ithaca: Cornell University Press.

Kwon, I. (1998) 'The New Women's Movement in 1920s Korea: Rethinking the Relationship between Imperialism and Women', *Gender and History*, 10, 3: 381–405.

Lazreg, M. (1988) 'Feminism and Difference: The Perils of Writing as a Woman on Women in Algeria', *Feminist Studies*, 14, 1: 81–107.

Lee, H. (1989) Han'guk yŏsŏng undongsa [A History of Women's Movement in Korea], Seoul: Chŏng'usa.

——(1996) *Han'gukŭi yŏsŏngundong ŏjewa onŭl* [Women's Movement in Korea: Yesterday and Today], Seoul: Chŏng'usa.

Lett, D. (1998) *In Pursuit of Status: The Making of South Korea's 'New' Urban Middle Class*, Cambridge, MA: Harvard University Asia Center.

Louie, M. (2000) 'Minjung Feminism: Korean Women's Movement for Gender and Class Liberation', in B.G. Smith (ed.) *Global Feminisms since 1945: Rewriting Histories,* New York: Routledge.

Moon, S. (2000) 'Overcome by Globalization: The Rise of a Women's Policy in South Korea', in S. Kim (ed.) *Korea's Globalization*, New York: Cambridge University Press, pp. 126–46.

——(2002) 'Carving Out Space: Civil Society and the Women's Movement in South Korea', *Journal of Asian Studies*, 61, 2: 473–500.

Nelson, L. (2000) *Measured Excess: Status, Gender, and Consumer Nationalism in South Korea*, New York: Columbia University Press.

Pak, Y.M. (1983) 'The Role of Labor Unions in the Female Labor Movement in South Korea', *Korea Scope*, 3: 3–12.

Park, K. (1999) 'Political Representation and South Korean Women', *Journal of Asian Studies*, 58, 1: 432–48.

Park, Y.O. (1977) 'The Women's Modernization Movement in Korea', in S. Mattielli (ed.), *Virtues in Conflict*, Seoul: Royal Asiatic Society.

Seth, M. (2006) *A Concise History of Korea: From the Neolithic Period through the Nineteenth Century*, Boulder: Rowman & Littlefield.

Sim, C. (1985) 'Yŏsŏng undong'ŭi panghyang Chŏngnib'ŭl wihan ironjŏk koch'al', [A Theoretical Consideration of the Direction of Women's Movement], *yŏsŏng* [Women], 1: 200–255.

Sin, I. (1985) Yŏsŏng, nodong, pŏp [Women, Labor, and Law], Seoul: P'ulbbit.

Smith, B.G. (2000) *Global Feminisms since 1945: Rewriting Histories*, New York: Routledge.

Soh, C. (1993) *Women in Korean Politics*, Boulder, CO: Westview Press.

Son, C. (1993) 'Kyŏngje palchŏnkwa yŏsŏng'ui chiwi' [Economic Development and Women's Status], in H.S. Im and K.S. Pak (eds), *Onŭl'ui han'guksahoe* [Korean Society Today], Seoul: Nanam.

Special Committee on Women (1998) *Yŏsŏng paeksŏ* [White Paper on Women], Seoul: Han'ullim.

Wang, Z. (1999) *Women in the Chinese Enlightenment*, Berkeley: University of California Press.

Yi, A. (1989) '*Chŏng chŏng-myong'ui samkwa t'ujaeng*' [The Life and Struggle of Chŏng chŏng-myŏng], *Yŏsŏng* [Women], 3: 255–80.

Yi, S. (1994) *Yŏsŏng undonggwa chŏngch'i iron* [Women's Movement and Political Theory], Seoul: Noktu.

12 'Riding a buffalo to cross a muddy field'

Heuristic approaches to feminism in Cambodia

Trudy Jacobsen

I was sitting at a pavement café near the central market in Phnom Penh early in 2008, enjoying a *kafé dteuk kok* (ice coffee), when two men at a nearby table began to speak. 'Look at that', said one. 'She might be the next President of the United States.' His friend turned to the TV, where a beaming Hillary Clinton was displayed. 'That's okay,' he said, 'that will never happen here.' And they laughed.

Those familiar with Judy Ledgerwood's work might be struck, as I was, by similarities between this anecdote and her experiences in rural Cambodia observing political campaigning before the 1993 elections (Ledgerwood 1996).[1] Why does the idea of women attaining high political office in Cambodia continue to attract either disapproval or ridicule? Many Cambodian men (and women) believe that women are biologically predisposed to being more timid and less capable (Lilja and Prom 2002: 48–9). Feminism is considered to be a foreign concept, one that sits uneasily with so-called 'traditional' Cambodian values. As a consequence, the women's movement in Cambodia has experienced significant obstacles in achieving its goals; one commentator remarked that the women's movement was 'like riding a buffalo to cross a muddy field'. This phrase is used in Cambodia when something is useful only in times of crisis; obviously, one would prefer to ride a buffalo than slog through mud to the other side of the field. It would, however, be considered undignified and embarrassing to be caught riding a buffalo at any other time.

Cambodia has experienced several periods of crisis during the twentieth century and each of these has moved Cambodian women's activism along its unique path. Cambodia achieved independence from France in 1953 after a century of colonial rule. Self-rule brought its own particular problems and within a few years the government, led by the hereditary monarch Norodom Sihanouk,[2] was marked by corruption and increasing popular dissatisfaction. To complicate an already tense situation, in the early 1970s Cambodia faced the overflow of the US–Vietnam war as the eastern parts of the country suffered air-raids that displaced large numbers of people. This combination of events facilitated the emergence of the brutal Khmer Rouge regime—a socialist political party with the now-infamous Pol Pot at its head. Between 1975 and 1979 the Khmer Rouge emptied the cities of residents and forced the population into agricultural work on communized land. The terror accompanying the implementation of these policies produced the infamous Killing Fields and their failure reduced Cambodia's population from around 10 million to less than 7 million. A Vietnamese-supported military government overturned the Khmer Rouge in 1979 and set about restoring a modicum of order to a traumatized nation. After decades of political and military instability—where people were variously exhorted to aspire to colonialist, monarchist, communist and socialist ideals—Cambodia emerged in 1993 with a democratically elected government under a UN-sponsored programme of recovery. During these years of chaos, it has been difficult for Cambodian women to forge an independent feminist movement—riding a buffalo is not a simple task. But, more importantly, as this chapter shows, Western-style feminism that draws from grass-roots activism has not developed a large support base in Cambodia.

Cambodian 'feminism' negotiating the space between colonialism and nationalism

There are distinct cultural and political reasons for the absence of Western-style feminism in the colonial and immediate post-independence years. During both these periods, for many Cambodians, women embodied the essence of Cambodia's cultural identity. On this premise, women who moved beyond 'traditional' social parameters were deemed to compromise the very core of Cambodian cultural identity. In addition, because the introduction of feminist politics coincided with colonial rule, it further reinforced the idea that a woman's movement was not 'really' Cambodian at a time of heightened nationalist enthusiasm. Simultaneously, the French tempered the principles of 'equality, liberty, and fraternity' in their unequal and unrepresentative rule of Cambodia and this adjustment for colonial conditions affected the manner in which a women's movement would be conceived there. The colonial regime's shifting codes of 'egalitarianism' made it possible to create the space for the idea that women should support men, rather than be in complementary or equal relationships with them—this sex hierarchy mirrored the unequal relationship in the colonizer/colonized roles of the French and Cambodians.

A typical example of the ambiguities generated around the notion of feminism in the colonial period is presented in the writings of a French woman, Andrée Viollis. In 1931, she travelled through Indochina and later published her observations in a book titled *SOS Indochine*. Viollis called for an awakening of Cambodian women—a process that would be led by their more enlightened Western counterparts, who would serve as 'moral instructors' (1935: 35). In this rhetoric, Cambodian women's awakening was a foreign project to be enacted upon an inferior Cambodia. This sense of colonialist superiority was also evident in the work of other women writers from the West, such as Virginia Thompson, who wrote in 1937 'Oriental women ... only begin to live when they become mothers' (Thompson 1937: 326). Yet, French colonial women simultaneously regarded these very same 'asleep', 'not-live' women with jealousy and suspicion because of their appeal to French men. Novels written at this time regularly depict the tragedy of a husband or fiancé, besotted by a calculating Cambodian woman of lax morals and exotic talents, facing financial exploitation and a ruined career (see, for example, Groslier 1994).[3] The contradictions inherent in the colonial experience ensured that there was little sense of solidarity built between French and Cambodian women around feminist issues. Ultimately, French women would have found it difficult to make a case for female emancipation without making a similar argument for freeing Cambodia from the tyranny of colonialism.

Accordingly, the first women's movement in Cambodia emerged from within the Cambodian nationalist movement of the 1940s and 1950s. This trend is in keeping with a pattern seen elsewhere in the world where nationalist and revolutionary movements often mobilized women to their causes (Mies 1986). However, as was commonly the case for women active in independence movements, Cambodian women found that the nationalists unequivocally placed men in a superior position and made no attempt to emphasize gender equality. For example, in 1945, the newspaper *Kampuchea* took the daring step of hiring several women writers, but their role was not to promote the empowerment of women in a feminist sense. Instead, these women were charged with inspiring patriotism in their fellow women whilst ensuring that they did not step out of the supporting roles accorded to them 'traditionally': 'Glorious and prosperous countries are not only composed of men but also of women who help out in all fields. ... So please fulfil your duties as good housewives' ('Khmer Daughters' 1945: 2). Kate Frieson points out that not all women shared this view; there are several articles from the era in which Cambodian women criticized such a standpoint, such as the author 'Woman Slave' who stated that women in 'modern' Cambodia should be encouraged to claim the same rights as their European counterparts in order for the country to reach the same level of development as elsewhere in the world (Frieson 2000). Moreover, wives of nationalist activists were clearly mobilizing for change in 1946, when a man calling himself a 'compatriot' wrote to *Kampuchea* complaining that wives were constantly disturbing the important work of male nationalists with their insistence that men share in domestic tasks (Frieson 2000).

Marshalling notions of 'tradition'

The peculiar brand of feminism at play in the early nationalist movement in Cambodia was directly related to the notion of a 'traditional' Cambodia. Cambodian history was 'resurrected' by French historians, epigraphists and archaeologists in the late nineteenth and early twentieth century and enshrined in the local education system. Cambodians aspiring to join the bureaucracy during the colonial era derived their knowledge of Cambodia's past refracted through the lens of this French colonial curricula, complete with biases of appropriate race, class and gender hierarchies. At the same time, a new class structure emerged from within this education system. Cambodians educated in the French colonial schools were the *neak che doeung*, the 'people knowing knowledge', and constituted a new kind of elite in Cambodian society and accrued privileges previously only the purview of the pre-colonial elites—the Buddhist *sangha* and the royal family (Edwards 2007: 136). The elite status garnered by the educated ensured that the non-elites trusted their judgement, believed their actions were correct and in the best interests of their social 'inferiors'. This group formed the core of the new Cambodian nationalist movement that sought to wrest control of the country from the French bureaucracy that had produced their elite status in the first place.

These newly educated elites sought an ideological foundation for their nationalist movement. They sought evidence of a Cambodian society that was free from external influence and quickly turned to the pre-colonial era for models of a 'traditional' Cambodian society. But this evidence had been selectively preserved. The rarefied culture of the royal courts with its strict hierarchies had been preserved, rather than the practices of ordinary people. Moreover, elite men who had embraced the more conservative strain of Theravada Buddhism, Dhammayut, inaugurated in the Siamese court in the eighteenth century, had authored this court material. Dhammayut came to Cambodia through the agency of King Ang Duong (r. 1848–59) and members of his court when they returned from exile in Siam in the 1840s and 1850s. The literature associated with this austere form of Buddhism includes the *cbpab thmei*, 'new codes of conduct' and several elegant compositions based upon Siamese *jataka*, tales of the Buddha's former lives. Significantly, King Ang Duong is credited with the authorship of two of the most misogynist pieces in this repertoire—the *Cbpab Srei*, 'Code of Conduct for Women' (1837), and *Rieong Neang Kaki*, 'The Tale of Lady Kaki' (1813). Both of these texts deliver stern warnings as to the ills that can befall families, communities and kingdoms should women fail to exhibit 'correct' behaviour. This meant unquestioning obedience and loyalty to one's husband even in the face of ill-treatment at his hands. Women were advised that they should 'learn how to behave towards your husband. Fulfil your duties and tasks every day so that they do not cause him disquietude. Oh my daughter, "the master of the room" is our superior: Never mistake it!' (Minh Mai 2001: vv. 5–7). The text goes on to admonish women against raising their voice to, surprising, or disagreeing with their husbands. Laughing loudly and making one's skirt rustle while walking was also classed as incorrect behaviour. In short, asserting oneself was not considered to be something a woman should do, whether in public or in the home.

There are at least two texts of the *Cbpap Srei* dating from the first half of the nineteenth century and other versions dating from the turn of the twentieth century (Jacob 1996: 70; Khing 1990: 90; Ledgerwood 1990: 82, 86; see also Jacobsen 2008: 119–23). The latter were attributed to popular Cambodian figures that in the 1920s and 1930s became synonymous with Cambodian cultural pride. One of these was the poet laureate Ind, who elected to remain in Cambodia rather than flee to Siam when the province of Battambang was removed from Siamese control in 1907. His *Supasit Cbpab Srei*, 'Maxims of the *Cbpab Srei*', was serialized in the journal *Kambuja Suriya* under the auspices of the Buddhist Institute

(Ind 1926: 46–80). The Buddhist Institute also recorded Phiroum Ngoy, a popular minstrel, performing several of his songs, many of which were based upon earlier *cbpab* and warned people against behaving inappropriately. These were transcribed and published in *Kambuja Suriya* as well (Ngoy 1932). The nineteenth-century literature that Cambodians at court wrote for entertainment of their fellows, and the commentaries that monks composed for the moral instruction of the masses, had little (if any) relation to everyday life. Yet it is this very literature that was taken to be indicative of Cambodian society before the imposition of colonial mores in the nationalist project: 'A woman is not considered civilized if she does not follow customs' ('Khmer Daughters' 1945: 2). If one wished to be considered patriotic, one embraced the social mores of the Cambodian past as dictated by the *neak che doeung*.

Feminism in post-colonial Cambodia

With the presentation of elite culture as 'truly Cambodian', it is not surprising that the first Women's Association reflected a domestic and supporting role for women rather than advocating equality with men on its establishment in 1949 ('L'Association des femmes Cambodgiennes' 1970: 52). Members were related to the men involved in the fledgling political scene that emerged in Cambodia in the 1940s and early 1950s. Another organization, the Women's Friendship Association, was established under the patronage of the royal family in 1958 (Frieson 2000). Here too membership was restricted to women with connections to elite men, although now 'elite' indicated acceptance within Prince Sihanouk's inner circle. Similarly, Cambodia's first woman minister, Tong Siv Eng, married to Pung Peng Cheng, a trusted associate of Sihanouk, had also formerly held a position as tutor to the royal children. The other three women to hold high office in the 1960s were likewise of elite status (see Jacobsen 2008: 185) by dint of their own birth as well as marriages to men who were involved themselves in the upper echelons of power in Cambodia.

Political agency in post-colonial Cambodia continued to reflect entrenched notions of social hierarchy rather than the aptitude of the individuals con-cerned. Membership of the Cambodian Women's Association dwindled in the 1960s until the organization petered out altogether ('L'Association des femmes Cambodgiennes' 1970: 52). Complicating the situation for Cambodian women was the prevailing view that they embrace modernity whilst ensuring that traditional Cambodian culture remained unsullied. This meant that adherence to 'traditional' codes of conduct, such as the ubiquitous *Cbpab Srei*, became more important than ever before. Thus, women were simultaneously told to participate in modern life *and* keep to the old ways of not putting themselves forward or 'above' a man. In 1963, a government publication, *Femmes du Cambodge* (Women of Cambodia), described the ideal Cambodian woman as follows:

The young Khmer woman today is by the side of her husband at receptions, informs herself of all aspects of national life and international events before expressing her point of view, interests herself in literature and music, goes often to cinemas, learns Western dances and follows fashion.

(Kingdom of Cambodia 1963: 37)

Consequently, very few women in mainstream Cambodian society in the 1960s deviated from roles as daughters, wives and mothers foremost, although they may have begun to work outside the home in order to supplement the family income and thus enhance the prestige of the family unit.[4]

After the coup of 18 March 1970 that deposed Prince Sihanouk and escalated the civil war, the Women's Association reflected the new political arrangements of the country. In the ensuing cabinet reorganization, those loyal to Sihanouk were replaced. Their family members were similarly reshuffled. Nou Neou, previously the undersecretary of state for tourism, was affected in this way. Deprived of her position, she set about reorganizing the Women's Association to reflect the new political elite. Whereas previously membership had comprised the relatives and associates of Prince Sihanouk's cronies, now membership was made up of those with connections to the men in charge of the Khmer Republic. Volunteers from the Women's Association and other organizations such as the Red Cross were kept busy distributing food and blankets and organizing shelter for the thousands of refugees escaping the ravages of bombing in eastern Cambodia and the civil war. These volunteers were almost exclusively the wives, sisters and daughters of high-level government and army officials; most ordinary women were too busy working, caring for young children and elderly relatives, and trying to hold their lives together under the onslaught to spare any time for philanthropy.

For many women, the 1970s were their first opportunity to participate equally with men in activities such as policing, training in weapons and training in field medical work. As the civil war drew on, women on both sides of the conflict were 'mobilized', either into civilian militia groups or guerrilla units in the communist resistance.[5] A 1973 document produced by the latter emphasized the key role that women played:

> At the front, women take part in combat, in medical teams, in destroying communications, in voluntary work teams. Behind the lines, women play a top-level role. Numerous guerrilla units have been formed entirely of women. Women take charge of various tasks, replacing men who have left for the front; village defense, making booby-traps, agricultural production, planning, medical work, etc.
>
> (CGPR 1973)

Meanwhile, female high school students and university co-eds joined the Patriotic Women's Youth Commandos, headed by Nou Neou, and were drilled like their male classmates in strategies for guarding important installations from the guerrilla forces ('Women in action' 1970: 27). Despite the increased importance placed upon women's equal participation in the conflict, the prevailing attitudes towards female agency precluded true equality. The reformed Women's Association had as its mandate that it would 'acquaint women of their responsibilities as young women, mothers and citizens' and 'make women understand the importance of their place in the family as well as in society' ('L'Association des femmes Cambodgiennes' 1970: 52). Government publications referred to the temporary abandonment of 'natural gentleness', the mobilized woman of Cambodia maintaining 'her gracious features, nevertheless being also firmly resolved to oppose the aggressors' and 'even the weaker sex is mobilized' (San Sarin 1970: 67; 'Mobilizing to fight' 1971: 38). Similarly, although young men and women were sent out on patrol together, it was the young women who, after the mission, 'put on the sarongs and started cooking' (Voss 1970: 50). Although their participation was encouraged, if not demanded, by the leaders of the government proper and the communist resistance, women in Cambodia were nonetheless expected to also attend to the duties and obligations that ensured the continuation of 'correct' gender roles in which women were associated with domesticity (Frieson 1991: 42).

Significantly, this did not change when the communist resistance took power on 17 April 1975 and established the state of Democratic Kampuchea, more commonly known as the Khmer Rouge period. Like preceding regimes, 'Angkar'—the decision-making body at the top of the Khmer Rouge hierarchy—appeared to embrace the concept of women at the forefront of every aspect of the new epoch in Cambodia's progress yet retained previous perspectives towards gender roles that precluded the development of true equality. This was because those at the top had been part of the group of educated elite Cambodians who in the 1940s and early 1950s had created Cambodian cultural identity. Thus while the Constitution of Democratic Kampuchea might refer to 'the men and women' of the nation (see, for example, Article 19 in Jennar 1995: 87) and Khmer Rouge songs laud the efforts of 'men and women soldiers, stirred like boiling water to build a new country', 'the newly liberated young men and women', and 'the troops—men and women' (Marston 2002: 120–2), roles that were associated with domesticity, such as the care of the sick, children and the elderly, fell to women. Teachers were predominantly women and nurses almost exclusively so. Perhaps most telling is the fact that the ministries of Social Action, Education and Culture were headed by women related by marriage to Khmer Rouge political elite men, whereas portfolios that required interaction with the outside world were allocated to men.

As had occurred in the 1950s and again in 1970 after the Khmer Republic had come into effect, a Women's Association was established during Democratic Kampuchea, organized to reflect the political hierarchy of the Khmer Rouge regime (see Jacobsen 2008: 231–2). Khieu Ponnary, wife of Pol Pot, was president of the Women's Association, mirroring her husband's position as Brother Number One. Although she held this, and other posts in the government, and was hailed as *me padevat* ('mother of the revolution') throughout the regime, there is no evidence that she ever designed or implemented programmes for the benefit of women in this capacity.[6]

There is very little indication of central planning for activities that would improve women's lives in Democratic Kampuchea. All women over a certain age (which seems to have varied from twenty in some places to twenty-eight in others) were automatically members of the Women's Association, as were married women; those who were under this age were members of the Youth Association. Both would hold meetings at which women were encouraged to 'build solidarity', work harder, and follow the orders of Angkar to the letter. Ros, now in her eighties, remembered that these meetings would go on for hours, sometimes late into the night; they could also start with no warning, as she and her work group were ordered to stop digging a canal after only 20 minutes and return to the village in order to attend one such meeting (Fieldnotes 2005). The Vietnamese delegation invited to visit Cambodia by the Women's Association in 1977 was bemused to find no real progress in terms of agriculture, industry, or the people's welfare (Kiernan 1996: 161). When a member of the delegation ventured to question the logic behind some of the policies put in place by the government, Khieu Thirith allegedly replied that the Vietnamese delegation '[did] not understand the problem of women at all' (Kiernan 1996: 162). It appears that a Women's Association existed in Democratic Kampuchea not as a platform for furthering women's concerns or an umbrella under which women could organize, but because all earlier post-colonial regimes in Cambodia, and the communist nations after which Democratic Kampuchea was modelling itself, had established one. The post-colonial leadership regarded the existence of a specialist women's affairs unit simply as a feature of modern constitutional government rather than a body charged with advancing women's rights.

After the fall of the Khmer Rouge and the establishment of the state known as the People's Republic of Kampuchea (PRK), the new leadership created the Women's Association for the same reasons.[7] Yet the Women's Association under the PRK differed from those that had gone before in key areas.[8] Perhaps one explanation for this is that more women survived the Khmer Rouge regime than men. On the one hand, the Khmer Rouge targeted men for punishment more often than women and, on the other, the greater physiological strength of men meant that more men than women made the journey to the Thai and Vietnamese border to escape. Thus, women comprised the majority of survivors living in Cambodia immediately after the Khmer Rouge period. Reconstruction of the country fell upon their shoulders. The burden was heaviest upon rural women, who, although accustomed to performing a range of activities, lacked the physical presence of men to carry out the most labour-intensive work. Animals, tools and equipment used in farming were also scarce. The collectivization scheme or *krom samaki* system and Women's Livelihood Groups implemented by the PRK government may have eased the burden for some women heads of household, but not all (see Jacobsen 2008: 238–48).

The new Constitution stipulated that the government would 'take concrete measures concerning women working outside the State sector' as well as those employed in the government itself. The Women's Association was the organ through which the state implemented such programmes (Boua 1981: 264).

Actual activities took many forms. The poor literacy rates of rural women were chief amongst the government's concerns and programmes addressing this and general education were implemented. Training was also provided so that women could work in state agricultural and industrial concerns safely and with increased productivity (Secretariat of State for Women's Affairs 1995: 15). Funding was sometimes forthcoming for women who wished to establish small businesses such as roadside vending stalls. Some women were able to ask the Women's Association for advice regarding family problems or in the event of emergency.

The extent to which women received assistance depended upon the representative in a particular area. Officially, the association maintained representatives throughout Cambodian society, from the village level, where matters of concern to women were taken to district-, provincial- and ministerial-level decision-makers, to the representatives who made recommendations to the Council of Ministers and assisted in the preparation of legislation that affected women, such as family planning (Desbarats 1995: 59; Secretariat of State for Women's Affairs 1995: 27). The Women's Association organized national congresses in 1983 and 1988 and ensured that International Women's Day was recognized each 8 March. Issues discussed at the congresses included education, female literacy and women's general needs in rural areas (Secretariat of State for Women's Affairs 1995: 26–7, 34–5).

Tradition redux

Although the Women's Association of the PRK period took many more concrete steps in the assistance of Cambodian women than any before, it was criticized for not doing more. Chanthou Boua, who returned to Cambodia in the early 1980s, wrote that the Women's Association did not seem to be making a difference and that although the new regime was turning out 'numerous, surprisingly forceful and capable' women, few were in positions of real importance. She attributed this to the fact that Cambodian women, before the civil war, had been used to working behind the scenes, without recognition, and accepted that men should have the senior positions; that Cambodian men were content to allow this situation to continue; and that many women were too traumatized by the events of the past decade (Boua 1982: 52). There was also nostalgia for the 1950s and 1960s, the time before the world turned upside-down. In the minds of many Cambodians, a return to the social mores of that 'golden age' would mean a return to the lives of imagined peace and prosperity they had had brutally torn from them during the Khmer Rouge years. This meant, above all, a return to the so-called traditional gender roles wherein the primary function of women was that of homemaker and caregiver, as mandated by the so-called traditional texts such as the *Cbpab Srei* (see Jacobsen 2008: 246–7; Ledgerwood 1990).

This nostalgia intensified when Cambodians who had been living in the West— in some cases for decades—and in refugee camps began returning to Cambodia following the signing of the Paris Peace Accords in September 1991. In order to make room for increasing numbers of male heads of household seeking employment, existing positions within the government had to be vacated. Women were the most affected by this policy. At the same time, partial privatization of state enterprises meant that revenue could no longer be channelled into state institutions such as the Women's Association. By 1992 the Women's Association was no longer receiving any direct government support and many of its programmes had fallen by the wayside. Staff were forced to seek employment in the private sector. Nevertheless, a core membership remained and organized a series of events for the 8 March 1993 International Women's Day, including a national summit on women's issues at which several were identified for the consideration of the government following the elections (Secretariat of State for Women's Affairs 1995: 28–32).

A fledgling civil society was preparing to take up the slack. In 1990, Mu Sochua established the first Cambodian non-governmental organization (NGO) with the advancement of women in leadership roles as its mandate—Khemara. Mu Sochua would later be minister for women's and veterans' affairs between 1998 and 2003 (Secretariat of State for Women's Affairs 1995: 17; Boua 1994). Khemara was the first organization to draw upon Western concepts of feminism in its approach and thus marked a departure from earlier women's organizations in Cambodia. The increasing awareness of human rights and the need to build measures that protected them was one of the more positive outcomes of the first few years of the 1990s during which the United Nations Transitional Authority in Cambodia (UNTAC) was mandated to prepare the population for democratic elections. The elections of May 1993 were preceded by mass education about peaceful political participation and the electoral processes and human rights. Many of the human rights organizations established between 1990 and 1994 had women's rights as a key aspect to their overall platforms. Cambodian women returning from the camps and exile in the West were keen members of these groups. Some had assimilated Western ideas of feminism and gender equality. In the context of the impending elections, this translated for the most part into activities based around political participation for women, organizing debates over issues in which women could voice their opinions and ask questions of candidates as to their views on matters affecting women.

Yet in one key way the women's movement of the early 1990s mirrored those of earlier years under other government systems—membership, and certainly leadership within it, was the domain of the elite. Cambodians who had lived in the West were perceived as socially superior to those who had not been so fortunate as to escape the Khmer Rouge regime and had lived under the PRK government. In some cases, 'returnees' were directly related to the inner circle that had surrounded Prince Sihanouk. The human rights group Lichado, for example, was founded by Kek Galabru, daughter of Tong Siv Eng, mentioned above, who returned having spent over twenty years in France. Similarly, an active member of the royalist party Funcinpec was Tioulong Saumura, also the daughter of a Sihanoukist in the 1950s and 1960s. The presence of these women at the forefront of the women's movement was accepted as a matter of course, not because of their feminist credentials but because their positions heralded a return to the social hierarchy of the 'golden age' before the civil war and the Khmer Rouge regime.[9] This is not to belie a genuine commitment to feminism and the Cambodian women's movement on the part of anyone concerned, but to point out that even after two decades of communism and socialism, pre-1970s notions of the elite dominated.

Any transnational character in Cambodian women's movements in the early 1990s reflected the individual networks of their leaders rather than any formal attempt at transnational linkage with existing women's movements in other countries. Aid organizations such as Unicef could provide women's rights advocates with access to country reports from elsewhere; foreign aid workers could explain feminism and female advocacy to their Cambodian counterparts. Yet without a pre-existing contact within an organization or with someone from the outside, no such resources were available to individuals. Thus Kek Galabru was able to draw on her networks in France for funding, approaches and ideas; her position as the daughter of Tong Siv Eng ensured that those who had known of and respected her parents would support her endeavours. Mu Sochua, well-known in the refugee camps along the Thai–Cambodian border and married to an American who was the country representative of the World Food Program in Cambodia for several years from 1989, was able to articulate her agenda for the improvement of Cambodian women's lives to a more receptive audience as she had a significant base of people to whom she was already known and trusted.

By 1995, there was such a proliferation of women's organizations in Cambodia that an umbrella organization, the Amara Women's Network, was established in order to coordinate projects and facilitate dialogue between them. Many of these targeted violence against women and the rehabilitation of abused women and sex workers; for example, Cambodian Women Against Violence, Koh Kor Island and the Women's Media Center. The Khmer Women's Voice Centre began producing a magazine, *Samlanh Neary* ('Women's Voice') in 1998 in which programmes, upcoming activities, and commentary on women's issues were published; two years later, the Women's Media Centre commenced radio transmission of programmes aimed at educating women in their rights, where to seek assistance in the event of violence perpetrated against them, and health issues including family planning (WMC 2001). Prior to the 2003 elections, a number of new NGOs, such as Women in Prosperity and the Women's Association for Peace and Development, were established in order to educate women on political participation and encourage women candidates to stand for election. Many of these organizations worked closely with the Ministry for Women's and Veterans' Affairs (MWVA) in formulating proposals to lay before the government in 2000. On 6 March that year, over 200 members of the Cambodian women's movement from all organizations and across political party lines marched through the main boulevard in Phnom Penh to the National Assembly, where they presented their proposal to the then first prime minister, Prince Ranariddh (WMC 2000: 11). A WMC staff member present at the march recalled 'we felt so proud to have achieved just that much—just to be let into the compound meant that we were being taken seriously' (Fieldnotes 2008).

Despite many programmes implemented by the Cambodian women's movement aimed at redressing gender inequality and improving the lives of women, feminism in general was not wholeheartedly embraced by Cambodian society in the 1990s. Indeed, many Cambodians viewed it as a foreign concept with no place in Cambodian society. Judy Ledgerwood (1996) has described how one political candidate in the lead up to the 1993 elections assured his audience that Cambodian women would never be permitted to become as loud and brash (and thus, un-Khmer) as American women. Politics, occurring in the world beyond the domestic sphere, was perceived as a male domain by Cambodians returning to participate in the 1993 elections and rebuild the utopian Cambodian society dimly remembered from before the war. It is therefore hardly surprising that we find neither women ministers nor women secretaries of state after the 1993 elections; in a reflection of the 'traditional' gender roles created in the nationalist project, however, there were five female under-secretaries of state (Jacobsen 2008: 260–1). This has been attributed to the (male) leaders of the main political parties contesting the election not wishing to risk losing potential voters by putting forward women candidates (Secretariat of State for Women's Affairs 1995: 18).

Similarly, the government was reluctant to send a woman as the head of the Cambodian delegation to the Fourth World Conference on Women in 1995, stating that the presence of an 'inferior woman' would insult the conveners as 'it means we don't give importance to the meeting'; moreover, if women were required 'to make a speech, take notes and answer questions ... they would be unable to manage' (Hill and Heng 2004: 108). The notion of women as the weaker sex, dependent upon a strong male figure for guidance (but very capable nonetheless), was as prevalent as it had been in the 1940s, despite fifty years and two successive regimes in which gender equality was an inherent component of political ideology. Women were expected to accept this arrangement because they were deemed responsible for safeguarding Cambodian culture, in which 'traditional' roles—male/female, patron/client, parent/child—should not be inverted. Upsetting these socially prescribed relationships would result in chaos, as had been proven by the Khmer Rouge regime.

Contemporary constructions of feminism

The Cambodian women's movement has had to tread carefully, choosing to emphasize the complementary nature of men and women, the harmony that this creates for families, and the role that the latter have played in Cambodia's past—by which two periods, that of Angkor (ninth to fourteenth centuries) and the Khmer Rouge period (1975–9) are specified. The Women's Media Centre pointed out in 2001 that the government seemed to view women 'like riding a buffalo to cross a muddy field' and asked why women, who had been 'actively involved in wars', were discouraged from running in local elections in favour of male candidates (WMC 2000: 17). Reference was made to the tenth-century temple of Banteay Srei, whose name means 'Fortress of Women'. Playing on the symbolism of the Angkor period, which resulted in the spectacular temples of the same name in northern Cambodia, in addition to the participation of women in combating the Khmer Rouge and rebuilding the nation in the 1980s, this trope conflated the glorious ancient past with more recent events in which women undeniably played a key role. The failure of the Cambodian government to recognize the efforts of women in the recent past could therefore be construed as a slight upon Angkor itself, and thus upon the Cambodian past in general.[10]

This does not mean, of course, that all (or, in fact, any) Cambodian men are misogynists or anti-feminists. Many do not understand what is meant by feminism. In the course of fieldwork in 2008, I interviewed Cambodian men and women as to their views on feminism. There is no directly translatable word for feminism in Khmer; the closest approximations are *satrei ach twer* (working for women) and *setthi neary* (women's rights). Some informants used these interchangeably, whereas others drew a distinction between the two. Others had not thought much about it. This was a common response from people I interviewed. Vuthy, a 45-year-old driver at an NGO in Phnom Penh, said that he had other things to think about, but he did not mind women working for more rights. I asked him if he would like to join them and be a fighter for women's rights. He laughed and said 'Of course not! I am a man.' I pointed out that men could assist the women's movement, and that a belief in *setthi neary* meant simply that men and women were equal and deserved equal treatment. He responded, 'But you and I are not equal. You have *bunn l'or* (high status). I am a driver. It has nothing to do with men and women' (Fieldnotes 2008).

Later that day, I spoke to 'Joe', a project officer in the same NGO, and asked him for his thoughts. He said that he strongly believed that men and women deserved equal treatment, but that women were naturally better suited to domestic tasks.

> They can organize and arrange things much better than men. They can have many thoughts and plans in their minds at once. Men can only think about one or two things. Men are also more likely to lose wealth, because they go drinking with their friends and then if they meet a girl at a restaurant they take a second wife even if she is not good and the family cannot afford it.

He then said that when he married, he would prefer his wife to stay at home, because her organizational skills would be best there. I asked why she could not use her skills in a career instead. He replied, 'But the family is more important than anyone's career' (Fieldnotes 2008). For 'Joe', women should remain in the domestic sphere not because men are superior, but because taking care of the family is actually more important and women are better suited to it.

Cambodian women I spoke to had some interesting perspectives on feminism. Srey Mom, a sex worker who caters only to Caucasian clientele and is therefore at the upper end of the sex sector hierarchy in Cambodia, had an interesting take on feminism. Over the past six years Srey Mom has been a regular informant of mine for my work and she has come to have a good understanding of gender theory and feminism in the West. In April 2007, I ran into her and explained that I was gathering some data on feminism and women's movements. She asked me if it was true that a feminist was a woman who made decisions for herself without anyone else. I said to some extent, yes. She then said:

> You said that in the West it is usually okay for a girl to have sex before she marries, that she can choose who to be her boyfriend [a euphemism for sex]. Right? So I want to know why Western women think I am not a feminist and want to give me help. Help for what? I decide what I do. I decide who is my boyfriend. So I am a feminist, like Western women.

I found it difficult to counter Srey Mom's argument on the spot. In black and white terms, elite sex workers such as Srey Mom do enjoy more 'freedoms' than their more traditional counterparts. She shares an apartment with three other girls who are also elite members of the sex sector. Sometimes one will have a steady boyfriend for some months and move in with him. Another woman, Bopha, said that being a sex worker allowed her to enjoy sexual activity, whereas if she was married to a Cambodian, she would have to suppress any enjoyment of the actual act. Western feminists are divided on the question of sex work and it may be hard for some to see any redemption in the sex sector, but my purpose in relaying this perspective is to give voice to a demographic of Cambodian womanhood that is always supposed to be downtrodden and powerless, whereas at least some of these women see their status as sex workers as empowering and liberating.

Other voices are equally thought-provoking. Paen, a 66-year-old *daun chi* or nun from Kompong Cham province, said that 'women are now trying to become higher than men; they do not realize that they are already the same' (Fieldnotes 2008). Perhaps this is an example of what Wazir Jahan Karim meant in arguing that Western assumptions of gender and its inequalities was not appropriate in non-Western civilizations in Southeast Asia (Karim 1992: 16). Debate over whether it is appropriate for Western feminism to be transplanted into non-Western contexts notwithstanding, it is clear that Cambodian society is not going to abruptly relinquish its view of appropriate behaviour for Cambodian women— which includes not complaining, accepting one's place in hierarchies and working selflessly for the good of the family; in other words, transcending individuality. This is because the country finds itself in relative peace for the first time in thirty years. More conflict is to be avoided. Also, abandoning cultural elements perceived as 'traditional' cannot be lightly undertaken when the cultural identity to which the elements belong was nearly eliminated by force between 1975 and 1979 during the Khmer Rouge's rule.

Yet until the idea of 'traditional' gender roles devised in the 1940s and 1950s is abandoned, feminism will continue to be perceived as a Western import that will destroy Cambodian culture. A better approach, and one which the Cambodian women's movement has adopted, is to rediscover positive models of Cambodian women in the past for others to emulate, thus preserving 'tradition' while negotiating a more active voice. In so doing, it may be possible to do more than invert the dominant perspective towards women's movements; it may yet become perfectly acceptable to ride buffalo not only across a muddy field, but also down the main boulevard.

Notes

1 Ledgerwood attended a political rally in which a male candidate who had returned from living in the United States in order to participate in the election decried the freedoms accorded to American women.
2 Sihanouk abdicated in 1955 in order to participate directly in Cambodia's fledgling multi-party political system after independence, after which he was known as 'Prince Sihanouk'.
3 There are several famous such cases involving French colonial officials. Léon Fonfrère, an officer in the military division posted in Cambodia, was abandoned by his mistress Ang Lava (also known as Marie Thérèse Fonfrère) in 1912. She took with her cash and property she calculated she was owed by Fonfrère to serve as dowry for her next alliance—with another French official in Cochinchina.
4 Of course, many women were choosing to leave mainstream society for the revolutionary movement in the countryside.
5 See, for example, *New Cambodge* 4 (August 1970): 23, 48; *New Cambodge* 11 (June 1971): 38; *New Cambodge* 3 (July 1970): 27; *New Cambodge*, 1 (May 1970): 27.
6 Khieu Ponnary is believed to have suffered from early onset dementia since the late 1960s, and seems to have spent most of the Khmer Rouge period living with her sister Khieu Thirith (married to Ieng Sary), not her husband.
7 The date given as the foundation of the new Women's Association is 2 December 1978, three weeks prior to date that the Vietnamese army and a select number of Cambodians who had fled the Khmer Rouge entered the country and removed the Khmer Rouge by force.
8 Other groups were established by and for women during this period in the border camps, such as the Khmer Women's association founded by Princess Norodom Marie Ranariddh in 1985 (Jeldres 2003: 76).
9 I was working at the UNTAC Human Rights Component in Phnom Penh when Kek Galabru came to consult Denis MacNamara, our head of component, prior to establishing Lichado on 10 December 1993. My Cambodian colleagues were awed, performing low *sompheah* and averting their eyes before her to indicate her superior status.
10 Banteay Srei is named for the exquisite carvings of *apsara*, female divinities, not (as is sometimes assumed) because a community of warrior women who dwelt there.

References

'Khmer Daughters' (1945) 'Khmer Daughers', *Kampuchea*, 190: 2, cited in and translated by K. Frieson (2000) in 'Sentimental Education: *Les sages femmes* and Colonial Cambodia', *Journal of Colonialism and Colonial History*, 1, 1: electronic journal.
'L'Association des femmes Cambodgiennes' (1970) 'L'Association des femmes Cambodgiennes', *Cambodge Nouveau*, 7: 52–5.
'Mobilizing to Fight' (1971) 'Mobilizing to Fight', *New Cambodge*, 10: 38–41.
'Women in Action' (1970) 'Women in Action', *New Cambodge*, 1: 27–9.
Boua, C. (1981) 'Observations of the Heng Samrin Government, 1980–82', in D. Chandler and B. Kiernan (eds) *Revolution and its Aftermath in Kampuchea: Eight Essays,* New Haven: Yale University Press.

—— (1982) 'Women in Today's Cambodia', *New Left Review*, 131: 45–61.

—— (1994) *Cambodia's Country Report: Women in Development, Prepared for the Second Asia-Pacific Ministerial Conference, Jakarta, 7–14 June 1994*, Phnom Penh: Secretariat of State for Women's Affairs.

CGPR (Cambodian Genocide Program Resources) (1973) 'Cambodian Women in the Revolutionary War for the People's National Liberation', Cambodian Genocide Program Resources. Online. Available HTTP: <http://www.yale.edu/cgp/kwomen.html> (accessed 24 June 2003).

Desbarats, J. (1995) *Prolific Survivors: Population Change in Cambodia, 1975–1993*, Tempe, Arizona: Program for Southeast Asian Studies, Arizona State University.

Edwards, P. (2007) *Cambodge: The Cultivation of a Nation, 1860–1945*, Honolulu: University of Hawaii Press.

Frieson, K.G. (1991) 'The Impact of Revolution on Cambodian Peasants, 1970–75', PhD thesis, Monash University.

—— (2000) 'Sentimental Education: *Les sages femmes* and Colonial Cambodia', *Journal of Colonialism and Colonial History*, 1, 1: electronic journal.

Groslier, G. (1994 [1928]) *Le Retour à l'argile*, Paris: Kailash.

Hill, P.S. and Heng Thay Ly. (2004) 'Women are Silver, Women are Diamonds: Conflicting Images of Women in the Cambodian Print Media', *Reproductive Health Matters*, 12, 24: 104–15.

Ind (1926) 'Supasit cbpab srei', *Kambuja Suriya*, 6, 4–6: 46–80.

Jacob, J. (1996) *The Traditional Literature of Cambodia: A Preliminary Guide*, Oxford: Oxford University Press.

Jacobsen, T. (2008) *Lost Goddesses: The Denial of Female Power in Cambodian History*, Copenhagen: NIAS Press.

Jeldres, J.A. (2003) *The Royal House of CAMBODIA*, Phnom Penh: Monument Books.

Jennar, R. (1995) *The Constitutions of Cambodia, 1953–1993*, Bangkok: White Lotus.

Karim, W.J. (1992) *Women and Culture: Between Malay Adat and Islam*, Boulder, CO: Westview Press.

Khing Hoc Dy (1990) *Contribution à l'histoire de littèrature khmère*, Paris: l'Harmattan.

Kiernan, B. (1996) *The Pol Pot Regime: Race, Power and Genocide in Cambodia under the Khmer Rouge, 1975–79*, New Haven: Yale University Press.

Kingdom of Cambodia (1963) *Femmes du Cambodge*, Phnom Penh: Ministère de l'Information du Gouvernment Royal du Cambodge.

Ledgerwood, J. (1990) 'Changing Khmer Conceptions of Gender: Women, Stories, and the Social Order', PhD thesis, Cornell University.

—— (1996) 'Politics and Gender: Negotiating Changing Cambodian Ideas of the Proper Woman', *Asia Pacific Viewpoint*, 37, 2: 139–52.

Lilja, Mona and Tevy Prom (2002) 'Female Politicians in Cambodia', in J.L. Vijghen (ed.) *People and the 1998 National Elections in Cambodia: Their Voices, Roles and Impact on Democracy*, Phnom Penh: Experts for Community Research, pp. 45–58.

Marston, J. (2002) 'Khmer Rouge songs', *Crossroads*, 16, 1: 100–27.

Mies, M. (1986) *Patriarchy and Accumulation on a World Scale: Women in the International Division of Labour*, London: Zed Books.

Minh Mai (2001) [c.19th century] *Cbpab Srei-broh*, Phnom Penh: Phsep pseay juon koan khmei.

Ngoy, Phiroum (1932) 'Cbpab kram thmei', *Kambuja Suriya*, 4, 7–12: 149–80.

San, Sarin (1970) 'For Victory', *New Cambodge* 5: 50–2.

Secretariat of State for Women's Affairs (1995) *Women: Key to National Reconstruction*, Phnom Penh: Secretariat of State for Women's Affairs, Kingdom of Cambodia.

Thompson, V. (1937) *French Indo-China*, London: Allen & Unwin.

Viollis, A. (1935) *SOS Indochine*, Paris: Gallimard.

Voss, T. (1970) 'A Visit to the Front', *New Cambodge*, 4: 50–1.

WMC (Women's Media Centre) (2000) *Gender in Election and Female Leadership at the Communal Level*, Phnom Penh: Women's Media Centre.

—— (2001) Information leaflet.

13 Rights talk and the feminist movement in India

Sumi Madhok

Progressive legalism, developmentalism and empowerment govern the discourse on women's rights in India. These occupy specific historical periods in India's colonial and post-colonial political history and are influenced in large part by prevailing domestic political imperatives and transnational trends. Feminist scholars and activists in India have engaged variously with these—challenging, critiquing, interpreting and expanding these with a view to retool them for feminist politics. As a result, these feminist engagements with rights provide a rich site for tracking the way in which not only rights operate within different discourses but also the use they are put to by different political constituencies. In attending to the specific discursive contexts within which rights have been invoked within the Indian feminist movement, I wish to draw attention to the political nature of rights, their curious workings and paradoxical outcomes, and to the political and legal conservatism that an avowedly progressive rights politics can result in. While many of these concerns are now well documented within elements of feminist scholarship within India and internationally, I suggest here that feminist scholarly reflections on 'rights worries' must be read alongside the increased vibrancy of the rights-based mobilizations in recent times. Despite their politically conservative outcome and workings, it is, in fact, the case that rights have been used forcefully and creatively in various grass-roots political mobilizations in India, paving the way, in some cases, for innovative public policy formulations. There must be a way, therefore, to provide an account for both the intended and the unintended conservatism of rights thinking and for the fast-fading faith in rights radicalism within intellectual circles, on the one hand, and their increasing articulation and continuing 'enchantment' within social mobilizations, on the other.

In this chapter, although I highlight some elements of feminist-inspired activism and thinking in India invoking progressive legalism, development and empowerment, it is important to note that these ideas continue to be subject to serious and careful scrutiny and debate within feminist thinking in India and this chapter is only a selectively organized reflection on some of these debates. Furthermore, many sophisticated accounts of the Indian feminist movement exist but, like all accounts, 'telling feminist stories' (Hemmings 2005) is not without its exclusions and 'glossing over' in favour of neat retellings,[1] and this chapter only too readily acknowledges its exclusions. This is therefore neither an account of the feminist movement in India nor an attempt to provide an exhaustive view of the rights struggles of different feminist groups (such as *dalit* feminists[2]) but is only a partial reading of some of the discursive contexts within which feminists in India have engaged with the question of rights.

Rights worries and feminist politics

The 'contemporary' or 'autonomous' feminist movement in India is often regarded to have come into its own in the 1970s (John 1996; Ram 2000; Phadke 2003; Menon 1999; Kumar 1999). The feminist movement which owed aspects of its emergence to the anti-colonial nationalist movement in undivided India attained its own organizational and mobilizational muscle amidst the political crises and social unrest which enveloped the post-colonial Indian state in the 1960s, culminating in the imposition of emergency measures by the federal government (1975–7) and suspension of constitutional liberties. This self-characterization of the feminist movement as 'autonomous' signified the 'coming into its own' through marking its independence from other social and political groups operating in the public arena and from the nationalist politics of social reform (Ram 2000). But this signification of the movement as 'autonomous' implicated 'women' as a self-contained and homogenous category and feminism as a form of identity politics, and laid the ground for serious internal challenge and critique, especially in the wake of nationwide debates on the formulation of Uniform Civil Code and the provisioning of parliamentary quotas for women which brought questions of intersectionality, elitism and secularism to the heart of feminist politics.

The several strains of the feminist movement in India have been concerned with a diverse range of issues related to the environment, sexuality, representation, health and civil rights (Kumar 1999), and there is a general concurrence that one can discern 'three waves' in the trajectory of the feminist movement (Gandhi and Shah 1992; also cited in Menon 1999). The first of these 'waves' encompassed women's participation in the anti-colonial nationalist-led movement; the 'second wave' witnessed the emergence of women as activists in the late 1960s within large class defined mobilizations taking to the streets in protests alongside other political formations; and the emergence of the 'autonomous' phase of the women's movement a decade later marked the 'third wave' of the women's movement in India (Menon 1999). The early years of this 'autonomous' phase of the movement focused on raising concerns about the gendered nature and application of laws and in pursuing legal reform, especially in relation to issues related to violence against women (Phadke 2003). In the 1980s, and as Flavia Agnes (1997) has pointed out, while there were a slew of legal reform measures undertaken by the federal state—mostly in response to the pressure mounted by feminist organizations who mobilized against state atrocities, rights violations and gender prejudicial legal judgements—these, however, fell short of delivering gender progressive legalism, informed as they were by prevailing gender orthodoxies and moralism. This period also witnessed the country-wide rise of identity politics, increasing thereby the pressure upon the women's movement to evolve strategies—intellectual and practical—to think more closely about not only identity politics and intersectionality in order to arrest its growing fragmentation but also to own up to its unacknowledged heteronormativity. In its anti-colonial and post-colonial defining of its roles, the women's movement had explicitly focused on reforming the heterosexual household, especially legislation governing conjugal relations, violence and property. It was only in 1997 that the Indian women's movements' congress passed a resolution recognizing rights of non-heterosexual groups (Menon cited in Phadke 2003). At the century's close, the women's movement found itself at the forefront of debates on aspects of sexualities, identities and citizenship—with sexual rights, parliamentary quotas and guaranteed citizenship entitlements becoming increasingly important.

While there is a clearly articulated rights discourse running through the several strands of feminist thinking in India, there is considerable disquiet and disagreement over entrusting the state with the task of securing and upholding rights. Much of this prevailing discomfort on the question of state-led promotion of women's rights owes in large part to the actual experience of rights, which have had less than an enviable record (Sunder Rajan 2003). Some elements of these rights worries are also generally shared by several strains within wider feminist thinking, with scholars pointing to the often contradictory effects of a rights politics: exclusion, heightened conflict and injuries (Brown 1995, 2000; Menon 2004; Crenshaw 2000). Within this literature, rights are critiqued variously for legitimizing existing hierarchies and upholding existing power relations, of being formal and empty of empancipatory content, for their universalizing and homogenizing moves (Brown 1995; Grewal 2005; Kiss 1997; Menon 2004). Feminists have also critiqued rights variously for being masculinist (Mackinnon 1982), for upholding bourgeois preoccupations oriented towards establishing sovereign and unencumbered persons who shy away from 'collective engagements' (Phillips 2009), for their abstract nature and exclusionary effects (Brown 2000) and of privileging political and civil rights—usually championed by the rich—over economic and livelihood rights which matter to the poor (Ilumoka 1994, 1996). Wendy Brown (2000) draws up a list of rights that women in the USA have secured, but these are, she writes, only 'mitigating' and 'not a resolution of subordinating powers', 'and the paradox of rights' is not only that they reinscribe, regulate and fix into place the very inequalities they seek to ameliorate but that they also operate differentially and, in so doing, ensure a positive relationship between great wealth and increased empowerment. Similarly, Spivak (2002: 174) writes that while human rights run on ideological pressure driven from the global North, they empower the rich and powerful across the global divide—resulting in 'epistemic discontinuity' between the human rights advocates located in the South and the subaltern groups whose rights they seek to defend. In the international arena, human rights are deemed by many as instruments of international relations used to police international alliances (especially during the Cold War and in its aftermath), are critiqued as a form of 'transnational governmentality' (Grewal 2005: 130) for managing, disciplining and representing the Third World, are regarded a 'central' element of US-led globalization, capitalism and of world trade (Mignolo 2000; Asad 2000) and, increasingly, articulated as central justifications within imperialist wars. In the last decade alone, two wars have been launched ostensibly on the pretext of securing and advancing human rights of women within these countries. While these rights worries make us more cautious of the rights politics and workings of rights, these are not, as I see it, calls either for a refusal of rights or a demand for a politics without rights or universal citizenship. As Sunder Rajan writes 'the expectation that rights would be all-powerful, cancelling at one stroke the inequities of history, is also at one level a recognition of the enormous cost of *not* having political rights or citizenship in the world today' (2003: 18). And furthermore, as Anne Phillips reminds us, feminist reservations must not blind us to the fact that it is precisely those aspects of rights which worry us the most—individualism and autonomy which are also its most useful, especially when negotiating the 'precise relationships between individuals and their religion or culture' (Phillips 2009: 10). The difficulties and worries inherent in desiring rights are captured by Gayatri Spivak (1999: 172) when she writes 'we cannot not want to inhabit this rational abstraction', drawing attention, thereby, at once to questions of 'constraint' underpinning both the desire and the gratification of rights (Brown 2000: 230). Spivak's concerns over rights appear most expansively in her *A Critique of Postcolonial Reason* (1999) in which she speaks of the 'incessant push and pull of self and other, rights and responsibility' (1999: 101) of rights and responsibility as dynamically entwined and engaged—neither assured, given nor fixed—and where the 'struggle' 'for rights is continuous and without resolution nor end' (2003: 18). In my view, feminist intellectual work on the institutional articulation and workings of rights must be accompanied by an attention to the ways in which rights languages are picked up and put to use in different political contexts by disparate and especially marginal groups so that we might produce accounts of how this manifold use complicates and expands current rights thinking. Rights are inherently political and must be seen as operating within fields of power and, therefore, the task is not one only of examining the discursive formulations and the political use that rights are put to but also one of investigating the political cultures that rights create (Brown 1995) and the new forms of subjectivities and subjection these produce.

Progressive legalism,[3] rights and gender

Two characterizations continue to attach themselves to the women's movement in India. The first is the assumption of voice by elite, middle-class and upper-caste women 'speaking for' (Alcoff 1995) and seeking to represent the aspirations of all Indian women, and the second constitutes the challenge posed by questions of cultural authenticity—of feminism being a Western import and an affiliative badge to be shrugged off. Both characterizations owe their theoretical and empirical origin to the nationalist anti-colonial struggles and have accompanied historical moments of intense identity, crafting both in colonial and post-colonial India. Anti-colonial nationalist discourses were replete with normative constructions of gendered identities and roles (Rai 2002) drawn from select elements of Brahaminical scriptural tradition and the question of women's rights was not only subordinate to but also easily displaced by questions of what constituted 'authentic' tradition. So, for instance, in the case of the discourse on *sati,* while women's rights ostensibly lay at the heart of it, this discourse was, as Lata Mani (1989) writes, not about women's rights at all but about what properly constituted 'Hindu tradition'. The legalism, progressive or otherwise, underpinning discourse on women's rights was entered into by both the colonial and the post-colonial state and by those who self-identified themselves as advocating the cause of women's rights—the chief element of this discourse was defining culture, tradition and a 'modern Indian' identity—one that while meeting the demands of nationalism and nation would not be in contravention with authentic culture/scriptural tradition. The debate on citizenship in post-colonial India has been similarly circumscribed by a careful balance between women's citizenship rights; that is, their public identities and their religious and cultural roles or their private identities (Kapur and Crossman 1996).

The unease with 'feminism' as a Western import comes in several variants in post-colonial politics, including from within some sections of the women's movement itself (John 1998b), re-emerged with renewed vigour in the religiously governed identity politics in the 1980s and 1990s (John 1998a). While it is entirely correct to posit questions in relation to the location of voice, leadership and political agendas, it is important to note that the women's movement, despite difficulties in relation to these, has displayed reflexivity and sensitivity to questions of poverty, power, social hierarchy and institutional elitism both in its campaigns and in the readings of its historical archives.[4] The suggestion that advocating women's rights and feminist politics, generally, is inauthentic because it draws upon Western feminist politics is weak on at least two counts. First, because the question of women's fundamental rights was itself raised within the context of the anti-colonial nationalist movement (Ram 2000; John 1998a). Despite the nationalist antecedents of rights demands, it is important to remember here that nationalism incorporated elite women in very specific ways—at once managing to appeal to women's rights and to their role as upholders of 'tradition'—and thus ensuring all the while that the public visibility and inclusion of women within organizational establishments—such as the 'All India Women's Congress' set up in 1927, the resolution on women's fundamental rights in 1925 and the sub-committee on women's role in the planned economy (John 1998a 2002; Dutta 2000)—was very much in line with the nationalist project of developing India through 'universalized discourses of citizenship and economic development' (Rai 2002: 15). Second, as Kalpana Ram (2000) writes, the attempt to represent the 'instabilities' within rights discourse in India in binary West/Indian/Asian value formulations does not quite fit the Indian political context, where the 'instabilities' are caused not by an absence of rights or the extent of their misfit (as the Indian state already guarantees fundamental rights to life, liberty and equality) but by questions of accountability and non-individuation of citizen identities.

The preoccupation with social reform did not lose its fervour with the overthrow of colonialism and the formal end of anti-colonial nationalism, and the post-colonial Indian state embarked upon a major constitutional exercise in the first decade of its independence. The chief legislative agenda and certainly the most controversial involved the reform of 'Hindu Personal Laws'—a select set of scriptural readings and practice which had received recognition under colonial rule and consequently rendered 'authentic' and 'uniform', and employed in the governance of personal affairs of Hindus. The constitutional and legislative activity of reforming these Hindu 'laws' resulted in the promulgation of the 'Hindu Code Bill' in 1956 and witnessed the restaging of some of the key elements of the debates voiced on the question of social reform in colonial India with legislative debates involving long drawn-out arguments on how best to complement universal citizenship guarantees with scriptural tradition (Parashar 1992)—and, as before, in this case 'tradition' trumped universal citizenship in particular matters. Citizenship thus became identifiably gender and religious specific. As opposed to the abstract individual citizen, the post-colonial female citizen in India has secure fundamental rights only where these remain unthreatening to her identity as a religious subject. And, therefore, the trouble with rights in the Indian case is not so much that their emancipatory potential is dissipated in their deployment—that is, collective identities' dissipation into individual identities (Brown 1995)—but rather it is in dependence upon pre-existing identities (such as religion) that they are rendered effete.

It was not, however, the ontological priority accorded to the female religious subject within the post-colonial citizenship discourses in India that mobilized intellectual and political response from within feminist quarters in its initial years, but those of gender prejudicial interpretation and application of legal equality by state institutions which drove the first campaigns of the contemporary movement. The two decades following the setting up of the post-colonial state witnessed the widespread crises of reflection and growing discontent over state-led developmentalism and reform, including formulation of explicit feminist reflections on the gendered nature, functionings and practices of institutions within state policy and laws (John 1998a). One of the earliest and most visible political campaigns launched by the 'autonomous women's movement' or the 'contemporary women's movement' (Kumar 1999) drew attention to the lack of correspondence between the formal laws which provided for gender equality and their actual institutional interpretation and application leading to a strong critique of state practices by the feminist movement. The gender institutional prejudice displayed by the police and legal bodies in the aftermath of the custodial rape of two women, Rameeza Bee and Mathura (Ram 2000; John 2002)—both occupying marginal subject positionings (one belonging to a 'tribal' community and the other a poor Muslim)—contravened constitutional principles of equal application of laws when both women were denied justice on the basis of their questionable moral standing. The gender prejudicial interpretation of law led to a decade-long campaign for legal reforms leading to what might be called successful outcomes, in the sense that almost each of these led to new legislation intended towards 'protecting' women against violence (Agnes 1997). In its initial phase, the contemporary feminist movement organized around questions of rape and dowry, both of which led to the recognition of two things: that while these campaigns attracted popular support, the legal changes required to translate this popular support into legal safeguards were marked by institutional resistance and non-progressive enactment (Kumar 1999; Agnes 1997). These initial campaigns were followed by others including domestic violence, prostitution, indecent representation of women, *Sati*, prevention of pre-natal sex selective diagnostic techniques, sexual harassment in the work place and those of political representation and quotas for women.

Perhaps it was with the reopening of the debate on the formulation and extension of a Universal Civil Code (UCC) that the privileging of 'women' as a stand-alone category and as a single axis of oppression and analyses came under considerable intellectual scrutiny. The early campaigns, focused as they were on highlighting the wronging of women's rights, did not weave complex analysis of the various ways in which complex identity vectors intersected each other (Ram 2000). The re-kindled debate over the application of Universal Civil Code to all citizens, irrespective of religious beliefs, coming as it did in the aftermath of the Shah Bano case,[5] drew attention to the gendered nature of citizenship with its coding of women both as 'unitary' and 'differential' categories and, in doing so, marking their difference from both men and other women (Sunder Rajan 2003). It also brought into ever sharper relief, the incompatibilities in modernizing imperatives of the State: between its commitment to secularism and the professed goal of gender equality (Jayal 1999). While there is no one feminist position on the UCC,[6] there exists generally a shared worry about the gender prejudicial nature of religiously based laws (Sunder Rajan 2003). The chief issue that divides the feminists is the extent of state involvement in initiating social reform—but this disagreement notwithstanding, the important question they raise, Sunder Rajan points out, is whether separate laws represent the best way both for recognizing difference and for ensuring respect for these (2003).

Developing women

Development was a key nationalist project (Rai 2002) and transferred seamlessly from being a key argument of anti-colonial politics to a central component of state strategy of post-colonial India. The historical trajectory of the first fifty years of the post-colonial Indian state, Sudipta Kaviraj has written, can be read in terms of the 'apparently contradictory trends' (2003: 155) and 'tendencies' represented by the logic of bureaucracy and that of democracy, both of which have their roots in colonial history. So while the logic of bureaucracy drew upon colonial governmentality and manifested itself in post-colonial developmentalism, the logic of democracy was a throwback from the nationalist movement and informs the democratic impulse of post-colonial politics. In independent India, while economic and social development was distinguished in Indian intellectual debates from the 1950s, development remained a general, all-embracing objective that all sections of society were expected to share. It was only much later that disillusionment set in with this general 'broad' idea of development and demands for a more sector-specific focus on development were voiced. The focus on women within state-led developmentalism became explicit once it became evident that they as a 'group' were not benefiting from various development initiatives—this evidence was provided in the first instance by the publication in 1974 of a state commissioned report titled 'Towards Equality', which documented widespread gendered inequalities across social, political and economic spheres.

The publication of the 'Towards Equality' report together with 'Shramshakti' in the first two decades of the autonomous women's movement, played a pivotal role in catapulting 'women' into development policy but also provided the feminist movement with empirical confirmation with which to reinforce their concerns and arguments. According to Mary John (1996), the publication of the 'Towards Equality' report weakened the 'acquiescent and nationalist' aspirations of the Indian women's movement, which had to adopt a more critical stance in the face of hard evidence revealing not only the glaring indifference of policy-makers and planners in taking into account of gender but also the absence of a 'women's' perspective in the overall development process. The 1970s also witnessed a growing attention to the dismal opportunities for women's participation in labour markets, to the sexual division of labour, the household, the gendered definition of 'work' and household production. Many of these concerns were reflected in the publication of 'Shramshakti' (John 1996), which focused on the informally and self-employed women and highlighted the vastly prejudicial and vulnerable conditions governing women's employment.

The publication of these public documents encouraged scholarly works which critiqued the gendered assumptions underpinning internationally financed development projects with their mandates to train women in the skills of good housekeeping and mothering (John 1996), and were, therefore, in step with the appearance of critiques within international development circles, which too were beginning to challenge the dominant representations of women within the 'development apparatus' (Escobar 1995). This increasing urgency to counter prevailing orthodoxies within international development policy and thinking led to the declaration of the UN decade for women (1976–85) and to a burgeoning academic scholarship on women's roles within development. There currently exists a well-established critique of the development discourse and its mobilization of specific forms of representations of Third World women (Escobar 1995; Mohanty 1991; Ong 1988; Apffel-Marglin and Simon 1994; Liddle and Rai 1998) and of various global spaces for advocating women's development. Chandra Mohanty, for instance, has written of the 'colonialist move' (Mohanty 1991) within feminist development thinking which portrays 'third world women' as 'passive' and as a 'victim', and Grewal and Kaplan (1994: 17) have spoken of 'global feminisms' who employ universalizing liberatory models of feminist politics which eclipse the 'diversity of women's agency'. In her critical assessment of the UN Conferences in the 1990s, Spivak (1999) too draws attention to the universalist-style UN feminism where Third World women are represented by the First World intellectual—the development practitioner and the policy-maker— who seek to develop them by speaking for their need to be developed. My aim here is not to rehearse these well-known arguments but I wish to simply draw attention to the international context of grave concern, discomfort and scholarly critique in which developmentalism found itself in the last decade of the twentieth century.

Even though the official acknowledgement of the rising prominence of the Women in Development paradigm within academic and practitioner development circles came fairly late within Indian state policy,[7] its influence was, however, not lost on the national policy circuits in India and reflections on the lack of women beneficiaries within development interventions gained ground. An outcome of these institutional reflections was the insertion of a chapter on women and development in the sixth five-year plan and, consequently, into state plans at the provincial level too. The Women's Development Programme (WDP) launched by the government of Rajasthan in April 1984 was a direct result of this attention to women within development policy thinking in India.[8]

The WDP drew on several sets of development ideas. It incorporated ideas espoused by the internationalist women's development frameworks, feminist conceptual frames and the development goals set by the Indian State in its sixth five-year plan. The development programme conceived its principal role and activities in consultative exercises with women's development experts, activists, researchers and non-government organizations, an exercise that resulted in the adoption of a development ethos markedly different than the 'top down', 'skill disbursement' nature of common development programmes of the time. This departure from other development programmes was reflected in its new focus. It shifted its emphasis away from the 'mechanisms' delivering benefits to the recipients of development policies, to the subjects of development—that is, to women. In a unique institutional arrangement, the state government of Rajasthan involved prominent feminist activists and NGOs in this development initiative with an explicit undertaking for the latter to take on the task of developing selected groups of rural women through specific training regimes into suitable agents of development or *sathins*.[9]

The originary and initial subject of the *sathin* emerged in two different discursive contexts, each based on different intellectual, historical and political trajectories. The first was a development vision authored by the state and the goal of its development script was unambiguous: to alter the existing subjectivities of the women elected as *sathins* in ways that would make them efficient and committed development workers. The second development vision was mediated by the feminist organizations roped in as partners who 'trained' the *sathins* through feminist consciousness-raising methods and thereby helped create a *sathin* subject not only able to articulate the specific and peculiar nature of her subject positioning but also one who had, as a result of the 'training', acquired the additional normative languages of self-improvement and development. The new subjectivities engineered out of the interlacing of differently constructed and layered hierarchies – the state development bureaucracy, the metropolitan women's groups and locally recognized power relations – lead the *sathins* to evolve creative strategies, both conceptual and practical, in order to define their new roles and make sense of their new and existing identities. An important intellectual idea that the *sathins* came into contact with and engaged creatively over was that of individual rights. I have described the process through which the *sathins* acquire, identify and engage with the moral language of rights elsewhere, but here it will suffice to say that the *sathins* encountered the moral language of rights for the first time through their participation in the WDP (Madhok 2003a, 2003b, 2005, 2007) and that my fieldwork documenting rights narratives of the *sathins* revealed three clear stages in their thinking on rights over their twenty years of participation within the WDP. The initial contact with rights-based ideas produced in their wake considerable moral dissonance and suspicion which in turn gave way in time to a 'new-found faith' in a state-centric discourse of rights and, finally, in the face of serious failings of the state, they are forced to weave their own theoretical and practical defence of the idea of rights independent of the state. These complex and active engagements with rights lead the *sathins* to review, reinscribe and challenge the inadequacies of their received development scripts but on a more confrontational path with the state.

Several writings on the Indian women's movement highlight the WDP as a unique project which led to subversive outcomes, especially in relation to the state developmentalism. What is less discussed, however, are the precise practices of metropolitan feminists who in seeking to 'develop' and 'empower' poor rural women disregarded their responsibility and accountability in the face of the injured subjectivities and bodies that resulted from this developmentalism.[10] Therefore, while analyses of the Indian women's movement and feminist interventions must not only be more reflexive in relation to the roles and positioning of the feminist interlocutors within existing power relations, especially those set into motion by the developmental state, but must also attend to the specific ways in which developmentalist discourses gain entry and the new subjectivities, vulnerabilities and the ever-more precarious subjects these create.

Empowering women

The discourse of empowerment comes bound with its own set of identifiable rights languages. The language of empowerment is used by both the political left and the right as a 'technology' to get the people to 'act in their own interests' (Cruikshank 1999). Within gender circles the emergence of empowerment frameworks is often identified with a specific phase of gender and development discourse known as the GAD approach, which provided 'the basis for feminist theorizing and action grounded in southern realities' (Parpart and Marchand 1995: 15). But there is no single understanding of empowerment even within the gender and development scholarship—these meanings range from those which invoke strong dependence on notion of 'self-help' to those who call for substantive structural changes for empowerment to take effect. Within the feminist movement in India, the question of women's empowerment has a strong presence with several groups advocating women's empowerment as a self-professed objective; for instance, the 'Self Employed Women's Association' (SEWA) upholds women's economic empowerment as an unambiguous objective, but has also mobilized metropolitan feminists into aligning themselves to the cause of 'empowering' rural women, as was the case with the WDP in Rajasthan. The WDP is an interesting case study for tracking the different forms the language of empowerment assumes. In its initial years, the WDP and its feminist partners advocated 'self-empowerment' of women to be achieved through a strong emphases on women's rights but, over the years, the WDP's programmatic interventions have been shorn of their radicalism and the feminist-mediated language of rights which the *sathins* had found so 'novel and even alien' (Madhok 2007) and this is now replaced by one which equates rights and empowerment with microcredit and the establishment of 'self-help' groups.

This shift in the languages and strategies of development are in a large measure an outcome of the growing ascendance of influence of neoliberal-led developmentalism where the ascendance of neoliberal discourses on self improvement have dovetailed with those of empowerment to articulate new understandings of citizenship. Although it is usually referred to in the singular, the actual experience of neoliberalism is marked by heterogeneity and there are now available detailed and gifted scholarship documenting this plural experience (Rofel 2007; Shakya and Rankin 2008; Rankin 2003; Rai 2002; Burawoy *et al.* 2000; Barrientos and Perrons 1999; Ong 1999, 2007). Along with its experiential heterogeneity, scholars have also pointed to the fact that it is neoliberalism's economic doctrine that dominates comment and not its politically prescriptive project (Brown 2003); they point out that although it is neoliberalism's political project which receives far less attention than its economic counterpart, it is nevertheless crucial in maintaining the former's legitimacy. For it is through its political rationality that neoliberalism produces 'prudent' (Brown 2003; Rofel 2007) subjects together with new ways of organizing sociality so that these reflect its economic rationality efficiently (Rose 1996; Lemke 2001). The doctrines of 'self-esteem', 'empowerment' (Cruikshank 1999) and 'self responsibility' (Rose 1996) are central to the ' "making up" of the modern citizen' and to the 'ethical reconstruction' of disadvantaged populations into 'active agents' (Rose 1996: 60).

The rise of neoliberal thinking has not only impacted development thinking in general, but has also led a perceptible change in representation of the 'Third World woman' within this literature. In other words, accompanying the standard descriptions of Third World woman, her poverty and her various needs and problems is also the shift in the responsibility for these. Increasingly, representations of poor women's *successful management* of the debilitating conditions of their poverty-stricken life (John 1996) through the exercise of their agential capacities fill the institutional reports of various development agencies including state institutions (Wilson 2007). The neoliberal turn within development discourse is most pronounced in the cooptation and reformulation of the feminist language of empowerment and of collective struggle over public resources into one of a private striving enabled through an active participation in market relations principally through microcredit schemes (Cruikshank 1999; Wilson 2007). This enthusiasm over micro enterprises and credit schemes, seen as they are as market-friendly replacements to the inefficient and costly state welfare provisioning are justified in terms of their empowering potential. Inderpal Grewal (2005) writes that rights are now firmly ensconced as a technique of neoliberal governmentality and traces the partnering of human rights with developmentalism to the announcement of the 'right to development' at the UNESCO meeting on 'human rights and establishment of New World Order', in 1978. The declaration marked the growing recognition that human rights and development were intimately linked, and that without some measure of development, human rights could not but thrive (Grewal 2005). While it cannot be denied that the various conferences on women's rights provided a site for transnational feminist organizing, it was also the case that only a narrow vision of women's rights was supported, primarily those that protected women against violence (Grewal 1998), but also that these rights were articulated and supported by countries signed up to neoliberal versions of economic and political citizenship (Marchand 2009).

While I am very sympathetic to analyses which investigate the actual operation of rights and what they actually do, I do believe we must exercise a degree of caution in regarding rights as always only oppressive and used only ever by the powerful. So while it is extremely important to document the precise nature and form of governmentalities—its languages and techniques in our historical present—we must at the same time also attend to the manner in which these proliferate outside of legitimate governmental spheres. For instance, in thinking about how the languages of rights and empowerment are employed within popular citizen mobilizations, we will have to make an analytical distinction between neoliberal subjectivities upholding the responsible, self-reliant, autonomous, rights-bearing subject and the demands for increased empowerment and rights voiced by the increasingly vibrant rights-based activism that is now emerging in many parts of India. Consider, for example, excerpts from an interview with a grass-roots worker involved in campaigning for the right to work drawn from my ethnographic study of 'rights scapes' and vernacular rights cultures (Madhok 2009, 2010) which examines rights narratives of grass-roots participants within large citizen mobilizations demanding rights to employment, food and information, *dalit* rights and those of indigenous peoples:

> On 5 June 2003, we attended a public rally at Jaipur where we demanded our *haq*. We said we wanted *'kam ka adhikaar'* (right to employment/work or employment guarantee). This right to work or employment guarantee is very important to us for in face of severe drought, successive crop failures, disappearance of water, food and livestock feed, how are we meant to live? ... The people are the wealth creators. ... and the government in guaranteeing a right to employment would only be giving us what is rightfully our due.[11]

Since the interview, the federal government in India has passed the National Rural Employment Guarantee (NREGA) in 2005. Under the provisions of the Act, the federal state is legally bound to provide one hundred days of employment to earmarked rural districts identified as the most vulnerable, thereby ensuring a basic subsistence for the poorest households.[12] Although the feminist movement in India has aligned itself to these rights mobilizations—and this alignment and support reinforces the inextricability of gender concerns from those of everyday livelihood, deprivation and indignity whilst also highlighting the gendered impact of these—this political alignment must still result in a close feminist analyses of these movements—of their gendered assumptions and prejudicial workings, their lack of internal democracy or, indeed, of how rights discourses gloss over gendered experiences of rights in relation to entitlement, articulation and even of attainment. I have argued elsewhere (Madhok 2009) that that these emergent 'rights-scapes' provide fertile opportunities for investigating how rights actually operate when coupled alongside strong claims for social justice and the new subjectivities and forms of subjection these create.

Conclusion

As I reflect upon the troubled nature of rights, their embeddedness in fields of power, their appropriation by multiple actors and groups not all progressive, their paradoxical functionings and operations, their socially regulative roles, and the dissatisfactions and despair they generate—dissatisfactions at the unfulfilled promise of juridical rights, and despair at their refusal, obstruction and contravention—I am also mindful of the fact that rights remain the 'only way for the disenfranchised to mobilize' (Cheah 2006: 172).We can, therefore, neither afford to give up on rights nor be less heedful of their implicated nature.

Scholars and commentators on the Indian women's movement have written of the myriad trials facing feminist politics in contemporary India.[13] In terms of the intellectual thinking and scholarly undertakings, there are, I believe, at least three areas that require attention. In a characteristically insightful article, Mary John (2002) writes that economic processes of liberalization and globalization represent different challenges for thinking about women and poverty and, consequently, require new intellectual ideas and frameworks. Whilst acknowledging the successes of the women's movement in earning not only recognition but also impacting policy provisioning, she writes that the movement needs to formulate new intellectual responses in the face of this changed 'constitutive context'. In addition to formulating sophisticated thinking in order to make sense of the social transformation under globalization, an analysis of the feminist movement must also, in my view, undertake scholarship which examines the different ways in which the languages of modernity have entered feminist discourse, the manner in which they have proliferated and taken up as well as the 'orientations, skills and politicized gestures' (Ram 2008: 10) these have given rise to. In her careful and sophisticated analysis of activism of *dalit*, Tamil women's engagement with modernity, Kalpana Ram (2008) points to the prevalence of a different notion of cosmopolitanism that she finds amongst the women activists—one that is not led by a concern for difference and pluralism—but instead by a 'partisan universalism', reflecting as it does the different histories through which these ideas have travelled. The critiques of enlightenment modernity and its ideas of progress and emancipation by post-modern and post-colonial scholars, Ram writes, have been both useful and productive and they have been somewhat quick in their analysis of modernity as always 'little more than a series of exclusions ... and the poor as only ever experiencing modernity as oppressive and external' (2008: 15). But as Ram (2008: 16) points out, there is a long history of modernizing the poor but little scholarship on the 'consequences' of these 'interventions, aimed precisely at re-shaping the subjectivities of poor women'. I read Ram here as calling for detailed ethnographic work which would not only outline the precise nature and consequences of these modernizing interventions but also document the creative languages and conceptual ideas used both by upper-class metropolitan women in their modernizing drives and, equally importantly, by poor and often rural women staking their wager as 'active claimants of modernity' (Ram 2008: 16).

And, finally, the women's movement in India as elsewhere has to take on board the growing threats to rights safeguards both nationally and in transnational contexts and also has to reflect more keenly on the increased militarization of socialities and the gendered impact of these—historically, this is one area which has been glaringly missing from feminist scholarship—arguably, an indicator of the nation-centric nature of feminist movements which permits grave silences on the question of human rights violations in the vast swathes of India's 'insurgency' hit states. Such an attention might mean that Irom Sharmila, a peace activist who is now on in her ninth year of indefinite fast and illegal confinement in protest against the draconian military laws in place in her home state of Manipur,[14] would gain recognition within the Indian feminist movement and her struggle for democracy and restoration of civil rights would be seen as a pressing area of feminist politics in India.

Notes

1 So for instance, within anthologies of Indian women's feminism, there is scant or little attention paid to the struggles of women under military laws in India and those who have explicitly rejected the identity of the nation-state, challenging it and exposing its brutal seams.

2 See Anupama Rao (2005) 'Gender and Caste' on *dalit* feminism.

3 'Does law have the capacity to pursue justice?' (Menon 1999: 285) has been a subject of serious debate within Indian feminist thinking and there are diverse positions on this, see for instance, Menon (1999, 2004); Parashar (1992); Kapoor and Crossman (1996); Kapur (2005).

4 See, for instance, Mary John (1996, 1998a, 1998b, 2002), Sunder Rajan (2003) and Kalpana Ram (2000).

5 The story of Shah Bano is as follows: Shah Bano, an elderly Muslim woman, went to the civil courts in India in order to press her demand for maintenance from her divorced husband. The legal judgement deposed in her favour and, in doing so, ignited

a political crisis of some significance—the chief elements of the debate did not dwell so much on Shah Bano's rights to a reasonable divorce settlement but rather on the autonomy of Muslim Personal Law from civil law and courts and the rights of Muslims to be governed by religious law in matters in personal and familial matters.

6 These positions according to Sunder Rajan (2003) include the following: range from unequivocal support for UCC, to support for internally led reform, for a combination of internal and state reform, to making UCC optional and even reversely optional, whereby, women have an option to choose between UCC and religious law.

7 While one could reasonably conjecture that the growing focus on women in development within international circles could not have been lost on national policy makers in India, it is useful to note that the 'Towards Equality' report made no mention of these international concerns with the first acknowledgement of this international dimension, Mary John writes, coming only with the publication of India's Country Paper prepared for submission to the Beijing conference (John 1996).

8 The *Women's Development Project Rajasthan*, DRDPR, Government of Rajasthan (1984).

9 The Hindi word '*sathin*' literally translates as a female companion.

10 The state, including its feminist partners in the WDP, harboured a shared assumption that the *sathin* would by virtue of her 'empowerment training' somehow be able to extricate herself from the prevailing power relations and gendered hierarchies and transcend her subordinate social positioning in order to achieve development goals of the WDP. Both the state and its feminist development partner upheld a transgressive politics for the fulfilment of development goals without too much soul searching on the personal costs of this transgression. For more on the instrumentalist conceptions of women's agency within development, see Madhok and Rai *Agency, Injury and Transgressive Politics in Neoliberal Times* (forthcoming).

11 Field interviews, Jhadla Village (Phagi Block), Jaipur District Rajasthan 2004.

12 For a conceptual discussion of NREGA, see Bhargava (2006).

13 See M. Krishnaraj (2003) and Mary John (2002).

14 See Bimol Akoijam (2005) for a detailed exposition of the 'Armed Forces Special Powers Act', 1956.

References

Agnes, F. (1997) 'Protecting Women Against Violence?: A Review of a Decade of Legislation 1980–89', in P. Chatterjee (ed.) *State and Politics in India*, Delhi: Oxford University Press.

Akoijam, B. (2005) 'Another 9/11, Another Act of Terror: The Embedded Disorder of the AFSPA', *Sarai Reader 2005: Bare Acts*, 481–91.

Alcoff, L. (1995) 'The Problem of Speaking for Others', in J. Roof and R. Wigeman (eds) *Who Can Speak: Authority and Critical Identity*, Champaign, IL: University of Illinois Press, pp. 97–119.

Appfel-Marglin, F. and Simon, S. (1994) 'Feminist Orientalism and Development', in W. Harcourt (ed.) *Feminist Perspectives on Sustainable Development: Shifting Knowledge Boundaries*, London: Zed Books, pp. 26–45.

Asad, T. (2000) 'What Do Human Rights Do? An Anthropological Enquiry', *Theory and Event*, 4, 4: electronic journal.

Barrientos, S. and Perrons, D. (1999) 'Gender and the Global Food Chain: A Comparative Study of Chile and the UK', in H. Afshar and S. Barrientos (eds) *Women, Globalization and Fragmentation in the Developing World*, NewYork: Macmillan, pp. 150–73.

Bhargava, R. (2006) 'Indian Democracy and Well Being: Employment as a Right', *Public Culture*, 18, 3: 445–51.

Brown, W. (1995) *States of Injury*, Princeton, NJ: Princeton University Press.

—— (2000) 'Suffering Rights as Paradoxes', *Constellations*, 7, 2: 230–41.

—— (2003) 'Neo-liberalism and the End of Liberal Democracy', *Theory and Event*, 7, 1: electronic journal.

Burawoy, M. et al. (2000) *Global Ethnography: Forces, Connections, and Imaginations in a Postmodern World*, Berkeley: University of California Press.

Cheah, P. (2006) *Inhuman Conditions: On Cosmopolitanism and Human Rights,* Cambridge, MA: Harvard University Press.

Crenshaw, K. (2000) 'Were the Critics Right About Rights? Reassessing the American Debate about Rights in Post-Reform Era', in M. Mamdani (ed.) *Beyond Rights Talk and Culture Talk*, Cape Town: David Phillip Publishers, pp. 61–74.

Cruikshank, B. (1999) *The Will to Empower: Democratic Citizens and Other Subjects*, Ithaca and London: Cornell University Press.

Dutta, N. (2000) 'From Subject to Citizen: Towards a History of the Indian Civil Rights Movement', in M.R. Anderson and S. Guha (eds) *Changing Concepts of Rights and Justice in South Asia*, Delhi: Oxford University Press.

Escobar, A. (1995) *Encountering Development: The Making and Unmaking of the Third World*, Princeton, NJ: Princeton University Press.

Gandhi, N. and Shah, N. (1992) *The Issues at Stake: Theory and Practice in Contemporary Women's Movement in India*, New Delhi: Kali for Women.

Gould, C. (2004) *Globalizing Democracy and Human Rights,* Cambridge: Cambridge University Press.

Government of Rajasthan (1984) *Women's Development Project Rajasthan: Concept Paper*, Jaipur: Department of Rural Development and Panchayati Raj.

Grewal, I. (1998) 'On the New Global Feminism and the Family of Nations: Dilemmas of Transnational Feminist Practice', in E. Shohat (ed.) *Talking Visions: Multicultural Feminisms in a Transnational Age*, Cambridge, MA: MIT Press, pp. 501–32.

—— (2005) *Transnational America: Feminisms, Diasporas, Neoliberalisms*, Durham: Duke University Press.

Grewal, I. and Kaplan. C. (1994) *Scattered Hegemonies: Postmodernity and Transnational Feminist Practices*, Minneapolis: University of Minnesota Press.

Hemmings, C. (2005) 'Telling Feminist Stories', *Feminist Theory*, 6, 2: 115–39.

Ilumoka, A. (1994) 'African Women's Economic, Social and Cultural Rights: Towards a Relevant Theory and Practice', in R. Cook (ed.) *Human Rights of Women: National and International Perspectives*, Philadelphia: University of Pennsylvania Press, pp. 307–25.

—— (1996) 'Beyond Human Rights Fundamentalism: The Challenges of Consensus Building in the 21st Century', *What Next Forum*, Draft Thematic Paper.

Jayal, N.G. (1999) *Democracy and the State: Welfare, Secularism and Development in Contemporary India*, Delhi: Oxford University Press.

John, M.E. (1996) 'Gender and Development in India, 1970–90s: Some Reflections on the Constitutive Role of Contexts', *Economic and Political Weekly*, 37, 41: 3071–7.

—— (1998a) 'Feminisms and Internationalisms: A Response from India', *Gender and History*, 10, 3: 539–48.

—— (1998b) 'Feminism in India and the West', *Cultural Dynamics*, 10, 2: 197–209.

—— (2002) 'Feminism, Poverty and Globalization: an Indian View', *Inter-Asia Cultural Studies*, 3, 3: 351–67.

Kapur, R. (2005) *Erotic Justice: Law and the New Politics of Postcolonialism*, New Delhi: Permanent Black.

Kapur, R. and Crossman, B. (1996) *Subversive Sites: Feminist Engagements with Law in India*, New Delhi: Sage.

Kaviraj, S. (2003) 'A State of Contradictions: The Postcolonial State in India', in Q. Skinner *et al.* (eds) *States and Citizens*, Cambridge: Cambridge University Press.

Kiss, E. (1997) 'Alchemy or Fool's Gold? Assessing Feminist Doubts over Rights', in M.L. Shanley and U. Narayan (eds) *Reconstructing Political Theory: Feminist Perspectives*, Cambridge: Polity Press.

Krishnaraj, M. (2003) 'Challenges Before the Women's Movement in a Changing Context', *Economic and Political Weekly*, 50, 43: 4536–45.

Kumar, R. (1999) 'From Chipko to Sati: The Contemporary Indian Women's Movement', in N. Meon (ed.) *Gender and Politics in India*, Delhi: Oxford University Press.

Lemke, T. (2001) 'The Birth of "Biopolitics": Michel Foucault's Lecture at the Collège de France on Neoliberal Governmentality', *Economy and Society*, 3, 2: 190–207.

Liddle, J. and Rai, S.M. (1998) 'Feminism, Imperialism and Orientalism: The Challenge of the Indian Woman', *Women's History Review*, 7, 4: 495–520.

Mackinnon, C. (1982) 'Feminism, Marxism, Method and the State: Towards Feminist Jurisprudence', *Signs*, 8, 4: 635–58.

Madhok, S. (2003a) 'Autonomy, Subordination and the Social Woman: Examining Rights Narratives of Rural Rajasthani Women', PhD dissertation, University of London.

—— (2003b) 'A "Limited Women's Empowerment": Politics, The State, and Development in North West India', special issue of *Women's Studies Quarterly*, *Women and Development: Rethinking Policy and Reconceptualizing Practice*, 31, 3&4: 154–73.

—— (2005a) 'Autonomy, Political Rights and the "Social Woman": Towards a Politics of Inclusion?' in C. Bates and S. Basu (eds) *Rethinking Indian Political Institutions*, London: Anthem Press.

—— (2007) 'Autonomy, Gendered Subordination and Transcultural Dialogue', *Journal of Global Ethics*, 3, 3: 335–57.

—— (2009) *Five Notions of Haq: Exploring Vernacular Rights Cultures in Southern Asia*, New Working Paper Series, Gender Institute, London School of Economics.

Mani, L. (1989) 'Contentious Traditions: The Debate on *Sati* in Colonial India', in K. Sangari and S. Vaid (eds) *Recasting Women: Essays in Colonial History*, New Delhi: Kali for Women.

Marchand, M. (2009) 'The Future of Gender and Development: Insights from Postcolonialism and Transnationalism', *Third World Quarterly*, 30, 5: 921–35.

Menon, N. (1999) 'Introduction', *Gender and Politics in India*, Delhi: Oxford University Press, pp. 1–36.

—— (2004) *Recovering Subversion: Feminist Politics Beyond the Law*, Urbana, IL: Indiana University Press.

Mignolo, W.D. (2000) 'The Many Faces of Cosmo-Polis: Border Thinking and Critical Cosmopolitanism', *Public Culture*, 12, 3: 721–48.

Mohanty, C.T. (1991) 'Under Western Eyes. Feminist Scholarship and Colonial Discourses', in C. Mohanty, A. Russo and L. Torres (eds) *Third World Women and the Politics of Feminism,* Urbana, IL: Indiana University Press.

Ong, A. (1988) 'Colonialism and Modernity: Feminist Re-presentations of Women in Non-western Societies', *Inscriptions*, 3, 4: 79–93.

—— (1999) *Flexible Citizenship: The Cultural Logic of Transnationality*, Durham: Duke University Press.

—— (2007) *Neoliberalism as Exception: Mutations in Citizenship and Sovereignty*, Durham and London: Duke University Press.

Parashar, A. (1992) *Women and Family Law Reform in India: Uniform Civil Code and Gender Equality*, New Delhi: Sage.

Parpart, J. and Marchand, M.H. (1995) 'Exploding the Cannon: An Introduction/ Conclusion', in J. Parpart and M.H. Marchard (eds) *Feminism/Postmodernism/ Development*, London: Routledge.

Phadke, S. (2003) 'Thirty Years On: Women's Studies Reflects on the Women's Movement', *Economic and Political Weekly*, 8, 43: 4567–76.

Phillips, A. (2009) *Religion: Ally, Threat, or Just Religion*, forthcoming.

Rai, S.M. (2002) *Gender and Political Economy of Development*, Oxford: Polity.

Ram, K. (2000) 'The State and the Women's Movement: Instabilities in the Discourse of "Rights" in India', in A.M. Hildson, V. Mackie, M. Macintyre, and M. Stivens, (eds) *Human Rights and Gender Politics. Asia-Pacific Perspectives,* New York: Routledge, pp. 60–82.

—— (2008) 'A New Consciousness Must Come: Affectivity and Movement in Tamil Dalit Women's Activist Engagement with Cosmopolitan Modernity', in P. Werbner (ed.) *Anthropology and Cosmopolitanism: Rooted, Feminist and Vernacular Perspectives*, Oxford: Berg.

Rankin, K. (2003) 'Anthropologies and Geographies of Globalization', *Progress in Human Geography*, 27, 6: 708–34.

Rao, A. (ed.) (2005) *Gender and Caste: Contemporary Issues in Indian Feminism*, New Delhi: Kali for Women.

Rofel, L. (2007) *Desiring China: Experiments in Neoliberalism, Sexuality and Public Culture*, Durham: Duke University Press.

Rose, N. (1996) 'Governing "Advanced" Liberal Democracies', in A. Barry, T. Osborne and N. Rose (eds) *Foucault and Political Reason: Liberalism and Rationalities of Government*, Chicago: Chicago University Press.

Shakya, Y. and Rankin, K. (2008) 'The Politics of Subversion in Development Practice: An Exploration of Microfinance in Nepal and Vietnam', *Journal of Development Studies*, 44, 8: 1214–35.

Spivak, G.C. (1999) *A Critique of Postcolonial Reason*, Cambridge, MA: Harvard University Press.

—— (2002) 'Righting Wrongs', in N. Owen (ed.) *Human Rights, Human Wrongs, The Oxford Amnesty Lectures, 2001*, Oxford: Oxford University Press.

Sunder Rajan, R. (2003) *The Scandal of the State: Women, Law and Citizenship in Postcolonial India*, Durham: Duke University Press.

Wilson, K. (2007) 'Agency', in G. Blakeley and V. Bryson (eds) *The Impact of Feminism on Political Concepts and Debates*, Manchester: Manchester University Press, pp. 126–45.

Index